Mr Stanley,
I PRESUME?

The Life and Explorations of HENRY MORTON STANLEY

ALAN GALLOP

SUTTON PUBLISHING

First published in the United Kingdom in 2004 by
Sutton Publishing Limited · Phoenix Mill
Thrupp · Stroud · Gloucestershire · GL5 2BU

British Library Cataloguing in Publication Data
A catalogue record for this book is available from the British Library.

ISBN 0-7509-3093-4

Title-page: Henry Morton Stanley, from *Leisure Hour*, 25 January 1873.

This book is dedicated to the memory of
Hazel Manson
who gave encouragement to everyone she met –
and who loved a good story

Typeset in 11/14.5pt Photina MT.
Typesetting and origination by
Sutton Publishing Limited.
Printed and bound in England by
J.H. Haynes & Co. Ltd, Sparkford.

CONTENTS

PREFACE

In 2002 the BBC asked viewers and listeners to name 100 men and women from history and contemporary life whom they considered to be the 'Greatest Britons'. Over thirty thousand people voted in the poll in which Sir Winston Churchill emerged as the figure the majority wanted as the top of their personality pops. Marie Stopes came in at 100th position; others nominated included Ernest Shackleton (11), Queen Elizabeth II (24), David Beckham (33), Captain Scott (54), Cliff Richard (56), J.R.R. Tolkien (92) and Dr David Livingstone (98).

Henry Morton Stanley (1841–1904) did not rate a mention. The man whom *The Times* identified on his death in 1904 as 'one of the greatest pioneer explorers and one of the most striking figures of the nineteenth century' had been confined to history's 'B' list during the last half of the twentieth century, making him an unsuitable candidate for inclusion in a table of the 100 most popular Britons. By 2002 there were insufficient numbers in Britain who were aware of Stanley and his achievements to vote him into their hall of fame.

The centenary of Stanley's death (in 2004) is a good time to reassess the life and accomplishments of this complex, controversial and most private of men; a man whose name will forever be associated with African exploration and the subsequent fever for colonisation of the land he named 'the dark continent'. It was his direct and indirect achievements that resulted in Africa's subdivision among European powers and inspired the 'Scramble for Africa'.

For most of his life, Henry Morton Stanley attempted to conceal his true identity and background. When challenged with the truth, he lied. It was only in later years when he had mellowed in appearance and manner that he agreed to confront ghosts from his past and begin drafting his memoirs. Even then, Stanley often felt a need to be economical with the truth, embellish facts or fail to mention people and events if they threatened to get in the way of his story.

Stanley died before completing his memoirs and it was left to his widow, a sensitive and capable woman, to finish the job using her husband's unpublished journals and notes. By the time they appeared in 1909, shady figures from Stanley's earlier life had begun to re-emerge, suggesting to Lady Stanley that they possessed evidence damaging to her late husband's heroic reputation. Miraculously, each was in a position to part company with their evidence, written or otherwise – providing Lady Stanley was prepared to buy the material and their silence. The possibility that her husband's reputation might be tarnished filled her with horror – and she succumbed to the blackmail. As a result, Stanley's memoirs are heavily edited and names and identities of important characters and incidents are omitted.

Stanley set out to present an honest account of his life. The ageing former explorer stated:

There is no reason now for withholding the history of my early years, nothing to prevent my stating every fact about myself. I am now declining in vitality. My hard life in Africa, many fevers, many privations, much physical and mental suffering, bring me close to the period of infirmities. . . . Without fear of consequences, or danger to my pride and reserve, I can lay bare all circumstances which have attended me from the dawn of consciousness to this present period of indifference. . . .

Who, then, was Henry Morton Stanley, the man who admitted: 'I was not sent into the world to be happy, nor to search for happiness. I was sent for special work'? Why did he live his life as a lie, denying his true identity and the fact that he was a poor Welsh boy, born a bastard, brought up in a workhouse, and tell the world he was an American? Who was this soldier who fought on both sides during the Civil War, this roving newspaper correspondent on the American frontier, this adventurer who walked across Africa searching for an elderly and broken Scottish missionary and, when he found him, enquired: 'Dr Livingstone, I presume?'

From what and from whom was he running when he marched from the Indian Ocean to the Atlantic to complete Livingstone's work, follow the mighty Congo River to the sea and claim a slice of Africa the size of Western Europe for a land-hungry European monarch? And why was he prepared to lead a daring rescue mission to relieve a mysterious and reluctant colonial official and his people from annihilation in equatorial Africa?

Stanley made a broad and deep mark on his generation. One hundred years after his death is not only a good time to re-evaluate his life and achievements but also, perhaps, to rehabilitate his reputation in a fair and objective way. To do this, it is necessary to go back to his earliest beginnings. . . .

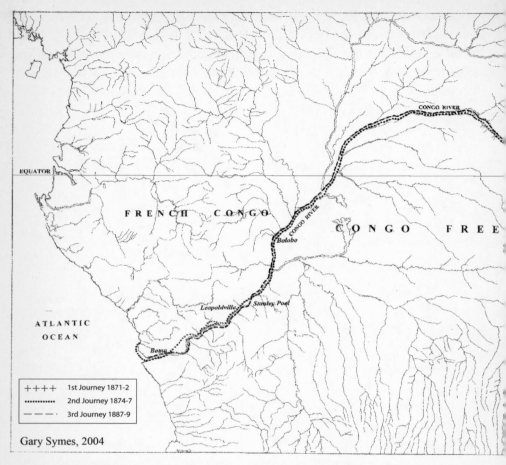

A map showing Stanley's three expeditions across central Africa. The first journey to find Dr David Livingstone was sponsored by the *New York Herald*. The second, an Anglo–American expedition to explore Africa, was sponsored by the *New York Herald* and the *Daily Telegraph*. The third was sponsored by public subscription to rescue and relieve Emin Pasha.

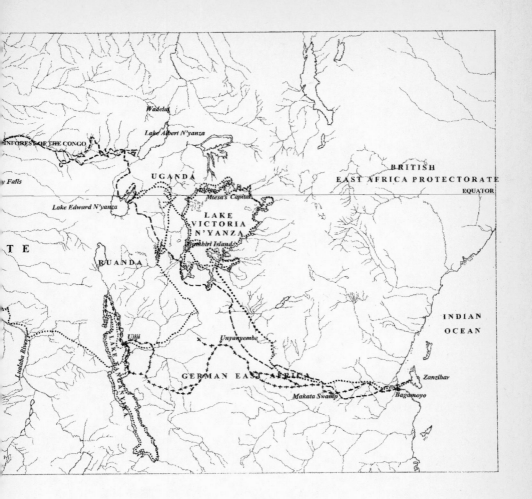

Wadelai

Lake Albert N'yanza

IN FOREST OF THE CONGO

y Falls

UGANDA

BRITISH
EAST AFRICA PROTECTORATE

EQUATOR

Lake Edward N'yanza

Mtesa's Capital

LAKE
VICTORIA
N'YANZA

RUANDA

Bumbiri Island

INDIAN
OCEAN

Lualaba River

LAKE TANGANYIKA

Ujiji

Unyanyembe

GERMAN EAST AFRICA

Zanzibar

Makata Swamp

Bagamoyo

Chapter 1

JOHN ROWLANDS – BASTARD

The ancient market town of Denbigh is one of the most historic in North Wales. Denbigh, or *Denbych*, derives its name from the Welsh language and means 'a fortified place'. Fortifications take the form of a ruined thirteenth-century castle, built in 1282 for Edward I, that look down on the town and rich pastures of the Vale of Clwyd.

Visitors in the vicinity of the High Street pass the fifteenth-century timber-framed archway of the Golden Lion Inn, the sixteenth-century County Hall and narrow cobbled alleys before arriving in front of No. 7 Highgate, a medieval stone gabled building which towers above the rest of the street. A steep path leads to Burgess Tower and the entrance to King Edward's old walled town. Tower Hill passes St Hilary's Terraces and an unusual medieval house with battlements along the top and the castle gatehouse, from which an unpaved track leads to the site where a tiny cottage known as Castle Row once stood. It was demolished long ago, but was where one of the Victorian world's most controversial figures is understood to have been born.

There is speculation that the baby baptised 'John Rowlands, Bastard', who in later life took the name of Henry Morton Stanley, may have been born in London. He wrote: 'One of the first things I remember is to have been gravely told that I had come from London in a band-box and to have been assured that all babies came from the same place. It satisfied my curiosity for several years as to the cause of my coming; but, later, I was informed that my mother had hastened to her parents from London to be delivered of me; and that, after recovery, she had gone back to the Metropolis, leaving me in the charge of my grandfather, Moses Parry, who lived within the precincts of Denbigh Castle.'

Old Moses Parry moved into the small, whitewashed cottage known as Castle Row in the shadow of the ruined castle in 1839 when the town had a population of some four thousand. He took the property because he was a butcher and needed a house with outbuildings that could double as a slaughterhouse for cattle bound for the meat market. Years later, Dr Evan Pierce, Denbigh's local physician and bard, told the *Denbighshire Free Press* he had been present at the cottage when Moses Parry's eighteen-year-old unmarried daughter, Elizabeth – known to many as Betsy – gave birth to a son on 28 January 1841. He claimed to have recited Welsh poetry to the mother while she was in labour. Less than a year before, Betsy had left home to enter service in London where, according to her son, she had 'thereby grievously offended her family'. By 'straying to London, in spite of family advice, Betsy had committed a capital offence' – in other words, she had become pregnant outside marriage; a serious and shocking thing to happen to a small-town chapel-going girl from Victorian Wales.

Denbigh's parish register confirms that John Rowlands's baptism took place in St Hilary's Chapel, Denbigh on 19 February 1841 and states he was 'illegitimate', with the parents named as 'John Rowlands, farmer, Llys, Llanrhaiadr and Elizabeth Parry, Castle, Denbigh'. However, a census taken in June of the same year shows no sign of Betsy and her baby living in the cottage, the new unmarried mother having fled from Denbigh in shame and disgrace with her son to return to London and work as a domestic servant. Baby John, though, was soon brought back to Wales to be cared for by his eighty-year-old grandfather and a pair of bachelor uncles in their Welsh-speaking household.

Moses, described as 'a stout old gentleman clad in corduroy breeches, dark stockings and long Melton coat, with a clean-shaven face, rather round, and lit up by humorous grey eyes', occupied the upper floor of the cottage with baby John, while Young Moses and Uncle Thomas inhabited the lower rooms. Young Moses later married 'a flaxen-haired, fair girl of a decided temper' called Kitty and 'after that event . . . [they] seldom descended to the lower apartments'.

Stanley never knew his father: 'I was in my "teens" before I learned that he had died within a few weeks after my birth.' This is the first of many untruths, inaccuracies or misleading statements the elderly Stanley made while relating the story of his colourful early life. 'John Rowlands, farmer', in fact, passed away thirteen years after his son's birth. He is known to have been a drunkard and his burial entry in the Llanrhaiadr Parish Register states that he died in May 1854 of 'delirium tremens', a severe psychotic condition that affects alcoholics. Rowlands contributed nothing to his son's welfare, upkeep or well-being. He showed no interest in the boy after his birth or, it would appear, in the young girl he is said to have impregnated in 1840.

A Denbigh legend, persistent since the mid-nineteenth century, suggests that James Vaughan Hall, a local solicitor, alderman and leading citizen may have been Stanley's real father. In 1840 Betsy Parry worked in a bakery shop next to offices Vaughan Hall shared with another solicitor in Vale Street. Vaughan Hall, who had a second home in London where *Pigott's Directory* states he was 'a Master Extraordinary in Chancery and Commissioner in all the Courts at Westminster', is said to have seduced the young baker's girl and when she discovered she was pregnant with his child, in order to safeguard his marriage and position in Denbigh society, bribed John Rowlands into claiming he was the father.

Many affluent Victorian middle-class employers considered servants and working girls 'fair game', and Vaughan Hall's frequent excursions to London to undertake official duties in Chancery while his wife remained in Denbigh, would have provided plenty of opportunity to seduce young women in his employ. Dr William Acton, who practised in London from 1840, noted in his book *Prostitution*: 'Seduction of girls from the lower orders is a sport and a habit with vast numbers of men, married and single, placed above the ranks of labour.'

Another local story suggests Betsy Parry was a girl with loose morals, an amateur prostitute who was having simultaneous relationships with both John Rowlands and James Vaughan Hall – and when her pregnancy was discovered, had no idea which man was the true father of her unborn child. Betsy went on to have more illegitimate children by two other men, one of whom she subsequently married. Her second illegitimate child, a daughter called Emma born in 1842, was to a man called 'John Evans, Liverpool, farmer, late of Ty'n' y Pwll, Llanrhaiadr'. One may well speculate that if Betsy had been employed as a servant at Vaughan Hall's London home, she could easily have been 'fair game' for the solicitor, resulting in the birth of one – possibly even two – children out of wedlock, with John Evans similarly bribed into falsely admitting he was father of the second offspring.

So, was young John Rowlands, born to Elizabeth 'Betsy' Parry in 1841, really John Vaughan Hall? It is unlikely the young man ever discovered the identity of his real father. The only thing certain was that the stigma of being born out of wedlock in a provincial Victorian Welsh market town was sufficient to leave a deep scar on the psyche of the strongest men –

and something that pursued the man, later known to the world as Henry Morton Stanley, for the rest of his life.

Stanley was aged four when he accidentally dropped a glass jug he was carrying to collect water from the castle well. It smashed to pieces and on hearing the crash grandfather Moses came to the door and 'lifted his forefinger menacingly and said, "Very well, Shonin, my lad, when I return, thou shalt have a sound whipping. You naughty boy!"' With that, grandfather Moses left the cottage to attend to some business in a nearby field where he promptly fell down dead. A jury at the inquest returned the verdict he had died through 'the visitation of God', which was their way of explaining any sudden fatality of this kind.

The death of Moses Parry was just the excuse Young Moses, Uncle Thomas and Aunt Kitty needed to rid Castle Row of their tiny nephew. The boy was transferred to the care of an elderly Welsh-speaking couple, Richard and Jenny Price, caretakers of the local bowling green 400 yards from Castle Row. Their cottage was appropriately named Bowling Green House and the two uncles agreed to pay the couple half a crown a week for his board and lodgings.

At infant school in the crypt at St Hilary's Church, the lad was never going to be tallest in the class, but the Prices' dismay at his increasing appetite resulted in the elderly couple asking the uncles for extra money for his upkeep. By now they were both married and were expected to bring home decent wages to keep their spouses happy. The wives told the Prices that times were hard, they could no longer afford to pay for the up-keep of their nephew and there was no room for him at Castle Row – 'so the old couple resolved to send me to the workhouse'.

In 1847, the Prices' son, Dick, was given the task of taking the boy to the St Asaph's Poor Law Union Workhouse under the pretence they were going to visit an aunt called Mary in Ffynnon Beuno 6 miles away. Stanley recalls:

The way seemed interminable and tedious, but he did his best to relieve my feelings with false cajoling and treacherous endearments. At last Dick set me down from his shoulders before an immense stone building, and, passing through tall iron gates, he pulled at a bell, which I could hear clanging noisily in the distant interior. A sombre-faced stranger appeared at the door, who, despite my remonstrances, seized me by the hand, and drew me within, while Dick tried to soothe my fears with glib promises that he was only going to bring Aunt Mary to me. The door closed on him, and, with the echoing sound, I experienced for the first time the awful feeling of utter desolateness.

St Asaph's Workhouse was an institution to which the aged poor and superfluous Welsh-speaking children of local parishes were taken 'to relieve the respectabilities of the obnoxious sight of extreme poverty, because civilisation knows no better method of disposing of the infirm and helpless than by imprisoning them within its walls'.

St Asaph's was created in 1837 and its operation ruled over by an elected board of 24 guardians representing 16 local parishes. The large red-brick workhouse was built between 1839 and 1840 at a cost of £5,499 16s 8d on a site 6 miles east of Denbigh and south of the village of St Asaph. It was intended to accommodate 200 inmates and for most of its early life its grey and dismal wings and dormitories were full to bursting. Its design followed the popular 'cruciform' layout with four separate accommodation wings, known as 'wards', for different types of inmate – male or female, young or old, infirm or able-bodied – radiating from an octagonal central house containing the institution's offices and the residence of the schoolmaster, James Francis – 'soured by misfortune, brutal of temper and callous of heart'.

Everyone entering the workhouse was subjected to a rigorous means test to assess 'suitability' for admission. Only 'deserving' cases were allowed in: the unemployed, the ill, the aged, orphaned families and individuals with nowhere else to go. Once inside, inmates were forced to undergo prison-like discipline, living in cheerless surroundings, eating plain and monotonous meals in silence. Visitors were not encouraged and occasional gifts left at the door by benefactors rarely found their way to inmates, being considered an unnecessary relaxation of workhouse regulations.

Inside the institution, young John Rowlands quickly found that the aged were subject to stern rules and assigned useless tasks, while children were chastised and disciplined in a manner that ignored the rules both of justice and charity. To the old, St Asaph's was a house of slow death; to the young, it was a house of torture. Paupers were the failures of Victorian society and their fate was to eke out the rest of their miserable existence within workhouse walls, picking loose fibres out of discarded ropes to be re-threaded into new coils.

Male and female inmates were lodged in separate sections of the workhouse, enclosed by high walls with every door locked, barred and guarded to preserve the questionable 'morality', a practice which went on in hundreds of similar institutions across the British Isles. Each inmate was required to wear regulation clothing made from cheap fabric: men were clad in grey blanket trousers, matching jacket and collarless cotton shirt with hair shaved close to the skull, the women in striped cotton dresses, their short hair making one inmate indistinguishable from another.

At 6 a.m. sharp, inmates were roused from their sleep and by 8 p.m. they were locked in their wards. Bread, thin soup, rice and potatoes were the daily diet. On Saturdays inmates had to undergo a severe scrubbing in a tin bath and on Sundays were forced to sit through long services on hard bench pews in the chapel. The routine was designed to afflict minds and break spirits, which it successfully achieved within a short space of time.

Like John Rowlands, the majority of workhouse children spoke only Welsh and lessons in the St Asaph's classroom were conducted entirely in that language, although religious instruction was given in English.

Meticulous records of daily life at the St Asaph's workhouse are stored at Hawarden Records Office. They give the names of every arrival and departure, details of those who absconded – and were dragged back – of visitors and comments about activities and incidents. In 1847, weeks after John Rowlands entered St Asaph's, a committee was formed to investigate conditions at the workhouse and report its findings to the Board of Education. It noted that young girls were brought into close association with prostitutes and 'learned the tricks of the trade'. Inspectors observed that 'the men took part in every possible vice', children slept two in a bed, an older child with a younger, resulting in their starting 'to practice and understand things they should not'. The inspectors' findings were subsequently published as a report by the Commission of Education in Wales, 1849, but comments about sexual depravity at St Asaph's were diluted.

Four decades after leaving St Asaph's, Stanley's resentment at how Dick Price had tricked him into the workhouse was still evident. 'Dick's guile was well meant, no doubt, but I then learned for the first time that one's professed friend can smile while preparing to deal a mortal blow, and a man can mask evil with a show of goodness. It would have been far better for me if Dick, being stronger than I, had employed compulsion, instead of shattering my confidence and planting the first seeds of distrust in a child's heart,' he recollected.

Not that young John Rowlands received any special treatment from James Francis, a former collier from Mold who had lost his entire left hand in an industrial accident years before and wound up as workhouse schoolmaster. He won the job over other applicants because he could communicate in broken English. According to Stanley, Francis was a violent and brutal man. 'The ready back-slap in the face, the stunning clout over the ear, the strong blow with the open palm on alternate cheeks, which knocked our senses into confusion, were so frequent it is a marvel we ever recovered them again,' he recalled. 'Whatever might be the nature of the offence, or merely because his irritable mood required vent, our poor heads were cuffed, and slapped, and pounded, until we lay speechless and streaming with blood.'

For young Rowlands and fellow youthful inmates, Francis's cruel blows with his bony right fist were preferable to deliberate punishment with the birch, ruler, or cane 'which, with cool malice, he inflicted' from a selection of instruments never far from his reach. Even the smallest classroom error caused Francis to reach for ruler or cane. Woe betide any child who managed wrongly to answer several questions in a row for 'then a vindictive scourging of the offender followed, until he was exhausted, or our lacerated bodies could bear no more'.

The boy's own first flogging from Francis happened on a Sunday evening during the early part of 1849. The eight-year-old was sitting with other children listening to Francis reading aloud from Genesis 41, a passage referring to Joseph, sold as a slave by his brothers and elevated to high rank by the pharaoh. Francis suddenly looked up from his Bible and demanded to know from John Rowlands who in the story had interpreted the pharaoh's dreams. The boy replied: 'Jophes, sir.'

The master thundered: 'Who?'

'Jophes, sir.'

'Joseph, you mean?'

'Yes sir, Jophes.'

Francis reached for his birch and ordered the boy to 'unbreech', unaware he had merely mispronounced Joseph's name. Stanley tells us that the master 'rudely tore down my nether garments and administered a forceful shower of blows, with such thrilling effect that I was bruised and bloodied all over, and could not stand for a time. During the hour that followed I was much perplexed at the difference between "Jophes" and "Joseph" as at the particular character of the agonising pains I suffered.

For some weeks I was under the impression that the scourging was less due to my error than to some mysterious connection it might have had with Genesis.'

Floggings were part of daily life at many workhouses, where it was not uncommon to see little wretches flung onto the flagstones in writhing heaps or standing with frightened eyes and humped backs to receive the shock of a sadistic schoolmaster's birch. Nothing exists to suggest that life at St Asaph's was any different.

The boy received another thrashing in 1851 when cholera was raging through North Wales and inmates were forbidden to eat fruit of any kind. John Rowlands and another boy were sent to town on an errand and on the journey back gorged on blackberries picked from a hedgerow. On their return to St Asaph's, tell-tale fruit stains on fingers and around mouths gave the game away and it was only a matter of time before Francis appeared in the dormitory doorway. He reminded everyone that he had expressly forbidden them to eat fruit and 'then, giving a swishing blow in the air with his birch, he advanced to my bed and with one hand plucked me out of bed, and forthwith administered a punishment so dreadful that blackberries suggested birching ever afterwards'.

Information on how the St Asaph's Workhouse was organised was meticulously recorded in the *North Wales Gazette*, which sent a reporter along every fortnight to cover meetings of the parish guardians. On 17 July 1850, the paper reported:

> Mr. J.J. Foulks thought there was a great deal of difference between the charge for the keep of the officers of the house and its inmates. The charge per head being 6*s* 6*d* and only 2*s* allowed for rations to the paupers. A discussion took place upon the subject but nothing particular was done towards remedying the complaint.

Details of the regime under which St Asaph's inmates suffered eventually reached the ears of the *Carnarvon and Denbigh Herald*, which in later years accused James Francis of 'coming in drunk' and 'taking indecent liberties' with female staff. Strangely, this was never mentioned in Stanley's account of his workhouse years.

Inmates were expected to fulfil difficult tasks, including sweeping the playground with brooms more suited to giants than little children, washing stone floors, hoeing the frozen ground wearing thin clothing that provided scant protection from the raw winter wind, and being forced to commit whole pages of text to memory during the space of an evening. 'In these and scores of other ways, our treatment was ferocious and stupid,' Stanley recalled.

'Ferocious and stupid', perhaps, but the overall standard of education at St Asaph's was often better than at other schools in the Denbigh area. Stanley says that by the time he had reached age ten, several boys had demonstrated qualities superior to others students at the best public schools. Naturally, he himself was one of them. One boy, named 'Toomis', was a born mathematician, while 'another was famous for retentiveness of memory'. George Williams was 'unusually distinguished' for quick comprehension, while 'Billy', with his big head and lofty brow, astonished Her Majesty's Inspector, who prophesied great things of him in future.

Notable workhouse visitors included a bishop, local parsons, the Chairman of the Board of Guardians and school inspectors who found most workhouse children to be above average in intelligence, their education based on religion and industry while in other schools the curriculum was more secular and less physical. Workhouse guardians attempted to turn St Asaph's boys into farmers, tradesmen and mechanics 'and instead of the gymnasium, our muscles were practised in spade industry, gardening, tailoring and joiner's work'. Several St Asaph's inmates went on to become businessmen, ministers of the Church, lawyers – and African explorers. Of himself at that time, Stanley writes: 'I, though not particularly brilliant in any special thing that I can remember, held my own as head of the school.'

The workhouse was also responsible for Stanley's zealous passion for order and cleanliness that remained with him throughout his life. When it was his turn to clean dormitories and make beds, he was seized with an all-consuming desire to arrange bed covers without a single crease, produce folds with mathematical precision, dust and polish cupboards and window sills until they were spotless and make dormitory flagstones shine like mirrors. Years later, the former workhouse boy would ensure his camps in the African interior were arranged in similar fashion and each occupant of a canvas tent brought its contents out to be aired before taking them back inside to be arranged with the same precision as those within his own tent.

Whether James Francis was as brutal as Stanley would claim in later life is open to conjecture. Indeed, it appears that young Rowlands was something of a teacher's favourite, often left in charge of the class when

Francis left the room or was called away. The schoolmaster is remembered as 'having a high opinion of young Rowlands and used to put him in charge of the boys in his absence', according to a *Denbigh Free Press* article published after Stanley's death.

> The boy was quite equal to the task of maintaining discipline. He would allow no one to question his authority. Rather than suffer anyone to take liberties with him, he would give the boys a good thrashing all round, and this he used to do so effectually that no one was found bold enough to dispute his authority. The boy was particularly fond of geography and arithmetic, and seemed never so happy as when, pointer in hand, he was allowed to ramble over the map at will. He seemed to the boys to have the latitude and longitude of each place at his fingers' ends. He was also a good penman, and on this account was often selected by the porter to enter the names of visitors in a book kept for that purpose and at times he was even invited into the clerk's office to help with the accounts.

The owner of a cake shop near the workhouse told the *Denbigh Free Press* that he remembered John Rowlands. 'Whenever [Francis] received a few shillings from friends to spend for the benefit of the workhouse boys, he used to visit her shop and generally brought Rowlands with him to carry the cakes home. He brought the boy with him . . . because he was very fond of the boy and thought much of him. Again and again he used these words with reference to Rowlands: "You mark me, this boy will be a great man some day."'

One of the most popular boys in the institution was Willie Roberts – 'a boy of about my own age. Some of us believed he belonged to a very superior class to our own. His coal-black hair curled in profusion over a delicately moulded face of milky whiteness. His eyes were soft and limpid, and he walked with a carriage which tempted imitation.' While confined to the infirmary 'with some childish malady where I lay for weeks', rumours circulated that Willie had died and his body been taken to the 'dead-house', a room set aside and sometimes used as a morgue.

On returning to St Asaph's, some boys suggested it was possible to view Willie's dead body,

> and prompted by a fearful curiosity to know what death was like, we availed ourselves of a favourable opportunity, and entered the house

with quaking hearts. The body lay on a black bier, and, covered with a sheet, appeared uncommonly long for a boy. One of the boldest drew the cloth aside, and at the sight of the waxen face with its awful fixity we all started back, gazing at it as if spellbound. There was something grand in its superb disregard of the chill and gloom of the building, and in the holy calm of its features. It was the face of our dear Willie, with whom we had played, and yet not the same, for an inexplicable aloofness had come over it. . . .

The sheet was drawn back further, to reveal scores of dark weals and bruises covering young Willie's body. The boys quickly replaced the sheet and withdrew from the dead house, convinced that Francis's brutality was the cause of their friend's death.

This author could find no trace of a boy called William – or Willie – Roberts having been admitted to or having died at St Asaph's workhouse between 1850 and 1854. Deaths were entered into workhouse records in a neat hand leaving no room for error. Either John Rowlands dreamt up the story while in a state of delirium in the infirmary, or an elderly man called Henry Morton Stanley invented the tale as yet another piece of fiction to add spice to the story of his early years.

In later life Stanley was adamant that 'there are two things for which I feel grateful to this strange institution of St. Asaph. My fellowman had denied to me the charms of affection, and the bliss of a home, but through his charity I had learned to know God by faith, as the Father of the fatherless – and I had been taught to read. It is impossible that in a Christian land like Wales I could have avoided contracting some knowledge of the Creator, but the knowledge gained by hearing, is very different from that which comes from feeling. Nor is it likely that I would have remained altogether ignorant of letters. Being as I was, however, the circumstances of my environment necessarily focussed my attention on religion, and my utterly friendless state drove me to seek the comfort guaranteed by it.'

John Rowlands was aged nine (although he wrote in his memoirs 'I must have been 12') when he came to realise a mother was indispensable to every child and that his own mother, Elizabeth 'Betsy' Parry, had been admitted to St Asaph's workhouse 'with her bastards', Robert, aged two and Elizabeth, aged one year old, on 3 December 1850. The boy's first feeling 'was one of exultation that I also had a mother and a half-brother and a half-sister, and the next one was of curiosity to know what they were like and whether their appearance portended a change in my condition'.

It was Francis who pointed out Betsy to her son when inmates were assembled in a hall. He indicated 'a tall woman with an oval face, and a great coil of dark hair behind her head' and asked the boy if he recognised her. He told the master he did not.

'What, do you not know your own mother?' asked Francis.

Apart from passing a few days with her following his birth eleven years before, he had spent the rest of his life with relatives, strangers and, for the last five joyless years, at St Asaph's. The boy directed a shy glance at the woman and thought she, too, was regarding him with a look of 'cool, critical scrutiny'. He had expected to feel tenderness for her but her expression was so chilling 'that the valves of my heart closed as with a snap'. The phrase 'honour thy father and mother' had been repeated to him scores of times, 'but this loveless parent required no honour from me. After a few weeks' residence my mother departed, taking her little boy with her, but the girl was left in the institution; and, such is the system prevailing, though we met in the same hall for months, she remained as a stranger to me.'

Betsy and her other two children were discharged from St Asaph's on 2 April 1851, but two months later her eight-year-old daughter 'Emma Jones, a deserted bastard' was admitted to the workhouse. Betsy had farmed her second child out to a family called Morris who lived near Castle Row. The child is described in workhouse day relief books as 'Emma Jones, alias Parry' and later as 'Emma Parry'. She remained at St Asaph's until discharged, aged fourteen, in March 1857 when it is recorded that 'she has gone upon trial to Mr. C. Owens, joiner, Rhyl', and it is to this half-sister that Stanley refers as 'the stranger'. Emma died in Denbigh, aged thirty-seven, in 1880. She lived long enough to boast about her half-brother's African exploits and, after marrying local man Llewellyn Hughes, named her second child Emma Stanley Hughes and her third Henry M.S. Hughes in honour of her 'American' relative.

Long hours locked in a dormitory gave John Rowlands time to read, write and draw. A local chaplain visiting the workhouse left some pictures of cathedrals and, with nothing better to do, the boy copied them and discovered he possessed a natural talent for drawing. Someone else gave him pencils and a drawing book and word soon travelled around the workhouse that young Rowlands was the institution's 'resident artist'. Word of his talent reached the Right Reverend Thomas Vowler Short, Lord Bishop of St Asaph's, who, on his next workhouse visit, rewarded the boy with a Bible in recognition of his diligent application to his studies; it was one of the first things the boy actually owned outright and could claim to be his and nobody else's.

Unlike his frame, the boy's talents in choral singing and public speaking began to grow. By his early teens, John Rowlands was still small in stature. Fellow inmates who had entered St Asaph's at the same time, began leaving the institution to enter service or take jobs with Denbigh employers. But no one came to claim young Rowlands and he remained at St Asaph's, becoming its oldest junior inhabitant.

He was thirteen years old when he learned an important lesson in dealing with other people; it was one he would always carry with him. One day Francis was absent from St Asaph's and John Rowlands was deputised to supervise a class. The sight of a slightly built boy standing in front of thirty other children made him a target for unruly pupils and those who preferred a day's play while their schoolmaster was away. A youth who had earlier bullied Rowlands in the playground decided to make the tiny temporary teacher's life more difficult and persisted in disrupting the class. Following Francis's usual practice, Rowlands ordered the boy to stand in the punishment corner. The boy refused and demanded a classroom fight. For once, Rowlands managed to come out on top and with the aid of a woollen scarf tied up the disruptive boy and 'conducted him to the opprobrious corner, where he was left to meditate, with two others similarly guilty. From the hour when the heroic whelp was subdued, my authority was undisputed. Often since have I learned how necessary is the application of force for the establishment of order. There comes a time when pleading is of no avail.'

The parting of the ways for John Rowlands and St Asaph's workhouse came suddenly and unexpectedly, but the precise circumstances are open to debate. It was an event which he later described as having 'lasting influence on my life' and had it not occurred, he might eventually have been apprenticed 'to some trade or other, and would have mildewed in Wales'. The account is almost certainly fictitious.

Stanley states that by the age of fifteen he had unconsciously contracted 'ideas about dignity' and that 'the promise of manhood was manifest in the first buds of pride, courage, and resolution'. Francis, however, had failed to notice any change in the boy. In May 1856 a new softwood table was delivered to the workhouse and its surface dented 'by some heedless urchin' who had climbed on it. When Francis discovered the damage he erupted into a rage and reached for his birch, intent on thrashing anyone in his sights.

The schoolmaster burst into the classroom demanding to know who was responsible for damaging the table. The inmates were ignorant that a new table had been delivered, let alone that it had been damaged. 'Very well then,' screamed Francis, 'the entire class will be flogged – unbutton!'

Francis began thrashing the children closest to where he was standing, gradually beating his way through the class. Normally young Rowlands would have been convulsed in fear as his turn approached, 'but instead of the old timidity and other symptoms of terror, I felt myself hardening for resistance. He stood before me vindictively glaring, his spectacles intensifying the gleam in his eyes.' Glowering at John Rowlands, he spat out: 'How is this? Not ready yet? Strip, sir, this minute; I mean to stop this abominable and barefaced lying.'

Calmly, the boy replied: 'I did not lie, sir. I know nothing of it.'

'Silence, sir. Down with your clothes.'

'Never again!' shouted the lad, surprised at his own audacity. Before anything else had time to sink in, Francis's one good hand grabbed the boy's collar, swung him into the air and down onto the bench where he was kicked in the stomach. Then the savage master lifted the boy and flung him onto some desks.

Stanley takes up the story of what happened next:

Recovering my breath, finally, from the pounding in the stomach, I aimed a vigorous kick at the cruel master as he stooped to me, and, by chance, the booted foot smashed his glasses, and almost blinded him with their splinters. Starting backwards with excruciating pain, he contrived to stumble over a bench, and the back of his head struck the stone floor; but, as he was in the act of falling, I had bounded to my feet, and possessed myself of his blackthorn. Armed with this, I rushed at the prostrate form, and struck him at random over his body, until I was called to a sense of what I was doing by the stirless way he received the thrashing.

The boy was puzzled about what to do next. His rage had disappeared and he began to think he should have taken his punishment. But why?

He had done nothing. Someone suggested the schoolmaster be dragged from the classroom and some boys pulled the lifeless figure towards his private rooms. Those remaining began to cry for fear of what might happen next.

John Rowlands had to find a way out of this mess. His friend Moses 'Mose' Roberts asked what they should do. It occurred to them that Francis might be dead and the wrath of the law would come down on them all – especially on John Rowlands. Mose said they must run away, but not before sending someone to check whether Francis was still breathing. A boy peeped into his rooms and found the schoolmaster had staggered to his feet and was washing his bloody face at the sink.

Together John and Mose slipped over the workhouse garden wall and took off across the fields. They ran with a belief that things could only get better. In fact they were soon to get much worse.

The story of how John Rowlands and Moses Roberts absconded from St Asaph's workhouse is uncannily similar to a parallel incident in Charles Dickens' *Nicholas Nickleby*. Substitute St Asaph's workhouse for Dotheboys Hall, James Francis for Wackford Squeers, John and Moses for Nicholas and Smike and readers are presented with a retelling of the classic story relocated to North Wales. The real circumstances surrounding John Rowlands's and Moses Roberts's departure from the workhouse were in reality very different.

The entry concerning John Rowlands's discharge recorded in parish workhouse records makes no mention of any conflict between the boy and his schoolmaster. Inmates absconding from the institution were always named and reasons for their leaving explained. Moses Roberts is shown to have 'run away' from St Asaph's on 24 July 1855 – almost a year before John Rowlands left. Records show Moses's conduct was 'good', but no effort seems to have been made to bring him back to the workhouse. At age fifteen he would soon have left to take employment.

No other boys were discharged on the same day that John Rowlands was permitted to leave – not 'run away' from – St Asaph's on 13 May 1856, ten years after admission. The entry reads: 'Gone to his uncle at the National School, Holywell'. Apart from mistakenly stating 'uncle' – actually his 'cousin' – the entry is correct. Denbigh legend has it that as John Rowlands left the workhouse, Francis stood at the doorway and handed him a shiny new sixpence as a farewell gift.

It is possible there was conflict between the schoolmaster and Moses Roberts, forcing the boy to run away, although nothing confirming this appears in workhouse records. The episode in which a student thrashes a schoolmaster, therefore, appears to be a fantasy invented by Henry Morton Stanley to give his workhouse reminiscences a thrilling climax.

Whatever the true circumstances, in 1863 Francis was committed to the Denbigh Lunatic Asylum, by which time John Rowlands was working as a lawyer's clerk in Brooklyn, New York – a world away from Wales and St Asaph's workhouse.

John Rowlands, aged about eighteen, wearing an ill-fitting suit bought with an advance in his pay from his first employer, James Speake of 'Speake & McCreary, Wholesale and Commission Merchants', New Orleans.

Chapter 2

THE OUTCAST

In Stanley's version of the story, John Rowlands and Moses Roberts were now on the run, still wearing rough workhouse clothing and identifiable to anyone searching for them. He states that they made their way through back roads towards Denbigh where Moses led them to 'a dingy stone house near a bakery' where a woman in the doorway recognised the boy. 'When Mose crossed the threshold he was received with a sounding kiss, and became the object of copious endearments. He was hugged convulsively in the maternal bosom, patted on the back, his hair was frizzled by maternal fingers, and I knew not whether the mother was weeping or laughing, for tears poured over smiles, in streams. The exhibition of fond love was not without its effect on me, for I learned how a mother should behave to her boy,' Stanley recalled.

The woman asked the boys whether they were in Denbigh on an errand – or had they run away? Moses related incidents leading to their departure from St Asaph's and then allowed his companion to introduce himself as 'the grandson of Moses Parry, of the Castle, on my mother's side, and of John Rowlands of Llys, on my father's side'.

She said she knew the family and asked if the boy planned to visit his paternal grandfather, old John Rowlands. The boy replied that he had indeed considered visiting him along with Young Moses, Uncle Thomas and his cousin, Moses Owen, who worked at a Church of England school at nearby Holywell. The woman told the boy that old John Rowlands was now a prosperous landowner, but a 'severe, cross and bitter' old man, unlikely to offer help. She said that the boy's father had 'died many years ago, 13 or 14 years, I should think'. He had, in fact, died two years before.

The following morning, the runaway grandson of wealthy farmer John Rowlands and son of the late John Rowlands, set off to visit his relatives, hoping they would take pity on him and welcome him into their home. He arrived at a large farm, stocked with well-fed animals, with an image in his mind of a severe and sour old man. He prayed it would be wrong.

Stanley recalled:

> Nothing is clear to me but the interview, and the appearance of two figures, my grandfather and myself. It is quite unforgettable. I see myself standing in the kitchen of Llys, cap in hand, facing a stern looking, pink complexioned, rather stout, old gentleman in a brownish suit, knee breeches, and bluish-grey stockings. He is sitting at ease on a wooden settee, the back of which rises several inches higher than his head, and he is smoking a long clay pipe.

He asked the boy who he was, what he wanted and sat back in his seat puffing on his pipe while the boy provided answers. 'When I concluded, he took his pipe from his mouth, reversed it, and with the mouth-piece pointing to the door, he said: "Very well. You can go back the same way as you came. I can do nothing for you, and have nothing to give you."'

This rejection, whether it happened as Stanley relates it or at another time in his young life, remained vivid in his mind into old age. He states: 'The words were few; the action was simple. I have forgotten a million things, probably, but there are some pictures and some few phrases that one can never forget. The insolent, cold-blooded manner impressed them on my memory, and if I have recalled the scene once, it has been recalled a thousand times.'

Later, the boy returned to Castle Row where Young Moses had become prosperous after acquiring his late father's butchery business. His wife Kitty received the boy 'with reserve'. He was given a meal, 'but married people with a house full of children do not care to be troubled with the visits of poor relations, and the meaning conveyed by their manner was not difficult to interpret'.

Next he knocked at the door of the Golden Lion, a pub kept by Uncle Thomas, but there was no room at the inn for a workhouse runaway and in a last-ditch attempt to find someone prepared to give him shelter, John Rowlands made his way towards Brynford and cousin Moses Owen the schoolteacher at the new National School who lived in lodgings next door.

Cousin Moses, 'a tall, severe, ascetic young man of 22 or 23', was surprised by his unexpected visitor. He asked the boy questions both academic and personal and appeared satisfied with the answers. To the boy's surprise, cousin Moses offered him a job as a classroom helper, payment to be made in clothing, board and lodging. Moses was unable to take the boy into the school immediately, so packed him off to his mother's home at Tremeirchion, where he was told she would provide clothes suitable for a young scholar. He would be sent for the following month.

At last, it appeared as if someone was prepared to admit an ex-workhouse boy into their lives, give him a chance – and, perhaps, some affection. The following day, full of high expectations, he walked to the village and a stone house called Ffynnon Beuno, or St Beuno's Spring, where a sign over the door told anyone who could read that Mary Owen owned the house and was licensed to sell groceries, tobacco, 'ale and spirituous liquors'. As he knocked on the door, the boy offered up a silent prayer that his aunt would be as gracious as her schoolmaster son seemed to be.

A woman with 'a bony and narrow face', who turned out to be Aunt Mary, opened the door and the boy handed over his letter of introduction scribbled by her son the previous evening. Its contents appeared both to surprise and annoy her and the boy felt she would rather not have received the news that he had come to stay.

In between serving ale and groceries to customers, Aunt Mary plied the boy with questions. Later, he overheard snatches of conversations with patrons and most were about how rash, extravagant and stupid her son Moses had been, offering this strange new boy in workhouse clothes a job and shelter in her home.

In return for board and lodgings, young John helped his aunt around the shop and farm. Over the following weeks he 'had abundant opportunities to inform myself of the low estimate formed of me by the neighbours'. By eavesdropping on conversations between men drinking his aunt's home-brewed ale, he learned he was the son of Aunt Mary's youngest sister, Elizabeth, also known as Betsy, now mother of three other children who 'had thereby shown herself to be a graceless and thriftless creature'.

Soon the boy also discovered that his situation at the house-cum-shop-cum-pub at Ffynnon Beuno was little better than he had endured at St Asaph's. To her four sons, Aunt Mary was the best of mothers, but her sister's young bastard she kept at arm's length until the requisite month had passed and the next part of the boy's life was to begin at the National School.

Wearing his first suit of smart school clothes, John Rowlands was driven to the school by his aunt in her pony and trap and the following day was appointed an assistant to his cousin who was in charge of the second class. He discovered that in some subjects, other boys were more advanced in their knowledge, but in history, geography and composition, young John Rowlands was best in the school. During evening hours, he was encouraged to study Euclid on geometry, algebra, Latin and grammar. He was allowed to read books from the school library and during weekends spent most of his waking hours engrossed in adventurous literature. The boy found it difficult to make friends. During his first few days at Brynford, boys learned 'of my ignoble origin' and workhouse background, resulting in taunts, jibes and social exclusion.

Although only in his early twenties, cousin Moses was a hard taskmaster, finding much to criticise in young John's efforts. 'With every spoonful of food I ate, I had to endure a worded sting that left a rankling sore. I was a "dolt, a born imbecile, and incorrigible dunce". When the tears commenced to fall, the invectives poured on my bent head. I was "a disgrace to him, a blockhead, an idiot" . . . and [he would] say: "I had hoped to make a man of you, but you are bound to remain a clodhopper; your stupidity is monstrous, perfectly monstrous . . . your head must be full of mud instead of brains. You must go back whence you came. You are good for nothing but to cobble pauper's boots."'

The boy's self-esteem plummeted. A long period of inactivity at the school had made him plump with a round face and rosy cheeks, which made him a target for more cruel jibes from students. Despite his academic achievements, the boy received no encouragement or praise from cousin Moses.

The violence began all over again. When Moses, wearing his 'kill-joy mask' ran out of spiteful words to hurl at John's head, he reached for a birch, boots or anything else that came to hand and hurled them towards his young relative. After nine months of verbal and physical abuse, the lad returned to Ffynnon Beuno for a long weekend, never to return to the National School. He helped on the farm and in the shop under the stern and watchful eye of Aunt Mary, always in the habit of reminding her nephew he would 'shortly be leaving'.

Quite where young John Rowlands would be going and with whom was never mentioned. He was encouraged to apply for a job as a platform assistant at Mold railway station, but nothing came of it, and Aunt Mary urged him to write to his Uncle Tom Morris and Aunt Maria in Liverpool to ask if they might find him suitable employment. Shortly afterwards,

Aunt Maria arrived and told Aunt Mary that there was plenty of work to be found in the city and that her husband, Uncle Tom, had influence with the manager of an insurance company. The boy's future as an office assistant was assured.

As the packet steamer carried the boy and Aunt Mary towards Liverpool and the coastline of North Wales disappeared from view, young John 'was astonished to see dozens of huge ships sailing, under towers of bellying canvass, over the far reaching sea, towards some world not our own'. In his tin trunk was a new Eton suit paid for by his aunt, an overcoat and little else. Soon, the smoke-filled horizon of Liverpool came into view and, as they approached, the boy saw a mass of houses, tall chimneys, towers and groves of ships' masts stretching as far as the eye could see.

They disembarked and boarded a public carriage that drove past berths where docked the scores of ships that sailed in and out of one of the world's largest seaports. The air was acrid with the fumes of pitch and tar and the noise from the horse-drawn traffic that bumped along the street was deafening. For a boy who had spent the first fifteen years of his life in the quiet of the Welsh countryside, Liverpool's clash and clamour came as a surprise.

The carriage stopped outside a hotel, where Aunt Mary handed the boy over to Aunt Maria who was waiting at the entrance. Aunt Mary could not stay; she had to return to Ffynnon Beuno, her business and customers. Reaching into her bag, she pulled out a sovereign and pressed it into John Rowland's hand. She told him to be a good boy and make haste to get rich. Then she was gone.

Aunt Maria ushered the boy into another cab and told the driver to head towards Roscommon Street in the city's Everton district. There Uncle Tom was waiting with cousin Teddy. Suddenly the boy had acquired more of a family than he had thought possible.

Uncle Tom was a genial man who had once occupied a responsible post with a railway company. Thanks to his influence, a man called Mr Winter had secured a position with the company and this same Mr Winter was said to be the man who would arrange for Uncle Tom's new nephew to begin a job in an insurance office. At some point, Uncle Tom had left the railway company and was now a lowly paid worker at a textile mill. Mr Winter, however, had risen to a managerial role and was in charge of an entire department. The reason why Uncle Tom toiled away at a poorly paid job while Mr Winter sat behind a large desk issuing instructions was not made clear to John Rowlands.

The boy's first days in Liverpool were spent exploring the busy streets leading from Everton to the docks. And then the day was announced when Uncle Tom would take the boy in his new Eton suit to call on the famous Mr Winter, through whose guidance the foundations of his future prosperity would be laid. Uncle Tom told John he had befriended Mr Winter some years earlier when he had moved in more affluent circles. Then Uncle Tom's influence had resulted in Mr Winter's promotion and his promise to repay the favour one day – and today was that day.

They arrived at a large detached house where Uncle Tom and John Rowlands were met with a great show of friendship from a man wearing smart business clothes who shook hands with the boy and his uncle. When it was time to state the reasons for their call, compliments were showered on the boy and uncle and nephew told to return the following morning 'to hear of something favourable'. On the journey home, Uncle Tom spoke enthusiastically about Mr Winter, his generous, influential friend. That month, they made the same journey to Mr Winter's house on twenty separate occasions. On each visit a different excuse was politely offered, until at the end of the twenty-first visit, Uncle Tom's patience snapped and he blurted out to his so-called friend: 'Now, damn it all! Stop that, Winter. You are nothing but an artful humbug. In God's name, man, what pleasure can you find in this eternal lying? Confound you, I say, for a damned old rascal and hypocrite! I can't stand any more of this devilish snivelling. I shall be smothered if I stay here longer. Come, boy, let's get out of this, we will have no more of this cheating fraud.'

Uncle Tom and his nephew strode out, the older man fuming all the way home, telling the boy: 'Never mind, laddie! We'll get along somehow without the help of that sweep.'

Back at Roscommon Street, Uncle Tom and Aunt Maria went into a huddle. When they emerged, it was to borrow the boy's sovereign to buy food to revive Uncle Tom's flagging spirits. The following week Aunt Maria 'borrowed my Eton suit and took it to the place of three gilt balls'. His overcoat went to the same place a few days later 'and then I knew the family was in great trouble'. The place was the pawnbroker's.

John Rowlands now walked through Liverpool's teeming streets with a different purpose, scanning shop windows for notices advertising job vacancies. There was little on offer – he was too young or too small, not smart enough or too late. But with the persistence for which Henry Morton Stanley would become famous in later life, he kept trying, finally landing a position in a haberdasher's shop at 5s a week. His duties included shop-sweeping, lamp-trimming, window polishing and taking care of the store's large and heavy wooden shutters, which he was required to take down each morning at 7 a.m. and replace at the end of the day.

The boy left the house early each morning, joining thousands of others trudging through the streets to their various tasks across the sunless and grimy city. In the evening he returned to Roscommon Street to eat a supper of cockles, shrimps or bloater and by 10.30 p.m. he would be in bed. After two months, the weight of the heavy shutters injured the boy's back but after a week off to recover he returned to work to find his job taken by someone else.

He was forced to tramp the streets again whereby he rapidly took on the appearance of an urchin. The need to find work drove him further in the direction of the docks where, with nothing better to do, he watched sailing ships come and go to all parts of the world. He saw grain, textiles, barrels, boxes and sacks unloaded from their holds and read the sailing notices pinned next to gangplanks stating where vessels were bound – New York, New Orleans, Demerara, the West Indies, Bombay, Calcutta, Shanghai, Melbourne and Sydney. The boy wondered what those cities were like and for the first time in his life, decided that he, too, wanted to sail away and explore the world. . . .

He found a job as a butcher's delivery boy at a shop close to the port. Duties included carrying baskets of fresh provisions to ships on the eve of sailing into the River Mersey and onwards to a hundred destinations around the globe.

Meanwhile, home life at Roscommon Street was getting harder. Money was scarce, space in short supply and the boy's relations with his older cousin Teddy, who resented John's presence, were causing tension in the small house.

Then, in the autumn of 1857, 'fate caused a little incident to occur, which settled my course for me'. The boy was sent to deliver provisions to the packet-ship *Windermere* along with an invoice addressed to its American skipper, Captain David Hartinge. While the skipper checked his provisions, the boy gazed admiringly at the rich furniture and gilded mirrors in his cabin.

The Captain noticed the boy admiring his surroundings and asked if he would like to live there. John Rowlands was overwhelmed to be talking to an American and shyly stammered that he knew nothing of the sea or seamanship. The seaman asked: 'What do you say to going with me as a cabin boy? I will give you five dollars a month, and an outfit. In three days we start for New Orleans, to the land of the free and the home of the brave.'

Without giving the matter a moment's thought, the boy signed up for the voyage on the spot. He would leave unhappiness at Roscommon Street and begin a new and better life in the United States of America. He would sail away from his past life, workhouse brutality, rejection by relations, hatred from cousin Teddy, his pauper's wardrobe and miserable jobs with dismal prospects. He would begin again in a place where nobody knew anything about him or his history. From now on he could be anyone he wanted to be and as soon as he arrived in America he would shake off his old life and reinvent himself as someone quite different to 'John Rowlands – Bastard'.

Uncle Tom and Aunt Maria greeted the news of his impending departure, scheduled for three days after Christmas 1857, with dismay. The boy insisted there was nothing for him in Liverpool and he had made up his mind. Without too much protesting, his relatives agreed to let him go.

On 28 December, sixteen-year-old John Rowlands arrived at the foot of the *Windermere*'s gangplank with a tin trunk containing his few worldly possessions. As he climbed on board, his mind was full of confusing thoughts – but one thing was certain: life could only get better.

A steam tug towed the vessel into mid-river, the sail was loosened, sailors hoisted the topsails and the *Windermere* headed out towards the Atlantic. John Rowlands, cabin boy, stood at the railings with scores of steerage passengers and watched Liverpool sink slowly into a grey streak on the distant horizon. Before him lay America – and a new and exciting life.

Chapter 3

THE *WINDERMERE*

At 1,107 tons, the triple-mast coastal packet-ship, *Windermere* was a sizeable vessel, equipped to transport 100 passengers – mostly British and European emigrants travelling on one-way tickets to try their fortunes in a new world – and a motley crew of thirty Anglo-Irish, Dutch and American seamen. The ship, owned by the Smith-Pilkington Line, regularly sailed between Liverpool and New Orleans, via Jamaica, a voyage taking anything up to sixty days to complete. On journeys to Liverpool she carried a cargo of cotton bales and on return voyages transported textiles and finished garments made from the same material at northern mills.

Once the ship had passed the north-western tip of Wales, it steered a southerly course into the chilly Irish Sea and down through St George's Channel before passing the south coast of Ireland and out into the rolling winter waters of the North Atlantic. The *Windermere* would not see land again for a further 3,971 nautical miles and fifty days when it would call into Jamaica to unload some passengers and freight and take on fresh supplies for the remaining 1,021 nautical miles to the port of New Orleans.

But when the *Windermere* was less than an hour into its long voyage and off New Brighton, it began sharply to rise and fall in Liverpool Bay's rough waters, causing its newest cabin boy to suddenly feel light-headed. As he gripped the handrail, the ship, sea and sky began to swirl around at speed, forcing the boy to confine himself to his bunk in the apprentice cabin on the main deck for the next three days.

On the fourth day, Captain Hartinge sent word below to remind his new cabin boy that he was not engaged on a pleasure cruise and had work to do. He was expected on deck immediately – or he could expect trouble. The message was delivered by 'a hoarse, rasping voice, whose owner seemed in a violent passion, bawling: "Now, then, come out of that, you — young Britisher! Step up here in a brace of shakes, or I'll come down a' skin your — — carcase alive!"'

With a swirling head and stomach that had not taken in food for three days, the boy was assigned deck-washing duties. Fear of more threats from the owner of the rough voice drove away any remaining nausea as he was urged to 'seize that scrubbing broom, you — joskin! Lay hold of it, I say, and scrub, you — son of a sea cook! Scrub like —! Scrub until you drop! Sweat you — swab!'

The boy snatched a look at the man issuing these crude commands. It was 'a kind of creature never dreamed of before by me'. His name was Nelson, second mate in charge of apprentice crew members, with a mission to make life as miserable as possible for his young charges.

After a day of deck scrubbing, John Rowlands was taken aside by an older boy called Harry, who warned him to avoid Nelson. Harry had undertaken an Atlantic voyage already on the *Windermere* and considered himself an expert seaman, having learned to get stuck into his work and never to answer back. John Rowlands's announcement that he was hired as a cabin boy and not a deck hand amused Harry. He told him that on his previous voyage two other lads had been induced to join the ship with promises of a similar job but ended up as deck skivvies for the entire journey. Once back in Liverpool, they were first down the gangplank, not even stopping to collect their wages, so keen were they to put as much distance as possible between the *Windermere*, Nelson's brutality and themselves.

Harry told John that while Nelson was dangerous, Chief Mate Waters was 'the very devil', a man prepared to punch anyone weaker than himself. Waters had taken a liking to Harry because he had been brought on board by his father, who insisted the Captain signed articles making him an official member of the crew. 'The skipper has to account for me when we get into port; but you may be blown overboard and no one would be the wiser,' said Harry. 'I am now as good as an ordinary seaman, though too young for the forecastle. I can furl royals as spry as any bucco sailor on board, and know every rope on the ship, while you don't know stem from stern.'

For a moment John thought he was back at St Asaph's, only this time it was a floating workhouse with a pair of sadistic ship's mates taking James Francis's place. Just as Francis had beaten inmates in his charge, so the ruffian mates stormed, swore, struck and kicked junior wretches on the *Windermere*. It was too late to climb over the rail and dive to freedom. They were now crossing the Atlantic – and John Rowlands couldn't even swim.

The workhouse boy learned that the rest of the crew also had nothing but contempt for land-lubbers working on the *Windermere*. Nothing pleased them more than seeing a boy doubled over with seasickness. If they encountered a lad going about his duties in one of the ship's corridors, they thought nothing of landing blows across his head or giving his rear a sharp kick. They enjoyed watching other seamen making lives a misery and the Captain rarely interfered.

Five days out of Liverpool, three stowaways – a pair of starving young Irish boys and a down-at-heel Irishman – appeared on deck. They were taken to the Captain who closely interrogated each one before dismissing them to the mercy of the crew. Nelson was first in line 'to warm their cockles', as he phrased it. The cries of the youngest lad were the loudest, but when he finally appeared on deck to beg for food, the remainder of the crew guessed from his roguish smile that he had been the least injured.

The arrival of the stowaways acted as a buffer between John and 'a considerable amount of inglorious mauling' which Nelson might otherwise have dealt out to the Welsh landlubber. The second mate was in the habit of chasing both Irish boys around the ship. Both were able to run, but there were few places to hide on the *Windermere* and when they were finally captured 'the cries of the innocents would be heart-rending'.

Henry Morton Stanley's account of his early years at the workhouse and on the *Windermere* make frequent reference to sadistic brutality and 'maulings'. The moral climate of the time prevented Stanley from describing the form the maulings took. They were, most likely, sexual. Homosexual rape of younger, weaker apprentice crew by older, stronger and undisciplined shipmates was common on merchant ships. Sexual activity between consenting males was frowned upon, but a blind eye was often turned by officers rarely present in quarters shared by the lower orders.

The boy gradually found his sea legs and even looked forward to sailing through the gales and tempests he heard about from shipmates. Somewhere in mid-Atlantic he encountered them, on a day when 'a shadow passed over the ocean, until it was almost black in colour; and then, to windward, I could see battalion after battalion of white caps rushing gaily, exultingly, towards us'.

Oilskins were passed around as waves began to lap over the sides and 'every "man jack" seemed electrified and flew to his duty with all ardour'. There was little an inexperienced landlubber could offer in such a situation, so he stood to one side, taking in the scene as men pulled on ropes and sails were lowered. Looking back, he recalled 'a gale at sea is as stimulating as a battle'.

Just as the boy was beginning to enjoy the experience of a storm at sea, a harsh voice told him to get back to swabbing the deck. It was Waters and the lad seized the first mop that came to hand and spent the rest of the storm soaking up what appeared to be the entire Atlantic Ocean as the mate's colourful language stung his sensitive ears.

'That first voyage of mine was certainly a remarkable one, were it only for the new-fangled vocabulary I was constantly hearing,' he recalled. 'Every sentence contained some new word or phrase, coined extemporate, and accentuated by a rope's end, or un-gentle back-hander, with gutter adjectives and explosive epithets.' Harry gave back as good a range of invective as he received – with interest – but John Rowlands was afraid to use similar language, which appeared to have been designed for people other than himself.

The remainder of the voyage took place under blue skies and the lad spent his time endlessly scrubbing paintwork, cleaning brass, painting, oiling, sloshing out the bilges and tarring. On Sundays, Nelson and Waters gave their spiteful invective a rest and 'there might have been worse places than the deck of the *Windermere* on a Sunday'. Quieter moments were few and far between. Before the end of the voyage both first and second mate felt the need physically to attack both junior and mature crew with spikes, ropes and the soles of their boots until the day before the ship entered the Mississippi. Suddenly the sadistic pair changed their attitude and began praising everyone they had mauled and beaten. Everyone agreed the pair were anxious they would be reported to the Captain and end up in a New Orleans jail.

The *Windermere* laid anchor off one of the four mouths of the Mississippi in mid-February 1858, fifty-two days after leaving Liverpool. On the following morning, a tug towed the ship upriver for 100 miles to New Orleans, where it joined hundreds of others lined up alongside sailing vessels and river steamers. Once the passengers had disembarked, a multitude of boarding house touts climbed on board and took possession of the entire crew, leaving Harry and John the only members on board who had travelled from Liverpool. They stood at the railing taking in the scene. The boy later recalled:

> The levee sloped down with a noble breadth to the river, and stretched for miles up and down in front of the city, and was crowned with the cargoes of hundreds of vessels which lay broadside to it. In some places the freights lay in mountainous heaps, but the barrels, and hogsheads, and cotton bales, covered immense spaces, though arranged in precise order; and with the multitudes of men – white, red, black, yellow – horses, mules, and drays and wagons, the effect of such a scene, with its fierce activity and new atmosphere, upon a raw boy from St. Asaph, may be better imagined than described. . . . I think it is one of the most vivid recollections I possess. Of the thousands of British boys who have landed in this city, I fancy none was so utterly unsophisticated as myself.

It was time to set foot on American soil and John Rowlands and Harry flew down the gangplank in the direction of Tchoupitoulas Street, New Orleans' main thoroughfare and some 'diggings' where Harry had friends. 'I was nearly overwhelmed with blissful feeling that rises from emancipation. I was free – and I was happy, yes, actually happy, for I was free,' Stanley wrote years later.

As they walked down the bustling street, the boys breathed in the balmy air and its rich mixed aroma of fermenting molasses, semi-baked sugar, coffee beans, pitch, tar, rum and whiskey. The people they passed seemed different to those in Denbigh and Liverpool; they possessed a sense of equality, confidence and independence.

They stopped at a boarding house where Harry was welcomed by the proprietor. He ordered dinner for them both – okra soup, grits, sweet potatoes, corn pone and mashed-pudding. Harry later paid for the meal 'with the air of one whose purse was deep beyond soundings'. He ordered a cigar and sat back in his easy chair puffing away like a millionaire.

It was time to explore. John was happy to follow Harry who headed in the direction of another house he knew where the proprietress 'was extremely gracious'. Harry whispered something to her and the boys were shown into a parlour 'where four young ladies wearing such scant clothing that I was speechless with amazement bounced into the room'. The naive Welsh workhouse boy had no idea what a brothel was or exactly what profession the young ladies were engaged in – 'but when they proceeded to take liberties with my person, they seemed to be so appallingly wicked that I shook them off and fled out of the house'. Harry followed and attempted to persuade his shipmate to return, 'but I would as soon have jumped into the gruel-coloured Mississippi as have looked into the eyes of those giggling wantons again. My disgust was so great I never, in after years, could overcome my repugnance to females of that character.'

They entered a waterfront saloon and Harry ordered whiskey – but John refused, telling his friend he belonged to the Band of Hope and had taken the pledge of abstinence. 'Well smoke then, do something like other fellows,' said Harry irritably, aware that the young pair stood out in the crowded bar. Wishing 'to appear manly', John called for a cigar, which he 'puffed proudly and with vigour', until he was overcome with nausea and rushed out to bring up his recently consumed dinner.

With no money in his pocket or anywhere to stay, the lad returned to the *Windermere* where he was discovered next day by Nelson who greeted him with 'Hello, you here still? I thought you had vamoosed like the Irish stowaways. Not enough physic, eh? Well, sonny, we must see what we can do for you. . . .' The boy was put to work cleaning brass fittings and spent the following days carrying out shipboard jobs, frightened to walk alone down the gangplank. Whenever he mentioned his wages, Nelson and Waters avoided the subject and raised threatening fists in his direction.

He decided to jump ship – which is what the Captain and his mates were expecting, so they might pocket his wages for themselves. He emptied his seabag onto the cabin floor and picked out the few contents he owned – some clothes, a pair of shoes and the Bible the bishop had given him at the workhouse. He dressed and lay on his bunk until a drunken Harry arrived and fell into a deep sleep. When it was quiet, he crept out into the night, down the gangplank and ran along the riverbank until he found a pile of cotton bales in the shadows. There he curled up and slept until daybreak. He was alone and adrift again.

Chapter 4

MEETING MR STANLEY

The penniless new émigré now had two choices – work or starve. He chose the former and set off in search of work among the mercantile stores lining Tchoupitoulas Street. By 7 a.m. he had walked the full length of the street without seeing a single sign in any window offering employment. At the end of the street he noticed a middle-aged gentleman with a silky black beard seated reading a newspaper in front of Store No. 3, his chair tilted at a leisurely angle against the door. He wore a dark alpaca suit and a tall hat and the boy assumed he was proprietor of the store, over which hung a sign announcing that these were the premises of 'Speake & McCreary, Wholesale and Commission Merchants'. The boy took a deep breath and asked: 'Do you want a boy, sir?'

Startled by the question, the man sat up and replied in a northern English accent: 'No, I do not think I want one. What should I want a boy for? Where do you hail from? You are not an American.' The boy told the gentleman more than he was expecting to hear: how he had arrived from Liverpool on a packet-ship, taken on as a cabin boy, tricked into becoming a deck hand, abused by older crew members, his pay withheld and, finally, how he had jumped ship the previous night.

The gentleman tilted his chair back again and noticing a book in the boy's pocket, asked if he could read. The boy proudly showed him the Bible presented at the workhouse and admitted that he could read. The gentleman read the inscription: 'Presented to John Rowlands by the Right Revd. Thomas Vowler Short, D. D., Lord Bishop of St. Asaph, for diligent application to his studies, and general good conduct. January 5th, 1855'. Returning the Bible, he pointed to an article in his newspaper and told the boy to read it aloud. The boy duly read out a newspaper story about a legislative assembly; the man then enquired if he could also write. 'Yes, sir, with a good round hand, as I have been told', and to prove it, he borrowed a pencil and copied out an address written on a label attached to some coffee sacks.

The gentleman appeared impressed with these accomplishments and called inside the store to ask when Mr Speake might be returning. A voice from within answered that he would be back after nine. 'Well, we have ample time before us. As I don't suppose you've breakfasted yet, you had better come along with me.'

As they walked along the wharf, the gentleman told John Rowlands that first impressions were important and he feared that if Mr Speake spotted cotton fluff on the boy's jacket and unkempt hair, he might not be induced to look at him twice or trust him with his grocery stock. After an American breakfast of waffles, doughnuts and coffee in a restaurant, he was taken for a haircut, wash and brush up before returning to the store to meet Mr James Speake, proprietor. At their meeting, Mr Speake asked if it were true he was seeking work, because if it was, he was prepared to offer a week's trial at 5 dollars – 'and if we find we suit each other, the place will be permanent. Are you agreeable?'

The boy struggled to express his thanks to the stranger and Mr Speake, but was lost for words. The men made light of it and the stranger told the boy he was about to go upriver but would soon return and expected to hear good reports of his progress.

As soon as the gentleman had gone, John Rowlands, newly appointed shop assistant at Speake & McCreary, New Orleans, began work alongside other assistants. From one he learned that the gentleman who had been instrumental in his good fortune was a commercial broker who, with his brother, acted as a middleman between upriver planters and merchants in New Orleans, Havana and the West Indies. The gentleman shared an office in the store and conducted a good deal of business with Speake & McCreary. From another he discovered that the gentleman was called Henry Hope Stanley, who lived with his wife in a fine house in St Charles Avenue and that he travelled regularly up and down the river on business.

The boy's first day as a shop assistant at Speake & McCreary included working with a pair of Mr Speake's slaves, Dan and Samuel. As well as general provisions, the store also sold clothing, brandy, liqueurs and syrups. Goods were stored in warehouses and in attics at the top of the building and as soon as they were ready for collection, Dan and Samuel carried them to a fleet of delivery drays parked outside. It was Dan and Samuel who introduced the boy to his first lodging house and when they walked together towards the spacious wooden building in Thomas Street that would become his home, he noticed that their tin lunch boxes appeared particularly heavy as they moved down the road.

The house was owned by a young black woman called Mrs Williams who said she was prepared to charge him a rent low enough to leave something over at the end of the week. The previous night he had slept on a bale of cotton like a criminal on the run. Today he had a job, new friends and, for the first time in his life, a room of his own in a respectable house in the great city of New Orleans. He was just wondering if life could get any better when Mrs Williams entered his room and 'in a most matter-of-fact way, assisted me to undress and took possession of my shirt and collar, saying they would be washed and ironed by morning, that I might look more "spruce"'. At the close of that momentous day, the boy knelt by his bed 'and was reminded to give thanks to Him, who, like a father pitieth his children and them that fear Him'.

Early the next morning the boy was at the store's front door. He loved his job and proved good at his work. A willingness to learn, take orders and jump to any task endeared him to Mr Speake. His confidence started to grow. For the first time in his life, someone was telling John Rowlands he was good at what he was doing. He was praised for his eager attitude and inwardly he swelled with pride, which was another new experience. Meanwhile, Dan and Samuel attempted to dampen his enthusiasm. 'Take it easy, little boss, don't kill yourself. Plenty of time. Leave something for tomorrow', they would tell him as they settled back on a pile of coffee sacks for an afternoon nap.

At the end of the week, John was called to Mr Speake's office and told his trial period had proved a success and he would be engaged as a junior clerk for $25 per month – a fortune for a boy who hitherto had only worked unpaid or been forced to hand his wages over to someone else. He worked out that he would be left with $15 to enjoy life at the end of each month and Mr Speake advanced the boy a month's pay to buy new clothes.

Within weeks of arriving in America, John Rowlands became a different boy in temper, spirit and personality. He discovered that he could express opinions and people welcomed his views. In the land of free speech, John Rowlands started to shake off his reserve, to live and talk like an American. 'My British antipathies and proclivities were dropping from me as rapidly as the littleness of my servile life was replaced by the felicities of freedom,' he recollected some thirty years later.

Eighteen months after leaving the workhouse and less than three months after sailing from Liverpool, he had fallen in love with America, his attic room, his job, the busy streets, tasty food and relaxed atmosphere which existed in the city that had accepted him as one of its own. For John Rowlands, New Orleans became the city in which the workhouse boy was allowed to flourish and grow into a healthy and spirited young man.

Henry Hope Stanley re-entered John Rowlands's life on his return from his upriver journey. He congratulated the boy on his smart appearance and confidentially revealed that Mr Speake was more than satisfied with his progress at the store. Mr Stanley handed his card to the boy and said he would be delighted if he could join him and Mrs Stanley for breakfast on Sunday at their St Charles Avenue home.

When John Rowlands arrived outside the pillared porticos and shady garden of Mr Stanley's home, he found his host waiting in an easy chair on the verandah. He greeted the boy warmly and showed him inside where he was introduced to 'a fragile little lady, who was the picture of refinement'. This was Mrs Frances Stanley, a woman now in her early thirties who had been beautiful in her youth, but whose vivacity had been robbed from her by years of illness. She greeted her young visitor and ushered him to a place at the table.

The perfectly groomed lady and her young guest impressed each other in equal measure. Although there were twelve others invited to the table that morning, John Rowlands felt 'there was an almost impassable gulf between me and them. Their conversation was beyond my understanding, mostly, though I could spell and interpret each word; but the subjects of their talk left me in the clouds.' Conversations with Mrs Stanley, however, were courteous and cordial and the lady of the house took pains to put the boy at ease.

A warm friendship grew up between John Rowlands and Henry Stanley and little by little the boy came to regard him as an older associate. To be in his company 'was an education for one so ignorant as myself' and the boy looked to the older man as a tutor and mentor.

Sunday breakfast with the Stanleys was the high spot of the boy's week. Mrs Stanley became more considerate at each meeting and she and her husband encouraged the boy to read widely, recommending books, which could be purchased cheaply in New Orleans, and loaning other volumes. Without the Stanleys, 'my love of books would have proved sufficient safeguard against the baser kind of temptations; but, with them, I was rendered almost impregnable to vice,' he wrote. Breakfasts were followed by visits to the Episcopalian church where Mr Stanley occasionally officiated as a lay-preacher. Later there was a chance to relax and talk for the remainder of the day in the comfort of their spacious home.

After three months, Mr Speake increased the boy's salary to $30 per month and informed his young employee that, thanks to John, the store had never been in such good order. It was while undertaking a routine check of warehouse stock that John Rowlands discovered something was wrong. Sacks and boxes that should have been heavy with the weight of provisions seemed strangely light. By turning his oil lamp on full, he noticed some coffee sacks appeared to have been bitten through by rats, but the quantity of beans spilt on the floor was out of proportion with the amount missing. When the boy took his lamp into storage lofts, he discovered wine and syrup barrels half empty and that entire boxes of biscuits and sardines had completely vanished. The boy checked the stock book, which revealed that incorrect sales figures had been entered into the records. So as not to cast suspicion on himself, he sought out Mr Speake and told him of the discovery.

The proprietor instructed staff to check the stock again, comparing goods in the warehouse with bills sent to customers. While searching the lofts, the boy moved a broom and discovered a lunch box hidden behind it. He reached down and found it heavy to lift. He flipped open the lid and found it full of golden syrup. A second lunch box nearby was full of Malmsey wine. They belonged to Dan and Samuel, who had been pilfering different goods each day, smuggling them out in their lunch boxes. On closer investigation, biscuits, sardines and other groceries were found concealed under floorboards and in dark recesses of the stockrooms.

Dan and Samuel had made themselves scarce in the gloomy shadows of the top floor loft and when questioned about missing items denied all knowledge, taking on an air of innocence. When challenged to produce their lunch boxes, they conveniently forgot where they had left them. When Mr Speake produced them and asked for the lids to be opened, they sank to their knees, confessed everything and begged forgiveness from their boss.

A constable was summoned and the slaves taken away 'to receive on the next day such a flogging as only practised State officials know how to administer'. Dan was reinstated but Samuel was sent into the fields to labour as a cotton picker.

Henry Stanley heard everything about his young protégé from Mr Speake and paid him an early morning call at Mrs Williams' boarding house. The older man was pleased to find the boy's room clean and tidy and he carefully scrutinised his collection of cheap editions of popular classics. When the boy returned to his lodging house the following evening, he found a large parcel waiting for him. It contained a dozen books in green and blue covers bearing the names of Shakespeare, Lord Byron, Washington Irving, Oliver Goldsmith, Ben Johnson and others – a gift from Mr and Mrs Stanley.

Yellow fever and dysentery raged through New Orleans in the autumn of 1859. Mr Speake was taken ill and after a few days died, aged forty-seven. Mrs Speake sold her husband's store to a pair of businessmen called Ellison and McMillan who dismissed the staff with the exception of the eighteen-year-old Welsh boy who had, by now, been promoted to the position of warehouse manager.

John Rowlands was now a confident young man about town. He had a responsible job with a regular income, a permanent address and a small circle of respectable friends with whom he was seen at church and promenading through the fashionable quarters of New Orleans. His only female companions at this time appear to have been the wives or daughters of his employers or customers and those he met at church. The boy was timid with the opposite sex, especially girls of his own age. He felt shy, uncomfortable and confused in their presence and was more at home with their mothers; particularly mothers interested in literature or tales from the darkest warehouse.

An example of how naïve he was at this time came when a new lodger arrived at Mrs Williams' house. The landlady thought the 'fair-haired lad of about my own age' would be better off sharing a room with John because he was English and recently arrived from Liverpool. The new roommate was called Dick Heaton. He had worked his passage to New Orleans as a cabin boy on the *Pocahontas*, where he had received the same rough treatment on the high seas as his new friend. Dick was clever and intelligent, 'though not educated'. John could not help noticing 'an unusual forward inclination of Dick's body, a leanness of the shoulders, compared to the fullness below the waist', causing him to remark casually that he walked more like a girl than a boy.

At night the boys shared a bed and John noticed that Dick was so modest he would only undress after snuffing out the candle. When he climbed into bed, he lay on the edge taking care not to come into contact with his bedfellow. In the morning he lay in bed fully clothed, which he explained by saying that during his sea crossing he had been thrashed for taking so long to get dressed 'and had scarcely dared take off his boots during the whole voyage'.

The boys traded stories about unhappy childhoods. John told Dick about his Atlantic crossing and Dick revealed he had protected himself from thrashings by padding the seat of his trousers with cotton while howling loudly as the kicks and blows showered down. If the new lodger mentioned other liberties the crew had taken on the journey to America, they remained unrecorded.

The boys spent their days off exploring New Orleans. One morning when John woke early to leave for the store, he noticed Dick, still asleep with 'what I took to be two tumours on his breast'. When Dick awoke he asked what was the matter. 'Pointing to his open breast, I anxiously inquired if those were not painful.' Dick rudely told John to mind his own business, but it slowly dawned on John – such were the buttoned up times in which they lived – that Dick was in fact a girl, disguised in boy's clothing.

The impostor admitted the truth, telling John 'her' name was Alice Heaton from Everton, Liverpool, who had lived with an ageing grandmother who had ill-treated her. She dreamed of running away from her harsh life and had heard wonderful stories about America. The girl had managed to scrape a little money together and stole more from her violent grandmother. She bought male clothing at a junkshop, got a boy's haircut and talked her way into a job on the *Pocahontas*. Somehow she had managed to avoid detection of her true sex on the Atlantic voyage.

It was time for John to leave for work. They agreed to continue talking later that evening, when John promised to think up a way of helping the boy who had suddenly become a girl to acquire a new identity. All that day the boy devised ideas in his head about how he might help her find employment and afford some feminine clothing. When he returned to the lodging house, Mrs Williams told him that 'Dick' had not been seen since early that morning. John waited hours for her return, but the girl who lived her life as a boy never came back to Thomas Street. Looking back, he reflected: 'I have hoped ever since that Fate was as propitious to her, as I think it was wise, in separating two young and simple creatures, who might have been led, through excess of sentiment, into folly.'

Henry Morton Stanley gives readers of his memoirs scant information about Henry Hope Stanley, the man he claimed would later adopt him and change his name from John Rowlands to his own. He fails to reveal that the older man was also British, born near Manchester in 1815, the son of John Stanley and Selina Howard. Henry Hope Stanley's father had died when the boy was very young and his mother had remarried a local Episcopalian clergyman, the Reverend Brookes from Mouton Eccles. At the age of twenty-one and like hundreds before him, he had crossed the Atlantic to seek a better life in America. A younger brother followed a year later. Perhaps the Stanley brothers had felt excluded from their mother's life once she had presented her new husband with a son, named James Howard Brooks?

Henry Hope Stanley arrived first in Charleston, South Carolina and later settled in New Orleans where he studied for the ministry, was ordained and preached at Episcopalian churches between Nashville and Savannah for the next two years. But the preacher lost his religious fervour and with advice from business members of his congregation, took up another life as a shopkeeper. Later he became a partner in a brokering business called the Commercial Cotton Press, which acted as an agent between upriver planters and New Orleans merchants. Mr Stanley also owned a large plantation called Jefferson Hall in Tangipahoa, near Arcola, which was managed in his absence by a widow with young daughters.

Mr Stanley married twice, the first time at age twenty-eight to a Texan girl who ran a boarding house to supplement their income. The first Mrs Stanley died from typhoid while her husband was absent on a business trip. By the time he returned home, his wife had been dead nearly a month.

Four years later during a visit to England to see his mother, Henry Hope Stanley met and married a pretty and petite teenage girl, Frances Mellor. The couple were unable to produce children of their own, so adopted two daughters, Joanna and Annie. By the time John Rowlands appeared on the scene, Joanna had already fled the family home, eloping with a coach driver. Stanley's memoir, however, states that Mr and Mrs Stanley were childless and had once visited an orphanage with a view to adopting a child 'but they had made no choice, from over-fastidiousness'.

The Stanleys' English origins, the death of the first Mrs Stanley and the existence of two stepdaughters do not merit any mention in Henry Morton Stanley's memoirs – unusual for a man who would later go into minute detail about people and incidents in accounts of his own exploits.

He relates a melodramatic story of how he discovered Frances Stanley seriously ill with fever while her husband was away on business. It was complete fabrication. He claims to have shared in a round-the-clock sickbed vigil with the family maid, Margaret, remaining in the house day and night. When morning came, the boy had to go to work, but told Margaret he would request leave and continue to help looking after Mrs Stanley in her husband's absence. In his account the store's new owner was outraged that the boy dared ask for time off and told him to go to the devil, so he resigned and returned to his seat outside Mrs Stanley's sick room. Her condition worsened and a doctor was summoned. There was little he could do. Margaret and John sat with her throughout. In another Dickensian moment, readers are told:

> With my heart throbbing painfully, and expecting I know not what, I entered on tiptoe. I saw a broad bed, curtained with white muslin, whereon lay the fragile figure of the patient, so frail and delicate that, in my rude health, it seemed insolence in me to be near her. It had been easy for me to speak of illness when I knew so little of what it meant; but, on regarding its ravages, and observing the operation of death, I stood as one petrified. . . . Margaret pushed me gently to the bedside, and I saw by the dim light how awfully solemn a human face can be when in saintly peace. Slowly, I understood how even the most timid woman could smilingly welcome death, and willingly yield herself to its cold embrace. . . . While listening at the door, I had wished that, in some way, I could transfuse a portion of my fullness of spirit into her, that she might have the force to resist the foe; for surely, with a little more courage, she would not abandon husband, friends and admirers, for the still company in the churchyard. . . .

Frances Stanley opened her eyes and told the young man: 'Be a good boy. God bless you!' Minutes later, she was dead.

By coincidence, Mr Stanley's brother arrived in New Orleans shortly afterwards and took charge of the burial arrangements and the running of the household. He assumed young Rowlands was some sort of domestic retainer and paid him no attention. Days later, Margaret sent a note to Mrs Williams' house telling John that the body had been embalmed, encased in a coffin and was due to be shipped upriver to Mr Stanley in St Louis.

Without the Stanleys and regular employment the boy grew increasingly despondent. He managed to secure odd jobs until he heard from a fellow lodger that the brig *Dido* needed deck hands to work on river routes. He was taken on as crew and earned enough for the fare to go in search of Mr Stanley.

In November 1859, John Rowlands purchased a ticket to St Louis where, within an hour of arriving, he discovered Mr Stanley had returned to New Orleans. With no money in his pocket for a return ticket, the boy went in search of more work. He learned that a barge was travelling downriver on a month-long voyage carrying lumber. Its owner needed an assistant to help with deck duties and assist the cook and John was taken on with the warning that there was no place on board for slackers and that he must be prepared to 'muck in' with everything from pulling the long oars to peeling potatoes and scouring pans.

Life on the barge gave the boy a chance to study the mighty Mississippi, its currents, eddies and whirlpools, unaware that these observations and impressions would one day be applied as knowledge and understanding to Africa's river systems and their waters' many moods.

The voyage ended when the barge arrived at lumberyards between Carroltown and New Orleans. It was a long walk into the city, but with determination and fortitude, the boy headed in the direction of Charles Street – and Henry Hope Stanley. He knocked on the door of the smart house and waited. The lock turned, the door opened and there stood 'the only friend I seemed to possess in the whole of America'.

His reception by Mr Stanley was remembered as being 'so paternal that the prodigal son could not have been more delighted'. The boy's absence from New Orleans had increased his affections for his friend: outside his company he was shy, silent and morose; with him he was different – confident, outgoing and conversational.

John entered the parlour he had sat in so often with the Stanleys and told the older man how he had shared Mrs Stanley's last moments, gone in search of work and of his voyage downriver on the barge. Mr Stanley listened carefully to the boy's story and said he would now take charge of his future. He had wondered what had become of John Rowlands, having visited the store and found he had left his job. Knowing how friendless and unsophisticated the lad was, he had searched the streets for him, and now they were reunited, he said he would oversee his education 'for the business of life' and be to him what a real father ought to be.

As a workhouse boy, he had often imagined what kind of a person he might have become with the support of loving parents. He daydreamed about how wonderful it would be if someone claimed him as their own son. Now it was happening. He recalled: 'Before I could quite grasp all that this declaration meant for me, he had risen, taken me by the hand, and folded me in a gentle embrace. My senses seemed to whirl about for a few half-minutes; and, finally, I broke down, sobbing from extreme emotion. It was the only tender action I had ever known, and, what no amount of cruelty could have forced from me, tears poured in a torrent under the influence of the simple embrace.'

Looking back to his early years, the Victorian explorer recollected: 'The golden period of my life began from that supreme moment!' Again, the truth was rather different.

Number 3 Store, Tchoupitoulas Street, New Orleans where John Rowlands met merchant Henry Hope Stanley in February 1858. *(Christie's Images)*

Chapter 5

LIFE WITH 'FATHER'

During the following days, Mr Stanley plied the boy with questions about his life. He had suspected he was an orphan and expressed surprise that his few blood relatives had not claimed him. Mr Stanley explained that he had always wanted a son and when John Rowlands appeared from nowhere, asking: 'Do you want a boy, sir?' the question seemed to give voice to his lifelong wish, although the shabby lad appeared far too big for this purpose. 'The long and the short of it is,' said Mr Stanley, 'as you are wholly unclaimed, without a parent, relation, or sponsor, I promise to take you for my son, and fit you for a mercantile career; and in future, *you are to take my name – Henry Stanley.*'

With that, the older man and occasional Episcopalian lay-preacher rose, dipped his hands in a basin of water and made the sign of the cross on the boy's forehead, speaking the words of the baptism ceremony, ending with a brief exhortation to bear the new name worthily. No documentary record exists of a formal version of this ceremony – making it unlikely that Henry Hope Stanley ever adopted John Rowlands and changed his name, legally or otherwise.

The older man set about the task of equipping his new 'son' for the position he hoped he would assume, kitting him out with new suits, linen, collars, flannels, shoes, boots, his first nightshirt and toothbrush – 'it had never entered my head before that teeth should be so brushed,' he recalled.

At the end of 1859, stepfather and stepson began a series of riverboat journeys from one city to another, one store to another, conducting business for the Commercial Cotton Press, now a significant enterprise with Henry Hope Stanley its principal partner. Over the next two years they travelled between New Orleans and the lower Mississippi tributaries, trading with country merchants and plantation owners. The boy learned fast and had a good memory. He was taught how to recognise the superiority of one grade of sugar over another, why one grade of flour fetched a higher price than an inferior variety, why Bourbon whiskey was better than rye and how to spot varying merits of coffee and tea. He also acquired the social graces and was taught how to deal honestly in business.

Riverboats and hotels along the Mississippi always had plenty to offer weary commercial travellers with diversions and distractions in barrooms, at gambling tables and cheap vaudeville theatres. They were not for Mr Stanley and his stepson. They carried a portmanteau of books, including classic texts, poetry and drama and as soon as they arrived in their cabin or hotel room, the volumes were unpacked and the next stage of young Stanley's education continued as diligently as if he had been at school.

The mobile library was replenished in each city and when not studying, the stepfather-tutor pointed out items of note en route. Mr Stanley also corrected the boy's verbal errors. He was determined to turn his stepson into a respectable gentleman who sounded every bit as correct as himself. If the older man ever found the lad daydreaming on the riverboat deck, he would enquire if he had finished reading a particular chapter or found a different answer to a problem set earlier that day.

They rarely mixed with other passengers or hotel guests, all of whom the older man looked upon as time-wasters, gossips and his intellectual inferiors. He told the boy: 'To squander time and youth among such fellows as congregate around barrooms and liquor counters is as foolish as opening my veins to let out my life blood.' For his part, Henry Stanley Jr loved every moment spent under the older man's tutelage. He was hungry for knowledge and was eager to study, converse and listen to his stepfather.

In New Orleans, Stanley and his stepson often travelled to Tangipahoa to stay at his country plantation, Jefferson Hall, and meet its caretaker-widow and her daughters. At weekends, father and son attended the local church. American historian Mary Willis Shuey recalls that when the pair arrived at the plantation they were immaculately dressed in their finest linen clothes and shiniest shoes. Thanks to nourishing food, Stanley Jr had gained weight and his new light-coloured clothes now fitted his stocky figure tightly.

Shuey informs us that merchant and planter families attended the church and during the summer months young Stanley was invited to join members of the congregation for country walks. It was on one of these walks that he learned from new friends that his stepfather was actively courting the widow at Jefferson Hall. The boy found it hard to accept that his stepfather would consider marrying again. In his view, no one who had known the warm, gracious and saintly second Mrs Stanley could ever consider replacing her with another. Everyone at Tangipahoa had been aware that Mr Stanley and the widow were becoming more intimate – apart from young Stanley.

Stanley senior began making excuses to prevent his stepson from joining him at Jefferson Hall. According to Shuey, the boy was jealous of his father's relationship with the widow and started a major argument. Relations were tense for weeks afterwards until their Mississippi travels resumed.

The tone of the relationship between stepfather and stepson now began to change and it appears as if Mr Stanley felt the need to distance himself from his clinging teenage stepson. On one of their Mississippi journeys, Mr Stanley outlined his plans for his stepson. They would continue to travel, trade and study until Henry Stanley Jr was ready to manage a mercantile store of his own. The store would probably be in a rural backwater somewhere along the Mississippi or Arkansas rivers, but with excellent navigation and regularly served by riverboats needing to replenish supplies from a store carrying the respected name 'H.H. Stanley & Son' above the door.

In September 1860, the Stanleys met a tall Southern gentleman on board a New Orleans river steamer. His name was Major Ingham, originally from South Carolina but now relocated to a plantation in Saline County, Arkansas. It was out of character for Stanley senior to develop polite acquaintance with anyone on a journey, but he appeared to enjoy Ingham's company, thanks to mutual friends and a shared love of business. The boy also warmed to Ingham's tales of wild animals living in forests around his plantation. By the end of the voyage, Ingham had invited the boy to spend a month with his family. Stanley senior thought it a good idea and promised to write to Ingham with details of his son's travel arrangements.

Once back in New Orleans, Henry Hope Stanley received a letter that had been awaiting his return from his brother in Havana urging him to come to Cuba to run his business while he recovered from an illness. This presented an ideal opportunity for the boy to visit Major Ingham's Arkansas plantation and scout around for suitable locations to open a general store along the Arkansas River. Stanley wrote to a Jewish friend called Altschul who lived near the Ingham plantation in Cypress Bend, requesting him to teach his stepson everything he needed to know about running a country store.

The boy viewed the idea with suspicion. He had been tricked by an older person before and saw this latest scheme as an opportunity for his stepfather to get him out of the way. He was disturbed by the speed with which his stepfather began making arrangements for the trip. Within days, steamer tickets to Havana and Arkansas had been purchased. The boy travelled with his father to the harbour to say goodbye. In his stepfather's stateroom, the boy was tongue-tied and lost for words. The man who had become his stepfather, who had changed and shaped his life, was now going to leave him indefinitely. As he prepared to walk down the gangplank, the older man gave the boy a photograph of himself along with a lock of his hair. Stepfather and stepson waved to each other as the steamer pulled away. The boy watched it until it became a small speck on the distant horizon.

Although Henry Stanley Jr received letters from his stepfather confirming his safe arrival in Cuba and expressing his desire to return home soon, the boy would never see Henry Hope Stanley again.

Henry Morton Stanley's version of his early life as a poor immigrant in New Orleans, meeting the man who would become his benefactor, quitting his job to sit at a sickbed and travelling up and down the great river in steamboats is a story straight out of the pages of Mark Twain.

Stanley's own version is questionable. Henry and Frances Stanley certainly existed, but the boy's relationship with them was more imaginary than real. Frances Stanley actually lived for twenty years after Henry Morton Stanley 'killed her off' in the pages of his memoirs. He treated his 'stepfather' in similar fictitious fashion. It is likely that the older man was an inspiration to John Rowlands and that he occasionally brought him to his home – a wonderful thing for a lonely boy who longed to be part of a family and needed a father figure and, perhaps, a mother figure, too. That is almost certainly as far as their relationship went.

It is plausible that the boy travelled along the Mississippi with the fascinating Mr Stanley – but as his assistant, not as a stepson. Yet John Rowlands looked on Henry Hope Stanley as the father he had never known. Deep in the heart of Africa a decade later, another man would take a similar place.

Chapter 6

THE SHOPKEEPER AT CYPRESS BEND

The Ingham plantation was surrounded by pine forest, with a comfortable family house made entirely from logs at its centre. Mrs Ingham and a retinue of black slaves were waiting on the porch to greet her husband and young guest.

After supper, the Major received a visit from his plantation overseer. Stanley tells us that he 'almost immediately contracted a dislike for him'. He found the man coarse, vulgar and haughtily guessed him to be 'one of those men who haunt liquor saloons and are proud to claim acquaintance with bar-tenders'. In turn, the overseer viewed young Stanley with similar disdain.

The boy spent his first weeks in Arkansas helping plantation slaves cut down trees to make room for new cotton plants. As trees came crashing down, slaves cut them into logs, then rolled them to a clearing ready to be taken to a sawmill. Young Stanley loved the work and being the token white boy in a team of black slaves. He rose early in order to get in a good day's work and returned exhausted to the plantation house at nightfall while slave gangs retired to less salubrious quarters on the edge of the forest.

The overseer resented the 'son' of a rich New Orleans merchant having such a wonderful holiday 'slumming it' alongside slaves. The boy noticed that whenever the obnoxious man arrived, the slaves became sullen, stopped talking and singing, keeping one eye on the man and the other on the 'black snake' bullwhip which he was fond of cracking in the air.

The slaves enjoyed having young Stanley around. While he worked alongside them, the overseer was restrained and less likely to crack his whip in their direction. When the lad was not present, the overseer became a foul-mouthed bully, picking on plantation workers and using his whip indiscriminately.

Things came to a head when the overseer arrived one day clearly looking for trouble. Young Stanley was helping a group carry a large log when the overseer muttered something to a slave called Jim. The slave's reply was obviously not polite enough for the overseer's ears and he flicked his whip onto the slave's bare shoulders, missing Stanley by inches. As Stanley pulled out of the way, Jim fell to the ground, followed by the massive log, which landed on another slave's foot. At the spectacle of such wanton cruelty Stanley's temper rose and he and the overseer 'became engaged in a wordy contest; hot words, even threats, were exchanged and had it not been for the cries of the wounded man who was fast by the log, we should probably have fought'.

The boy marched off in search of Ingham who was lounging in his rocking chair on his porch. To Stanley's surprise, the genial gentleman remained seated, calmly informing the boy that such things were outside his province, work in the field being left to the overseer's discretion. He told the boy not to excite himself over things he knew nothing about.

Such blatant injustice was too much for the hot-headed young Stanley, who refused to remain at the plantation a day longer and announced he was leaving immediately for Cypress Bend. It took the boy two days to hike 40 miles along forest tracks to the small swampland community, where he discovered the long wooden single-storey store in a clearing. Mr Altschul, the proprietor, had been expecting young Stanley, although he was unsure when exactly he would arrive.

The proprietor took the boy on a tour of the store which was actually a country house divided into four apartments, three of which contained all manner of things sold in a general store with the fourth room used as an office by day and a bedroom for the storekeepers at night.

Young Stanley commenced work at the shop in November 1860, working as an assistant. His previous retail experience in New Orleans and knowledge gained from observing his stepfather at work turned the boy into an ideal provincial shopkeeper. Customers were many and varied – European immigrants, rich landowners, cotton barons, poor dirt farmers and illiterate labourers. Store work proved as routine and undemanding as Cypress Bend itself, a dismal backwater where little of note occurred apart from a weekly duck shoot on the river. When anything did happen, everyone knew about it and who was responsible. Newcomers usually decided to leave the place as soon as possible. The food was terrible and the young shop assistant quickly became bored with his diet of cornbread and greens swimming in grease, salt pork and heavy biscuits. He despised the swamplands, the need to use slave labour on plantations, the wealthy customers not as refined as his stepfather and the poorer ones who made no effort to improve their knowledge through books and learning.

Malaria was rife throughout Cypress Bend and Stanley suffered his first attack within a week of arriving. It began with violent shaking and a feeling that his blood had turned to ice. No amount of blankets or hot water bottles could warm him. Two hours later, the coldness turned into hot fits, perspiration and delirium. This was followed by nausea and total exhaustion that could last a week. It was not uncommon for swampland people to be incapacitated with malaria two or three times each month. The illness would incapacitate Stanley many times in later life, sapping his strength and reducing his frame to skin and bone. The first attack reduced the stocky-framed boy to 95lb and it took weeks to regain the weight, only to lose it again to another bout of malaria.

Stanley states that the arrival of letters from his stepfather in Cuba at Cypress Bend became less frequent. One of the last he received informed the boy that Mr Stanley expected to travel to New Orleans 'in about a month' and would be coming out to Cypress Bend to see how his stepson was progressing in his new career. No further letters arrived. He and his stepfather 'were destined never to meet again. He died suddenly in 1861 – I only heard of his death long after.'

Again, Stanley distorts the truth. Henry Hope Stanley lived for a further seventeen years, dying from a heart attack in November 1878 – not 1861 – shortly after his wife's death. This means that in retirement, the educated and highly informed British-born merchant would have been aware of the fame which came to the young man who took his name and became the most celebrated newspaper correspondent and African traveller in the world. There is no evidence that the two met again.

Little is known about Henry Hope Stanley after he parted company with the boy who claimed to be his stepson. At the outbreak of the American Civil War, Henry and Frances Stanley went home to England, returning after peace was declared. Mr Stanley resumed his business and moved to a new house in the New Orleans suburb of Arcola.

There were opportunities in later life for Stanley to have contacted the couple, but he chose not to. Either he had completely misunderstood the depth of his relationship with the older man or an irreparable gulf had developed between Mr and Mrs Stanley and himself, destroying any prospect of future contact for good.

Mary Willis Shuey writes that Mr Stanley refused to talk about his 'stepson'. When he died in November 1878, Henry Hope Stanley left an estate worth $138,000 – and not one penny went to the former workhouse boy.

In 1861, newspaper readers across the United States from New York to California and North Dakota to Louisiana knew that the country was on the eve of civil war. But Henry Stanley, the 21-year-old shop assistant at Altschul's general store in Cypress Bend, only read a small weekly parochial paper carrying news of births, deaths, marriages, church socials and tips on preventing racoons from entering cabins. He was unaware that the southern states of Alabama, Georgia and Louisiana were demanding independence from the rest of the Union and that the northern states were against the notion. It was not until March 1862 that the young man began dimly to comprehend that 'something was transpiring which would involve every individual'. By eavesdropping on conversations at the store, Stanley learned that 'confederate' southern states had set up their own government, appointed a president and were pushing Arkansas to join them.

Dan Goree, son of a Cypress Bend planter returning home from college, brought young Stanley up to date with what was happening in the outside world. Dan told him that Abraham Lincoln's election to the presidency had created hostile feelings in the South because of his opposition to slavery. Lincoln's abolitionist policies would ruin plantation owners, including many in Arkansas. The call would soon come for boys to sign up for the southern cause and go to war against the Yankees – an enemy every Southerner was convinced could be thrashed with a few licks of a whip. Dan said he would be one of the first to sign up and invited Henry to follow his example.

Across the country, young men were enlisting for the southern cause. News reached Cypress Bend that a patriotic plantation owner was raising a volunteer company, to be called the Dixie Greys, and that scores had already signed up. Young Stanley viewed the coming conflict as the end product of someone else's folly and nothing to do with a Welsh boy. He avoided conversations about the Dixie Greys, and entertained ideas of getting out of America and returning to Wales where he could offer his retail experience to shopkeepers in Denbigh, Swansea or Cardiff.

People began asking Stanley when he might be leaving Altschul's store to train with Dan and the Dixie Greys. He explained that he was not an American citizen and had no desire to fight in a war that did not concern him. Cypress Bend citizens were not convinced by his argument.

Stanley resolutely dismissed thoughts of war, preferring to spend his time trying to attract the attention of various young ladies in Cypress Bend. He had grown a small moustache in an attempt to make himself look older and it would remain on his top lip for most of his adult life. The boy still found it hard to converse with girls, but one local young woman appeared different. Her name was Margaret Goree, Dan's cousin, a shy, sweet-tempered and friendly girl interested in the boy's stories from literature and tales of his travels up the Mississippi. She visited the store with her mother and while Mrs Goree toured the shelves in search of provisions and household goods, Margaret sat shyly at the counter sipping sarsaparilla and making eyes at Henry.

One day Stanley received a parcel at the store, which he half suspected might be a gift from Margaret. He carefully untied the ribbons and opened the box, the contents of which he discovered to be 'a chemise and petticoat, such as a Negro lady's maid might wear'. The boy had been sent Arkansas's equivalent of a British white feather signifying cowardice and his fear of the coming conflict. A girl with whom he was only casually acquainted and had thought was interested in him as a person and whom he hardly knew, was now responsible for forcing him to fight in someone else's war.

Within a matter of days, young members of the 6th Arkansas Regiment of Volunteers – known as Dixie Greys – boarded a river steamer bound for Little Rock with a cargo of inexperienced farmhands, schoolboys, sons of plantation owners and a 5ft 5in tall shop assistant, once known as John Rowlands and now answering to the name of Trooper Henry Stanley – accidental Confederate.

They were sworn into the service of the Confederate States of America for a year, issued with heavy flintlock muskets, knapsacks and a light grey uniform and told to make themselves ready for a fight. The boys had signed up for the cause for a variety of reasons – many were the sons of passionate patriots who had joined to please their fathers, others were seeking glory and excitement, while the majority just needed an excuse to escape the tedium of daily life in the swamplands of Cypress Bend.

Chapter 7

DIXIE GREYS AND YANKEE BLUES

Stanley later admitted that enlisting in the Confederate service had been 'a grave blunder'. There would be occasions in the following six years when he wished he had followed his earlier instincts and returned to Wales; but it was too late. He was now billeted in a bell-tent with others from Cypress Bend, including Dan Goree, plantation men, clerks, cotton growers plus a collection of neighbours 'and a rustic lout or two'.

All too soon the Dixie Greys were on the move to the battlefront, marching through the streets of Little Rock to cheers from crowds of admiring females and worrying amounts of young men yet to sign for the Confederate cause. They carried everything in heavy backpacks – a spare uniform, undergarments, blankets, toiletry articles, plus a heavy musket, bayonet and a canteen of water. The full kit weighed 60lb and after an hour or two marching under the hot August sun, the first flush of enthusiasm soon wore off.

By sunset, the entire regiment was suffering from blistered feet and aching limbs. Older and more experienced soldiers poked fun at recruits limping so badly they lagged at the back of the long line of men. They finally fell into camp after dark and Stanley recalled that 'pains and aches darted through every tortured limb, feet blistered and bled, our backs scorched and our shoulders inflamed. No bed that I have ever rested on gave me a tithe of the pleasure afforded me now by the cold, damp pastureland.'

The next day was a halt in camp and an orderly suggested that recruits lighten their loads by sorting through their packs and discarding everything not essential on the battlefield. Hundreds of personal items and thousands of little luxuries were thrown onto a bonfire. Stanley threw his share onto the burning pile, but kept his photograph of Henry Hope Stanley and the lock of his hair – 'very trivial and valueless to others, but my own particular treasures to be looked at every Sunday morning when we smartened up'.

The following week found Stanley in another camp 60 miles from Little Rock. An epidemic raged through the tented village caused by typhoid, swamp malaria, fatigue and meagre rations. Over the following days, fifty soldiers died and the same number lay in hospital tents receiving treatment. Twice as many died the week after without ever setting foot on a battlefield.

Other regiments reinforced the Dixie Greys, including cavalry and artillery. Together they moved across Arkansas, up the banks of the Mississippi where on 7 November 1861 they experienced their first battle at Belmont – as observers, held in readiness on high bluffs overlooking the battlefield and not as combatants. The battle went on for ten hours and the Dixie Greys watched as 641 Confederate comrades were killed and 610 fell on the Yankee side.

Trains and cattle trucks transported the Dixie Greys to Cave City, Kentucky, where they remained encamped until the following February. Soldiers in the area numbered 22,000 men and it was a case of every man for himself when it came to finding decent food. Stanley won a reputation as an efficient scavenger after little items that helped make camp life more bearable.

While exploring the surrounding countryside at Christmas, Stanley was told about a farm owned by a Yankee sympathiser. In one of the meadows he spotted earthen mounds thought to conceal potatoes. From one of the barns he heard the clucking of hens – the perfect ingredients for a festive dinner for Dixie Greys sharing his tent.

Stanley borrowed a mule to help carry the spoils back to the camp, journeying to the farm under cover of darkness. Tying the mule to a tree, he headed in the direction of the earthen mounds and began burrowing into the side with his bayonet. Soon he smelled apples, which were better than potatoes as they could be cooked as dumplings. He half filled a sack and moved to another mound covering a winter supply of potatoes. He raked out enough to fill the sack and then heaved the load back to the mule. It was now time to go in search of a chicken or two.

Stanley discovered the rest of his dinner in the barn, wrung the neck of a goose, a duck and a pair of fowl. It was time to return to his mule, but he heard the unmistakable grunt of pigs in an outbuilding and stole across the meadow to a sty containing plump shoats. The thought of roast pig was irresistible and he climbed into the sty and snatched a piglet by the heels – setting off a terrifying clamour of grunts and squeals from the remaining porkers.

Determined not to lose his prize, with the pig under one arm and the rest of the poultry over his shoulder, Stanley fled through the darkness towards the mule. Suddenly a light appeared in the farmhouse door and a figure emerged carrying a shotgun. A shower of buckshot whistled around his ears that encouraged him to run faster. On arrival at the now loudly braying mule, he slashed the pig's throat with his bayonet and crammed it into another sack. Still holding the rest of the poultry and with apples and potatoes thumping the side of the animal, Stanley galloped towards camp, buckshot flying through the air. Stanley's midnight raid provided a Christmas feast for twenty soldiers and, emboldened by success, in the weeks that followed he ventured further into the surrounding countryside to relieve more farmers of 'excess' stock and produce.

In February 1862, advancing Yankee regiments forced southern contingents to evacuate their camp and march through the snow to Bowling Green, where they were packed into railway cars and shipped off to Nashville. From there, they marched 250 miles south before climbing into more cattle trucks transporting 55,000 troops to Corinth, the Confederacy's most important rail junction. There they would defend the Memphis and Charleston railroad from attack – although word rapidly spread that they were soon to spring a surprise attack on the enemy, who had landed on the Tennessee River some 24 miles away, near a log-built Methodist meeting house called Shiloh, a Hebrew word meaning 'a place of peace'.

Chapter 8

SHILOH

O n April 2, 1862, we received orders to prepare three days' cooked
rations. Through some misunderstanding, we did not set out until
the 4th; and, on the morning of that day, the 6th Arkansas
Regiment . . . marched from Corinth to take part in one of the bloodiest
battles of the West,' wrote Stanley. The Dixie Greys left tents and
knapsacks behind and after two days' march and two nights of
bivouacking, living on sodden biscuits and raw bacon, spirits were low.

The battle of Pittsburg Landing – better known as the battle of Shiloh –
became the second great engagement of the American Civil War.
Confederate Generals Johnston and Beauregard planned to advance an
army of well-prepared troops into the Tennessee River and send Yankees
running all the way home. On the day of the planned assault, 43,000
scruffy, hungry soldiers turned up for a fight. Southern forces, a quarter
of them under the age of twenty, would be reinforced by 20,000 men
from General Van Dorn's regiments. Together, 60,000 Confederate soldiers
would charge an anticipated strength of 49,000 Yankees. Early victory
was predicted and the Yankees were expected to lay down their arms and
surrender. It was to be the turning point that would cover the South with
glory and bring defeat and humiliation to the armies of the North.

In the grey light of dawn, the Dixie Greys rose from their damp bivouac
and formed into lines. General Johnston told fellow officers: 'Tonight we will
water our horses in the Tennessee.' The men stood in line for half an hour
while preparations were made further along the 3-mile front, the Dixie
Greys in the centre. As dawn broke, it promised to be a clear and sunny day.

On Stanley's right stood seventeen-year-old Henry Parker. While men
stood at ease, Parker pointed with his boot to some wild violets on the
ground and suggested it might be a good idea to put some in their caps
because 'the Yanks won't shoot me if they see me wearing such flowers,
for they are a sign of peace'. Parker and Stanley picked a few violets and
the two soldiers arranged them in their caps.

The order passed down the line to load their ancient flintlock muskets and prepare cartridge pouches for use. The loading procedure was slow and laborious, taking 30 to 40 seconds to complete and many soldiers lining up with the Dixie Greys were aware that the enemy used Enfield and Minie rifles which were quicker to fire and reload.

The soldiers were instructed to shoulder arms and commence marching. Silently, the Dixie Greys trudged through a thin forest just as the sun was rising. As they passed over grass and beneath peach trees, Stanley thought how wonderful a spot it would be for a Sunday picnic with Margaret Goree.

Firing was heard from the front followed by an explosive burst of musketry that sent ammunition flying through the air and slamming into trees. The men were ordered to surge forward and although they could hear the enemy and their gunfire, the Yankees were nowhere to be seen. The Dixie Greys were told to aim low and shoot – but at what? Shadows?

They advanced and directly ahead Stanley suddenly saw 'little globes of pearly smoke streaked with crimson, breaking out from a long line of bluey figures in front'. All hell broke loose. Stanley wrote that the sound 'suggested . . . a mountain upheaved, with huge rocks tumbling and thundering down a slope, and the echoes rumbling and receding through space. Again and again these loud explosions were repeated, seemingly with increased violence, until they rose to the highest pitch of fury, and in unbroken continuity. All the world seemed involved in one tremendous ruin.' The Dixie Greys were in confusion as they slowly reloaded, fired and advanced step by step – and with every forward movement, the enemy took a backward step, quickly loading and firing as they withdrew.

While the sound of muskets, rifles and over sixty cannon was deafening, an order to 'fix bayonets on the double' was heard. Yelling at the top of their lungs, the Dixie Greys surged forward close to Shiloh church. Stanley said the yelling helped release pent-up feelings and 'transmitted encouragement along the attacking line. I rejoiced in the shouting like the rest. It reminded me that there were about 400 companies like the Dixie Greys, who shared our feelings. Most of us, engrossed with the musket-work, had forgotten the fact; but wave after wave of human voices, louder than all other battle-sounds together, penetrated to every sense, and stimulated our energies to the utmost.'

Their savage yells combined with the sight of thousands of young men surging forwards set the Yankees – mostly Illinois and Iowa farm boys –

on the run. The Dixie Greys gave chase and soon came in sight of the Yankees' tented camp, which was cleaner, neater and more modern than their own. Stanley thought that the battle must be nearly over and allowed himself a moment's respite to catch his breath.

Southern regiments were urged to advance further towards other Yankee encampments. A furious hail of bullets met them from a line of soldiers who quickly rid them of the notion that the day was practically over. Opposing armies of blue and grey blazed away at each other.

The order was given: 'Lie down and continue firing.' Stanley and a dozen others threw themselves to the ground behind a fallen tree as shells buzzed around like angry bees and bullets thudded into the trunk. A man next to Stanley was shot in the face and another received a bullet through his head.

A cry of 'Forward, forward!' was heard and slowly the men in grey struggled to their feet, bent their bodies and moved towards the noise and confusion. A boy's voice near Stanley cried for them to stop. It was young Henry Parker, who had been hit in the foot. The soldiers urged him on, telling him that standing still was the worst thing he could do. So the boy with violets in his cap hobbled on towards enemy gunfire and was never seen alive again.

By 10 a.m. the Dixie Greys had won new ground and were again in sight of the enemy fleeing into the distance. Something hit Stanley in the region of his belt buckle, knocking him winded to the ground. The clasp on his belt was dented but the ball had failed to penetrate the metal and enter his body.

The land around him was strewn with bodies and the debris of war. The Dixie Greys had advanced further and Stanley set off in search of them, using the bodies of his dead and wounded comrades which 'lay as thick as the sleepers in a London park on a Bank Holiday' as his signposts.

He caught up with them at about 1 p.m. as they were preparing another assault. They lay behind fallen trees, logs and in hollows before rising and racing forward. By mid-afternoon, the battle was at its height and the Southern regiments were pushing the Yankees into the Tennessee River – the mission they had been told could easily be achieved using bullwhips.

The Yankees released their big cannon shells, which screamed overhead and landed in the middle of the battlefield, scattering men, limbs and muskets in all directions. Exhaustion overcame many of the Dixie Greys, and about fifty sought shelter in an abandoned enemy camp, where they hungrily snatched up bits of food dropped suddenly when the enemy had evacuated the tented village.

The noise of battle subsided and when night fell only stray shots were heard in the darkness. The men went to a pond to fill water bottles and bathe their wounds. It was stained red with blood. Stanley collapsed onto an enemy camp bed and in his sleep, relived the day's events.

Wounded and dead from both sides lay out in the open that night. A Confederate soldier later said: 'You could hear the screams of the injured. They screamed for water. God heard them and the heavens opened and the rain fell.' As lightning flashed over the fields of Shiloh, vultures could be seen feeding indiscriminately on the ungathered blue and grey carcasses.

By dawn, the Dixie Greys were certain that although they had still to drive the Yankees into the swamps and reinforcements had yet to arrive, Confederate forces had won a great victory the previous day. At daylight, Dixie Grey stragglers set off in search of their company. They found them, hungry, exhausted and ill prepared for what lay ahead. Gunfire began again and 22,500 reinforcements and gunboats that had arrived during the night joined the soldiers of the North. The men in grey were confronted with hundreds of men in blue advancing directly towards them, aiming, shooting, reloading, aiming, shooting, reloading. . . .

The Confederates were pushed back over ground they had fought hard to win the previous day and thousands turned tail and ran towards Shiloh church. Others sought shelter from the relentless hail of bullets.

Stanley found himself in an open, grassy space, with no trees behind which to shelter. He spotted a shallow hollow some twenty paces ahead and made a dash for it. So absorbed was he with the blue figures directly ahead that he did not notice where his companions were going. When they were no longer either side of him, he assumed they had moved towards more trees. But they had withdrawn. He rose from the hollow, 'but to my speechless amazement, I found myself a solitary grey, in a line of blue skirmishers! My companions had retreated! The next I heard was, "Down with that gun, or I'll drill a hole through you! Drop it, quick!"'

Half a dozen Yankee soldiers – with strong *German* accents – raised rifles in his direction. The game was up and Stanley dropped his musket and pointed to the violets in his cap. Two men grabbed him and marched the boy in grey 'into the ranks of the terrible Yankees. *I was a prisoner!*'

The battle of Shiloh is remembered as one of the bloodiest of the American Civil War. The final number of dead or missing was between 13,246 and 23,746 on the Yankee side and 10,500 Confederates. Both sides claimed victory, although the Confederates were first to retire from the battlefield, and heavy casualties immobilised both sides for nearly a month. As many men fell at Shiloh on 6/7 April 1862 as had fallen when Wellington's troops met Napoleon's force at Waterloo in 1815.

Chapter 9

A Prisoner at Camp Douglas

'Drive a bayonet into the — —! Let him drop where he is!' The orders were barked out by an excited German, a member of a small platoon made up of European settlers eager to fight for their newly adopted homeland. Before the latest Confederate prisoner was shredded by razor-sharp bayonets, two 'ruddy-faced Ohioans' intervened, claimed Stanley as their prisoner and frogmarched him from the battlefield. His knapsack containing letters, the photograph of Henry Hope and the lock of his hair were left in the hollow in which he had sought refuge from the madness all around.

Stanley claims that as he was taken from the battlefield he spoke to his Yankee captors about their respective causes. He learned that Yankees were not the robbers politicians had made them out to be, but decent fellows who, like himself, would have preferred to be anywhere else but in a war. Now he was their prisoner he expected to be treated decently as he was directed to other captives taken on the battlefield.

They were bundled onto steamers and dispatched upriver to St Louis from where they were herded into railway trucks and taken to Camp Douglas on the outskirts of Chicago – the northern military's best-kept secret prison camp, a grim hellhole where more would die in its overcrowded, unsanitary, brutal conditions than on many a field of battle.

The prison pen was a square enclosure, a bleak cattle yard, walled high with planking on top of which were sentry boxes. Over eight thousand prisoners were housed in twenty large wooden barns standing 30ft apart in two rows, each measuring about 250ft by 40ft and accommodating up to 300 tired, wounded, hungry and lice-ridden men. Inside each barn was a wide platform on each side, raised 4ft from the rough floor. These platforms formed continuous bunks for about sixty men, allowing 30in per prisoner. Two more rows were accommodated on the hard floor.

Prisoners were told to form into military-style companies and elect 'officers' to draw rations and oversee the running of each barn.

Trooper Stanley of the 6th Arkansas Regiment found himself 'Captain' of his barn's right-hand platform and the berth below. Blank books were handed to each 'Captain' with instructions to note the names of everyone in their company. Stanley was responsible for 100 captives and on production of his ration book, he was assigned meagre supplies for his men for distribution in the billet.

Disease swept through Camp Douglas's miserable prison barns so that within a week of arriving, scores of men in Stanley's billet were suffering from dysentery, cholera and typhoid. Medicine offered by the Confederate government to ease their soldiers' suffering was seized by prison authorities as 'spoils of war'. Soon the company's size began to dwindle as sick and dying men were carried off, never to return.

Filthy latrines were located next to open sewers at the rear of the barns and rain washed raw sewage into drinking water supplies. 'Each time imperious nature compelled us to resort to them, we lost a little of that respect and consideration we owed our fellow-creatures,' Stanley recalled. Crowds of sick men, who had fallen to the ground with weakness, wallowed in filth, breathing in the stenchful atmosphere. Those not so far gone prayed for death. Dead wagons arrived daily to collect more bodies, which were piled one upon the other like so many carcases of frozen mutton.

On the same day as the dead wagon carted away two full loads, Stanley was told that if he was tired of being a prisoner he could be released – by the simple expedient of switching sides, exchanging his disease-infested rags for a new blue uniform worn by soldiers of the North. At first he refused but over the following weeks he realised that if he remained at Camp Douglas he would either succumb to illness and die or be locked up in the hellhole for many more months. On 4 June 1862, Stanley together with a handful of other men negotiated their release, enrolled in the US Artillery Services, took an oath of allegiance to the government of the North – 'and was once more free to inhale the fresh air'.

Chapter 10

WHEN JOHNNY CAME
MARCHING HOME

Three days after donning the new blue uniform of the Northern army, Trooper Stanley of the US Artillery became ill with dysentery. The deprivations of Camp Douglas had finally caught up with him. He attempted to hide his symptoms, but a high fever erupted and he was confined to a field hospital in Maryland. On 22 June he was discharged from army service 'a wreck', just two weeks after being sworn in as a Yankee soldier. Stanley described his condition as being 'as low as it would be possible to reduce a human being to, outside of an American prison', his only possessions were a pair of blue army trousers, a dark serge coat and 'a mongrel hat' to keep his head warm.

He set off to walk to goodness knows where. Disease racked his body and he had to keep stopping every few hundred yards to catch his breath. At night he curled up in a ditch while his fever burned and he bled internally. 'I thought I ought to die, according to what I had seen of those who had yielded to death,' he wrote. 'As my strength departed, death advanced; and there was no power or wish to resist left in me. But with each dawn there would come a tiny bit of hope, which made me forget all about death, and think only of food, and of the necessity of finding shelter.'

It took Stanley a week to walk 12 miles to Sharpsburg, Maryland where he came to a farm and collapsed in a barn. His lips were scaled with fever, eyes swimming and his face burning hot under a week's dirt – 'the wretchedest object alive'. A week later, the sick ex-soldier slowly awoke from his fever to find that he was lying on a mattress, wearing a clean cotton shirt, his body washed from top to toe. A farmer had found him, taken him to his home and cared for the sick man. Thanks to a stranger's care and kindness, Stanley slowly gained strength until he was able to assist the farmer gather in the crops and partake of a harvest supper.

Stanley stayed with the farmer and his family until mid-August. When it was time to leave, the farmer drove him to town, gave him the price of the railway fare to Baltimore – and a new life away from the battlefront.

The peace and quiet of rural Maryland allowed Stanley to earn his keep working on other farms, on oyster schooners and performing odd jobs that allowed him to scrape the fare together for a one-way sea passage back to England. So it was that five months after being discharged as unfit for active service, Henry Stanley again sighted Liverpool's tall masts and quayside buildings. It was exactly five years since the penniless workhouse boy had boarded the *Windermere* for New Orleans. Now he was back, aged twenty-one, and just as penniless, pulling into Liverpool docks in the ship *E. Sherman* and entertaining high hopes of a reunion with his mother.

Stanley admitted to being 'very poor, in bad health, and my clothes were shabby'. If he could find her, what would Betsy make of her son, John Rowlands? Would she be pleased to see the lad she had last glimpsed as a small boy at St Asaph's workhouse twelve years before? Would she throw her arms around his neck, as he had seen other mothers do when their sons returned from war? Would she try to be a proper mother and make up for the missing years? Had she been thinking of her John, wondering what had become of him? These were some of the thoughts running through his mind when Johnny came marching home. . . .

He made his way to the village of Glascoed, near Denbigh where his mother and her husband, Robert Jones – father of her two youngest sons – together ran the Cross Foxes public house. Betsy Parry, or Mrs Elizabeth Jones as she now preferred to be known, had become a respectable member of the Glascoed community, with no scandalous evidence of illegitimate children to disturb her. She had become plump and matronly in her early middle age. A local artist had recently sketched her standing in the gateway of her garden with her dark hair tied into a bun, wearing spectacles, a long apron and a nearly completed woollen sock hanging from a knitting needle in her hands.

'With what pride I knocked at the door, buoyed up by a hope of being able to show what manliness I had acquired, not unwilling, perhaps, to magnify what I meant to *become*; though what I was, the excellence of my present position, was not so obvious to myself! Like a bride arraying herself in her best for her lover, I had arranged my story to please one who would, at last, I hoped, prove an affectionate mother,' he wrote.

The young man was ill prepared for the shock he was about to receive. He was abruptly told that he 'was a disgrace to them in the eyes of their neighbours, and they desired me to leave as speedily as possible'. Because it was late in the day, he was allowed to stay for one night before being shown the door the following day with a shilling in his pocket for the fare back to Liverpool. His mother's parting shot to her son was: 'Never come back to me unless you can come better dressed and in better circumstances than you seem to be in now.' The door slammed shut behind him.

Stanley celebrated his twenty-second birthday in New York, where he signed on for jobs on merchant ships travelling to the West Indies, Spain and Italy. A fragment from his notebook at this time reveals an intriguing entry: 'Wrecked off Barcelona. Crew lost in the night. Stripped naked, and swam to shore. Barrack of Carbineers . . . demanded my papers!'

By the end of 1863, he was in Brooklyn, New York having landed a position as a clerk with Judge Thomas Hughes. Another notebook fragment from this time shows that there were few dull moments in his life: 'Boarding with Judge X——. Judge Drunk; tried to kill his wife with hatchet; attempted three times. I held him down all night. Next morning, exhausted; lighted cigar in parlour; wife came down – insulted and raved at me for smoking in her house!'

Still seeking adventure, Stanley signed up for thirty-six months' service as a member of 'Uncle Sam's web feet' – President Abraham Lincoln's name for the Union Navy – possibly making him the only man ever to have served in both Confederate and Union armies as well as the Union Navy. He joined the training ship *North Carolina* in New York on 19 July 1864 and was later transferred to the warships *Moses H. Stuyvesant* and *Minnesota*.

Although Stanley was no coward he was not anxious to see active service again following his experiences at Shiloh and Camp Douglas. He was aware that the Navy wanted to recruit on-board ship's writers – clerks responsible for keeping daily records of shipboard life including accounts, logs and correspondence. Sailors combining seamanship with penmanship skills were a rarity, held the rank of petty officer and were not required to take up arms. Ship's writers spent time below decks, away from trouble, providing Stanley with time to read and to indulge his latest passion – writing.

It was thanks to the Union Navy that Stanley began his first true occupation as an observer and reporter of great events. He would later become the maker of events – the subject as well as the story – but his journalistic career actually began on the deck of the *Minnesota*.

By January 1865 the American Civil War was drawing to a close. The Union Navy had begun a blockade of 3,500 miles of Confederate coastline and the *Minnesota* was one of sixty warships and ironclads assigned to positions facing Fort Fisher, the last Confederate stronghold on the Atlantic coast and defending the port of Wilmington, North Carolina. Their job was to bombard the fort with cannon fire while Union sailors and marines prepared to land, attack enemy infantry positions, capture the fort and go on to wreak havoc in Wilmington.

Bombardment commenced on 13 January and cannon fired on the fort ceaselessly for two days. On 15 January, 2,000 sailors and marines were transported ashore with orders to capture the fort 'in a seaman like manner'. The landing party was engaged in bloody hand-to-hand combat and hundreds were killed or wounded during the two-day engagement, eventually won by troops from the North. The engagement played a decisive role in crushing the Confederacy.

Henry Stanley watched the entire skirmish from a grandstand position next to one of the *Minnesota*'s cannon. He later went below to write up his personal account of the battle for Fort Fisher, which he offered as a freelance contribution to Northern newspapers. Stanley tells us that he was 'most handsomely rewarded' for his copy.

Three months later, General Robert E. Lee's armies surrendered to the supreme commander-in-chief of the North, Ulysses S. Grant at Appomattox Court House, Virginia. The American Civil War was over; 600,000 lives had been lost.

Chapter 11

LEWIS NOE AND TROUBLE IN TURKEY

It was while serving on the *Minnesota* that Stanley became friends with a fifteen-year-old enlisted sailor from Sayville, Long Island, called Lewis Noe who joined the warship as a messenger at Hampton Road, Vermont in June 1864. Lewis Noe entered Stanley's life as his young and impressionable admirer. Stanley developed an infatuation for the boy. He kept a photograph of Noe in his collection for the remainder of his life and the name of his younger friend would crop up in a significant way nearly a decade later – and finally following Stanley's death.

In an interview with the *New York Sun* eight years afterwards, Noe described Stanley as 'full of aspirations for adventure, told marvellous tales of foreign countries and he urged that when we should leave the service I should accompany him on a proposed tour in Southern Europe. Being of a romantic turn of mind, I was pleased at the suggestion.'

Stanley had been planning his return to Europe for some time. He wanted to visit famous sites from classic literature and anticipated exciting adventures along the way which he would turn into articles to sell to the same newspapers that had published his Fort Fisher copy. The problem was that Stanley still had seven months of his navy contract to run and was impatient to move on. The only way to leave the service was to desert – and Lewis Noe intended to join the adventure.

They planned their desertion carefully. The *Minnesota* was scheduled to enter the navy dockyard at Portsmouth, New Hampshire, for repairs in February 1865. Noe claimed that Stanley forged passes carrying the Commodore's signature and permitting the sailors to pass through the shipyard's main gate. Once outside, they swapped uniforms for civilian clothes paid for in advance from workmen at the yard.

Stanley and Noe jumped ship on 10 February 1865 and set off for New York where Noe returned to his family in Long Island – who immediately dispatched him back to the city with orders to return to his ship. In New

York he met Stanley who warned the boy that 'disgrace and punishment waited me if I should go back'.

Noe claimed that Stanley had devised a plan by which Lewis would sign up for the army, give his 'bounty money' – a joining fee – to Stanley, desert, re-enlist with another unit and hand that money to Stanley and so on until they had sufficient funds for a passage to Europe. Noe declined, stating that Stanley 'was angry at me for my refusal, and finding that neither persuasion nor scolding would swerve me from my resolution, he set to work to procure employment. . . . His pleasing address, engaging manners, neat penmanship, and with all, his intelligent conversation and air of confidence enabled him to get a position, I believe in a law office.'

Following employment on a Long Island farm, Noe eventually enlisted as a private in the 8th New York Mounted Volunteers under the name of Lewis Morton. He remained with the unit until the close of the war when he was discharged. Meanwhile, Stanley was making enquiries about what had happened to his young companion, calling on Noe's parents who informed him that their son was back in uniform.

Hungry for adventure, Stanley was not prepared to wait for Noe to reappear. He boarded a westbound train heading towards frontier towns, Indian camps and Mormon settlements in Missouri, Utah, Colorado and Nebraska. Along the way he knocked on the doors of city, town and county newspaper editors offering his services as a freelance reporter. With press clippings from the battle for Fort Fisher as his only credentials, he nevertheless managed to pick up occasional commissions. When not pursuing writing assignments, he landed other jobs at a printing works and a gold mine to fund his travels.

It was in Mohawk City in the spring of 1866 that Stanley met a fellow freelance reporter called Harlow Cook who, like himself, yearned to travel outside America. Their first meeting was an auspicious one and demonstrates the self-confidence and high principles Stanley had discovered within himself in early maturity. Cook recalled: '[Stanley] had made himself notorious, and shown his character, by making a man twice his size kneel and ask his pardon for something said reflecting on his character. He was the hottest blooded man I ever saw. He never stopped for consequences. He put a pistol to the man's head, and said, "Retract, d—n you", and the big fellow flipped down and retracted.'

Together, Stanley and Cook planned to use their meagre earnings to undertake an extraordinary epic journey to Asia Minor, an expedition unheard of by ordinary Americans during the 1860s – particularly travellers planning to visit this little-known region with limited funds. The expedition would travel by ship from Boston to Smyrna (Izmir) in the Turkish Aegean and overland in the footsteps of Marco Polo to Constantinople, some six centuries after Marco's own journey in search of Kublai Khan. They would cross into Armenia, visit Yerevan and push onwards to Tblisi, cross the Caucasus and traverse the Caspian Sea before ending up on Marco's famous Silk Route to Bukhara, Samarkand – and who knows where after that? An ambitious onward journey into India, Tibet and China was certainly discussed along with a route that would eventually take them around the world.

The expedition would be expensive, but Stanley had been careful with his earnings. He had begun to keep an occasional journal and recorded: 'I have practised a rigid economy, punished my appetites, and, little by little, the sums acquired through this abstinence began to impart a sense of security, and gave an independence to my bearing which, however I might strive to conceal it, betrayed that I was delivered from the dependent state.'

The third person accompanying them on their adventure was to be Lewis Noe, acting as their 'attendant'. Along the route, Stanley and Cook planned to gather material for their articles and a book they would write about their experiences and encounters. First they had to get out of their frontier backwater and return to civilisation. Deciding that their great journey might as well begin there and then, they floated down the mighty Platte river in a flat-bottom raft of their own construction.

In Denver they purchased wood, tools and rope and within a few hours had constructed a flimsy craft that would carry them down the rapids. It was 6 May 1866 and melting mountain snow had swollen the river into a raging torrent passing through Indian territory. They attempted to talk each other out of the seemingly foolhardy exploit, but arrived at the conclusion that if they were unable to travel down the Platte river, they would certainly be unable to face the challenges of Asia.

Fuelled by apprehension and adrenalin in equal measure, Stanley and Cook lashed down their provisions, loaded the rifles that would protect them from any savage Indians they might encounter along the banks and pushed their raft to the water's edge. Curious onlookers told them they were mad to undertake so patently suicidal a mission. Others said that several unsuccessful attempts to follow the river had already been made. Previous rafters had given up but those who continued had all met disaster when underwater rocks smashed craft to matchwood, projecting passengers into the raging current.

The farewell party helped push the raft and its intrepid two-man crew into the water and it shot off around a bend in the river. It turned over twice, but the rafting reporters managed to catch it, drag it to the shore, dry their supplies and relaunch the raft back into the raging waters.

At one of the drying-out posts they met an army patrol seeking deserters from Fort Laramie. The soldiers arrested both men and marched them to the fort for questioning. Cook recalled how they were escorted to the colonel's office, where Stanley immediately turned on his heel and walked back towards the door. The colonel threatened to put him under arrest and Stanley told him to go ahead 'if you have men enough to take me'. Stanley and Cook walked out without a backwards glance and resumed their hazardous journey. They arrived in St Louis soaking wet – but alive – five days later, where they caught a train to New York to rendezvous with Lewis Noe.

Cook was far from impressed with Noe, whom he later described as 'a weak, dish-water kind of a boy . . . no backbone to him, no character at all'. According to Cook, Noe was 'a chit of a boy and with no signs of a man about him. Stanley was young, but manly, and easily 50 years ahead of Noe in everything.' Cook said that Noe was taken along to act as 'our servant'; Noe would later state that Stanley introduced him to Cook as 'his half brother. . . . This part I was compelled to play on our travels abroad, whenever Stanley's caprice suggested it.'

Stanley visited Noe's parents and urged them to allow their son to take part in the adventure. Noe admitted that he longed for adventure and heard Stanley tell his parents that

he desired to educate me and give me the polish that could be obtained by intercourse with the world. He told of diamonds, and rubies, and precious stones, and rich India shawls and other fabrics in Central Asia, the real value of which the natives knew scarce anything, which could be procured for us for insignificant sums of money, and could be sold at enormous profit. He professed to have acquired abundant means in Colorado, and was willing to pay all my expenses for the pleasure of my companionship. My parents were in humble circumstances, and naturally they desired to promote the welfare of their son and they gave their consent.

By 10 July 1866 Stanley, Cook and Noe were in Boston where they boarded the barque *E.H. Yarrington* for the long voyage to Turkey. Once on board, Noe claims he was 'a little surprised, after the rose coloured prospects Stanley had held out to me, when he expressed a wish for me to work my passage on the vessel, for which he stated he had made arrangements. . . . My faith was so unbounded in his wisdom, his integrity and love for me, that I readily acquiesced. With my previous experience, I was enabled to make myself serviceable on the voyage.' For his part, Cook later confirmed that the trio part-worked their Atlantic passage, stating: 'Stanley and Noe understood the ship, and I wanted to. So we would turn in and help once in a while for the sport of it.'

At Smyrna, Noe was in for another shock when he found 'the exchequer of the expedition was not of the large proportions I had supposed from Stanley's representation. . . . With what little means he and Mr. Cook had, they purchased a couple of sorry horses, a few cheap cooking utensils and other things to make up the meagre outfit. This being accomplished, the whole amount of money left did not exceed the value of $5 in gold.' Noe recalled that he had been expecting a 'finely equipped Arab horse' of his own but 'was compelled to trudge along on foot' while Stanley and Cook rode the horses.

On their second day out of Smyrna, Noe decided to play a prank on Cook who was sitting dozing in the sunshine next to a bunch of dry bushes. To Stanley's amusement, Noe crept up and set the bush alight. The fire soon spread, bringing a group of excitable local people to the scene with their policeman. Noe ran off in the direction of Smyrna, but Stanley and Cook were arrested and taken to a guardhouse. Hours later they were released and Stanley returned to Smyrna to find Noe, where the boy said that Stanley's 'flattering words and professions of love reassured me, and I consented to go with him again'.

Noe found that instead of being a travelling companion he was to be 'a beggar and a slave' for a remorseless master. His duties were to perform any menial service Stanley and Cook directed, to cook and steal. Stanley instructed Noe: 'Remember you are here to do my bidding. If I tell you to cut a man's throat, you do it.'

When Noe attempted to escape, he was taken into a pomegranate forest by Stanley, his shirt ripped from his back, tied to a tree and

on my bare skin, he scourged me with a whip which he cut from trees and on which he left the sharp knots, until the blood ran from my wounds. . . . Each blow caused the most excruciating agony, which continued for hours. While he was tying me he looked significantly at his revolver, which was lying on the ground, and said he wished me to understand that I was in his power. Before he commenced his whipping, he asked me if I knew what he was going to do. I told him I did not. Said he, 'I am going to give you the d——dest thrashing you ever had.' I then asked what I had done to deserve a whipping. He said that 'whipping does boys good, whether they have done anything or not.' . . . When he had concluded, he comforted me by saying: 'I think you are a good boy, just the one I want for a companion. We will let the matter drop, for I am satisfied.'

Did Stanley derive sexual satisfaction from taking a whip to his young companion? Noe's remarks were made several years after the event when Henry Morton Stanley's name was on the lips of every newspaper reader and Noe was seeking a profitable way of discrediting his former friend. By that time, Stanley's accounts of his African travels had made numerous references to using the whip to deter native porters from deserting his caravan. Some critics observed that while the whip was a good deterrent, Stanley's overuse of it on the shoulders and backs of half-naked native bearers was not always necessary. Did he derive masochistic gratification from inflicting pain? Was Stanley a repressed homosexual, something as bad, perhaps worse, than being born a bastard in Victorian England?

The travellers were in need of fresh horses 300 miles further into their journey. Noe recalled a plan hatched by Stanley to hijack an approaching Turk riding one horse and leading another by its reins. Cook had been lagging behind and was not party to what happened next.

Stanley, who had learned some of the local language from a phrase book, engaged the Turk in conversation. Pointing in Noe's direction, he asked the Turk if he wanted to buy a girl dressed in boy's clothing. As the Turk began groping Noe, Stanley raised his sabre and struck it over his head. The Turk was wearing a fez made from thick pasteboard, which stopped the sabre's force. He began struggling for his life and reached for a knife, which he attempted to stick into Stanley's heart. 'Shoot him, Lewis – shoot him, or he'll kill me!' Stanley yelled and Noe, fearing he would be left at the mercy of the Turk, levelled his rifle and pulled the trigger. Nothing happened. Whoever had last used the weapon had failed to reload it, forcing Noe to club the Turk across the back of the head with its stock.

The Turk escaped up a nearby hill. His knife had cut the inside of one of Stanley's hands and the wound needed medical attention. Stanley and Noe jumped on the Turk's horses just as Cook appeared riding one of the party's original animals. They rode their animals into the ground, only stopping once they considered themselves out of danger.

By this time the Turk had rounded up a force from his village and set out to retrieve his horses. The three travellers were easily located sitting around a smoking campfire and were overpowered. The Turks tied them up and marched them to their village, where they were held prisoner and beaten. On the first night of their imprisonment, Noe was taken out by three of the Turks and gang raped.

The travellers were moved to a larger town where they were thrown into jail and charged with highway robbery. When they appeared before a local court, Stanley asserted that their Turkish captors had robbed the companions of everything they owned – clothes, blankets, weapons, papers and 'a great deal of money'. The presiding magistrate ordered the Turks to be searched and, sure enough, some of their property was found hidden in their garments. Stanley and company were freed without charge – and the Turks arrested.

Stanley turned the episode into a story for Turkey's English language paper for expatriates, and it was published in the *Levant Herald* on 17 October. The paper also syndicated the piece to other newspapers in the United States and England:

OUTRAGE ON AMERICAN TRAVELLERS IN TURKEY

When about seven hours from Afuna Karahissar on 18 September, en route for Tiflis and Tibet, via Erzeroum from Smyrna, I and my two companions, Mr. Cook of Illinois and a youth of New York, were attacked by a band of robbers, hailing from the village of Chihissar, headed by a fellow named Achmet of Karahissar and robbed of all our money, valuables and clothing to the tune of about 80,000 piastres . . . after robbing us, they conveyed us as prisoners in triumph to Chihissar, accusing us of being robbers, which brought down on our devoted heads unparalleled abuse from the villagers; the women pelted us with stones; the children spat at us; the men belaboured us unmercifully with sticks, clubs and fire tongs. Not comprehending in the least what

direction affairs had taken, I must say, for myself, that I was plunged
into a state of stupefaction, not unmingled with rage as to how and
why we were thus treated. We had instantly acquiesced in all their
demands, and were as docile as lambs in their hands, and though when
attacked we were armed with the best Sharpe's rifles and Colt revolvers,
we had offered no resistance. When night arrived, they bound us with
cords drawn so tight around our necks that it nearly produced a
strangulation, in which suffering condition they allowed us to remain
12 hours. (A passage here occurs relating to the treatment of the boy.)
No explanations that they can render can gloss over the wanton cruelty
and malignant treatment to which we had been subjected. Next, two of
them conveyed us, bound with the most daring effrontery imaginable,
to a small town called Rashikeui with a statement that we were robbers,
where of course, we, powerless to explain the mystery which hung over
us, were treated as prisoners, accompanied by the most cruel abuse;
chains were hung around our necks, like garlands, for the night. . . .
We were sent to Afiuna-Karahissar, where we received the benefit of an
interpreter, in the person of Mr. Poloso, agent of the Ottoman bank at
that place, who acquitted himself very creditably in that capacity; the
fruits of which that we were immediately freed from 'endurance vile'. . . .
All the robbers were arrested and will be tried according to law. The
American minister at Constantinople has demanded full repayment of
the money stolen, the public trial of the prisoners, and the exaction of
the full penalty of the law upon the ruffians who assaulted the boy.

The trio made their way to Constantinople to do as tens of thousands of
distressed tourists far from home have done ever since – throw themselves
at the mercy of their embassy. Unannounced, they turned up at the doors
of the American Embassy demanding to see the American Consul-General
and enlist his aid.

The Consul-General was out of town and Stanley was sent to the
residence of his deputy, Edwin Joy Morris. According to Morris, Stanley
arrived wearing 'neither shirt nor stockings and he showed other evidences
of great suffering'. The American diplomat had read Stanley's article in the
Levant Herald and later stated that he had 'lost no time in taking the
necessary steps . . . for the protection and relief of my countrymen'.

Morris and Stanley returned to the embassy where Noe and Cook were
waiting. Morris described their condition as 'most miserable – if ever the

condition of men presented the traces of cruel treatment, theirs did'. He advanced Stanley a loan to procure an outfit for himself and his companions, handing over a cheque for £150. Morris failed to ask Stanley for security for the loan, offering it as charity, trusting it would be repaid in the future. But Stanley offered security 'in the name of his father', who he said was a lawyer living at 20 Liberty Street, New York who would settle the sum. After Stanley had left Turkey, notice came from New York that no such person lived at that address.

Using the diplomat's money, Stanley purchased conventional clothes for Noe and Cook and, according to Morris, for himself 'a kind of semi-navy officer's coat and vest, with gold lace on the sleeves, and Turkish buttons' stamped with the Turkish crescent and star. Wearing his new outfit, Stanley paid a call at Abdullah Frères' studio – 'photographers to his Imperial Majesty the Sultan' – and commissioned a three-quarter length *carte de visite* photograph of himself casually leaning on a low pillar and looking for all the world like a high-ranking naval officer on shore leave.

The US Navy battleship *Ticonderoga* was docked at Constantinople on a goodwill visit at the time and Stanley had seen officers from the ship wearing their uniforms as they browsed through the bazaars. His new uniform could have passed as American naval issue, providing admirers did not examine its buttons too closely. Stanley could see that a uniform gave those wearing it an assurance of dignity and bearing of the kind he did not innately possess. It was different in cut and style to the rough uniform he had worn with the Dixie Greys and he knew it would work wonders for his reputation when he was spotted wearing it in the streets of Constantinople, New York – or Denbigh.

Stanley and Noe were allowed to leave Turkey, while Cook remained to conclude the legal action against the Turks. Cook was happy to see the back of Noe, whom he described as 'the whining little pup', and later collected the 80,000 Turkish piastres the expedition party falsely claimed had been stolen from them. Instead of pressing ahead in the footsteps of Marco Polo, Stanley and Noe announced their intention to return to America. No ships were scheduled to leave Smyrna for American ports at that juncture – but a steamer was departing for Marseilles, from where they could easily sail onwards to Liverpool and work their passage across the Atlantic, putting the whole unfortunate Turkish misadventure behind them.

Chapter 12

ANOTHER HOMECOMING

In the seven years and ten months between the time John Rowlands
set sail from Liverpool and returned from Turkey as Henry Stanley,
Uncle Tom and Aunt Maria Morris had moved from Roscommon
Street. They now lived in a smaller home in Davies Street, 1½ miles away
in Liverpool's Whitechapel district – and the last thing they expected to
find on their doorstep on a grey, wet autumn morning was their 24-year-
old nephew 'John' with a young American stranger.

Stanley explained that he was planning to visit Wales, hoping to be
reconciled with his mother, and said he would be obliged if Lewis Noe
could lodge at Davies Street until his return. Uncle Tom and Aunt Maria
could hardly say no and agreed to provide lodging for the boy, who
understood nothing of what was said in the Welsh-speaking household or
why the Morrises addressed their nephew as 'John'.

It was only after Stanley had departed for Wales that Noe learned of his
companion's mysterious past and true identity from Uncle Tom and Aunt
Maria in the 'humble circumstances' of their Liverpool home. He recalled:
'I remained for some weeks with his uncle and aunt and was most kindly
treated by them, though they were ill able to bear the burden of my
support. I frequently urged Stanley by letter to send me means to reach
my home, but without success and was unable to leave Liverpool until I
received means from my parents.'

Meanwhile, a young man of below average height, with a light
moustache and sporting the dark blue uniform of a foreign military
officer, was walking through Denbigh's narrow streets, politely lifting
his hat and wishing passers-by 'a very good mornin' to you, Sir, and
you, too, Ma'am' in an American drawl. The courteous young
American with noble bearing, charm and impeccable manners
impressed the locals. For most, this was the first time they had met,
let alone spoken to, an American – and they liked what they heard
and saw.

Was it coincidence, or the act of a young man keen to earn extra shillings, that Stanley's story from the *Levant Herald* about being robbed and assaulted was now published in one of Denbighshire's local newspapers, the *Flintshire Observer*, on Friday 2 November 1866? The piece, published from the paper's Holywell editorial offices shortly after Stanley's return to his hometown, identified 'Mr Henry Stanley' as 'one of the number' involved in the incident, stating that he was an American. The story provided no further information about the author, his true identity or the fact that he was in Wales seeking reconciliation with his mother and no longer known as John Rowlands. Stanley was hoping she might be more welcoming once she learned of the hardships he had endured in Turkey – and saw him wearing a smart foreign military uniform.

With these thoughts in his mind and his mother's previous parting words never to return until he was better dressed still ringing in his ears, Stanley made his way to the Cross Foxes public house in Abbot Street, Glascoed, where he politely asked to see the landlady, Mrs Jones. While someone went to fetch the lady of the house, the young man in uniform remained in the public bar. When Betsy appeared the first thing she saw was the back of her unexpected visitor. She asked how she could help, and the stranger turned and said: 'Hello, Mam.'

The landlady scrutinised the stranger and recognised that it was her son, John Rowlands, who stood before her – not the sickly ragamuffin who had turned up at her door fresh from a prison camp four years earlier, but a smart, tanned, bright-eyed 24-year-old who, by the look of the uniform, had made something of himself.

The meeting proved a turning point in the relationship between Betsy and her son. Although they were never to become close, Stanley managed to convince his estranged mother that he wanted nothing from her apart from her acceptance and a chance to get to know his stepbrothers Robert and James and stepsister, Emma. His efforts paid off and Stanley spent the rest of November, the Christmas and New Year holidays at the Cross Foxes, regaling his mother, her husband, his younger brothers and sister with exciting fireside stories of his life and adventures. Letters to Lewis Noe in Liverpool, including one dated 25 December 1866, inviting the young American to 'come on to Wales and see his folks. He strongly urged me to do so – indeed, he insisted upon it.' However, Noe remained in Liverpool with Uncle Tom and Aunt Maria.

Stanley revisited the scene of his earliest childhood at Denbigh Castle again – this time as a tourist. On 14 December 1866 he wrote the following untruth in the Royal Denbigh Bowls Club visitors' book:

John Rowlands formerly of this castle, now Ensign in the United States Navy in North America belonging to the US Ship *Ticonderoga* now at Constantinople, Turkey. Absent on furlough.

Before leaving to rejoin Noe in Liverpool, Stanley could not resist putting on his fake uniform again and paying a call on staff and inmates at St Asaph's workhouse. James Francis had been dead for several years and the schoolmaster was now a Captain Thomas, who was impressed when the young man turned up to talk to junior inmates. Writing in the *Denbigh Free Press* only days after Stanley's death in 1904, G.T. Miller, a former workhouse guardian, recalled: 'Captain Thomas praised Stanley for what he had done; that he was not ashamed to acknowledge having been reared in the workhouse after raising himself to the position he then held and pointed out to those present what could be done by lads having grit and energy in them. Captain Thomas also thanked Stanley for giving the children the treat, and said he was proud of him.'

While still with his 'folks' in Denbigh, Stanley received another letter from Lewis Noe pleading for money for a passage home to America and revealing that he knew everything about his friend's identity and early life in Wales. The letter prompted Stanley to rush back to Liverpool in January 1867 for a heated argument with Noe in the front parlour of his aunt and uncle's home. According to Noe, Stanley 'commenced a tirade against me with his uncle and aunt in Welsh. His uncle interjected: "Speak English, so that the boy (meaning me) can understand what you say. I don't want anything said so that Lewis cannot take his own part."'

On 12 January 1867, Stanley wrote to Noe's parents giving them a long account of their Turkish journey and urging them to send money to their son. By 18 January Stanley had suddenly left Uncle Tom and Aunt Maria's home and was himself back on the high seas aboard the steamer *Damascus* heading out across the Atlantic. He wrote a short letter to Noe, posted during a transit stop in Londonderry, telling of his plans to head west to Missouri where he intended to land a job as a newspaper reporter.

Noe's parents managed to scrape money together and forwarded it to their hapless son on the other side of the Atlantic. He sailed home in March and in April received a letter from Stanley in St Louis informing him that he was working as a 'special correspondent' with the *Missouri Democrat* for a weekly salary of $15, plus expenses, 'writing up North-western Missouri, and Kansas and Nebraska'. This sparsely populated region was larger than the United Kingdom and infamous for hostile Indians on the warpath with new settlers, ramshackle and lawless towns with cowpoke populations, lively saloons and a scattering of US army forts to help keep a fragile peace. For Henry Stanley, 'special correspondent', this all spelled adventure and opportunities to create lively and imaginative copy direct from the heartland of America's frontier. In keeping with the popular tradition of the time, it also permitted him to add a middle initial to his name, allowing his stories to be credited to the impressive-sounding 'Henry M. Stanley' – the letter M sometimes standing for 'Moreland' and at others for 'Morton'.

Chapter 13

HANCOCK, HICKOK AND THE WRONGED CHILDREN OF THE SOIL

The *Missouri Democrat* prided itself on the variety of stories it published from across the Midwest for its St Louis readers. It was one of the first to carry profiles of leading personalities of the day – and the more flamboyant the characters, the better the *Missouri Democrat*'s editor liked them. Through detailed descriptions and lively reporting, correspondents were encouraged to transport readers from their comfortable St Louis living rooms into the heart of the story.

The hunt for news and memorable personalities directed Stanley towards tracks being laid by the new Union Pacific Railroad Company, an organisation created five years before to lay 1,006 miles of track westwards at the rate of 4 miles daily from Omaha to meet the Central Pacific's track heading east from Sacramento. As the railroad pushed west through miles of prairie, land was assigned either side of the track every 70 miles to build movable cities, known as base camps, to accommodate the hundreds of engineers and labourers employed on the line. Scores of others also moved into the cities to help relieve railwaymen of their hard-earned wages – prostitutes and their pimps, liquor sellers, gamblers and gunmen. The cities became known as 'Hell on Wheels'.

Now aged twenty-six, Stanley visited several base camps for the *Missouri Democrat*, including North Platte, Nebraska, which had been established by the railroad company eight months earlier. After stepping from one of Union Pacific's platform cars he reported:

Every gambler in the Union seems to have steered his course for North Platte and every known game under the sun is played here. Every house is a saloon, and every saloon is a gambling den. Revolvers are in great requisition. Beardless youths imitate to the life the peculiar swagger of the devil-may-care bullwhacker and blackleg. . . . On account of the immense freighting done to Idaho, Montana, Utah, Dakota and Colorado, hundreds of bullwhackers walk about and turn the one-street into perfect Babel. Old gamblers who revelled in the glorious days of 'flush times' in the gold districts declare that this town outstrips them all yet.

In August 1867 he arrived at another 'Hell on Wheels' known as Julesburg and described it for his *Missouri Democrat* readers:

At night, new aspects are presented in this city of premature growth. Watchfires gleam over the sea-like expanse of ground outside the city, while inside, soldiers, herdsmen, teamsters, women, railroad men, are dancing, singing, or gambling. I verily believe that there are men here who would murder a fellow creature for five dollars. Nay, there are men who have already done it, and who stalk abroad in daylight unwhipped of justice. Not a day passes but a dead body is found somewhere in the vicinity with pockets rifled of their contents.

Stanley was always devising methods of earning extra cash to keep him afloat until his *Missouri Democrat* wages arrived – often weeks late due to the distance they had to travel and the difficulty of locating a 'special correspondent' always on the move between one frontier story and the next.

In between Union Pacific reporting assignments, Stanley found himself in Jefferson City, Missouri, where in February 1867 he came up with a plan to supplement his income by satisfying the public's appetite for everything foreign. If it proved successful, he intended to take the idea on the road to wherever he might be reporting. His scheme was to hire halls where the public would pay an admission charge to hear a lecture by:

The American Traveller!

HENRY STANLEY,

who was cruelly robbed by the Turks on September 18, 1866, and stripped by overwhelming numbers, of his arms, passport, letter of credit, and over $4,000 in cash, will lecture on his travels and adventures in Turkey and Life in the Orient!!

There was space for the date, starting time and venue to be entered before the posters went on to tell the public various truths and lies:

Mr Stanley has served in the American navy, from January 1862, till the fall of Wilmington, at which he was present in January 1865. He then took a grand tour through the interior of Asia Minor, from which he has just returned. During his lecture he will appear in the costume of a Turkish naval officer. He will also show to the audience a Saracenic Coat of Mail; Needlework by a Turkish maiden; Turkish fez, and the elegant cap of a Greek pirate; a Turkish Chibouque; a piece of skull from the tomb of Sultan Bajozetr, commonly called the 'Lightning' or 'Thunderer', a whitestone from Mt. Olympus near the ancient city of Troy, of which Homer and Virgil sung, about 2,000 years ago. There will also be on exhibition, a firman, signed by the present Sultan of Turkey, Abdul Azziz. Also, a passport signed by our Secretary of State, William H. Seward. Mr Stanley will repeat the Moslem call to prayer, after the manner of Muezzin, in the sacred Arabic language used by 14,000,000 people. The lecturer will close the exercise of the evening by singing a Turkish song, à la Turque.

Stanley totally misread the public's fascination for foreign travel because the lecture was a disaster, attracting only eight people, later described by one of Stanley's journalist friends as 'four deadheads and four who paid'. It would be several more years before Stanley would mount a platform and deliver another lecture – and then in very different circumstances.

Between March and November 1867, 'special correspondent' Stanley was given a choice assignment in the region's western territories, one highly suited to his aggressive, energetic and ambitious nature. He was sent to join an expedition headed by Gettysburg battle hero, Major-General Winfield Scott Hancock, to drive warring Plains Indians – Kiowa, Comanche, Sioux, Arapaho and Cheyenne – from their ancestral hunting grounds to make way for white settlers, new townships, army forts, roads and railroad tracks. The Indians were on the warpath, there was bitter conflict between white men and red and the US government wanted an end to the problem.

Indians did not want white settlers on territory that had been theirs for centuries or white men to pass through their land. They protested that every time settlers entered sacred territory, blood was left behind. The

Indians were invited to sit around a table and negotiate. They were given promises and presents and treated like children. White settlers claimed that Indians had attacked and burned overland mail stations, murdered their employees and captured their stock. Kansas settlers were killed in their homes and others intimidated by Indians. There was bitterness on both sides.

As Commander of the Department of Missouri, Hancock planned to march 450 miles deep into Kansas and Nebraska Indian country with a force of 1,500 men made up of eight troops of cavalry, seven companies of infantrymen, one battery of light artillery and a *Missouri Democrat* correspondent. The 7th Cavalry would be under the command of the army's most celebrated, courageous, impulsive and vain officer, General George Armstrong Custer, who at the age of twenty-three was the Union army's youngest general, famed for daring raids behind Confederate lines during the Civil War.

A letter to tribal agents announced Hancock's intention to enter sacred lands 'to convince Indians . . . that we are able to punish any of them who might molest travellers across the Plains, or who may commit other hostilities against the whites. We desire to avoid, if possible, any troubles with the Indians and to treat them with justice according to the requirements of our treaties with them. . . . I will be pleased to talk with any chiefs whom we may meet.' Indian agents were instructed to send messengers to settlements, read out the letter and invite the Indians to send representatives to meet Hancock and his men at the Arkansas River.

At Hancock's camp, Stanley was summoned to the General's tent, where he found 'a hale, hearty, and tall gentleman in the prime of life'. A dispatch to the *Missouri Democrat* ran:

Major-General W.S. Hancock left Fort Riley on March 28 with about fifteen hundred men, consisting partly of cavalry and partly of infantry. He proposes from what I can hear to proceed to Fort Larned. . . . On his arrival he will invite the chiefs of the different tribes of hostile Indians to a council, where, together, they will discuss terms of a peace agreeable to both parties. If they cannot agree he then proposes, by force of warfare, to bury the hatchet.

Stanley's articles from the western territories were signed either 'Stanley' or 'S' in accordance with an 1863 ruling that correspondents attached to the Army of the Potomac identify themselves by name. Articles in the *Missouri Democrat* penned by other correspondents remained anonymous, making Stanley one of the earliest reporters to receive a prestigious byline next to his work. The credit also brought Stanley's name to the attention of other editors, a fact on which he would capitalise at the end of 1867.

Stanley disagreed with Hancock's policy as soon as he joined the troops. He could tell from his first meeting that the Major-General totally misunderstood Indian ways. Hancock had burned down a Cheyenne village for no other reason than that he wanted to be seen as superior to the Indians. War drums now beat out the message over the plains that more blood would be spilt.

Neither the army nor the Indians appeared in a glowing light in Stanley's dispatches. He criticised the army's inability to capture Indian war parties or persuade them to sit down and talk. He described Indians as 'remorseless savages'. But he was intrigued by the reputation of an express rider Hancock had engaged to transport information from one part of the expedition to another. He was 'widely known for courage, endurance and faithfulness' and named James Butler Hickok – commonly called 'Wild Bill'.

The reporter went in search of Wild Bill in Hancock's camp, hoping to write a profile of this interesting character. His *Missouri Democrat* description was one of the first to bring Hickok's name and fame to public attention and helped shape the image of a man who would later become one of the best known figures from America's Wild West:

He ['Wild Bill'] is one of the finest examples of that peculiar class known as frontiersman, ranger, hunter, and Indian scout. He is now thirty-eight years old, and since he was thirteen the prairie has been his home. He stands six feet one inch in his moccasins, and is as handsome a specimen of man as could be found. We were prepared, on hearing of 'Wild Bill's' presence in the camp, to see a person who might prove to be a coarse and illiterate bully. We were agreeably disappointed however. He was dressed in fancy shirt and leathern leggings. He held himself straight, and had broad, compact shoulders, was large chested, with small waist, and well-formed muscular limbs. A fine, handsome face, free from blemish, a light moustache, a thin pointed nose, bluish-grey eyes, with a calm look, a magnificent forehead, hair parted from the centre of the forehead, and hanging down behind the ears in wavy, silken curls, made up the most picturesque figure. He is more inclined to be sociable than otherwise; is enthusiastic in his love for his country and Illinois, his native State; and is endowed with extraordinary power and agility, whose match in these respects it would be difficult to find.

Stanley asked his first question: 'I say, Mr Hickok, are you willing to mention how many men you have killed, to your precise and certain knowledge?' Hickok thought for a moment and said, 'I assume you mean white men; after all, nobody counts Indians, or Mexicans and so forth. Well, I am perfectly willing to swear a solemn oath on the Bible tomorrow, that I have killed substantially over one hundred – and not one without good cause!' In reality, Hickok is known to have killed fewer than ten men – some in suspicious circumstances – but he was so adept with his guns that only a fool would have disputed his claims.

When Hancock's expedition arrived at Fort Larned on 7 April, news was waiting that tribal representatives would come for a meeting on 10 April. Eight inches of snow fell on the 9th. To save horses from dying in the intense cold, guards were instructed constantly to walk the animals around the parade ground. If they stopped, they would freeze to death.

No Indians arrived on the day appointed for the conference. Hancock sent word that he and his men would visit their settlements, but a message got through that the Indians had been delayed but were now on their way – they had come across a herd of buffalo and decided to stock up on supplies of meat and skins.

On the evening of 10 April, fifteen Cheyenne chiefs – 'dog soldiers' as Stanley disparagingly called them – arrived at the camp. A tent was erected for the chiefs, a campfire built and Hancock and his officers assembled there. The chiefs asked for time to collect their thoughts, and while they were doing that, asked for food to be brought.

They emerged in front of the fire, but proceedings were further delayed while the chiefs filled and smoked their pipes. They were then ready to 'talk'. Hancock assured them that he had not come to make war and told them what he expected in future. He expressed disappointment that more chiefs had not come and informed them that he would set out next day to visit their territory.

The expedition ventured deep into Indian country and on the way encountered what Custer described in *My Life on the Plains* (1874) as 'one of the finest and most imposing military displays, prepared according to the Indian art of war, which it has ever been my lot to behold. It was nothing more nor less than an Indian line of battle drawn directly across our line of march – as if to say, thus far and no further.'

All of this provided Stanley with wonderful copy for the *Missouri Democrat*. He observed several hundred mounted Indians in front, plus others stationed at the rear acting as reserves, wearing their brightest colours, heads covered in war bonnets, lances decorated with crimson pennants, bows strung and quivers full of barbed arrows. Each possessed hunting knives, tomahawks, rifles or revolvers – kindly supplied by the US Indian Department. Custer remarked that this displayed 'the wonderful liberality of our Government, which not only is able to furnish its soldiers with the latest improved style of breech-loaders to defend it and themselves, but is equally able and willing to give the same pattern of arms to their common foe'.

Stanley rode close to Hancock and heard him give the order for the infantry, artillery and cavalry to form a line of battle, determined that although war was the last thing on his mind, they should at least be prepared for a fight. The order was given for the cavalry to draw sabres and 'as the bright blades flashed from their scabbards into the morning sunlight, and the infantry brought their muskets to a carry, a most beautiful and wonderfully interesting sight was spread out before and around us, presenting a contrast which, to a military eye, could but be striking'. After moments of 'painful suspense' Hancock rode forward and enquired the object of the hostile display confronting his men, telling the chiefs that if war was their object, he was ready. The chiefs admitted they did not want a battle and Hancock announced that his men would move forward as planned and camp nearby.

In June, Stanley described an Indian's scalping procedure to his readers, adding: 'It is a horrible sight and the operation is one, we earnestly hope, will never be performed on our worthy self. While writing, we assure you that our scalp is intact, but how long it will remain so, we cannot as yet inform you. . . .'

Hancock's effort to forge a peace was a failure; if anything, he made matters between the white and red man worse following the death of four Indians, two of whom had been sent by friendly tribes and killed by mistake.

Before beginning the next part of his assignment, Stanley found time to send word to Lewis Noe:

> I am with Hancock's Command hunting Indians. . . . I am a Special Correspondent. Copies of my articles will be sent to you. When in Liverpool, I promised you any curiosities I could get as I always think of you and I have already succeeded in getting a bow and twenty arrows from a Comanche Chief . . . I will send anything else I get as soon as I reach St. Louis. You need not write to me, as we are moving into the interior of the territories and are on 'the war path'. My deep respect for all and in the meantime, God bless you. Your brother, Henry.

The second part of Stanley's frontier assignment required him to report on the proceedings of the Indian Peace Commission, headed by General William Tecumseh Sherman. This was the man responsible for the celebrated Civil War 'march to the sea' in which 62,000 Yankee troops had cut a wide swathe as they moved from Atlanta to Savannah, tearing up railroad tracks, burning farms and destroying supplies to reduce the Confederacy's war-making potential. The red-haired officer was now in overall command of the army between Canada and Texas, the Mississippi and the Rockies and, having been ordered by Congress to go west and bring peace to the frontier, was in no mood to show leniency towards the Plains Indians.

Stanley joined peace commissioners visiting reservations, concluding treaties and handing out presents – including more rifles. The Indians listened, but still failed to understand why they should move from ancient lands to be herded on to tiny reservations. A pow-wow between commissioners and leading chiefs was held at the end of the Union Pacific tracks near Platte City, Nebraska in August 1867.

Stanley predicted that Sherman 'will be the soul of the party. His views will probably have controlling weight. Cautious, calculating, with a dash of statesmanship in him, he is a valuable acquisition to the country at this time. He is perfectly aware of the responsibility attached to his present commission. He is aware that all the people wish peace, and the results of the conference will be looked for with unusual interest. We earnestly hope that peace may be secured although we have grave doubts that it would be a lasting one.' The Indians were represented by chiefs who spoke of the problems brought by white settlers to tribal lands, the damage caused by the railroad, of their reliance on buffalo herds wandering across their territory, of how white men plundered their animals, and of their reluctance to leave 'the old ways' and their fear of the breaking up of their tribes.

Stanley reminded *Missouri Democrat* readers scathingly that for their part the American government had urged Indians to raise stock and herd sheep on their lands:

> The country is admirably suited for it; the Indian temperament will rejoice in such a pursuit. . . . When the Navajos begged the government to send them $20,000 worth of sheep in lieu of blankets, promising they would ever after weave blankets for themselves, what did the excellent government of the United States do? Sent them blankets. Yet there was no remorse of conscience, no memory of the countless flocks and herds which the soldiers of the United States had taken from the Navajos; no such thing – only a sullen determination not to encourage the industry of a tribe which could make blankets before which the Eastern fabric is a rag, and the English whitney a dish cloth. For the same reason probably the government may be reluctant to place herds of sheep in the hands of these wronged children of the soil, but I hope to God there will be a higher sense of justice.

When Indians at Medicine Lodge Creek, Kansas, signed the final treaty, Sherman asked newsmen reporting the occasion, including Stanley, to act as official witnesses to the event.

Hancock's peace expeditions and the treaties brokered by Sherman were spectacular failures. Indian wars went on for a further twenty years during which other peace commissions tried – and failed – in their purpose. But the experience of witnessing and reporting stirring events as they unfolded on the American frontier and rubbing shoulders with America's highest-ranking military officials allowed Stanley to produce penetrating, profound and often prophetic copy for the *Missouri Democrat*.

The *Missouri Democrat*'s editor permitted Stanley to syndicate his dispatches to other journals, providing the St Louis newspaper published them first. Stanley's form of popular journalism found favour with the *Chicago Republican*, *Cincinnati Commercial*, *New York Tribune* and – most famously – the *New York Herald*.

City publications were hungry for frontier news and reporters based in those remote areas were as important to editors as foreign correspondents. Stories about western life were always sensational, appealing to readers in crowded cities, for whom America's frontier was like a foreign country, populated by individuals living in a landscape different to their own who often looked, spoke and behaved in another way. Stories were written in a racy style, with plenty of gory detail and lots of colour, ingredients to be found in abundance in Stanley's early dispatches from America's vanishing frontier.

Major-General Winfield Scott Hancock. (*Library of Congress*)

Chapter 14

MR BENNETT AND THE
NEW YORK HERALD

T he $15 weekly salary from the *Missouri Democrat* plus freelance fees earned from other newspapers, boosted Stanley's earnings to $90 per week and he recorded in his journal that 'by economy and hard work, though now and then foolishly impulsive, I have been able to save three thousands dollars, that is, six hundred pounds'. It was time for the frontier reporter to move on and head for New York, the Mecca of American journalism. In December 1867, he wrote: 'I ventured . . . to throw up my engagement with the *Democrat*, proceed to Cincinnati and Chicago, and collect my dues, which were promptly paid to me; and in two cases, especially the *Chicago Republican*, most handsomely.' He caught a train to New York with high hopes of landing a staff job on the *New York Tribune*. The editor was complimentary about Stanley's work but had no vacancy for 'such an indefatigable correspondent' at that time.

Disappointed, Stanley crossed over to the editorial offices of the *New York Herald* on Broadway and Ann Street 'and by a spasm of courage' asked to see the boss, James Gordon Bennett Jr, editor-in-chief and son of the paper's founder and proprietor, James Gordon Bennett 'the Elder'. Stanley's card was passed to Bennett, who recognised the name of the reporter who had sent important dispatches from the frontier 'and I was invited to his presence. I found myself before a tall, fierce-eyed, and imperious-looking young man [Bennett was aged twenty-seven at the time, a few months younger than Stanley] who said, "Oh, you are the correspondent who has been following Hancock and Sherman lately. Well, I must say your letters and telegrams have kept us very well informed. I wish I could offer you something permanent, for we want active men like you."'

James Gordon Bennett 'the Elder', as he became known after handing the reins of his paper to 25-year-old 'Junior' in 1866, was a Scottish-born

American who was instrumental in shaping the face of journalism in the United States. Bennett had been destined for the priesthood and attended a Catholic seminary in Scotland before sailing to Canada in 1819. He eventually settled in New York where he became a correspondent for the *New York Enquirer* and *Morning Courier*. He was admired for his bold writing style, producing articles on cultural, economic and political topics. His first newspaper, the *Globe*, was founded in 1832 and the following year he became owner and editor-in-chief of the *Pennsylvanian* in Philadelphia.

With a start-up capital of $500, he launched a new independent paper called the *New York Herald* in May 1835. The first four-page edition was written entirely by Bennett, who was aided by two compositors and a printer all working out of a cellar in Wall Street. It sold for 1 cent per copy and became known as 'the penny paper'.

The *New York Herald* faced financial problems from the start, competing against established titles in the city. Its offices were burned out twice and Bennett was robbed and threatened by gangsters. He succeeded by industry, persistence, a rapidly growing circulation (it eventually achieved the largest circulation of any newspaper in the United States) and high advertising revenue. Bennett pioneered aggressive news gathering, developing the art of interviews as a reporting technique and covering issues others considered unworthy of their time. In June 1835, the *New York Herald* was the first American newspaper to carry a Wall Street financial article and to print a vivid, colourful and factual account of the great fire that destroyed a large section of the city later that year. The paper was also first to appoint foreign correspondents, receive copy via telegraph, mail trains and ocean-going steamships, commission more than sixty writers to cover the American Civil War, report on proceedings in the police courts, establish a society section and to feature sporting and artistic events in depth. Bennett also pioneered the use of illustrations in his paper.

Bennett knew what New Yorkers wanted to read in their newspapers and introduced other subjects of which he decided they should also be aware. He turned the *New York Herald* into the publication with the largest editorial staff, printing more pages than its rivals and the journal for which every American reporter aspired to write. By 1860, the paper was printed on the world's most technologically advanced presses producing 50,000 copies overnight, in time to be on the breakfast table of every well-informed New Yorker. This self-styled 'Napoleon of the newspaper' who – in his words – infused his journal with 'life, glowing eloquence, philosophy, taste, sentiment, wit and humour', brought his son into the business to learn about newspapers from the ground floor up with a view to surrendering control on his retirement. At the time the paper was turning in annual profits of over $400,000.

Bennett Jr had been given an expensive foreign education and returned to New York at the outbreak of the Civil War to enlist in the navy. After discharge, he joined the newspaper as his father's assistant, becoming managing editor in 1866 and taking over as editor on his father's seventy-first birthday the following year. Bennett Jr was a gifted editor, possessing all his father's flair for tuning into public taste. He was also extravagant, enjoyed life at New York's best restaurants, moving in city society and spending large sums on circulation-building promotions. Like all editors, Bennett wanted exclusive stories on his news pages. The first two pages of the *New York Herald* were given over to classified advertisements, so Bennett's exclusives were designed to appear from page 3 onwards with new instalments published in prime positions on subsequent days alongside Bennett's own editorial comment columns.

Legend states that thanks to New York's vaudeville comedians, Bennett's unceasing daily news exclusives and exposés introduced a new phrase into American and, later, British popular culture. The punch line to topical jokes cracked by a host of comedians ended with audiences responding loudly with the chant: 'Oh, Gordon Bennett!' In time, the phrase crossed the Atlantic, where London's music hall audiences adapted it to 'Oh, Gawd!'

Stanley boldly asked Bennett if he might cover a military campaign about to be waged in Abyssinia (modern-day Ethiopia) against an emperor who had imprisoned missionaries and envoys whom the British government was sending armed soldiers to rescue. In Stanley's opinion, the brave mission promised all the hallmarks of a cracking series of articles for the *New York Herald*. Bennett, however, had his doubts and said he did not think the story had sufficient interest for American readers. He then asked, 'On what terms would you go?'

Stanley replied that he would travel either as a staff writer for a moderate salary, or as a freelance receiving higher rates for all material published with the right to syndicate articles to other papers. Bennett was alarmed by this last remark, stating that the *New York Herald* did not have a policy of sharing news. 'We would be willing to pay well for exclusive intelligence. Have you ever been abroad before?', asked the editor. Stanley avoided mentioning he was still a British subject (he would swear an oath of allegiance to the United States in 1885) and a 'foreigner' from Wales, admitting only that he had visited Europe several times as well as Asia Minor.

Bennett made Stanley a proposition: cover the assignment on a trial basis, defraying his own expenses, 'and if your letters are up to standard and your intelligence is early and exclusive, you shall be well paid by the article, or at the rate by which we engage our European specials, and you will be placed on the permanent list'. Stanley agreed and Bennett sent his London representative a cable stating that a new correspondent would be sending his office dispatches from Abyssinia via telegraph. 'Thus I became what had been the object of my ambition, a regular, I hope, correspondent of the *New York Herald*,' Stanley wrote in his journal.

On the morning of 22 December, Stanley transferred £300 from his American bank to the Lombard Street branch of the National Westminster Bank, leaving the remainder in the United States. He received letters of introduction from General Sherman, realising that as both a stranger and 'an American' he would need all the help he could muster among English officers on the expedition. Hours later he was on board the steamer *Hecla* heading out into the Atlantic. First stop was Liverpool and then he took a train to London to draw funds from his bank, boarded another train to Dover for a cross-Channel ferry to the French coast and then travelled overland to Paris.

From his room at the Boulevard de Strasbourg on 1 January 1868, Stanley wrote a note to Lewis Noe: 'To Brother Lewis – Prince of Boys – & Best of companions. A Happy New Year's Day to you, Louis & a hundred more of the same sort. In your rejoicings forget not the exiled friend & Brother. Henry.' Later he travelled south to Marseilles where he boarded a steamer to Alexandria. From there he headed south to Suez, the Red Sea and Abyssinia – his first visit to the hinterland of a place he would later call the 'Dark Continent' . . . Africa.

Chapter 15

THEODORUS AND MAGDALA

Greed was the only reason Britain was interested in Abyssinia in the mid-1800s. The country's ruler, Emperor Theodorus (pronounced 'Todoros') had declared himself emperor following battles with feudal chiefs and claimed to be of the lineage of King Solomon. In 1851 he proclaimed himself 'Messiah' over everyone, was victorious over Egyptian, Palestinian and Arabian enemies and gained a popular following among his people. His fame spread abroad and on the strength of his reputation as a powerful monarch in an important if relatively unknown part of Africa, his friendship was sought by European and Asian traders willing to visit Abyssinia to win profitable contracts, particularly for their armaments manufacturing industries.

The British sent an envoy called Plowden to manage their interests, 'promote commerce, suppress the slave trade, watch and counteract foreign intrigue'. Plowden become a favourite of Theodorus, advising him on how to create a more effective army, purchase the best weaponry and be more successful in battles with his Islamic neighbours. To expand his empire, Theodorus began attacking areas on the fringes of his territory. He brought in foreign weapons engineers to advise on building a cannon foundry, explosives experts to advise on setting up a gunpowder factory and arms manufacturers to procure guns.

Plowden told his government that Egypt was acting as an aggressor, capturing Theodorus's men and selling them as slaves. The British envoy was murdered by rebel forces while observing a border conflict and, as a token of thanks for the favourable way in which he had been treated by the Emperor – and in the interests of ongoing relations – Queen Victoria appointed a replacement. When Captain Charles Cameron arrived to present his credentials at the court of Theodorus in February 1862, he brought gifts from Queen Victoria, including a silver revolver, inscribed:

Presented by Victoria, Queen of Great Britain and Ireland –
To Theodorus, Emperor of Abyssinia, as a slight token of her gratitude
for his kindness to her servant, Plowden, 1854.

Theodorus was delighted the monarch from across the seas had sent such a fine gift. He allowed British missionaries to enter his country and more businessmen to trade with Abyssinia. Unbeknown to Victoria's diplomats, Theodorus was a tyrannical monster along the later lines of Uganda's Idi Amin and Emperor Bokassa of the Central African Republic. Anyone suspected of treason would be removed, never to be seen alive again.

The Emperor became a feared man. By the time his treachery was discovered, Captain Cameron had nearly completed the process of establishing a treaty between the countries, with the result that Abyssinia was preparing to open a London embassy. Cameron helped Theodorus to draft a letter to 'his friend' Queen Victoria, expressing the hope that 'lasting goodwill may exist between our two countries, which will redound to the glory and advantage of both'.

The letter arrived in Whitehall, was read by Foreign Office staff and filed in a pigeonhole – where it remained unread by anyone else. Seventeen months later, by which time word had reached England of Theodorus's brutality, the Emperor was still waiting for his reply. He summoned Cameron and threw him in prison. Three months later, acknowledgement of the Emperor's letter arrived from London, without reference to future cooperation or aid. Slighted, Theodorus instructed his thugs to beat Cameron's servants and British missionaries 'as you would a dog'. Their work was so effective that two missionaries died. The rest were gaoled alongside Cameron and any remaining Europeans fled from Abyssinia or went into hiding.

From his cell, Cameron managed to smuggle out a letter to *The Times* explaining his situation. The newspaper accused the government of standing by while a British citizen was fed bread and water, beaten, tortured and chained to a wall. Britain made threats to Theodorus, but Cameron and the missionaries remained in chains. A minor official was sent to plead for their release. He brought a new letter from Queen Victoria but Theodorus did not think it was sufficiently respectful for a 'Messiah'. More Europeans were imprisoned.

Then the British government declared war. English mercenaries offered their services to capture hostages and deliver them to freedom while reports circulated that a squadron of cavalry would be dispatched to rescue the unfortunates. In the end an imperial army comprised of 13,000 dragoons and foot soldiers, Bengali and Punjabi infantry and artillery, Madras and Bombay sappers, 8,000 Chinese labourers, thousands of horses, hundreds of camels and a herd of elephants was sent together with hospital ships, arms, ammunition, donkeys, saddles, chains, halters, tents and enough food to keep an army well fed for months.

The entire rescue mission was masterminded by the Commander-in-Chief of the British army in Bombay, General Sir Robert Napier, a brilliant military strategist and former civil engineer. Napier had learned lessons from the disaster at the Crimea and was longing to put them to good use. This was his opportunity and his orders from London were succinct: 'Failure is not an option. Locate Theodorus before the summer rains in June, liberate the prisoners and leave Abyssinia.'

In November 1867, an advance force from the British–Abyssinian rescue expedition landed on the beach at Zoulla in Annesley Bay (now Mitsiwa, Eritrea) on the southern shores of the Red Sea – at the same time that Henry Morton Stanley was reading about Theodorus's outrages in American newspapers and making up his mind to quit the *Missouri Democrat* and travel east to find a new job in New York.

Stanley was about to enter the competitive world of the foreign correspondent in which every reporter would be doing their utmost to scoop rivals and get their stories published first. This would not be easy from Abyssinia, where terrain was rugged, communication difficult and the nearest telegraphic station was 1,000 miles away in Suez. Correspondents travelling with Napier's army were expected to entrust articles to official couriers travelling back to Zoulla, from where they would be carried on Suez-bound steamers to be telegraphed to London. Stanley's copy was destined for New York and an editor who demanded correspondents file stories before anyone else. How they did it was up to them.

In Suez, Stanley's first call was to the city's telegraphic officer to discuss a private arrangement to transmit his dispatches before those of his rivals. He wrote in his journal: 'My telegrams are to be addressed to him [the telegraphic officer] and he will undertake that there shall be no delay in sending them to London, for which services I am to pay handsomely if, on my return, I hear that there has been no delay.'

From Suez, Stanley headed south to Annesley Bay, where the former fishing village had been transformed into a military port. Troops and horses were already heading 400 miles inland towards Theodorus's fortress at Magdala (a Hebrew word meaning 'tower of strength') situated 5,000ft above sea level 'amid gigantic mountains piled one upon another . . . a region of indescribable wilderness and grandeur . . . an almost impregnable stronghold'. It was from here that Theodorus planned to defend his kingdom with forces and weapons of his own.

In Abyssinia, Stanley joined an exclusive group of newspaper correspondents covering what newspapers predicted would be a 'small British war'. Gentlemen of the press included representatives from *The Times*, *Morning Post*, *Daily News*, *Daily Telegraph* and the flamboyant George A. Henty of the *Evening Standard*, later dubbed the 'prince of story tellers' for his writing of fictional 'ripping yarn' stories for schoolboys. Stanley confided to his journal that the British press corps might look down on an American correspondent, but he quickly learned that they 'consisted of some remarkable literary lights . . . they all messed together, and though there were contrasting elements in their natures, yet they seldom disagreed; in fact there was more harmony in the Press tent than in any other bell-shaped domicile in the army. I hope I shall not be traducing these good gentlemen, as I bear them much love and respect, if I give them the credit of being the most sociable mess in the army, as well as the most loveable and good tempered.'

While Stanley did not wish to 'traduce' his press colleagues, he certainly expected to scoop them with his Abyssinian dispatches, hoping they would not stumble across his private arrangement with the Suez telegraphic office until it was too late and his *New York Herald* pieces had appeared.

The press corps caught up with expeditionary forces, riding over the barren plains on horseback. The route presented the army with numerous problems, which they overcame thanks to the tactics of General Napier. Sometimes the track completely disappeared and troops had to climb over rocks, descend into deep gullies and clamber up the side of ravines in order to advance in the right direction. Under Napier's supervision, ropes, pulleys and elephants were used to haul supplies, ammunition and animals up the slopes and similar methods employed to lower them down again on the other side. Elephants could carry 1,800lb with ease, fed on a daily diet of 35lb of bread and 40lb of straw. The weather was hot and humid and tropical storms drenched the soldiers. The terrain was dusty one minute, soaking wet and muddy the next. As British forces edged closer to Magdala, Theodorus was preparing for battle, with 10,000 armed men, 20 giant cannon and enough supplies to keep them going for months.

On 10 April – Good Friday – Napier's expeditionary force sighted the fortress in the distance and prepared to lay siege. The huge oval rock platform, a mile and a half in length and three-quarters of a mile wide, rose above a narrow plateau. It provided Theodorus with a grandstand view of approaching forces and he greeted them with cannon fire and a charge by 3,500 wild and furious men who came screaming down the mountain road.

While Theodorus's crazed army rolled forward like an oncoming wave, Stanley noted that Napier 'sat on his charger serene and impassable, surrounded by a group of men who were not nearly so unaffected as their chief'. His men were instructed to hold fire until an order was given. Stanley observed: 'Closer the Abyssinians drew, until we momentarily expected to see them launch their spears, and annihilate the Sappers.' They came nearer, but still no order was heard. Just as Theodorus's men were in the act of launching spears towards the British, the order to fire was given. As gunfire from the army's rifles cut down the approaching enemy, rockets were launched from tubes. Those not cut down by the rifles' bullets turned and fled in fear of the rockets. Stanley observed Napier leaning from his saddle giving encouragement to his men. In next to no time the battle was over, gunfire ceased and the British army set up camp for the night. Stanley recorded:

> Before rolling ourselves up in our rugs, and while thinking of the events that marked the day, our ears caught the sounds that betokened the presence of beasts of prey. In ravenous packs, jackals and hyenas had come to devour the abundant feast spread out by the ruthless hand of war. Stranger lullaby than that which lulled us to sleep that night man never heard, and the last sounds our dulled ears caught were the jackal's shrill whelp, the hyena's sonorous bay, mingling with the lichowl's mournful 'tu-whit-tu-whoo'. It was the nightmare battlefield of Shiloh all over again.

One officer and thirty-one privates were wounded in the encounter. A detachment was sent to count the bodies of Theodorus's men and bring in the wounded. Stanley accompanied them and reported: 'A frightful scene was presented to our eyes. The significant sounds of the past night had prepared me in a measure for some horrors, but reality exceeded my conception tenfold. The beasts of prey had been at work upon the bodies. They had revelled in the unusual abundance of flesh. . . . Carefully the dead were counted and buried where they fell, and most carefully the wounded, who had lain in torture and pain the livelong night and had feebly warded off savage jaws, were conveyed . . . to the hospital.' Of the Abyssinians, 75 wounded were treated in the tented hospital and 560 were buried.

Theodorus had witnessed the battle from his mountain eyrie and knew his chances of victory were slim. Word was sent up the mountain that Napier demanded immediate release of all prisoners, 'unconditional surrender to Queen Victoria' of the Emperor and the fortress of Magdala. Assurances were sent that the Emperor and his family would not be harmed.

Theodorus demanded better terms from 'the English commander who serves a woman' (Queen Victoria), stating: 'Rather than surrender, I will fight to the death. Can you not be satisfied with the possession of those you came for, and leave me alone in peace?' He called for the captives to be brought from their cells. Standing before them in his best robes, Theodorus ordered the gates to be opened and with Consul Cameron at their head, 61 weak and filthy men, women, children with 187 servants and 323 animals slowly walked out of the fortress and down the mountain road to freedom. Stanley wrote: 'These were the captives for whom the Crusade had been undertaken; these were those whose graphic letters had drawn tears from Christendom.'

Rumour circulated that Theodorus had fled from his mountain, making his way to the valley below by a secret path on the other side. Napier put a $50,000 bounty on the Emperor's head – dead or alive – and ordered his soldiers up the mountain road. Stanley was taken to the edge of a precipice 'and looking in that direction, I saw a sight which for ever beggars description . . . I am no lover of the horrible or the disgusting. But if you can conceive 308 dead [Africans], piled one upon another, stripped, naked, in a state of corruption, with gyves and fetters round their limbs, you will save me the unpleasant task of describing the scene.' An eyewitness told Stanley that prisoners had been manacled and either sabred or shot by Theodorus's men as they lay helpless on the ground. Pleas for mercy went unheeded and 'they were butchered to the last soul'.

For Napier, this gruesome sight was the last straw. Troops making their way up the mountain were ordered to attack the fortress and root out the Emperor's remaining followers. Soldiers of the Royal Engineers and the King's Own Regiment were assigned the task – carefully observed by Stanley – and they captured the stronghold in less than two hours. As they burst through Magdala's gates, chaos was everywhere. A man was seen next to a haystack holding a revolver. When he saw soldiers approaching, he turned and ran. As soldiers gave chase, they heard shots and after rounding a corner found the man on the ground, his smoking revolver still in his hand. A soldier picked up the weapon and noticed a silver plate attached identifying it as a gift from Queen Victoria to the Emperor of Abyssinia. The dying man was Theodorus himself. Knowing the battle was lost, he had decided that death was better than imprisonment and had placed the revolver in his mouth and fired. British soldiers standing around the body cheered over it as if it had been a dead fox.

Theodorus was 'clad in coarse upper garments, dingy with wear, and ragged with tear, covering undergarments of clean linen. The face of deep brown was the most remarkable one in Abyssinia; it bore the appearance of one who had passed through many anxious hours. His eyes, now overspread with a deathly film, gave evidence yet of the piercing power for which they were celebrated . . . and thus was it that we saw the remains of Theodorus, Emperor of Abyssinia . . . dead by his own hand.' The battle was over; the British had won another victory. Detachments were ordered to all parts of the fortress to quell pockets of resistance and free remaining captives. Hundreds were released from cells, many too weak to walk. Scores of them kissed the hands of their liberators.

Stanley noticed an excited crowd ahead who had discovered Theodorus's treasure tents. The ground was strewn with an assortment of precious items and an ugly mob of soldiers, former prisoners and Theodorus's followers were attempting to plunder the treasure trove. The mob smashed open the stone coffin of a priest and stole a diamond cross from the body. Thousands of pounds worth of goods were grabbed, including gold, silver and brass crosses, pots made from precious metals, diamond-encrusted goblets, Bohemian cut glass, French china, Staffordshire pottery, fine wines, ornamental textiles, Persian carpets and furs made from lion, leopard and wolf skins. Meanwhile, a separate group jostled around Theodorus's body attempting to tear off pieces of his bloodstained shirt. Napier gave orders that the body be left alone and prepared for burial. He then ordered all buildings within the fortress to be blown up or burned.

Napier then marched his men back to camp, ordered plundered booty to be brought to the front of his tent and officers told to select mementos they considered most appropriate for their troops and mess halls. Fifteen elephants and 200 mules were loaded with 'miscellaneous articles'. The rest were auctioned and £5,000 divided between those participating in the Magdala campaign. Each soldier ended up with a few extra pounds in their pay as they turned about-face to march the 400 miles back to the coast.

The siege and capture of Magdala produced exciting copy for the *New York Herald*. It was now time to get the news back in the fastest possible way. On the return journey, Stanley sought a messenger prepared to carry his dispatches to the coast and onwards to his telegraph contact at Suez. A British officer supervising the correspondents got wind of Stanley's plan and informed him that all dispatches penned by reporters must travel in the same official bag. No single reporter would be given preference and the government in London must receive news of the Magdala victory first – and newspaper readers second. Fuming, Stanley attempted to devise other plans to outsmart fellow reporters and his military watchdog. But by the time they arrived at the coast, he had failed to come up with a scheme and his dispatches went into the official bag with the rest.

Stanley was determined to be first to the telegraphic office when the steamer arrived in Suez. Then the vessel hit a sandbank in the Red Sea and was grounded for four days under a boiling sun. The combination of heat and too much whiskey caused a pair of officers on board to disagree over something trivial and insist the matter be settled by a duel to the death on the main deck. Seeing an opportunity for a story about the stupidity of British upper-class officers unable to hold their liquor, Stanley offered to mediate and talk the officers out of the duel. Once effects of the alcohol had worn off, both men realised their foolhardiness and separately thanked Stanley for saving one – or both – of their lives.

At last the steamer passengers sighted Suez, only to be told by the harbourmaster that they must be quarantined for five days as reports of cholera in Abyssinia had reached the port authorities; the official bag containing all the journalists' reports was also held in quarantine. Unlike other correspondents, Stanley had made a copy of his dispatches. That night he secretly bribed someone on the quayside to deliver them to his friend at the telegraphic office, where they were cabled to London and on to New York, marking Stanley's first foreign 'scoop' for the *New York Herald*.

The other pressmen remained in ignorance of Stanley's actions. When released from the steamer five days later, they were informed that the cable link between Alexandria and Malta had snapped and would not be repaired for weeks. By the time Stanley's articles about the sacking of Magdala and Theodorus's death had been splashed across the *New York Herald*, Bennett had syndicated the articles to London newspapers, making their own correspondents' dispatches obsolete. It would be another week before official military dispatches confirming the defeat found their way to Whitehall, making Stanley as popular with his press colleagues and British politicians as a cat with fleas.

Not for the first time, politicians denounced the *New York Herald* while other publications accused the paper of making up the story. When the reports were later confirmed, accusers suddenly fell silent. Nor, in a curious foretaste of what would happen to the *New York Herald* and its front-rank correspondent four years later, were there any words of apology. Bennett was delighted with his scoop and in Alexandria on 28 June 1868, Stanley proudly wrote in his journal: 'I am now a permanent employee of the *Herald* and must keep a sharp look out that my second "coup" shall be as much of a success as the first. I wonder where I shall be sent next . . . ?'

The body of Emperor Theodorus following his suicide at Magdala in 1868.

Chapter 16

ROMANTIC INTERLUDE

Bennett ordered his new star foreign correspondent to remain in Suez and report on the progress of the new multi-million dollar canal, now three-quarters completed and due to open the following November after eleven years' construction work. Ferdinand de Lesseps, 'in his 64th year, though his appearance is that of a man little past middle age', was the wealthy chief architect of the project. De Lesseps was delighted to hear that the *New York Herald* was interested in his 90-mile-long shipping waterway linking Port Said on the Mediterranean coast with Suez and the Red Sea in the south. After all, the company building the canal, Compagnie Universelle du Canal Maritime de Suez, was owned by international shareholders, but America's Rothschild banking empire was financing the venture to the tune of the $77 million finance.

De Lesseps made sure that Stanley was given access to managers and engineers to gather the facts he wanted about the Suez Canal. Everywhere the reporter travelled along the canal route, staff emphasised that American shipping lines with vessels plying the commercial routes to Indian Ocean, East African, Arabian and Asian destinations would benefit. Once the shortcut provided by the canal was open, they would be able to shave thousands of miles and many weeks off sailing times, instead of travelling around the Cape of Good Hope. Stanley learned that British merchant and military ships serving India would also cut 9,300 miles from their journey and be able to sail from England to Bombay in thirty days – half the previous sailing time.

Because American and British ship owners were reluctant to alter routings and pay additional costs to take vessels through the canal, de Lesseps' company needed positive exposure for the project to persuade them to change their minds. Newspapers on both sides of the Atlantic had shown a high degree of cynicism towards the Suez Canal and a positive article in the *New York Herald* would be just the thing to help bring them around. Stanley's enthusiastic comments that work completed on the canal was 'positively wonderful' and his prediction that 'common sense will prove that as the voyages shorten so will the trade expand' did the trick. Days after the article appeared on 12 August 1868, de Lesseps began receiving positive enquiries from American shipping lines about using the canal.

'Your correspondent', as Stanley referred to himself, became one of the first writers to travel in a steamer down a 45-mile stretch of canal already completed, his description of the journey part travelogue, part civil engineering report, with plenty of space devoted to 'human interest' – curious people encountered en route. These included a pair of Parisian ladies 'whom we found out afterwards to belong to the class of the *demi monde* who had come to ply a nefarious trade in the desert. . . .' Stanley concluded: 'In eighteen months, the whole world will meet on the isthmus of Suez to bless the able President of the Suez Maritime Canal Universal Company and consecrate the means whereby 500 million human beings hitherto enveloped in the dreary night of Mussulman bigotry and paganism are brought into closer contact to the civilizing influence of Europe and America. Inshallah! Inshallah!'

So delighted was de Lesseps with Stanley's full-page article and prediction that 3,000 vessels would pass through the canal annually, that he sent 'Monsieur Henri' a personal invitation to cover the opening ceremony, to be performed by Princess Eugénie, wife of Napoleon III, and still a year and a half away.

From Suez, Stanley was ordered to Crete, where Ottoman Turks controlled parts of the island and native unrest resulted in frustrated attempts to restore power back to the Greeks. To Stanley's chagrin, the Cretan visit produced little more than an article putting the conflict into context. There was no rioting, desecrating of mosques or open combat between Turks and Greeks to be found anywhere in Crete's narrow streets or rocky mountains.

Disappointed at not being in the thick of a fight again, Stanley took off to visit the small Aegean island of Syra in the Cyclades in search of copy. It was August and the height of summer when he arrived in the town of Hermopolis seeking a guide to show him around. A genial English-speaking local called Christo Evangelides was given the job and on their travels noticed how Stanley mentioned more than once how attractive he found the island's young ladies. 'You should marry a Greek girl,' said Evangelides and, uncharacteristically, Stanley confesses to his journal that up to that moment it had never entered his mind to take a wife. 'Yet the suggestion was delicious from other points of view. A wife! My wife! How grand the proprietorship of a fair woman appeared! To be loved with heart and soul above all else, forever united in thought and sympathy with a fair and virtuous being. Whose very touch gave strength and courage and confidence! Oh dear! How my warm imagination glows at the strange idea,' he wrote.

Stanley set out to explore the island. One evening he set eyes upon 'a young lady who came as near as possible to the realisation of the ideal which my fancy had portrayed, after the visions of marriage had been excited by Evangelides' frolicsome talk. She, after a formal introduction, subsided on a couch, demure, and wrapped in virgin modesty.' The girl was called Virginia 'and it well befitted her', Stanley recalled. She was sixteen years old. Spotting Stanley's evident interest in the young girl, Evangelides began telling the girl's parents about the American visitor.

The girl's mother, a Frenchwoman, demanded to know if Stanley was already married. Stanley stammered that he had hardly thought about the subject, prompting the response from Virginia's mother: 'I hope you will think of it now; there are many fair women in Greece – and Greek women makes the best wives.' The girl's mother promised to find a nice wife for the young visitor and as he left he pondered on Virginia's Franco-Grecian parentage and what language he might use to woo her. The girl spoke no English and Stanley naïvely observed, 'but she is fluent in French. Here then comes another obstacle. I could make no love in French, without exploding at my own ignorance of it. But there is no doubt that, so far as beauty goes, Virginia is sufficient.'

Stanley was invited to dine at the home the Greek beauty shared with her family, who were all summoned to weigh him up as a suitor for Virginia. The following day it appeared to be general knowledge to everyone – except Stanley – that the marriage was as good as concluded, that he only had to name the day. He blurted out that he wanted the ceremony to take place the following Sunday.

That night Stanley called at Virginia's home where he found her mother had cooled towards the idea of marriage to an American roving reporter. She wanted to know about his background. What was he to tell her? Was he to dredge up ghosts from his past? She asked Stanley to be patient 'until all reasonable assurances had been given that I was what I represented myself to be'. Virginia's parents went about their enquiries, including contacting various referees in the United States supplied by Stanley. He then began to ponder whether he wanted to surrender his freedom 'to wander where I liked, at a moment's thought, with only a portmanteau to look after' and settle down.

On 11 September, close to the date when he was due to leave Greece and return to a new assignment in Turkey, Stanley gave a dinner party for Virginia and her family at the Hotel d'Amerique. Virginia was 'lovelier than ever' and he knew that evening he had fallen in love. Next day, he was a guest at their home and 'had the honour of being seated near her. We exchanged regards, but we both felt more than we spoke. We are convinced that we would be happy together, if it is our destiny to be united.' On 13 September, Stanley boarded the *Menzaleh* bound for Smyrna. He told his diary: 'Virginia was quite affectionate, and, though I am outwardly calm, my regrets are keener at parting than I expected. However, what must be, must be. . . .'

In Turkey, a telegraph message instructed Stanley to go immediately to Barcelona 'and wire for instructions on reaching France'. On 27 September, he wrote letters to Virginia's mother informing them 'that they must not expect my return to Syra unless they all came to a positive decision and expressly invited me, as it would be an obvious inconvenience – and likely to be resented at headquarters'.

Chapter 17

THE GOOD DOCTOR

So geographers, in Afric-maps
With savage-pictures fill their gaps,
And o'er unhabitable downs
Place elephants for want of towns.
Jonathan Swift, 'On Poetry' (1733), l. 177f

By 1871 it had been two years since anything had been heard from Dr David Livingstone, the world's best-known missionary, traveller, geographer and 'Her Majesty's Consul to all the native states in the African interior'. The last letter, received by the British Consul in Zanzibar in May 1869, was brought on foot by a messenger who had hiked 900 miles from Ujiji, on the shores of Lake Tanganyika. Livingstone complained about the disreputable conduct of a buffalo driver sent to deliver animals and requested the British Consul to be kind enough to send 30 pieces of sheeting, 40 pieces of blue cloth, £420 of red coral beads and a pair of new shoes.

Snippets of conflicting information about Livingstone arrived in Zanzibar from time to time. Some men who had deserted Livingstone near Lake Nyassa turned up in Zanzibar claiming that hostile tribesmen had killed the doctor. Obituaries began appearing in some British newspapers, while others demanded to see a body before they would believe the news. The Royal Geographical Society chose not to believe it and raised £1,200 for an expedition that aimed finally either to prove or disprove the theory.

Other information said that Livingstone was old, sick and in a state of utter destitution, stranded at the mercy of Arab slavers at a village deep in the interior and with no means of getting out. By 1871, following a disastrous expedition up the Zambezi River, Livingstone's lustre as the subject for sparkling news copy had begun to wane and more cynical newspapers now speculated that the doctor was dead, lost, or – most fantastic of all – attached to an African princess and nicely settled down somewhere in the interior.

Livingstone's African expeditions and discoveries had turned him into a travelling hero. He was the first European to cross the African continent from coast to coast, admired for missionary zeal and bravery as the roving representative of a rich, powerful and moral nation chosen by God to bring progress and liberty to those living in darkness in the darkest of all continents. He was known to be headstrong, stubborn, but totally committed to his work. And now he was missing. . . .

David Livingstone was born in March 1813, one of five sons and two daughters of poor parents, Neil and Agnes. They lived together in a tiny single room at the top of a whitewashed tenement building called Shuttle Row in the industrial town of Blantyre, near Glasgow. Shuttle Row housed twenty-four families, each living in the cramped accommodation built for workers at a local cotton mill. Neil, a God-fearing, teetotal Sunday school teacher, worked as a lowly paid tea salesman, handing out paper bags full of tea with one hand and religious tracts with the other. After two sons died in infancy, Neil earned extra funds by putting his three remaining lads to work at the mill. At the age of ten, David was employed as a piercer, a job perfectly suited to a child's small, delicate hands, scuttling about under spinning jennies, joining together pieces of broken thread. The job was dirty and noisy and employees worked from 6 a.m. to 8 p.m. six days a week for 2s 6d.

Despite tiredness and aching limbs, David attended evening school between 8 and 10 p.m. on weekdays, where he learned to read and write. From his first wage packet, his mother allowed him to buy a Latin grammar book. Back at Shuttle Row, he would read until midnight before falling asleep, repeating the process again next day.

The earnest young mill piercer was promoted to spinner at the age of nineteen, working a spinning jenny on which he propped books so that he could read sentence after sentence as he operated his machine. Fellow spinners were amused by his attempt to weave and learn at the same time, but he was determined to improve his knowledge and get out of Blantyre as quickly as possible.

Young Livingstone's head was always in a book and he read widely about plants, animals, travel, science and religion. His father disapproved of all books except religious texts, saying they were ungodly and undermined the Almighty's power. So as not to antagonise Neil, David saved his other books to read at the spinning jenny, taking only religious works to Shuttle Row.

In later years Livingstone admitted that his life had changed after reading Thomas Dick's *The Philosophy of a Future State*, which propounded the theory that Christian belief and complex scientific issues were intimately linked. It was this book, not the Bible, which led nineteen-year-old Livingstone to devote his life to God. He wrote: 'It is my desire to show my attachment to the cause of Him who died for me by devoting my life to His service.'

Livingstone toiled at the mill for thirteen years, finally leaving at the age of twenty-three when he trudged through the snow to Glasgow to begin studying for a medical degree at the Andersonian University. He would never regret his mill years, stating that the experience was an important part of his early life and if he had his time again, he would live 'in the same lowly state and pass through the same hardy training'.

His medical education was costly and money was needed for lodgings, training fees, books and food. Livingstone had set his heart on a career as a medical missionary in China, a mysterious and exotic land, that would satisfy his desire to please God as well as his romantic longing to travel to remote corners of the earth. He found a room in Glasgow's Rotten Row for 2s a week and began an intensive period of study. Between terms, he returned to mill work at Blantyre, attempting to save money for remaining medical school fees.

In the course of his second session in Glasgow, Livingstone applied to the London Missionary Society, the LMS, offering his services as a missionary-physician in China. He had learned that the organisation's objectives were to take the gospel to the world's heathens using missionaries from different Churches and allowing converts to choose the form of worship they considered most in accordance with the word of God. The Society's aims were identical to Livingstone's own and his father approved, too. His application was accepted and in September 1838 he was called to London to meet the organisation's directors.

After passing his first medical examinations at the age of twenty-five, he was accepted by the LMS and sent to begin his missionary training in Chipping Ongar, Essex. There he studied Latin and Greek. But Livingstone wanted to learn Chinese, the language he expected to use when his real missionary work began, only to be informed that the directors would not consider sending anyone to the Orient while an opium war was raging. The West Indies were proposed instead, but he turned the offer down, suggesting South Africa as an alternative.

Livingstone had heard about the work of Robert Moffat, a fellow Scot who had established a number of South African mission stations away from the traditional Cape Colony. During a fund-raising visit to Britain, Livingstone met Moffat and asked outright if he, too, might be suitable for the South African mission field. Moffat recalled: 'I said I believed he would, if he would not go to an old station, but would advance to unoccupied ground, specifying the vast plain to the north, where I had sometimes seen, in the morning sun, the smoke of a thousand villages, where no missionary had ever been. At last Livingstone said: "What is the use of my waiting for the end of this abominable opium war? I will go at once to Africa." The directors concurred, and Africa became his sphere.'

In 1840, the LMS brought Livingstone south for more medical experience before he returned to Glasgow to sit his final examinations. On 8 December he boarded the *George* for a three-month voyage to Cape Town. Dr David Livingstone's personal mission and lifelong love of Africa and its people were about to begin.

For the next fifteen years and for a salary of £100 a year, Livingstone was constantly on the move in and out of Africa's interior, creating a dual reputation as a missionary dedicated to saving souls and an arch-enemy of Portuguese and Arab slave traders. An exhausting 700-mile journey by ox-cart brought Livingstone to Moffat's mission station at Kuruman, Bechuanaland (now Botswana), the most remote in southern Africa and located on a lion-infested plain. This would be his home for the next two years and he immediately fell foul of white colleagues with whom he disagreed on every issue under the hot African sun.

Livingstone's life nearly came to a grizzly end in February 1844 near his second missionary station at Mabotsa, 250 miles away from Kuruman. In a letter to his parents, dated 27 April 1844, he writes about lion attacks at a nearby village:

... one of the lions destroyed nine sheep in broad daylight on a hill just opposite our house. All the people immediately ran over to it, and, contrary to my custom, I imprudently went with them in order to see how they acted, and encourage them to destroy him. They surrounded him several times, but he managed to break through the circle. I then got tired. In coming home I had to come near to the end of the hill. They were then close upon the lion, and had wounded him. He rushed out from the bushes, which concealed him from view, and bit me on the arm so as to break the bone. It is now nearly well, however, feeling weak only from having been confined in one position for so long; and I ought to praise Him who delivered me from so great a danger. I hope I shall never forget His mercy. You need not be sorry for me, for long before this reaches you it will be quite as strong as ever it was. Gratitude is the only feeling we ought to have in remembering the event. Do not mention this to any one. I do not like to be talked about.

In order not to distress his parents, Livingstone deliberately understated what had happened. The lion had, in fact, leapt out, knocked him to the ground, seized his shoulder and crushed the bone of his upper left arm, leaving him crippled for life in that part of his body. For the next thirty years, he experienced pain whenever he lifted his left arm above shoulder height.

Livingstone did not mention that an elderly native nearby had saved his life by diverting the lion with a shot from his double-barrelled shotgun. The shot missed but caused the animal to leave the doctor alone and turn on the unfortunate African, biting into his thigh. The lion then went on to attack another man before falling dead from the effects of shots fired earlier. Livingstone tended his own wounds and was weeks recovering from the experience, travelling back to Kuruman to convalesce.

In a letter to a friend, Livingstone had observed that daughters of European missionaries possessed 'miserably contracted minds' and he was considering 'sending home an advertisement to the *Evangelical Magazine*, and if I get very old, it must be for some decent sort of widow'. But soon after Moffat and his family returned to Kuruman from England Livingstone was making 'the necessary arrangements with Mary, the eldest daughter of Mr. Moffat'. They were married in January 1845.

Mary Moffat was twenty-three years old and had spent nineteen of them living with her parents in African mission stations. She was plain, unworldly and unsophisticated, qualities which Livingstone found admirable. She was a good housekeeper, could cook, clean, make clothes and would be the perfect wife for the kind of man she had known all her life – a missionary.

The marriage may initially have been one of convenience, but later letters written by Livingstone to his wife show their relations soon turned to love. Neither the doctor nor Mary had many suitors to choose from miles from civilisation. He needed a partner to help with his work and she needed an excuse to get away from her domineering mother and have a home of her own. Marriage was the perfect solution for both of them.

Describing his wife in a letter to a friend, he said that the best wife for a missionary was 'a plain, commonsense woman, not a romantic. Mine is a matter-of-fact lady, a little thick black haired girl, sturdy and all I want'. To another he wrote that Mary was 'a good deal of an African in complexion with a stout stumpy body'.

Mary Livingstone was a good missionary partner but did not enjoy an easy married life to the man from Blantyre. She would bear him five children – Robert, Thomas, Agnes, Oswell and Anna – but life together was hard and her health suffered. When pregnant for the fourth time in 1850, she crossed the Kalahari Desert with her husband. She lost the baby and suffered partial paralysis afterwards. The other children caught malaria and, when they finally reached Kuruman again, were so weak they could hardly stand.

In later years, Livingstone would admit: 'I did not feel it to be my duty, while spending all my energy on reaching the heathen, to devote a special portion of my time to play with my children. But generally I was so exhausted with the mental and manual labour of the day that in the evening there was no fun left in me. I did not play with my little ones while I had them, and they soon sprung up in my absences, and left me conscious that I had none to play with.'

Against her parents' wishes, Livingstone took Mary, who was pregnant again, on another journey of exploration in 1851. His excuse was that there were thousands of primitive natives in the interior who needed to hear God's word. Mary was required to assist him with this task. His true motivation, however, was somewhat different. As well as saving souls, Livingstone also wanted to explore Africa's deep interior and follow the course of its rivers. He was curious to know what lay inside the heart of the dark continent – and if he could save souls along the way, so well and good. He told London Missionary Society directors that it was 'imperatively necessary to extend the gospel to all the surrounding tribes. This is the only way which permits the rational hope that when people do turn to the Lord it will be by groups.'

Wherever Livingstone went, his dutiful wife followed. The intense heat, jolting wagon, insects, shortage of fresh food and water took their toll on the woman, who gave birth to their third son shortly after their return. Mary pleaded with her husband to give her more security and the children a proper education. She wanted to return home to Scotland.

Livingstone refused to give up Africa and in April 1851 told his directors that 'it has occurred to me that, as we must send our children to England, it would be no great additional expense to send them now along with their mother. . . . To orphanise my children will be like tearing out my bowels. . . . If I were to follow my own inclinations they would lead me to settle down quietly with . . . some small tribe and devote some of my time to my children; but Providence seems to call me to the regions beyond, and if I leave them anywhere in this country, it will be to let them become heathens. If you think it right to support them, I believe my parents in Scotland would attend to them otherwise.'

Instead of waiting for a reply, Livingstone took his family to Cape Town and put them on a British-bound ship, unaware of what provision, if any, might be available to support them on their homecoming. When the Livingstone family arrived in Cape Town they were mistaken for paupers. Livingstone had not bought new clothes for himself or his family for ten years. One commentator described them as being dressed 'somewhat in the style of Robinson Crusoe'.

William Cotton Oswell, a big-game hunter and amateur explorer with a private income and whom Livingstone later described as 'the best friend we have in Africa', gave Mary £200 to buy new clothing for her and the children to wear on the journey home.

Once in Scotland, Mary and her children lived on the brink of poverty, staying in a series of dark and damp lodgings. They began by moving in with Livingstone's parents who now lived in a small cottage in Hamilton. It was a disaster. Neil and Agnes Livingstone were elderly, set in their ways, and observed a quiet and strictly religious way of life, which was disrupted when the daughter-in-law they had never met, arrived unannounced with four children in tow, all under the age of seven. After six months Mary left, telling her in-laws that they should not attempt to find out where she was going or enquire after the children. In a letter to LMS directors, Neil stated that he wanted nothing further to do with her 'until there is evidence she is a changed person'.

Mary and the children moved from place to place, sometimes staying with her husband's friends, sometimes renting rooms paid for from an LMS pittance. Two years passed without any word from Livingstone mentioning a homecoming. His letters told Mary not to spoil the children and to be patient because 'patience is great virtue'. He told his poverty-stricken children that he had seen women in chains, so they should think themselves lucky that Jesus had been kind to them.

By the end of the fourth year of separation, Mary Livingstone was in despair. She had turned to the LMS, her husband's parents and his friends and they had all let her down. Next she turned to the bottle, which became her close companion for the next ten years. By 1854 she was ill, destitute and unable to pay the doctor his fees. She wrote another letter to her husband pleading with him to come home.

Between 1849 and 1851, Livingstone took several diversions from missionary work, undertaking surveying and scientific expeditions into Africa's unexplored interior. In August 1849, this resulted in his discovery of Lake Ngami, a shallow expanse of water situated beyond the Kalahari Desert at the south-western corner of the 10,400 km sq Okavango Swamp, in an area known today as Botswana. Thanks to his rich friends William Cotton Oswell and Mungo Murray, who together funded the expedition, Livingstone was one of the first Europeans to set eyes on the lake. His account was published in the March 1850 edition of the *Missionary Magazine*, generating positive publicity for the LMS and recognition from the Royal Geographical Society, the RGS, which awarded him a gold medal and £25 prize. The expedition forged a lifelong association between Livingstone and the RGS, which championed his interests in England and encouraged his inclinations to spend more time exploring – and less time engaged in missionary work.

Livingstone was eager to promote his African trinity, 'the three Cs' – Christianity, commerce and civilisation – which he fervently believed would open up Africa, turn its people away from primitive rituals, convert them, encourage trade which would create benefits, bring education and a way of life which better mirrored England's civilised ways. In a letter to his brother-in-law, Robert Moffat, he wrote: 'I shall open a path into the interior, or perish. I never have had the shadow of a shade of doubt as to the propriety of my course, and wish only that my exertions may be honoured so far that the gospel may be preached and believed in this dark region.'

In November 1853, Livingstone had arrived at the approaches to the Zambezi River in the country of the Makololo people. With only a small group of Makololo and little equipment, he journeyed north-westwards for six months searching for a route to the Atlantic coast that would permit legitimate commerce and weaken the slave trade. After an arduous journey, he reached St Paul de Loanda (Luanda) and collapsed at the house of a British Commissioner. Soon after arriving, he became ill with fever and dysentery and had to be nursed back to health.

As soon as he was well enough to travel, Livingstone collected his Makololo people and headed back towards the Zambezi. He had been absent for nearly a year. Three weeks later he was off again to explore the Zambezi to its mouth on the Indian Ocean.

On previous expeditions, Livingstone had been within four or five days of a vast waterfall east of Sesheke village and known locally as 'mosi-oa-tunya' – or 'the smoke that thunders'. He was resolved to be the first white man to look on it. On 16 November 1855, Livingstone first heard and then saw the grandeur of 47 million gallons of Zambezi River rushing and roaring headlong every minute over the 1¼ mile wide, 355ft deep falls. He later described the scene as 'so lovely, it must have been gazed upon by angels in their flight'. He named the rushing torrents Victoria Falls, after his Queen living thousands of miles away in distant England – a land which he was now beginning to feel he ought to visit again.

Livingstone emerged on Africa's east coast on 25 May 1856, sixteen years after first setting foot on the continent and almost four years after setting out on his 5,000-mile journey on foot to follow the Zambezi's course. During that time he had encountered a myriad of problems that African travellers before and after would experience: hard work, fatigue, privation, fever, attacks on life, danger and separation from family and friends. There was also the ever-present heat, torrential rain, huge areas of mud, demands by tribal chiefs for hongo (payment in the form of cloth, beads and brass wire in return for permission to pass through their territory), porters deserting, food shortages, delays by hospitable chiefs and inhospitable tribesmen, demands on missionary and medical skills and threats of malaria which brought the good doctor to a standstill on more than thirty occasions during those first sixteen years.

It was time to return home.

In December 1856, a *Times* reporter observed Livingstone on the voyage home and noted that when he boarded the ship *Frolic*, he had difficulty speaking a single sentence in English, 'having got out of the language habit years before'. The report continued:

> Dr. Livingstone has been absent from England for 17 years. He crossed the great African continent almost in the centre, from west to east; has been where no civilised being has even been before, and has made many notable discoveries of great value. . . . He is rather a short man [Livingstone was 5ft 8in], with a pleasing and serious countenance, which betokens the most determined resolution. He continued to wear the cap he wore while performing his wonderful travels. On board ship he was remarkable for his modesty and unassuming manners. He never spoke of his travels, except in answer to questions.

On the voyage, Livingstone received news that his father, Neil, had died. London Missionary Society directors also sent him a terse letter discouraging further exploration, while expressing 'appreciation upon which for some years past, your energies have been concentrated, but are nevertheless restricted in their power of aiding plans connected only remotely with the spread of the Gospel. The financial circumstances of the Society are not such as to afford any definite period, to venture upon untried, remote, and difficult fields of labour.'

In the days and weeks following Livingstone's arrival, he was awarded the RGS Patron's gold medal, made a freeman of half a dozen cities, awarded an honorary doctorate at Oxford, was received by Prince Albert and Palmerston, the Prime Minister, accepted 2,000 guineas collected by public subscriptions in England and Scotland, was wined and dined by the great and the good, wrote and published his book *Missionary Travels and Researches in South Africa* and became the best known missionary on the planet. The press called him 'devoted . . . a truly apostolic preacher of Christian truth'. People expecting to see a saint mobbed him in streets and in churches. Dr David Livingstone was becoming a legend in his own lifetime. And wherever he went, he wore his distinctive blue peaked cap.

On 13 February 1858, Livingstone was summoned to an audience with Queen Victoria and turned up wearing his usual black coat, blue trousers and cap. A newspaper reported:

> The Queen conversed with him affably for half an hour on the subject of his travels. Dr. Livingstone told her Majesty that he would now be able to

say to the natives that he had seen his chief, his not having done so before having been a constant subject of surprise to the children of the African wilderness. He mentioned to Her Majesty also that the people were in the habit of inquiring whether his chiefs were wealthy; and that when he assured them she was very wealthy, they would ask how many cows she had got, a question at which the Queen laughed heartily.

Although Livingstone could now house his family in better accommodation and take care of his children's education, they had to share him with hundreds of others during the fifteen months he spent in England. He had been separated from them for four and a half miserable years and was now unable to spend as much time with them as he wished. Everyone wanted Livingstone as a guest, to give a lecture or chair a meeting. Occasionally Mary was at his side. When not travelling, he was writing – and wrestling with the problem of how to separate himself from the LMS while still maintaining a presence in Africa.

Sir Roderick Murchison, a fellow Scot and president of the Royal Geographical Society suggested to Foreign Secretary Lord Clarendon, that Livingstone be appointed a consul with a roving commission taking care of territories extending from Africa's east coast and inland to the west. This would make him a government employee, include a salary of £500 per year, relieve him of his missionary duties and allow him to conduct new expeditions into the interior on behalf of the RGS. Murchison believed that missionary work stood in the way of good exploration and he secretly hoped Livingstone would not spend too much energy saving souls, preferring him to use his time more productively seeking new discoveries.

Livingstone felt that his next expedition should follow the course of the Zambezi River as far as Victoria Falls where regular trade could be established between the Makololo people and other tribes dwelling on the Batoka plateau. He was certain that missionaries, settlers and traders could live in perfect harmony with local tribes and that new converts would be made across a great sweep of Africa.

In December 1858, Parliament voted £5,000 for 'Dr. Livingstone to embark on a voyage of discovery upon the Zambezi' exploring Eastern and Central Africa. The money was spent acquiring a small 'tin kettle' of a steamer, built in collapsible sections that could be bolted together and used to navigate the river and discover as much as possible about the region's agricultural potential and mineral wealth.

Other expedition members included a naval commander, a geologist, an official artist, an engineer and Livingstone's younger brother, Charles, an American-educated Nonconformist minister who had not seen his older brother for eighteen years. Charles was engaged as the expedition's 'moral agent', Livingstone's personal assistant and official photographer, this despite the fact that the younger Livingstone was inexperienced with a camera. A 25-year-old Scottish physician called Dr John Kirk also joined the group as 'economic botanist'. He had served in the Crimean War and came to the venture highly recommended by Edinburgh doctors and the Royal Botanical Gardens at Kew. Later he would figure prominently in events surrounding Livingstone and Stanley.

Mary Livingstone, unwilling to be separated from her husband for another day, completed the party. Now that the family had sufficient money for several years of independence, they placed their children in the care of guardians and left them in Scotland, apart from the youngest, Oswell, aged seven, who would travel to Africa with his Pa and Ma.

On 10 March 1858, David and Mary Livingstone, their young son and members of the expedition, sailed from Liverpool on the Colonial Office steamer *Pearl*. Also on board were the prefabricated sections of the steam launch Livingstone had purchased with his government grant and called *Ma Robert*, the native name given to Mary Livingstone following the birth of her eldest son, Robert. This time Livingstone was travelling to Africa as 'British Consul at Quelimane for the Eastern Coast and independent districts of the interior and commander of an expedition for exploring Eastern and Central Africa, for the promotion of commerce and civilisation with a view to the extinction of the slave trade'. A tall order.

Everyone suffered seasickness on the voyage, but they recovered, apart from Mary, who continued to vomit and remained in her cabin. Days later Livingstone confirmed that Mary was pregnant again, rendering her unable to travel into the interior. She would leave the *Pearl* at Cape Town and remain with Oswell at her parents' missionary station in Kuruman before returning to Scotland. It would be another four years before Livingstone would see his wife again. The rest of the expedition party were quietly pleased as they felt that the African interior was no place for a woman and small child.

The *Pearl* arrived at the wide mouth of the Zambezi in the Mozambique Channel on 14 May 1858. There had been tension on board.

Commander Norman Bedingfeld, in overall charge of the *Pearl* and her navigation, had fallen out with the ship's master, Captain Duncan, over her course. Following a stand-up argument between the men – one a Royal Naval officer and the other a merchant seaman – Livingstone intervened, taking Duncan's side and causing Bedingfeld to request his release from the expedition. He was soon on his way back to England, relieved he no longer had to deal with people he had come to detest, particularly Livingstone.

When the engineer George Rae bolted parts of the 'tin kettle' *Ma Robert*, together and lowered her into the river, there was more disappointment. The vessel consumed too much fuel and leaked. Her furnace had to be ignited hours before the steamer became serviceable; she 'snorted' so offensively that expedition members renamed her *'The Asthmatic'* – and she moved so slowly that canoes passed her.

Over 300 miles further up the Zambezi, the little tin kettle became holed above the waterline and expedition members had to abandon the vessel and continue on foot. The thermometer registered 130 degrees and the terrain was rough, with huge boulders piled one on top of another. Everybody was falling out with each other. Charles Livingstone, the most idle man in the party, complained about trivial matters. He had taken a dislike to the expedition's young geologist and its official artist. Livingstone senior also began acting out of character, criticising both men. They, too, were sent home.

Livingstone told the remaining group that he would travel onwards alone, but Dr Kirk insisted on accompanying him. Native porters refused to travel. They were exhausted, disillusioned, their feet covered in sores and blisters – but Livingstone pleaded with them to continue. They told him that they had thought their master had a heart, but now they could see that he had none and told him to his face that he was mad.

Livingstone and Kirk discovered something that would have become apparent if the *Pearl* had covered this part of the journey – rapids, running over a series of treacherous waterfalls, higher than a tree and known locally as Cabora Bassa. Navigation by boat was now impossible. What made matters worse was that the porters seemed to know all about the waterfalls but had said nothing to their master, who raged at them in an unchristian fashion, telling them they could remain there forever as far as he was concerned. His hopes of finding a navigable route along the Zambezi were now in ruins.

There was only one thing for it: return to the *Pearl*, sail back and explore another river called the Shire, said to be fed from a large inland lake which flowed into the Zambezi 100 miles from the coast. Livingstone reasoned that if the lake could be found and claimed by the expedition as a new discovery, the unfortunate detection of the Cabora Bassa rapids might be discounted. He also hoped that banks either side of the Shire might be suitable for settlement and trading and he might save the expedition and his diminishing reputation.

On 20 December 1858, the *Pearl* chugged 200 miles downriver to the point where the Shire flowed into the Zambezi. They entered the new and uncharted river and continued without mishap for several days, discovering more rapids and waterfalls along the way, which Livingstone named the Murchison Falls after Sir Robert Murchison of the Royal Geographical Society.

The expedition turned east where they discovered a magnificent inland lake, Lake Shirwa, which Livingstone described in a letter home to his daughter, Agnes, as 'very grand . . . all around it are mountains much higher than any you see in Scotland. . . . The country is quite a highland region, and many people live on it. Most of them were afraid of us.'

Livingstone considered the Shire Highlands perfect for European settlement. They were fertile, well irrigated, easy to reach – the perfect location for a missionary settlement and trading post. But despite having contributed a large sum of money towards the expedition, the British government was starting to lose interest in Livingstone and Africa, declining to become further involved with the region.

Livingstone's health began to deteriorate. On the journey back to the mouth of the Zambezi, painful haemorrhoids caused him to lose blood from his bowels. His diary entry for 14 October reads: 'Very ill with bleeding from the bowels and purging. Bled all night. Got up at one a.m. to take latitude.' But there was also better news. On 4 November, family letters reached him. His diary reads: 'A letter from Mrs. L. says we are blessed with a little daughter of 16th November 1858 at Kuruman. A fine healthy child. The Lord bless and make her His own child in heart and life!' Little Anna Mary Livingstone had been nearly a year in the world before her father heard of her existence.

On 31 January 1860, Livingstone and party rendezvoused with the naval ship *Gorgon*, which brought a new prefabricated steamer called the

Pioneer to replace the *Ma Robert*. The naval ship sent out the signal: 'I have steamboat in the brig – wife aboard.' Mary had left the new baby in Scotland, where she had returned after giving birth to Anna at her parents' mission in Kuruman. Thanks to royalties from her husband's writing, Mary had more funds to support her family. Despite her husband's fame and renown, life was still hard for Livingstone's wife and her children. Letters to her husband revealed that she had lost her Christian faith and entered a period of 'spiritual darkness'. His replies were full of tenderness and encouragement, although none gave any impression that he was expecting her to leave the children and rejoin him in Africa, travelling on the *Gorgon* with a missionary party Livingstone had encouraged to establish mission stations along the Shire.

On the outward voyage, Mary had been drinking again, often becoming difficult and hysterical. She borrowed money from other passengers to buy more alcohol and when one refused she shouted abuse. Everyone on board knew that Mary was a disturbed woman and of little value to her husband's work in Africa.

As Livingstone's expedition continued on the *Pioneer*, he discovered the full extent of the grievances Mary had been harbouring since he had left her in Cape Town in May 1858. She now openly and loudly reproached him for deserting her and the children, failing to make provision for their education or providing a proper home for their expanding family. She blamed him for being the cause of their eldest son, Robert, becoming a problem child and running away from boarding school. She accused her husband of being the reason why she had lost her faith and why she had turned to the bottle and away from God.

A week after returning to the Zambezi delta, Mary succumbed to malaria. She remained in her cabin and many on board the *Pioneer* thought she was drunk again. Her condition worsened; she was vomiting every quarter of an hour which prevented the quinine prescribed by her husband from being absorbed into her body. She became delirious, fell into a coma and Livingstone recognised that his wife was close to death.

Livingstone sat next to her bed throughout, weeping like a child. Mary died, aged forty-one, on 27 April and was buried in the shadow of a huge baobab tree at Shupanga. A guard stood vigil next to the grave until a stone cairn could be built to protect the body from wild animals. Two weeks later, Livingstone wrote in his journal: 'For the first time in my life I feel willing to die. — D.L.'

The loss of his wife did not prevent Livingstone from completing the last stage of the Zambezi expedition. Remaining expedition members were kept occupied preparing to assemble and float his portable paddle steamer *Lady Nyassa* on the waters of Lake Nyassa and prevent the region's slavers from making further headway down the Shire.

Civil war had been raging through the Shire Highlands and the area was in the grip of famine. There were so many corpses floating in the river that the steamer had to stop to clear bodies from the floats. Livingstone wrote: 'Wherever we took a walk, human skeletons were seen in every direction.' What had once been a green, fertile and populated valley 'was now literally strewn with human bones'. Livingstone decreed: 'The destruction of life . . . however great, constitutes but a small portion of the waste and made us feel that unless the slave trade – that monster iniquity which has so long brooded over Africa – is put down, lawful commerce cannot be established.'

Dr Kirk and Charles Livingstone now became ill and returned to England. On the voyage home, Kirk noted his impressions of Livingstone in his journal: 'Dr. L. is a most unsafe leader. He never thinks of getting back. All he cares for is accomplishing his object at any risk whatever. It is useless making any remark to him . . . I can only say that his head is . . . what is termed "cracked".'

A letter was received from the Foreign Secretary, Earl Russell, informing Livingstone that the six-year-long expedition was to be cut short and remaining members recalled to England. Russell stated that Livingstone was not at fault, but because the Zambezi was not navigable by ship, the government no longer shared the doctor's optimism about economic and political development in the region. He had not accomplished the objectives for which it had been designed and the expedition had cost more than expected.

The Times, previously complimentary towards Livingstone, was not so kind to the doctor on 20 January 1863: 'We were promised cotton, sugar, indigo . . . and of course we got none. We were promised converts and not one has been made. In a word, the thousands subscribed by the Universities and contributed by the Government have been productive only of the most fatal results.'

The Zambezi expedition was not a total failure. It had collected a mass of scientific information about the Zambezi and its feeder rivers, including the Shire, and their navigability. It had ascertained the capacity of the soil along the route and found it admirably adapted for the cultivation of indigo and cotton as well as tobacco, castor oil and sugar. Highlands above the Shire were proven to be free of tsetse fly and mosquitoes. And the party had discovered Lake Nyassa and was able to assess the region's potential for European settlement and trading opportunities. The expedition had provided the foundation upon which the British Central Africa Protectorate would be established in 1893, which later became Nyasaland and, in 1966, the Republic of Malawi.

Livingstone could have sailed directly home to visit his motherless children – including his youngest daughter, whom he had yet to see – and face the critics awaiting his return. Instead, he planned to allow the dust to settle and quietly slip home to England after everyone had time to forget his failure. He returned to Zanzibar, travelling up the eastern coast of the Indian Ocean in the *Lady Nyassa* manned by a small native crew; there he planned to sell the steamer and use the money to part-fund more explorations.

On reaching the mouth of the Zambezi, Livingstone spied the British man of war HMS *Orestes* whose commander offered to tow the doctor and his steamboats all the way to Mozambique. The doctor was assigned quarters on the ship, but chose to remain on the *Lady Nyassa*, something he regretted when a violent typhoon nearly wrenched his steamboats from their tow lines at *Orestes'* stern. From Mozambique, Livingstone made his way to Zanzibar in the *Lady Nyassa*, where he hoped to sell the vessel for something like the £6,000 he had originally paid for the craft. Offers were made but none of them was anything like the asking price Livingstone expected to recoup from the sale. In a bold move which would buckle the sea legs of the most experienced sailor, Livingstone decided he would sail *Lady Nyassa* across the Indian Ocean to Bombay, where he would renew attempts to sell her.

Rae, Livingstone's Scottish engineer, said he had been offered another job with good prospects and would not be making the voyage, leaving the doctor to recruit a crew to perform duties of stoker, carpenter and general deck hands. Seven local natives, none of whom had ever been to sea, were hired to cook, clean and perform other duties which might arise. One was a young man called James Chuma, a former slave who had worked at mission stations and who would be associated with Livingstone for the rest of the doctor's life.

With 14 tons of coal in her hold, the *Lady Nyassa* set out on 20 April to cross 2,500 miles of ocean. Livingstone was convinced he could cross it in eighteen days and they made good headway before hitting calm waters, rendering the sail useless. A full head of steam only created sufficient power to creep across the water. The crew became ill as the sea became glassy calm and sharks swam around the little steamer. One month later, a breeze sprang up and gathered in intensity. Livingstone knew that the annual monsoon was only days away and he needed to sight land before the full impact of the weather sank his little tin kettle.

They finally crept into the port at Bombay on 13 June, fifty-five days after leaving Zanzibar – thirty-seven days more than Livingstone had expected to take to cover the distance. The *Lady Nyassa* was so small that no one at the port noticed its arrival and the authorities remained unaware until Livingstone went ashore to ask where he should berth his steamer.

Before travelling home to England, Livingstone arranged for Chuma and another native boy called Wikatani to be taken in at a local mission school. Then he set about finding a buyer for the *Lady Nyassa*. By the time Livingstone left Bombay, the steamer was still unsold, forcing him to entrust her to an agent for safekeeping in the expectation that he would arrange the vessel's sale and transfer money for its asking price into the doctor's bank account.

In July 1864, instead of travelling north to Scotland for a reunion with his children, Livingstone checked into London's Tavistock Hotel. No sooner had he arrived, than he began building bridges with former associates in the hope of mounting another expedition. He met members of the Royal Geographical Society, visited several receptions where he noted that the ladies were 'wonderfully beautiful – rich and rare were the gems they wore' and called on Gladstone whom he found 'affable'. There were no official receptions or banquets for the African hero this time, no mobbing in the streets or royal audiences.

Livingstone finally reached Scotland in August and knocked at the door of his mother's cottage in Hamilton. She did not recognise her son who had aged considerably since she had last seen him. Here he met his daughter, Anna Mary, now aged six – 'a nice sprightly child' – for the first time. The following day his other children came to the house. He wrote: 'Agnes, Oswell and Thomas came. I did not recognise Tom, he has grown so much. Has been poorly a long while; congestion of the kidney, it is said. Agnes quite tall, and Anna Mary a nice little girl.'

A doctor recommended an operation to remove the haemorrhoids that had troubled him ever since his first great journey in Africa, but Livingstone declined because he thought the story would find its way into the newspapers and he hated the idea of the public speaking about his infirmities.

The launch of a new Turkish frigate on the Clyde gave Livingstone a rare opportunity to take his seventeen-year-old daughter Agnes on an outing. Following the ceremony, Livingstone and daughter shared a railway carriage with the Turkish ambassador. They were cheered at the railway station. 'The cheers are for you,' Livingstone told the ambassador. 'No,' said the Turkish diplomat, indicating the crowd, 'I am only what my master made me; you are what you made yourself.'

Livingstone and Agnes accepted an invitation to stay at Newstead Abbey, near Nottingham, previously the residence of Lord Byron and now home to William Webb, a former big-game hunter who had originally met the doctor in southern Africa. Webb was aware that Livingstone needed someone to care for him while he regained his energy and wrote his next book, *A Narrative of an Expedition to the Zambezi and its Tributaries*. The book was a careful account of the last expedition, conveniently failing to mention the arguments, dismissals and resignations but concentrating on the geography, flora and fauna. Because Charles Livingstone had loaned his diaries, he benefited from being credited as co-author and received royalties from American sales.

Livingstone remained at Newstead Abbey for eight months, writing and getting to know his teenage daughter, who helped copy his manuscript. It was at Newstead that the doctor received news that his eldest son, Robert, aged eighteen, had joined the American army and had died in a prison camp. The restless youth had left school, intending to join his father on the Zambezi where they would together discuss his future. He arrived in Natal penniless and discovered it would be impossible to reach his father in such a remote region. He was press-ganged into joining a Boston-bound ship and on arrival forced to enlist in an army embroiled in fighting a civil war. He was in the thick of the conflict as a private with the 3rd New Hampshire Regiment and in letters to Agnes expressed regret at the course his life had taken. In America he had traded on his father's name, but after enlisting assumed the name 'Rupert Vincent'. In a letter to his father he confessed: 'I am convinced that to bear your name here would lead to further dishonours to it.' Robert was wounded by Confederate gunfire at Laurel Hill, Virginia and, like Henry Morton Stanley, taken prisoner and sent to a prison camp in North Carolina, where he died in December 1864 shortly before his nineteenth birthday. He is buried in an unmarked grave in the American national cemetery at Gettysburg, Pennsylvania.

On 5 January 1865, Livingstone received a letter from Sir Roderick Murchison of the Royal Geographical Society:

> My dear Livingstone – As to your future, I am anxious to know what your own wish is as respects African exploration. Quite irrespective of missionaries or political affairs, there is at this moment a question of intense geographical interest to be settled: namely the watershed, or watersheds of South Africa. Now, if you would really like to be the person to finish off your remarkable career by completing such a survey, unshackled by other avocations than those of the geographical explorer, I should be delighted to consult my friends of the Society, and take the best steps to promote such an enterprise. . . . Various questions might be decided by the way, and if you could get to the west, and come out on that coast, or should be able to reach the White Nile, you would bring back an unrivalled reputation, and would have settled all the great disputes now pending . . . I have heard you so often talk of the enjoyment you feel when in Africa, that I cannot believe you now think of anchoring for the rest of your life on the mud and sand banks of England.

Livingstone accepted, stating he was not yet ready to hang up his compass but would only return to Africa as a missionary and not 'simply as a geographer'. The region would also place him right at the heart of the Arab slave trade where he hoped to suppress its activities and do as much harm to the 'industry' as possible.

He left England for the last time on 13 August 1865 and returned to his beloved Africa via Bombay after collecting £2,300 for the sale of the *Lady Nyassa*; £4,000 less than the vessel's true value, but the best that could be raised in the circumstances. He was advised to invest the money in an Indian bank until he needed it. Two years later the bank collapsed, resulting in the loss of the entire £6,000 Livingstone had sunk into the steamer in which he had risked his life to sail from Africa to India.

Livingstone headed into the dark continent on his final journey in March 1866 as a single white man travelling with thirty-six natives from the different regions through which he expected to pass. They included Abdullah Susi and Amoda who had cut wood to power the boiler on board the *Pioneer* and James Chuma and Wikatani, whom Livingstone had arranged to be taken in at a Bombay mission school while he was seeking a buyer for the *Lady Nyassa*. Compared to other European expeditions, this was a small party. It also included an assortment of pack mules, donkeys, buffalo, cows and camels to carry supplies, tents, navigational equipment plus cloth and beads with which to trade throughout the journey. He was exhilarated to be back on the move and wrote in his journal: 'The mere animal pleasure of travelling in a wild unexplored country is very great. . . . The sweat of one's brow is no longer a curse when one works for God.'

The doctor planned to march inland along the Rovuma River and, after passing Lake Nyassa's southern shore, head north towards Lake Tanganyika where he expected to find the source of the Nile. Early into the march, Livingstone discovered that some of his men were troublemakers who treated their animals badly, others were thieves and so idle that a group of Johanna porters, originating from the Comoros Islands, were ordered back to the coast.

As the remaining party advanced, the horrors of the slave trade became more evident. Women were found dead, tied to trees, lying shot or stabbed because they had been unable to keep up with the rest of the party. To prevent them becoming the property of someone else, their 'masters' had killed them.

Rain, hostile tribes, illness and the slave trade all played their part in delaying Livingstone's expedition. By 8 August, he had reached Lake Nyassa and the scores of slave colonies along its banks. He attempted to cross the lake, but slave owners had commandeered all the dhows and refused to loan their vessels, forcing him to walk around the southern shore, where he witnessed further massacres and destruction of native settlements.

To advance without delay, Livingstone had to travel with Arab slavers. Not only did this guarantee safe passage through hostile territory, but also provided an opportunity to learn about the slave trade and its evils at first hand. He also wrote to his family in Scotland and Dr Kirk in Zanzibar entrusting them to Arabs making their way out of the interior towards the coast. A letter, addressed to the Foreign Office in London, stated that he had discovered two more lakes, Moero and Bangweulu, and that the latter 'might be the source of the Nile'. He wrote: 'I am standing on the threshold of the unexplored.'

Back in Zanzibar, the Johanna porters ordered back to the coast were telling stories that the great African traveller had been murdered by a savage who had crushed the doctor's skull with an axe somewhere along the shores of Lake Nyassa. The story began appearing in newspapers; first to break the news was the British-owned *Times of India*, which reported on 13 March 1867: 'The hopes raised by the news and rumoured safety of Dr. Livingstone have speedily been dispelled, and there can be no longer doubt that he was killed by a savage of the Mafite tribe. . . .'

The Johanna men were closely questioned by British consular staff, who asked them about the territory where the murder was purported to have taken place. The diplomats were satisfied that the land they described was the same territory that Dr Kirk had passed through with Livingstone during the Zambezi expedition. They grudgingly accepted that the grim news might be true.

On 10 December 1866, Dr Edward Seward of the British High Commission in Zanzibar sent a telegraph to the Foreign Office:

My Lord, I send you the saddest news . . . if the report of some fugitives from his party be true, this brave and good man has 'crossed the threshold of the unexplored' – he has confronted the future and will never return. . . . On his sad end being known, the British flag was lowered at this Consulate . . . I may state that no papers, effects or relics of Livingstone are likely to be recovered.

The *Times of India* article was reproduced in English and American newspapers, prompting the obituary writers to reach for their pens. But not everyone believed the story. Sir Roderick Murchison wrote to *The Times* in London casting serious doubts on the rumour started by the Johanna men. To confirm the story one way or another, Sir Roderick called on the government to dispatch an expedition to ascertain the truth. Volunteers were called for, hundreds applied, and a hand-picked group was selected under the command of Edward Daniel Young, a naval warrant officer and Lieutenant Henry Faulkner of the 17th Lancers. They left London on 11 June 1867 and in December reported back that while they had not seen Dr Livingstone, they could produce ample and satisfactory evidence that the story of his murder 'was a tissue of the greatest falsehoods'.

In February 1867, letters written by Livingstone the previous year were delivered to Sir Roderick Murchison. They explained that he had been ill and had been staying for a long period with an Ajawa chief called Mataka until his health improved. He said that slave traders, who would murder him if his presence in Mataka's camp was discovered, had prevented him from communicating earlier.

Another letter in Livingstone's hand was received by the British Consul in Zanzibar dated 30 May 1869. It stated that he was now at Ujiji, an Arab trading community on the eastern shores of Lake Tanganyika and working hard tracing various water courses flowing in and out of the lake in the hope of proving, once and for all, where the source of the Nile was located.

Then the trail went quiet again, apart from rumours in Arab circles confirming that Livingstone was still in the Lake Tanganyika region and now in a state of utter destitution. The majority believed that because there had been no recent letters, sightings or clues, there could only be one conclusion – 'that the illustrious man had passed the threshold of the unexplored, that bourn whence no traveller returns'.

Livingstone was neither lost nor dead – but he had come close to being both on several occasions. Malaria, anal bleeding and ulcers on his feet had made walking impossible. In July 1871, the doctor attempted to purchase canoes from Arab traders in order to continue his explorations. He had been staying in the town of Manyuema, when he had heard rifle shots in a market and witnessed hundreds of people being driven into the Lualaba River by Arabs, who fired indiscriminately into the crowd. With the cruel objective of frightening tribes into obedience, the Arab slavers massacred over four hundred people at Manyuema that day, plus hundreds of others in surrounding villages.

Sickened by what he had seen, Livingstone returned to Ujiji, where on his last visit in 1869 he had left 3,000yd of calico and 700lb of beads paid for by the Royal Geographical Society and sent on Dr Kirk's instructions to use as barter. He arrived at the lakeside looking like a living skeleton to discover that an Arab, Sherif Bosher, charged by Dr Kirk to deliver the goods, had sold them and used the proceeds to buy ivory and slaves. He had been told that Livingstone was dead. A tribal war was raging in the vicinity and the doctor's hopes of receiving further supplies from Zanzibar were dashed.

Livingstone would now have to rely on the goodwill of Arab slavers. He was old, broken, destitute, ill and in need of a Good Samaritan – who finally arrived, not in the form of an angel with wings, but in the shape of a young white man marching towards him at the head of a large caravan and under the stars and stripes of the American flag.

Livingstone relaxing in a hammock made from the Stars and Stripes, from *Punch*, 24 August 1872.

Chapter 18

'FIND LIVINGSTONE!'

In October 1869, Stanley was in his Madrid apartment resting after covering republican disturbances across Spain. His Spanish assignment followed on after the *New York Herald* asked him to file dispatches from Greece, Turkey, Lebanon and Egypt. He was told to go to the paper's London office to receive 'secret' instructions from bureau editor, Colonel Finlay Anderson. In London, Anderson told Stanley that there was a possibility that Dr David Livingstone, the Scottish-born missionary and traveller, might be making his way out of Africa's interior towards Zanzibar. There were rumours he might be dead, while other stories claimed he was alive but in poor health. Stanley was to sail to Aden and await further instructions, and when – if – positive information arrived, he was to use discretion about travelling to Zanzibar to meet and interview the elderly doctor.

With days left before departing for Aden, Stanley found time to visit Denbigh to see his mother, half-brothers and sister. Now that he was a well-paid, fashionably dressed and polite young American reporter with a great future ahead, Betsy had found room in her life for her boy and was pleased to introduce him to respectable friends in the neighbourhood. Stanley's 25-year-old half-sister, Emma Parry-Jones, was also proud of her 'American' half-brother and introduced him to her friend Catherine – 'Katie' – Gough-Roberts, the nineteen-year-old daughter of 'retired gentleman solicitor' Thomas Gough-Roberts, who lived just outside the town. Katie found the young man interesting and agreed to allow Stanley to write to her while he was on his Aden assignment.

Back in London, Stanley raced around bookshops buying everything he could lay his hands on about Africa. He purchased works by former African explorers, John Hanning Speke, Samuel White Baker, Richard Francis Burton, James Bruce, Mungo Park and Livingstone himself. This working library would provide the reporter with valuable information on how to put together an expedition into the interior.

Arriving in Aden in November 1868, Stanley found nothing new had come to light about Livingstone since he had left London. He directed polite but deliberately vague letters to the British Consul in Zanzibar seeking news of Livingstone, avoiding any mention of the fact that he was a reporter hoping to land the scoop of the century. He also wrote to the American Consul, Francis Webb, who replied promising to share any intelligence about Livingstone with a fellow American.

To while away the time sitting it out in hot and dusty Aden, Stanley turned his Magdala dispatches into a book he planned to publish at a later date. He also wrote to Katie Gough-Roberts – addressed as 'My dear Miss Roberts' – and studied his books about African exploration. However, Stanley's Aden sojourn proved a waste of time. There was no news about Livingstone. He returned to London and checked into the Langham Hotel near Oxford Circus, where he was told to await further instructions. There he received an unexpected visit from Thomas Gough-Roberts, Katie's father, who made it known that he held the young man in high regard and considered Stanley eminently suitable as his prospective son-in-law. He also mentioned that whoever married his daughter could expect a generous dowry of around £1,000 to help them in their married life.

It was from the Langham Hotel on Easter Sunday 1869 that Stanley sat down to compose a long and heartfelt fifteen-page letter to Katie, owning up to his workhouse background, his strained relationship with his mother, how he had run away to sea and his 'adoption' by Henry Hope Stanley. He admitted to being ambitious, stating that he intended to make something of himself – and could achieve it more easily with a wife, 'not a pretty, doll faced wife, but a woman educated and possessed with energy. With her aid and encouraging presence . . . I would defy the world.' He begged to know how he should address Katie because 'Miss Roberts is so formal, almost unkind. Address me by my name, Henry'.

Stanley returned to Spain to report the continuing revolution that would eventually drive Queen Isabella from her throne. One of his liveliest Spanish dispatches was written from the balcony of a Saragossa hotel overlooking barricades designed to keep revolutionaries in and mounted artillery out. From this vantage point and with bullets whistling through the air, Stanley observed the battle for thirty-nine hours.

In June 1869, Stanley allowed himself a little self-congratulation in his journal:

So well have I performed my duty, surpassing all my contemporaries, that the greatest confidence is placed in me. . . . How have I done this? By intense application to duty, by self-denial, which means I have denied myself all the pleasures, so that I might do my duty thoroughly, and exceed it. Such has been my ambition. I am fulfilling it. Pleasure cannot blind me, it cannot lead me astray from the path I have chalked out. I am so much my own master, that I am master over my own passions.

The telegram delivered to Stanley's Madrid apartment on 16 October 1869 was short and abrupt: 'Come to Paris on important business – Bennett.' Five hours later Stanley was on his way to Paris, where he arrived the following evening. He went directly to the Grand Hotel and knocked at the door of James Gordon Bennett's suite. What followed next has entered newspaper legend:

'Come in,' called a voice and on entering Stanley found Bennett sitting up in bed.

'Who are you?' he asked.

'My name is Stanley,' he reminded the man he had met only once before; but in all probability, Bennett had enjoyed a few aperitifs, glasses of wine and a cognac or two over dinner and his recollection may have been clouded. . . .

'Ah, yes! Sit down; I have important business in hand for you,' said Bennett, motioning Stanley to a chair. He then asked: 'Where do you think Livingstone is?' Stanley had to concede that he had no idea and acknowledged that the doctor might even be dead. Bennett had other ideas.

'Well, I think he is alive, and that he can be found, and I am going to send you to find him.'

'Do you really think I can find Dr Livingstone? Do you mean me to go to Central Africa?' Stanley enquired somewhat naïvely.

'Yes; I mean that you shall go, and find him wherever you may hear that he is, and to get what news you can of him, and perhaps the old man may be in want – take enough with you to help him should he require it. Of course you will act according to your own plans, and do what you think best – BUT FIND LIVINGSTONE!'

Stanley gently asked if Bennett had seriously considered the great expense 'likely to be incurred on account of this little journey?'

'What will it cost?' asked Bennett abruptly.

'Burton and Speke's journey to Central Africa cost between £3,000 and £5,000, and I fear it cannot be done under £2,500.'

'Well, I will tell you what you will do. Draw a thousand pounds now; and when you have gone through that, draw another thousand, and when that is spent, draw another thousand, and when you have finished that, draw another thousand, and so on; but, *FIND LIVINGSTONE!*'

Surprisingly, Bennett did not expect Stanley to sail directly to Africa to search for the doctor. He instructed his reporter:

I wish you to go to the inauguration of the Suez Canal first, and then proceed up the Nile . . . and as you go up, describe as well as possible whatever is interesting for tourists; and then write up a guide – a practical one – for Lower Egypt; tell us about whatever is worth seeing and how to see it. Then you might go to Jerusalem . . . then visit Constantinople and find out about that trouble between the Khedive and the Sultan. Then – let me see – you might as well visit the Crimea and those old battlegrounds. Then go across the Caucasus to the Caspian Sea . . . from there you may get through Persia to India; you could write an interesting letter from Persepolis. Baghdad will be close on your way to India; suppose you go there, and write up something about the Euphrates Valley Railway. Then, when you have come from India, you can go after Livingstone. Probably you will hear by that time that Livingstone is on his way to Zanzibar; but if not, go into the interior and find him. If alive, get what news of his discoveries you can and if you find he is dead, bring all possible proofs of his being dead. That is all. Good night and God be with you.

Stanley's version of his Parisian meeting with Bennett makes no reference to the fact that he had already been posted to Aden hoping to hear something of Livingstone's movements. It also fails to mention that *New York Herald* founder, James Gordon Bennett 'the Elder', now ailing, in retirement but still casting influence over the content of his newspaper, was Scottish by birth and took an interest in the achievements of fellow Scots at home and abroad. Hitherto, column inches in the paper devoted to Livingstone's story had been at the insistence of the old man, whose instincts had been correct: American readers were indeed fascinated by stories about Livingstone's work in

Africa, and Bennett 'the Elder' wanted his paper to be first with the big story of his discovery when it broke. Sharing his father's nose for news and public taste, Bennett Jr was happy to go along with a scheme to find the sick old man missing in the jungle and he knew that Stanley was just the reporter to go and get the news – exclusively.

Off went Stanley to cover his shopping list of foreign assignments, all the time monitoring what might – or might not – be happening in Africa. It took a year to complete his tasks.

From Paris he crossed the Channel and hurried to Denbigh to see Katie and ask her father's blessing to marry his daughter before leaving on his Suez assignment, taking his bride on a working honeymoon. Thomas Gough-Roberts was horrified by the suggestion and refused to give his permission. Perhaps he was uncomfortable with what Denbigh's citizens would have made of a hastily arranged marriage, which in those parts usually meant one thing – the girl was pregnant. Or perhaps Thomas disliked the idea of home-loving Katie travelling from one strange place to another, unable to put down roots anywhere for long. She would be visiting hostile locations and be separated from her husband for long periods while he went in search of news in dangerous places. What if he were killed, and Katie made a widow before she had time to become a proper wife? No. Thomas told Stanley that marriage must await his return when his roving life might cease for a while and the wedding of one of Denbigh's most prominent citizens could be organised properly.

Although Stanley was disappointed, he believed that he and Katie were now 'betrothed' and he would continue writing to her as often as he could during his travels.

The Suez Canal Company welcomed Stanley back to Egypt and he was present on 17 November 1869 when this new route of commerce was opened to sea traffic from all over the world. Stanley was on the deck of one of the first ships to sail through the canal, following a yacht carrying Empress Eugénie, the Austrian Emperor, the Crown Prince of Prussia and other international VIPs. He told *New York Herald* readers: 'A beautiful morning ushered in the greatest drama ever witnessed or enacted in Egypt. It is the greatest and last, so far, of all the magnificent periods which Egypt has witnessed.'

He floated along the Nile as one of seventy special guests of the Khedive and wrote a fascinating piece – 'twenty-three days of most exquisite pleasure, unmarred by a single adverse incident'. Then on to Jerusalem where he observed a vast archaeological dig beneath the city and saw the foundation stones of Solomon's Temple.

It is interesting to note that in the same edition of the *New York Herald* to carry Stanley's Suez Canal article, a story from London reported that the Royal Geographical Society had received a twelve-page letter from Livingstone in New Bangweolo, South Central Africa. In it he claimed to have found the source of the River Nile 'between 10–12 degrees south latitude or nearly in the position assigned by Ptolemy, the second-century Greek astronomer'.

By February 1870, Stanley had returned to Turkey in circumstances considerably different to those of his previous visit four years earlier in the company of Lewis Noe and Harlow Cook. In Constantinople he had a debt to settle, repaying the £150 loan given to him in 1866 by Edward Morris, the US Consul in Turkey after the encounter with bandits. Morris had not asked Stanley for security, trusting that the loan would be repaid in the future. Stanley now wanted to make amends, repay the debt – and seek Morris's assistance.

Morris recalled: 'The uncouth young man whom I first knew had grown into a perfect man of the world, possessing the appearance, the manners and attributes of a perfect gentleman. Instead of thinking he was a young man who had barely seen 26 summers [Stanley was in fact aged twenty-nine at this time] you would imagine that he was 35 or 40 years of age, so cultured and learned was he in all the ways of life.'

In Constantinople, Morris gave Stanley letters of introduction to other ambassadors whose path he was likely to cross along the way and a Winchester .44 Henry Rimfire rifle, which he would carry into the African interior in his search for Livingstone.

Dispatches were filed from Crimea, Odessa, Tiflis and Teheran and in August 1870, Stanley arrived in India where he looked forward to his next big assignment and confessed to his journal: 'I feel very ignorant about most things concerning Africa.'

Stanley was also ignorant of what was happening in Denbigh. As he was making arrangements to sail from Bombay on the first leg of his voyage to Zanzibar, his 'betrothed', Katie Gough-Roberts, was making her own arrangements – to walk down the aisle with Urban Rufus Bradshaw, a 22-year-old Denbigh architect. Stanley had continued to correspond with Katie from places he had visited on assignment, but she was not prepared to await his return to Wales. He had been unable to tell her precisely when he might be back – it might have been the following month or the next year – so she switched affections from the unreliable trouble-shooting reporter to the security of a provincial Welsh architect. Stanley's half-sister, Emma, appears to have been the cause of the problem. A letter unearthed by the author in the Royal Geographical Society's London archives from a Welsh writer calling himself 'Morien the Bard', claims that Emma had become jealous of Katie's relationship with Stanley and told her that her half-brother had secretly married while out of the country, driving her into the arms of another man.

With his preliminary assignments completed, it was now time for Stanley to search for Livingstone, although there was still no news of his whereabouts. In October he sailed in the barque *Polly* from Bombay to Mauritius, a six-week-long voyage, during which Stanley made friends with the Scottish first mate, William Lawrence Farquhar from Leith, whom he engaged to accompany him on the expedition. Afraid that Farquhar might reveal the true purpose of his new employer's reason for visiting Zanzibar, Stanley told the seaman he was travelling into the interior to explore a little-known river. Livingstone's name was never mentioned and Farquhar asked no questions. Stanley and Farquhar boarded the brigantine *Romp* for a seventeen-day voyage to the Seychelles and then the whaling brig *Falcon* for the final nineteen days to the island of Zanzibar, where they arrived eighty days after leaving Bombay.

On 6 January 1871, fifteen months after receiving his instructions from Bennett, Stanley landed in Zanzibar. He expected to find further instructions and funds from his editor waiting with the US Consul, Captain Webb. There was nothing. By now, Stanley's money was running dangerously low and he was expected to employ large numbers of native porters, kit out his expedition with food and equipment and transport the entire operation 25 miles across the Zanzibar Channel to the mainland. He estimated that he would need around $20,000 – and all he could summon up was $80 from his own pocket.

Former US naval officer Webb came to the rescue. Not only did he provide Stanley with accommodation at his residence, he also used his influence among Zanzibar's expatriate community to introduce the reporter to people with possible knowledge of Livingstone's movements. He helped Stanley raise money for his expedition from business sources on the island, whose owners were happy to assist a writer from America's most respected daily newspaper. As far as they were concerned, the word of a *New York Herald* correspondent was good enough and Stanley wrote them drafts in the name of James Gordon Bennett Jr as his guarantor. As cheques and letters of credit were unrecognised in Zanzibar, money was provided in the form of gold coins, the only currency accepted in the island's markets and bazaars.

Stanley wanted as few people as possible to know his true reason for coming to Zanzibar. He was happy for it to be known that he was a newspaper correspondent, but as far as the majority of the island's population was concerned, he was there to mount an expedition to the mainland to explore the Rifiji River. Before long, everyone in Zanzibar knew that the white American had arrived in order to enter Africa and everyone – especially the island's European population – wanted details.

To hear the latest rumours about Livingstone, Stanley began visiting Zanzibar's consular officials, including Dr John Kirk, Livingstone's old partner on the Zambezi expedition and now Acting British Consul on the island. Kirk was not the most cooperative of men, considered by many to be aloof and self-important. Stanley sensed that Kirk was not entirely convinced by his story of exploring the Rifiji River. At a consular reception one evening, Stanley gently introduced the subject of Kirk's earlier travels with Livingstone in the hope that he might warm to the subject. Kirk was guarded when asked where he thought the doctor might be and said he was last heard of somewhere 'between the coast and Nayamweze' (Kirk was referring to the town of Unyamwezi, but for some reason was either unable to pronounce it or Stanley misheard what Kirk had said). 'Of one thing I am sure, nobody has heard anything definite of him for over two years. I should fancy, though, that he must still be alive,' Kirk volunteered.

Stanley confided to his journal: 'Kirk gave me a very bad opinion of Livingstone; he says that he is hard to get along with, is cross and narrow minded; that Livingstone ought to come home and allow a younger man to take his place; that he takes no notes or keeps his journal methodically; and that he would run away, if he heard any traveller was going to him.'

Stanley was alarmed to hear that Dr Kirk had sent a 'Livingstone caravan' into the interior, paid for by the Royal Geographical Society and made up of forty-two native bearers. They had departed three months previously carrying thirty-five bales of goods and letters from home, hoping to meet Livingstone somewhere on the caravan path to the coast. No news of their progress had been received.

Sources in Zanzibar led Stanley to believe that Livingstone might be making his way to Ujiji on Lake Tanganyika and the reporter renewed his resolve to march there as fast as possible or meet the doctor somewhere en route – and preferably before news reached him that the *New York Herald* reporter was on his way. He recorded that 'my impression of him is that he is a man who will try to put as much distance as possible between us'.

Stanley admitted: 'I was totally ignorant of the interior and it was difficult at first to know what I needed in order to take an expedition into Central Africa.' The first thing required was a direct route to bring him 900 miles westwards to Ujiji. After crossing the Zanzibar Channel to Bagamoyo on the mainland, the expedition caravan would traverse a variety of terrain, depending on weather and local conditions, taking them deep into the interior. Stanley would carefully record the distance covered and the time taken to march from one camp to the next in hours and minutes. There would be over ninety separate entries for camps between Bagamoyo and Ujiji.

Much of Stanley's information about the route was culled from books about African exploration written by his predecessors Burton and Speke, which also gave him the background knowledge to estimate the amount of ground it was possible to cover in a single day, the stores and provisions needed and how to budget for a potentially lengthy expedition. The books gave Stanley clues about the type of terrain he might encounter – flat, hilly or mountainous, safe or dangerous, where extra supplies might be purchased from tribes along the way and whether they were friendly or hostile. He noted that explorers travelling this path before had paid porters and bartered with tribes using coloured cloth, beads, brass wire and lead shot and that a plentiful supply of each must be purchased in Zanzibar's markets.

The number of porters to be recruited and how to go about selecting those who would not desert was another consideration. Zanzibar's European community had little idea of what was required as none of their number ever ventured off the island. So the question of how much food must be purchased to feed a hundred men for days, weeks and months went unanswered until Stanley engaged an Arab merchant called Sheikh Hashid to address the problem.

Sheikh Hashid, 'a man of note and of wealth in Zanzibar', had dispatched his own caravans into the interior and was acquainted with prominent traders. He visited the market with Stanley and together the men bartered for the kind of beads preferred by different tribes as currency, some favouring white over black beads, brown over yellow, red over green, green over white and so on. Eleven different varieties were purchased and packed into twenty-two sacks, which were delivered to the storeroom of Captain Webb's house. Stanley later noted: 'The women of Africa are as fastidious in their tastes for beads as the women in New York are for jewellery.'

Next came the wire, a valuable trading commodity, which tribal men used 'for the adornment of their wives, who wear it in such numerous circlets round their necks as to give them at a distance an appearance of wearing ruffs. Wristlets of copper, brass and iron, and anklets of the same metal . . . are the favourite decorations of the males.' Sheikh Hashid told Stanley that while beads and necklaces stood for copper coins in Africa, good quality cloth was the equivalent of silver and brass wire of gold. Over 300lb of coiled brass wire, almost the thickness of telegraph wire, was purchased.

Stanley's shopping list also included provisions, cooking utensils, rope, twine, tents, ammunition, guns, hatchets, medicine, bedding, a tin bath, plus twenty-two donkeys and pack mules to haul some of the goods through the interior. A large boat measuring 25ft long and 6ft wide capable of carrying twenty people plus 'stores and goods sufficient for a cruise' was purchased for $80. A smaller one, 10ft long and 4ft 6in wide, with room for six passengers, was bought for $40. The entire shopping expedition produced goods weighing 6 tons (it would later increase to 8½ tons) and Stanley confessed that he 'was rather abashed at my own temerity'. He reasoned that a modern explorer travelling deep into the African interior needed to transport 'just what a ship must have when about to sail on a long voyage. He must have his slop chest, his little store of canned dainties and his medicines, besides which, he must have enough guns, powder and ball to be able to make a series of good fights if necessary. He must have men to convey these miscellaneous articles; and as a man's maximum load does not exceed 70 lbs, to convey 11,000 lbs requires nearly 60 men.' Supplies were broken down into 116 individual loads.

The bill so far totalled $8,000 and in one of his dispatches to the paper aimed directly at James Gordon Bennett, Stanley later admitted to his chief that 'the expense which you were incurring frightened me considerably; but then "obey orders if you break owners" is a proverb among sailors and which I adopted. Besides, I was too far from the telegraph to notify you of such an expense or to receive further orders from you; the preparations for the expedition therefore went on.'

Stanley thought of everything, including the possibility of arriving at Ujiji to find Livingstone was somewhere on Lake Tanganyika. With boats of his own, he could set out in pursuit of his quarry if necessary. To make each boat lighter, Stanley stripped each of its boards and replaced them with a double canvas skin, well tarred. The boats were then cut into sections which could be bolted together, each piece weighing 68lb. A number of canvas boats fitted to frames were also assembled.

A cockney third mate called John William Shaw, who had been discharged from the American ship *Nevada* in Zanzibar under suspicious circumstances, asked Stanley for a job. He was an experienced navigator and Stanley 'saw no reason to refuse his services and he was accordingly engaged for $300 per annum, to rank second to William Farquhar'. Like Farquhar, Shaw was not told the true reason for the expedition. Instead, Stanley spun them a yarn about marching to Lake Tanganyika where he would measure its depth and report back his findings to his American superiors.

Together with his white companions, Stanley went in search of twenty armed guards prepared to walk into the interior with them. Men who had previously travelled with Burton and Speke were available for hire, familiar with the ways of the white man and able to induce others to join the expedition. One man, called Seedy Mbarak Mombay but known to one and all as 'Bombay', was considered the best. Stanley described him as 'a slender, short man of fifty, or thereabouts . . . his face rugged, his mouth large, his eyes small and his nose flat', and he indicated his willingness to head the marching party to Ujiji for $80 a year, half in advance, plus a muzzle-loading rifle, a pistol, knife and hatchet. Six other 'faithfuls' from Speke's party were also engaged and Bombay rounded up a further eighteen 'fine looking men, far more intelligent in appearance than I could have ever believed African barbarians could be'. The men were each paid $36 per annum or $3 per month and issued with a flintlock musket, powder horn, bullet-pouch, knife and hatchet, plus powder and ball for 200 rounds.

Stanley would engage porters to carry everything the expedition's regiment of donkeys and pack mules was unable to transport across

Africa. To help lighten the load, Stanley issued instructions for a cart to be constructed, 5ft long and 18ins wide. The cart would have a capacity of 280lb – equivalent to that of four human porters – and was intended to carry heavy ammunition boxes, but would prove useless deep in the interior.

On the eve of departure, Stanley was summoned to the palace of Sultan Seyd Burghash, where an Arab horse was presented to the American visitor. The Sultan also gave Stanley letters of introduction to agents, representatives and merchants in the interior, expressing the hope that on 'whatever mission I was bound, I should be perfectly successful'. Later that evening, a Zanzibar-based American presented Stanley with a bay horse imported from the Cape of Good Hope.

On 4 February 1871, twenty-eight days after arriving in Zanzibar, the organisation and bales of equipment of the *New York Herald* expedition into the African interior were complete. At noon, four large Arab dhows were ready to make the short crossing to Bagamoyo and the men, their loads and animals were all on board. Only Farquhar and Shaw were missing. They were found in a quayside bar, sitting drinking as if they had all the time in the world. Stanley threw them out, reminding both that they were under contract. Shaw said he was having second thoughts about crossing to the mainland, unsure of what lay ahead. Stanley reminded him he had been paid half of his wages as an advance and it was too late to change his mind. Sullenly, the two white men climbed into one of the dhows.

An American flag, especially sewn for the *New York Herald* expedition by Mrs Webb, was raised at the masthead and a farewell committee waved hats and handkerchiefs as the dhows entered the Zanzibar Channel. Rank jungles, fetid swamps, fly-infested grasslands, fever, deserting porters and warring tribes all lay ahead and Stanley was prepared for everything – apart from the possibility of *not* finding Livingstone alive. This was an option he chose not to consider as the dhows nosed their way towards the African mainland. Instead, he pondered on the fact that one month ago he had been a total novice at putting a caravan together. Now he was in charge of a large expedition heading into the interior on an important mission – and as the man at its head he was all too aware that its success or failure fell entirely on his shoulders.

Chapter 19

'FORWARD, MARCH!'

Within twenty-four hours of setting up camp in Bagamoyo, two donkeys and a coil of wire had gone missing. The loss was put down to the 'many dishonest prowlers of the night' operating in the coastal town. It was to be the first of many raids on the expedition's supplies. A search also began for a further 140 '*pagazi*' – native porters or carriers – to travel with the expedition. It took two months to find them, during which time unscrupulous African and Arab traders tried continually if unsuccessfully to swindle and mislead Stanley.

Stanley was astounded to learn that the Royal Geographical Society-funded 33-man caravan, which Dr Kirk had mentioned in Zanzibar and dispatched into the interior three months previously, had travelled no further than Bagamoyo. Instead, the men had spent the last hundred days 'living in clover . . . thoughtless of the errand they had been sent upon and careless of the consequences'. The Consul's party only bestirred themselves when word of Dr Kirk's imminent arrival at Bagamoyo forced them to move on. After routine visits to local Arabs and taking a courtesy cup of tea in Stanley's tent, Kirk and a group of friends took off to hunt big game – ignorant of the fact that his own caravan had left only the day before and that Stanley would soon be hard on its trail.

By the time Stanley was ready to begin his march to Ujiji, the expedition had swelled to nearly two hundred men, split into five separate caravans, each marching three or four days ahead of the one behind. The first two caravans would act as an advance party, sending word back to those following days behind about what lay ahead. The first two and fourth caravans were under the protection of Zanzibari soldiers, the third under Farquhar, and the last under Stanley's personal command.

The first caravan departed on 18 February, consisting of 24 *pagazi* and 3 soldiers. The second, made up of a further 28 *pagazi*, 2 chiefs and 2 soldiers headed into the interior three days later. On 25 February, the third caravan left, supervised by Farquhar and comprising 2 *pagazi*,

10 donkeys, 1 cook and 3 soldiers. Caravan four departed on 11 March, made up of 55 *pagazi*, 2 chiefs and 3 soldiers.

On 21 March, Stanley's caravan prepared to depart with 28 *pagazi*, 10 of them carrying the boat sections, 12 soldiers under the command of Bombay, 1 tailor, 1 cook, Selim (Stanley's personal interpreter), 1 gun bearer, 17 pack mules, 2 horses, 1 guard dog called Omar who would guard Stanley's tent at night and John Shaw – called 'Bana Mdogo' or 'little master' by the men – riding a donkey in rear-guard. 'Total number, inclusive of all souls, comprised caravans connected with the *New York Herald* expedition, 192', Stanley recorded in his journal.

The entire expedition was made up of 3 Europeans, 45 Zanzibaris, 140 *pagazi*, a tailor (required to fix canvas tents, cloth and mend clothing owned by the three Europeans), Stanley's personal cook, interpreter and gun bearer, 27 pack animals, 2 riding horses, some goats and, according to his journal, 'every needful article for a long journey that the experience of many Arabs had suggested. And that my own ideas of necessaries for comfort or convenience, in illness or health, had been provided'.

It was time for the fifth caravan to depart. Everything was ready. Stanley mounted one of the two fine horses given to him before leaving Zanzibar, called for the American flag to be borne aloft by one of the men at the front and gave the order: 'Forward!' The long march away from civilisation and into Africa's dark interior had begun – at last.

A crowd of onlookers gazed as the expedition passed by, the soldiers singing and the American flag fluttering in the warm breeze. Stanley was full of excitement and admitted: 'my heart, I thought, palpitated much too quickly for the sober face of a leader. But I could not check it; the enthusiasm of youth still clung to me – despite my travels; my pulses bounded with full glow of staple health.' Stanley estimated that it would take three months for the expedition to reach the trading town of Unyanyembe several hundred miles west and another month's march to Ujiji.

The bay horse – known as 'Bana Mkuba' or 'the big master' – provided good service to Stanley, allowing him to gallop at full speed from the rear of his column to the head in minutes. The 'road' was nothing more than an earthen track, passing at first through small farming communities in which 'men and women in the scantiest costumes' worked the fields. After three days on the march, the expedition sighted an abundance of wild animals, including red antelope and hippopotami bathing in the muddy waters of a river. A bridge had to be built across the water, which was too deep for the animals to traverse. Saddles and a thick layer of grass provided a secure floor for nervous creatures. While the men set about their work, Stanley amused himself peppering the necks and skulls of the hippos with his rifle. Fortunately, he soon became bored with his target practice, using his time to better effect observing their behaviour in the water and on sandbars.

The next few days took the expedition through a mixture of terrain – 'a noble expanse of lawn and sward . . . as one may find before an English mansion', groves of ebony trees teeming with guinea-fowl, open plains, dense forests full of jays, green pigeon, ibis, turtledoves, pheasant, quail and moorhens, some of which ended up in that evening's cooking pot. By 23 April, the expedition had marched 125 miles into the interior.

At native settlements along the way, local chiefs demanded presents in return for allowing the caravan to pass through their land. Gifts of cloth, beads and brass wire were expected, and many chiefs attempted to exhort more from Stanley than he was prepared to give, causing delay after delay until a compromise was reached enabling the men to continue. Some chiefs invited Stanley's party to lodge overnight in their villages, graze the animals and cook meals over tribal fires. Others were not so keen for the strange travellers to linger in their territory, accepting presents and then urging them to move on as fast as possible fearing the white man and his caravan might rape their women, kill their children and plunder store houses. Territory covered during the expedition's early days provided members of the caravan with an abundance of fresh meat, but the deeper they progressed into the interior, the more they had to rely on supplies they were carrying.

At nightfall, Stanley's tent was first to be erected, a woven carpet laid across the ground along with a Persian rug and bear skin, his wood and canvas camp bed brought in along with a folding camp chair, a bag containing his journal, notebooks, pencils and reading matter and his tin bath filled with cool water. Omar the guard dog was positioned outside the front flap and allowed nobody to enter on pain of a chewed leg. Early on in the expedition, Stanley had found that he was receiving a constant stream of visits from members of the party who entered his tent uninvited to examine his things. It was Omar's job to ensure that no one entered, whether his master was 'at home' or not.

A messenger from the fourth caravan brought word that some *pagazi* had been taken ill and wanted Stanley to send '*dowa*' (medicine) to them. Stanley, who carried a well-stocked medicine chest equipped to deal with almost any injury or minor emergency, mounted his horse and rode ahead to the next caravan where he found one *pagazi* suffering from inflammation of the lungs and another with fever. He ordered all the men to rest for twenty-four hours and rode back to his own caravan, catching up with caravan number four again the following day. The men were still sick, so Stanley ordered them to remain another day in camp while he went ahead with his own men. Three days passed without further news from the straggling caravan. Shaw and Bombay were sent back to ensure that all was well. They returned on the fourth day with members of the sick caravan trailing behind pleading for more rest.

In pouring rain, Stanley's party marched on into dense jungle, which was difficult for the expedition's ammunition cart to negotiate. Ahead they could see the land steeply rising and falling into deep valleys. Stanley called a halt to the day's march to build camp for the night. It rained unceasingly for hours, ending at nightfall when an army of natives appeared from the forest wanting to trade. The head of the tribe appeared with a gift of rice for the 'rich' leader. Sensing trickery, Stanley told him through his interpreter that if he was so rich, why did the chief bring such a simple gift. The chief pleaded poverty – and so did Stanley. He gave him a piece of simple cloth in return for the rice. After the day's soaking, which drenched both men and supplies, Stanley was in no mood to waste time with a chief who considered him a soft touch.

At daybreak, the caravan found that the grey Arab horse presented by the Sultan of Zanzibar had died. The magnificent animal had shown signs of illness in the rain the previous day, and now lay dead in the mud. Stanley ordered his men to cut open the animal. Inside its stomach, twenty-five short, thick, white worms stuck like leeches to the lining while its intestines were alive with scores of long white worms which would eventually transform themselves into tsetse fly, an insect deadly to all bloodstock.

Stanley ordered the animal to be buried deep in the ground, provoking uproar from the chief who had called on the caravan the night before and now demanded payment in the form of 8 yards of cloth in return for allowing the dead horse to rest in his soil. The chief arrived with his entire tribe to collect his 'fee'. Again Stanley refused to pay, offering to dig up the carcass, fill in the hole and allow the dead horse to fester, stink out the valley and bring sickness to the village. The chief relented, told Stanley his horse could remain in the earth and quickly went on his way.

At nightfall, Stanley's men heard deep groans coming from the animals. On investigation, Stanley's bay horse 'Bana Mkuba', the 'big master', was found suffering. Stanley stayed with the animal through the night but as dawn broke over the interior, it died. When its stomach was opened it was discovered that death had been caused by internal rupture of a large cancer, which had affected the larger half of the coating of its stomach and extended up to within an inch or two of its larynx. Stanley had lost two valuable horses within the space of fifteen hours. Now there were none.

Several days passed and nothing further was heard from the lagging caravan. A *pagazi* in Stanley's group deserted, the interpreter, cook and tailor all fell ill with fever, men developed severe sore throats and by nightfall, ten men lay sick in the camp. Stanley had no option but to remain where he was until the men recovered. When the caravan behind finally caught up, the men begged their master for more rest. Stanley was impatient. He had now lost several days due to adverse weather and sickness. Taking the more healthy men from caravan four and his own group, Stanley sent them on as his new advance column while he remained with the sick men, some of whom he suspected of being more lazy than ill.

To rouse men 'from the sickened turpitude they had lapsed into', Stanley sounded the alarm by hitting a tin pan with an iron ladle, signifying that they would soon be on the march and anyone left behind must fend for themselves. The entire caravan fell into place, and once again Stanley had a full complement of men, even if some of them were walking wounded. It took twice as long to reach the next camp and, somewhere along the track, another *pagazi* deserted, taking a property tent, 10lb of beads and some cloth with him. Two men were sent back to find him and bring him back to the caravan, while the remainder rested.

The caravan now entered a stinking jungle, with acrid odours from plants and decaying vegetation. The *pagazi* became dispirited and Stanley was forced to speak sharply in order to get them to move. He marched to the front of the column, pulling ten fully laden donkeys behind. Shaw was in charge of the cart 'and his experiences were most bitter, as he informed me he had expended a whole vocabulary of stormy abuse known to sailors, and new ones invented *ex tempore*. He did not arrive at that night's camp at far end of the putrid forest until two-o-clock the next morning, totally exhausted.' Another camp was created for men and animals to recover. The local chief, 'a white man in everything but colour', sent a gift of fat sheep and grain in return for a demonstration by Stanley of loading and firing his Winchester rifle.

The next few days were easier; the men were rested and able to buy good food from tribesmen. And then the caravan came across a chain slave gang travelling towards the coast. Stanley reported that the slaves 'did not appear to be in any way down-hearted, on the contrary . . . were it not for their chains, it would have been difficult to discover master from slave. The chains were ponderous – they might have held elephants captive; but as the slaves carried nothing but themselves, their weight could not have been insupportable.'

Meanwhile, men dispatched to bring back *pagazi* who had deserted with the tent, beads and cloth were unceremoniously dragging him back into Stanley's camp, the pilfered booty intact. The man had been captured by a local tribe who had tied him to a tree and were about to kill him when Stanley's men arrived to claim him and the goods, paying for his deliverance with some of the stolen beads.

Stanley convened a campside court, comprising eight *pagazi* and four Zanzibaris who would decide what punishment would be meted out to the thief. 'Their unanimous verdict was that he was guilty of a crime almost unknown among *pagazi*, and it was likely to give bad repute to the carriers, they therefore sentenced him to be flogged with the "Great Master's" donkey whip, which was carried out to the poor man's crying sorrow.' Stanley ensured punishment was conducted in full view of the entire caravan, an example to each that desertion and theft were punishable offences. When another *pagazi* deserted later, he was also hunted, dragged back to camp, given two dozen lashes and locked in chains.

One of the main obstacles encountered on the march through the interior was the notorious Makata swampland, a disease-ridden area extending over 45 miles, taking days to cross as the expedition party and its animals waded deep in rancid water and black mire. At night, camps were made on mounds of high ground rising from the swamps, but mud and filth were everywhere in evidence, and Stanley knew it would only be a matter of time before his men would succumb to fever brought on by their long exposure to slough and quagmire.

Stanley himself felt the first pangs of fever one morning at 10 a.m. He recalled: 'First, general lassitude prevailed, with a disposition to drowsiness; secondly came the spinal ache which, commencing from the loins, ascended the vertebrae, and extended around the ribs, until it reached the shoulders, where it settled into a weary pain; thirdly came a chilliness over the whole body, which was quickly followed by a heavy head, swimming eyes and throbbing temples, with vague vision, which distorted and transformed all objects of sight. This lasted until 10 p.m. and the mukunguri [fever] left me, much prostrated in strength.' A short time later, Stanley was attacked with dysentery 'which brought me to the verge of the grave'. From a stout and fleshy person weighing 170lb, he was reduced to a skeleton weighing a mere 139lb. Stanley's guard dog, Omar, also became ill from inflammation of the bowels and later died.

Shaw was the next casualty followed by Bombay and other *pagazi*. The remaining men moved at a pace so slow, Stanley thought they had completely stopped. He knew he had to get his men out of the swamp-lands before they could rest and recover, so to 'encourage' them to trudge forward 'I was compelled to observe that when mud and wet sapped the physical energy of the lazily inclined, a dog-whip became their backs, restoring them to a sound – sometimes to an extravagant – activity'. At the far side of the swamp, the caravan rested for four days.

With temperatures exceeding 128 degrees, Stanley's caravan trudged onwards towards the foothills of the steep Usagara Mountains, where in 'a filthy village' swarming with flies and insects and 'well grounded in goat dung, and peopled with a wonderful number of children for a hamlet that did not number 25 families', he stumbled across the third caravan. Its leader, Farquhar, lay ill in his tent with swollen legs (Bright's disease). 'As he heard my voice, Farquhar staggered out of his tent, so changed from my spruce mate who started from Bagamoyo, that I hardly knew him at first. His legs were ponderous, elephantine, since his leg-illness was of elephantiasis or dropsy. His face was of a deathly pallor, for he had not been out of his tent for two weeks.'

Stanley called for a camp to be built on a cool hillside far away from the stinking village and arranged for Farquhar to be carried up by four men. As he lay on a camp bed in Stanley's tent, Farquhar told his commander that he had no idea what had caused his illness or his legs to swell to such an immense size, preventing Stanley from correctly diagnosing what medicine might be administered to reduce the swelling.

What was Stanley to do? Should he hold up the march in the hope that Farquhar might recover? Or should he leave him on the hillside with plentiful supplies until he was well enough to find his way back to Bagamoyo – and possibly die in the process? Stanley decided to secure Farquhar to a donkey to carry him up mountain passes, through valleys and uninhabited wilderness ahead.

By now John Shaw should have caught up with the rest of Stanley's caravan with the handcart but 'Bana Mdogo', the 'little master', was nowhere to be found. A messenger told Stanley that Shaw was too ill to walk and a strong and burly Zanzibari called Chowpereh was instructed to take one of the donkeys for him to ride and a second for the load on the cart. The *pagazi* carried a message from Stanley to pitch the cart into the nearest ravine, gully, or river and return to the caravan.

The expedition waited but after four hours there was still no sign of Shaw, forcing Stanley to hike back to find him. Back down the track, Stanley came across the incredible sight of Chowpereh carrying the cart on his head – wheels, shafts, body and axle all complete. The Zanzibari found it easier to transport the cart in this way instead of pulling it over the rough terrain. Stanley ordered the African to push the cart over the track and into some tall reeds. No longer would it hold up his progress. Shaw followed some distance behind, sitting on the donkey sound asleep. Stanley bawled him out, accusing him of holding everyone up, to which Shaw wailed that he had done his best and a row between the men erupted on the mountainside.

There were more desertions followed by back-trailing expeditions to find the culprits, bring them to camp and clap them in a growing chain gang of runaways. More donkeys died and Stanley was forced to give his own beast to Farquhar, whose condition worsened by the day. To give the man a rest out of the sun, Stanley sent Farquhar ahead to the next village with a *pagazi*. He wrote in his journal: 'To save the expedition from ruin, I was reluctantly compelled to come to the conclusion that it were better for me, for [Farquhar] and all concerned that he be left with some kind of Chief of a village, with a supply of cloth and beads, until he got well, than that he make his own recovery impossible.'

Farquhar and his *pagazi* found their way to a settlement on the slopes of the Mpwapwa Mountains, where Stanley's caravan caught up with them. Arrangements were made with the village chief for Farquhar to stay for an extended period with a renegade *pagazi*, called Jako, who was freed from his chains and given instructions to take care of the sick white man and attend to his needs. He was left with a quantity of beads, cloth, a rifle, 300 cartridge rounds, a set of cooking pots and 3lb of tea.

As the caravan advanced, they occasionally met others heading in the opposite direction, some carrying hundreds of ivory tusks. On 12 April, an Arab called Salim Bin Rashid in charge of a caravan told Stanley he had recently been at Ujiji and stayed in a hut next to one occupied by Livingstone. He described the doctor as 'looking old, with long grey moustaches and beard, just recovered from severe illness, looking very wan'. He also told Stanley that Livingstone planned to visit a country called Manyuema as soon as he was well enough to travel.

The news revived Stanley's flagging spirits and he immediately dashed off a short dispatch for the *New York Herald* – his first since departing from Zanzibar – which he handed to a messenger to carry back to the coast for transmission to London and New York. The dispatch was just a few lines long but stated that 'positive intelligence of the safety of Dr. Livingstone' had been received and that 'the authority of the statement is unquestionable and its truth certain'.

It took five months for the few lines to reach New York and Bennett, who had all but given up on his African correspondent. Cautiously, Bennett tucked the short item away on page 7 of his newspaper on 19 September 1871. But he used the story to announce to the world for the first time that 'a party of Americans is hurrying into the interior with the object of rescuing the doctor from his perilous position'. News of the *New York Herald*'s search for Livingstone was now in the open. The eyes of newspaper readers and rival papers waited anxiously for the next dispatch. God help Stanley if he failed to find the man.

On 18 May, another Arab trader encountered along the route told Stanley that the '*musungu*' (white man) was off on his travels again and was now one month's march from Ujiji. 'He has met with a bad accident, having shot himself through the thigh while out hunting buffalo. When he gets well he will return to Ujiji', Stanley was told.

By mid-June, the *New York Herald* expedition had joined forces with an Arab caravan headed in the same westerly direction. One of the Arabs volunteered alarming information about Livingstone: 'You are asking me about the *musungu* whom people call "Dochter Fellusteen" [Dr Livingstone]? Yes, I lived near him about three months ago at Ujiji. His men have all deserted him, except three slaves, whom he was obliged to buy. . . . He used to beat his men very hard if they did not do instantly what he told them. At last they all ran away; no one would stop with him. He had nothing with him, no cloth nor beads to buy food for a long time; so he had to go out and hunt buffalo every day. He is a very old man and very fat, too; has a long white beard. He is a great eater. . . .'

So Livingstone was now fat, with a long grey beard and beat his slaves. It sounded unlikely. Stanley began to wonder if this man was the one he had read about, whom he felt he knew in person and was now searching for in the heart of Africa. On 16 June, a fourth witness who had personally seen Livingstone said: 'He is a very old man, with a beard nearly white. His left shoulder is out of joint from a fight he had with a *suriba* [lion]. He has gone to Manyuema with some Arabs . . . he is returning to Ujiji soon, owing to a letter he received from the "Balyuz" [Consul]. They say that although he has been out here so long he has done nothing. He has fifteen bales of cloth at Unyanyembe, not yet sent to him.'

Four days later and three days away from Unyanyembe, the head of a caravan bound for the coast confirmed: 'Yes, there is a *musungu*, a very old man. . . . Lately a caravan coming from Ukonogo brought the news that he was dead. I don't know whether the news be true or not.'

On 4 July 1871, Stanley sat down in his tent at Kwihara, near Unyanyembe, and wrote his first lengthy dispatch from the African interior for the *New York Herald*; the piece told the expedition's story so far, describing the circumstances surrounding the search for Livingstone, Stanley's travels prior to arriving in Zanzibar, his attempts to buy equipment and supplies in an African market, to recruit men prepared to walk 900 miles and back and the trials and tribulations of marching through the interior. It was a long article, designed to fill a page or more of the newspaper. The final paragraph of the dispatch read:

If at Ujiji in one month more I shall see him, the race for home shall begin. Until I hear more of him or see the long absent old man face to face, I bid you a farewell; but wherever he is be sure I shall not give up the chase. If alive, you shall hear what he has to say; if dead, I will find and bring his bones to you.

Stanley carefully placed the handwritten dispatch into an envelope, sealed it and passed it to one of his men acting as a messenger, who would run back to Zanzibar along paths and through swamps already trodden. Five months and three weeks were to elapse before readers of the *New York Herald* would open their newspapers and read the page 3 extended headline: 'Dr. Livingstone – The Expedition of the New York Herald in Quest of the Great African Traveller – Description of the Undertaking – Livingstone Reported at Ujiji – Special Report of the Herald Commissioner Directing the Expedition'. As was Bennett's usual policy, the name of the reporter was not mentioned.

Cockney John William Shaw and Scotsman William Lawrence Farquhar, travelled with the *New York Herald* expedition from Zanzibar – and were not told the real reason for the journey. Neither man returned.

Chapter 20

'MIRAMBO IS COMING!'

In early July 1871, Stanley caught up with the same Royal Geographical Society-funded caravan detailed to find Livingstone which he had stumbled across lazing in Bagamoyo. This time they were lazing in Unyanyembe, where they had arrived a month earlier, filling every waking hour with the arduous activities of sleeping, dozing or merely resting. In addition to carrying a packet of registered letters from family, friends and the RGS dated 1 November 1870, other essential supplies were waiting to be delivered to Livingstone, including bales of cloth, twelve boxes of wine (a strange item to send to a man who rarely drank alcohol), provisions and luxuries including tea and coffee.

In order to keep watch on the doctor's goods, Stanley suggested that the Society caravan join his own. Seeing how well fed men in the white man's caravan appeared to be, they agreed. But it was impossible for the enlarged group to continue. A feared tribal warlord called Mirambo, head of a confederation of mercenaries known as the 'Ruga-Ruga' and named by Europeans as 'the African Bonaparte', had been mounting attacks on caravans between Unyanyembe and Ujiji, stealing goods and butchering men. Stanley's proposed route passed directly through Mirambo's country and no other recognised pathways led to Ujiji.

Unyanyembe's Arabs were united in thinking that Mirambo's mercenary forces, then just twenty-seven hours' journey away, would be easy to conquer. They told Stanley that a combination of his Zanzibaris and their own fighting men would see the tyrant off in a couple of weeks and 'I was tempted in an unlucky moment to promise them my aid, hoping that by this means I would be enabled to reach Livingstone sooner than by stopping at Unyanyembe awaiting the turn of events.'

Stanley hand-picked fifty men, loaded them with bales, beads and wire, and told them to head off towards Ujiji. The Society caravan remained at the camp – its members lazing around, as usual. When it was time to depart Bombay was missing, to be discovered six hours later, 'his face faithfully depicting the contending passions under which he was labouring – sorrow at parting from the fleshpots of Unyanyembe'. In other words, he had been in the company of one of the town's ample supply of prostitutes and was reluctant to leave and start marching all over again. Stanley demonstrated his fury by beating Bombay with his cane until he pleaded for mercy.

The Zanzibaris with Stanley and Shaw joined a small army of others employed by the Arabs, armed with guns and ammunition, ready to march to Zimbizo, one of Mirambo's strongholds. As they marched, they sang:

Hoy! Hoy! Where are ye going? Going to war! Against whom? Against Mirambo! Who is your master? The White Man! Ough! Ough! Hyah! Hyah!

Six hours into the march, Shaw collapsed and had to be carried to the first night's camp, where arrangements had been made to rendezvous with an army put together by Arab traders, a fighting force of 2,255 men comprising slaves, soldiers and Zanzibaris from the *New York Herald* expedition. They were armed with a mixture of flintlock muskets, German and French double-barrelled shotguns, English-made Enfields, American Springfields, plus 'spears and long knives for the purpose of decapitating, and inflicting vengeful gashes in dead bodies'.

The fighting force steathily surrounded Zimbizo in readiness for a surprise attack. Mirambo's mercenaries were ready for them, lying in wait and first to open fire. Stanley's soldiers recovered and stormed the gates, capturing the village plus two others, plundering them for ivory, slaves and grain (all of which the Arabs claimed as their 'loot'). They then set fire to them. More villages were captured and torched in the days that followed.

Stanley's fever returned and from his sick bed he issued orders that none of his men should take part in further raids until he was well enough to accompany them. No sooner had Stanley lapsed into a coma than some of his men raided another village in which Mirambo and his son were reported to be hiding. Scores of men, including many of Stanley's best Zanzibaris, were killed. The rumour had been true: Mirambo and son had been in the village and after hearing that a raiding party was approaching, had escaped into long grass surrounding the settlement. When the raiders emerged victorious carrying ivory tusks, bales of cloth and over two hundred slaves, Mirambo's forces rose up on each side of them and finished them off with spears. Only a handful of men returned to tell the tale.

Stanley wrote: 'The effect of this defeat is indescribable. It was impossible to sleep, from the shrieks of the women whose husbands had fallen. All night they howled their lamentations and sometimes might be heard the groans of the wounded that had contrived to crawl through the grass unperceived by the enemy.'

Still weak from fever, Stanley remained in his tent, but was woken by one of his men claiming that everyone outside was running away. Stanley was helped from his camp bed and looked outside to see the backs of hundreds of people retreating from camp. A terrified Arab called to Stanley as he ran past: 'Bana – quick – Mirambo is coming!'

Stanley caught sight of Shaw saddling one of the donkeys and preparing to flee. Only seven of Stanley's fifty men travelling with the raiding party remained; the rest had fled. A weakened Stanley was helped onto another donkey and, surrounded by the loyal followers, rode away suffering intense pain in the process. One thought was in Stanley's mind: 'The full and final accomplishment of my mission', which now appeared doubtful.

As they fled through the night, Shaw fell from his animal and refused to remount. Stanley instructed that he be dragged back to the animal with men running either side to make sure he remained seated. They arrived back at the village from which the raiding party had set out the previous day, where deserters sheepishly made themselves scarce.

Still weak after his fever, Stanley confronted Arab leaders the following day and berated them for their cowardice, the desertion of their men and for encouraging Mirambo to come after them. Rather than travel another mile with Arab caravans, Stanley announced he would take an alternative route that would circumnavigate the warlord's territory. He wrote in his journal: 'Very few people know anything of the country south; those whom I have questioned concerning it mentions its "want of water" and robber *Wazavira* [tribesmen] as serious obstacles; they also say that settlements are few and far between. . . . I have a good excuse for returning to the coast, but my conscience will not permit me to do so, after so much money has been expended. And so much confidence has been placed in me. In fact, I feel I must die sooner than return.'

Before taking any route, Stanley needed new men to replace the deserters and those who had been killed, or been released from the caravan at Unyanyembe. Only thirteen of the original party were left, too few to carry over a hundred loads plus Livingstone's goods. As he set about the task of hiring extra manpower, a caravan arrived from the coast with news that William Farquhar, whom Stanley had been forced to leave behind in Mpwapwa, was dead. Farquhar's health had recovered but as he had attempted to rise from his bed, he had fallen backwards and died. Superstitious about having the body of a white man in his village, the chief ordered a man to take Farquhar's body into the jungle and bury it. The man was unable to lift Farquhar's great weight, so dragged the body outside the village confines, where he left it without any covering for jackals and worms to eat.

By 22 August, Mirambo's forces were on the warpath again – and heading for Unyanyembe. Stanley's caravan worked feverishly to make their settlement defensible, boring loopholes through which to fire their muskets in the 3-feet thick stout clay walls. Around 150 men crowded into the courtyard of Stanley's primitive quarters, with enough food and water for six days. Stanley noted: 'Tomorrow Mirambo has threatened he will come. . . . I hope he will come, and if he comes within range of an American rifle, he shall see what virtue lies in American lead. . . .'

On 26 August, word reached the settlement that Mirambo's forces were just 2 miles away. A reconnaissance group was sent to spy out their whereabouts. However, the group was spotted and the warlord sent back word that he 'wanted a day off to eat the beef he has stolen from them'. He told the group to return the following day when he promised them 'plenty of fighting'. When the spies returned the next morning they discovered that Mirambo and his men had left the area. Stanley resumed the business of hiring men and successfully recruited fifty Wangwana tribesmen. He left seventy loads behind at a safe place and under guard at Unyanyembe, including inessential personal items.

On 30 August, it was Shaw's turn to refuse to work. To Stanley's annoyance he remained sitting listless in his tent. In the hope of galvanising Shaw into action, Stanley revealed to him the true nature of their mission. 'I told him that I did not care about the geography of the country half as much as I cared about FINDING LIVINGSTONE', Stanley wrote in his diary. He told Shaw: 'Don't you see what reward you will get from Mr. Bennett if you will help me? I am sure, if ever you come to New York, you will never be in want of a fifty-dollar bill. So shake yourself; jump about; look lively.'

The following week an Arab named Mohammed presented Stanley with a little boy slave named 'Ndugu M'hali' ('my brother's wealth'). Stanley did not care for the name and called the chiefs of his caravan together and asked them to give him a better one. One suggested 'Simba' (a lion), another said he thought 'Ngombe' (a cow) would suit the boy child, while yet another felt he ought to be called 'Mirambo', which raised a loud laugh. After looking at his quick eyes and noting his agility, one of the chiefs suggested the name 'Ka-lu-lu'. 'Just look at his eyes, so bright! Look at his form, so slim! Watch his movements, how quick! Yes, Kalulu is his name.' *Kalulu* is a Kisawahili term for the young of the blue buck antelope. 'Let his name henceforth be Kalulu, and let no man take it from him,' said Stanley. Clearly, the boy had no parents and afraid that he would otherwise almost certainly end up in perpetual slavery – or in an African equivalent of St Asaph's workhouse – Stanley agreed to find him a good home somewhere along the route.

On 20 September, Stanley led fifty-four of his men out of Unyanyembe for the march to Ujiji by the southerly detour route. He had still not fully recovered from his fever but had no wish to remain in the region a day longer. Compared to the caravan that had marched into the interior from the sea, this new one travelled light, carrying goods for themselves and Livingstone including cloth, beads, ammunition, a single tent, one bed, a medicine box, a sextant, books, tea, coffee, sugar, flour, candles, canned meats and sardines, one load of cooking utensils and 'some miscellaneous necessities'.

When the camp awoke the next day, Stanley learned that twenty men were missing, including the man charged with taking care of Livingstone's letter bag. A delegation was sent back towards Unyanyembe with orders to find the men and bring them back with a long slave chain. Towards nightfall, nine men were dragged into camp. The rest were never found. As instructed, they returned 'with a strong chain, capable of imprisoning within the collars attached to it at least ten men'. Livingstone's bag carrier also drifted into camp; he had not absconded at all, just walked at a slower pace than the rest of the men.

Stanley addressed the caravan and the slave chain was shown to them. He informed them that he was the first white man who had taken one on his travels 'but, as they were all so frightened of accompanying me, I was obliged to make use of it, as it was the only means of keeping them together. The good need never fear being chained by me – only the deserters, the thieves, who received their hire and presents, guns and ammunition, and then ran away. I would not put anyone this time in chains; but whoever deserted after this day, I should halt, and not continue the march till I found him, after which he should march to Ujiji with the slave-chain around his neck.' They confirmed they had heard and understood what their master had said. Nevertheless, the head count the following morning showed that a further two men had deserted – one a man who had absconded twice previously. By the evening they had been discovered, dragged back, flogged and chained.

More men became ill with fever and Shaw was so sick that he twice fell from his donkey, the second time remaining face down in the dirt and hot sun for over an hour. When Stanley found him, he sat up and wept like a child. Stanley asked Shaw if he wanted to return to Unyanyembe and Shaw said he could travel no further, wished he had never come and thought that life in Africa would be different. Stanley told him that his patience had run out, that Shaw was 'simply suffering from hypochondria' and would surely die if he returned.

Arrangements were made to transfer Shaw on a litter to Unyanyembe and four men from a local village were hired to carry him. The men stood in two ranks, flags were lifted and Shaw was carried away towards the north while Stanley's caravan, minus a dozen sick men left behind at the village, 'filed off to the south, with quicker and more elastic steps, as if we felt an incubus had been taken from us'. As Stanley had predicted, John Shaw would live for another month in Unyanyembe, before succumbing for the last time to Africa's heat and fever.

The caravan moved deeper into the interior throughout the remaining days of September and October. There was more fever, friendly and hostile encounters with local tribes, hunts for fresh meat and, on 3 November, a meeting with a group of travellers approaching from the opposite direction. The oncoming caravan consisted of eighty members of the Waguhha tribe from Lake Tanganyika. An interpreter found out that an elderly sick white man, with hair on his face and wearing clothes similar to Stanley's, had arrived at Ujiji from Manyuema. They had last seen him eight days ago. Stanley wrote: 'Hurrah! This is Livingstone! He must be Livingstone! He can be no other; but still, he may be someone else – someone from the west coast. . . . But we must now march quick, lest he hears we are coming and runs away.'

Stanley asked his caravan if they were prepared to march to Ujiji without a single halt – apart from overnight camps – and promised to reward each man with a length of his finest cloth. They answered in the affirmative and set off with renewed vigour. A week later and travelling lighter thanks to unscrupulous chiefs who relieved the caravan of most of their cloth and beads before they could pass over their lands, Stanley was two days away from Ujiji. He recorded in his journal: 'Patience my soul! A few hours more, then the end of all this will be known! I shall be face to face with that "white man with the white hairs on his face, whoever he is!"'

At camp on the evening of 9 November, Stanley summoned the boy Kalulu to his tent. In just a short time, the lad had become Stanley's own manservant and gun bearer, waiting on his master at table, joining him on hunting expeditions and making sure that no one unauthorised entered his tent. The boy was a fast learner and, although small in stature, he had become an important member of Stanley's entourage now that Farquhar and Shaw were gone. Kalulu was ordered to set out a new flannel suit that Stanley had brought along to wear on the day he expected to meet Livingstone. The boy was told to oil his master's boots, chalk his sun helmet and fold a new red and white *puggaree* (cloth band) around the crown of the hat 'that I may make as presentable an appearance as possible before the white man with the grey beard, and before the Arabs of Ujiji; for the clothes I have worn through jungle and forest are in tatters'. He closed his journal entry for that day with the words: 'Good night; only let one day come again, and we shall see what we shall see. . . .'

The 236th day out from Bagamoyo and 51st day from Unyanyembe, 10 November promised 'a happy and glorious morning, the air is fresh and cool' and Ujiji only a six-hour march away. Towards mid-morning, the caravan approached the summit of a steep mountain and from the top they gazed down on Lake Tanganyika – the end of their journey. Stanley insisted that the caravan move quickly 'lest news of our coming might reach the people of Ujiji before we come in sight and are ready for them'.

They descended and saw 500 yards below the lakeside settlement where Dr David Livingstone was last known to have resided. All thoughts of the distance marched, hills ascended and descended, forests, jungles, thickets and swamps traversed, hot sun, blistered feet, fevers, dangers and difficulties now vanished. Was the old Scottish doctor down there? Had word of Stanley's arrival travelled ahead and the old man fled from sight? Or had he died in Africa's heat, from disease or from a multitude of hardships encountered trudging across the dark continent?

Stanley gave the order: 'Unfurl the flags and load your guns!'

'We will, Master, we will,' the men responded eagerly.

'One, two, three— FIRE!' A volley from fifty guns announced that Stanley's caravan had arrived at Ujiji. The American flag was held high by one of the tallest men and the caravan marched down, to be greeted by hundreds of people coming from their homes wondering what all the noise was about. They surrounded the caravan and shouted words of welcome: 'Yambo, yambo, bana! Yambo, bana! Yambo, bana!'

The crowd parted to let them through. 'Good morning, Sir,' said a voice in English. Stanley swung around, startled to hear English spoken from among a sea of black faces. A man dressed in a long white shirt and with a turban around his head was smiling. 'Who the mischief are you?' asked Stanley.

The smiling man replied: 'I am Susi, the servant of Dr Livingstone.'

'What! Is Dr Livingstone here?'

'Yes, sir.'

'In this village?'

'Yes, sir.'

'Are you sure?'

'Sure, sir, sure. Why, I leave him just now.'

'Good morning, sir,' said another voice.

'Hello,' said Stanley. 'Is this another one?'

'Yes, sir.'

'Well, what is your name?'

'My name is Chuma, sir.'

'And is the doctor well?'

'Not very well, sir.'

'Where has he been so long?'

'In Manyuema.'

'Now, you Susi, run and tell the doctor I am coming,' ordered Stanley, whereupon Susi darted off like a madman.

The crowd was now so dense that movement was difficult. Susi returned and said the doctor was surprised to hear that a white man was approaching and he had returned to find out his name. Ahead stood a large 'tembe', a house constructed from mud, wood, palms and other native materials. In front of it was a group of Ujiji's Arab merchants. Behind them, standing on a verandah, was an elderly white man wearing a blue cap. Was it *the* man? Stanley confessed: 'What would I not have given for a bit of friendly wilderness, where, unseen, I might vent my joy in some mad freak, such as idiotically biting my hand, turning a somersault, or slashing at trees, in order to allay those exciting feelings that were well-nigh uncontrollable. My heart beats fast, but I must not let my face betray my emotions, lest it shall detract from the dignity of a white man appearing under such extraordinary circumstances.'

Stanley did what he considered most dignified in the circumstances. 'I pushed back the crowds, and, passing from the rear, walked down a living avenue of people, until I came in front of the semicircle of Arabs, before which stood "the white man with the grey beard".' The supreme moment in Stanley's life was now only seconds away. With little Kalulu just a few feet behind, the thirty-year-old American reporter slowly advanced in the noon sunshine, noticing that the 59-year-old white man was pale 'wearied and wan, with grey whiskers and moustache, and wearing a bluish cloth cap with a faded gold band on a red ground round it, and has on a red-sleeved waistcoat, and a pair of grey tweed trousers'.

Here, at last, was the object of his search. What should he say to him? 'My imagination had not taken this question into consideration before. All around me is the immense crowd, hushed and expectant, wondering how the scene will develop itself.' Stanley decided to exercise restraint and reserve, resisting the temptation to run to him, admitting that he is 'a coward in the presence of such a mob – [I] would have embraced him, but that I did not know how he would receive me; so I did what moral cowardice and false pride suggested was the best thing – walked deliberately to him, took off my hat, and said: "*Dr Livingstone, I presume?*"'*

* The famous phrase: 'Dr Livingstone, I presume?' has entered popular legend, but some historians have cast doubts on whether Stanley actually uttered the words. The diary Stanley kept throughout his search for Livingstone, available on microfilm at the British Library and used extensively by this author, has a missing page – the page on which he records his meeting with Livingstone and his first exchange of words with the doctor. There is no reason to suggest that Stanley did not say the words, as they appeared in the *New York Herald* dispatch written shortly after the first meeting. Stanley went through the remainder of his life insisting that he had used the phrase, although Livingstone's own recollection of the same meeting made no mention of words used when the two men met for the first time in the African interior.

'Yes,' said he, with a cordial smile, lifting his cap slightly, speaking his first words to a white man for six years.

The men replaced their hats and shook hands. Stanley then blurted out: 'I thank God, doctor, I have been permitted to see you.'

'I feel thankful that I am here to welcome you,' the doctor answered.

One of the biggest news stories of the nineteenth century had just broken.

Bombay and Mabruki, two porters experienced in travelling with caravans into the African interior.

Chapter 21

LIFE WITH LIVINGSTONE

Stanley found himself gazing at Livingstone almost in disbelief that he had actually found the needle in the haystack. 'Every hair of his head and beard, every wrinkle of his face, the wanes of his features, and the slightly wearied look he bore were all imparting intelligence to me – the knowledge I craved for so much ever since I heard the words [from Bennett] "Take what you want but *Find Livingstone!*" What I saw was deeply interesting intelligence to me . . . I was listening and reading at the same time.'

Livingstone caught sight of Stanley's caravan standing in the hot sun and said: 'Let me ask you to share my house with me. It is not a very fine house, but is rainproof and cool, and there are enough spare rooms to lodge you and your goods. Indeed, one room is far too large for my use.' Stanley gave orders for the storing of the goods and purchase of rations and Livingstone instructed Susi and Chuma to assist. He directed Stanley to a verandah enclosing his *tembe*, a cool and shady spot away from the heat. And then the conversation began, although Stanley later confessed that he forgot what was discussed in all the excitement, possibly about the road he had taken from Unyanyembe. 'I know the doctor was talking, and I was answering mechanically,' he recalled.

Stanley recorded his first impression of Livingstone:

a man of unpretending appearance. . . . He has quiet, composed features from which the freshness of youth has quite departed, but which retain the mobility of prime age just enough to show that there yet lives much endurance and vigour within his frame. The eyes, which are hazel, are remarkably bright, not dimmed in the least, though the whiskers and moustache are very grey. The hair, originally brown, is streaked here and there with grey over the temples; otherwise it might belong to a man of thirty. The teeth above show indications of being worn out. The hard fare . . . has made havoc in their ranks. His form is stoutish, a little over the ordinary in height, with slightly bowed shoulders. When walking he has the heavy step of an overworked and fatigued man. On his head he wears the naval cap, with a round visor with which he has been identified throughout Africa. His dress shows that at times he has had to resort to the needle to repair and replace what travel has worn. Such is Livingstone externally.

The crowd outside Livingstone's *tembe* began to disperse and Stanley instructed his own men to prepare for a long and well-earned rest at Ujiji. He called for Livingstone's letter bag to be brought forward and correspondence that had left Zanzibar exactly 365 days before was finally delivered. Livingstone's face lit up when he took some letters from the bag and saw they were from his children, friends and colleagues at the Royal Geographical Society. He put them back and Stanley urged him to read his correspondence. Livingstone responded: 'I have waited years for letters and have been taught patience. I can surely afford to wait a few hours longer. No, tell me the general news: how is the world getting along?'

While a crimson tablecloth was spread, hot dishes laid out and tea poured from a silver pot containing 'best tea' from London, Stanley told the doctor about the opening of the Suez Canal, Grant's election to the US Presidency, laying the Atlantic telegraphic cable, wars, revolutions, insurrections and the state of the British and American nations. Livingstone had lost his appetite weeks ago and his stomach refused everything but tea, but now he and Stanley ate like vigorous, hungry men 'and, as he vied with me in demolishing pancakes, he kept repeating: "You have brought me new life – you have brought me new life."'

Suddenly remembering something forgotten in the excitement, Stanley sent Kalulu to 'bring that bottle; you know which, and bring me the silver goblets. I brought this bottle on purpose for this event, which I hoped would come to pass. Though often it seemed useless to expect it.' A bottle of vintage Sillery champagne from the famous and ancient vineyards of the Montagne de Reims, was brought to the *tembe*, its cork pulled and a silver goblet of the sparkling drink handed to the doctor.

'Dr Livingstone, to your very good health, sir.'

'And to yours,' replied Livingstone, all the time wondering who this American stranger was, who had sent him and what he wanted from an old and ailing Scotsman hundreds of miles away from civilisation.

The men talked and ate all afternoon. Livingstone related how, on returning to Ujiji, he had discovered that his goods had been sold by the man charged with taking care of them; he had assumed Livingstone was dead and had sold them, using the money to buy ivory. The doctor was now reduced to poverty, relying on the dubious kindness of Arabs. He had been suffering from dysentery and unable to retain his food. The shadows outside the *tembe* grew longer. Stanley left Livingstone alone to read his letters, bade the doctor goodnight and retired to a cool room within the house to write up his journal.

He awoke early next morning, a thousand questions running through his head desperate for answers. Now that Stanley had found Livingstone, he knew he needed proof to convince the rest of the world that his discovery was true. His first task would be to admit his true purpose in coming unannounced to Ujiji and who had sent him. Stanley wrote:

> I will ask him to write a letter to Mr. Bennett and to give what news he can spare. I did not come here to rob him of his news. Sufficient for me is that I have found him. It is a complete success so far. But it will be a greater one if he gives me letters for Mr. Bennett and an acknowledgement that he has seen me. . . . I think, from what I have seen of him last night, that he is not such a niggard and misanthrope as I was led to believe. He exhibited considerable emotion, despite the monosyllabic greeting when he shook my hand.

Despite the early hour, Livingstone was already up and about. He had read his letters from home, which brought both good news and bad. 'Now doctor, you are probably wondering why I came here,' said Stanley. 'It is true,' said Livingstone; 'I did not like to ask you yesterday, because I thought it was none of my business.'

'You have heard of the *New York Herald*?'

'Oh, who has not heard of that despicable newspaper?' said Livingstone – and how Stanley must have flinched at the word 'despicable', later excised from all retellings of the famous encounter. Stanley explained how James Gordon Bennett had sent Stanley in search of the doctor 'to get whatever news of your discoveries you like to give – and to assist you, if I can, with means'.

Livingstone said he was obliged to Bennett 'and it makes me feel proud to think that you Americans think so much of me'. On observing

Stanley's large bathtub being brought into the *tembe*, his personal knives, forks and crockery being unpacked for breakfast and laid out on a Persian rug, Livingstone remarked that his new American friend must surely be a millionaire. In turn Stanley inwardly reflected on his good fortune and the fact that had he travelled directly from Paris to Africa after receiving instructions from Bennett and not been delayed at Unyanyembe by Mirambo's warriors, he might have lost Livingstone. Instead he had found the doctor, missionary, explorer and honorary consul and spent the rest of the day – and many of those that followed – sitting on the verandah and under the palms at Ujiji listening to his story.

On what Stanley understood to be 11 November 1871, he completed a long dispatch about his march through the interior and ultimate discovery of Livingstone to the *New York Herald*. He dated the piece 10 November, the day he shook Livingstone's hand for the first time, and began writing the article that night, finishing it the following day after the doctor had provided the reporter with more information. Livingstone's own account of his meeting with Stanley at Ujiji records the date as 3 November, which is correct. Stanley had become confused about dates as a consequence of earlier bouts of fever which had left him incapacitated for days at a time. He only discovered the date of their meeting was wrong days later when Livingstone himself corrected him, by which time the dispatch was on its way to the coast. The famous 'meeting date' of 10 November, however, remained unchanged in Stanley's notebook.

It took eight months for Stanley's triumphant dispatch to be carried 900 miles to the coast by a messenger careful to avoid Mirambo's marauding mercenaries. From Zanzibar it travelled by steamer to Bombay, from where it was telegraphed to the newspaper's London office, which in turn forwarded it to New York where it finally appeared in the *New York Herald* on 2 July 1872 under the headline 'LIVINGSTONE – Finding the Great Explorer – A Picture for History, The Grasp of the Two Explorers'. The paper's London bureau immediately appreciated the immensity of the story. Under the headline 'The Glorious News', Stanley's article was prefaced by a piece from the London bureau chief stating:

It is with the deepest emotions of pride and pleasure that I announce the arrival this day of letters from Mr. Stanley, Chief of the Herald Exploring Expedition to Central Africa. I have forwarded the letters by mail. Knowing, however, the importance of the subject and the impatience with which reliable news is awaited, I hasten to telegraph a summary of the Herald explorer's letters, which are full of the most romantic interest, while affirming, emphatically, the safety of Dr. Livingstone.

Under the terms of the arrangement between the *New York Herald* and the *Daily Telegraph* in London, the dispatch appeared in the British newspaper the following day under the headline 'Dr. Livingstone's Safety – Outline of his Discoveries'. The news was now out and by 4 July, Independence Day in the United States, the story of the American newspaper's great scoop was headline news around the world.

During his time with Livingstone at Ujiji, Stanley experienced a series of recurrent nightmares over which he had no control. What if Bennett had forgotten his 'special correspondent' in Africa and given him up for lost? What if Livingstone's story was no longer hot news in New York, replaced by another of Bennett's whimsical topics? Despite instructions to 'take a thousand dollars, and when that is spent, take another, but *Find Livingstone!*', had the proprietor been frightened off by the sums Stanley had spent on the expedition and refused to honour loans taken out in Zanzibar on the paper's behalf? What if the 'swift and trusty' messengers employed to run back to the coast with Stanley's handwritten dispatches were captured and killed by Mirambo's men or refused to travel further than the fleshpots of Unyanyembe? What if the messenger became ill and died somewhere along the pathway to the coast – or simply gave up and dumped the dispatch in the jungle? These and other anxieties were always at the back of Stanley's mind as he sat under the verandah at Livingstone's *tembe* and listened to the doctor's story of his ill-fated African expedition and his belief that 'in the broad and mighty Lualaba he has discovered the head waters of the Nile'.

Livingstone's health and spirits improved with each new day. Stanley recorded: 'Life had been brought back to him; his fading vitality was restored, his enthusiasm for his work was growing up again into a height that was compelling him to desire to be up and doing.' Stanley gently introduced the question of Livingstone returning home to rest from his travels, reacquaint himself with his family, enjoy the adulation that would be bestowed on him, receive honours, give lectures, encourage commerce, speak out against slavery – and get some false teeth to replace his decayed and worn ones. Livingstone was firm in his reply: 'No; not until my work is ended . . . I should like very much to go home and see my children once again, but I cannot bring my heart to abandon the task I have undertaken, when it is so nearly completed. It only requires six or seven months more to trace the true source that I have discovered. . . . Why should I go home before my task is ended, to have to come back again to do what I can very well do now?'

Livingstone told Stanley how after exploring 600 miles of watershed along the Lualaba, tracing all the principal streams discharging into its central line of drainage, his men had mutinied and refused to go further. Before continuing he had had to trudge 700 miles back to Ujiji to collect stores – only to find them sold and the proceeds gone.

The doctor's African tales were carefully recorded by Stanley in his reporter's notepads by day and at night he would return to his room in the *tembe* and, by the light of an oil lamp, transcribe them into riveting personalised articles, which were then passed to other messengers to rush back to the coast. Eleven long and exclusive dispatches of varying length about Stanley's quest for Livingstone and accounts of the doctor's African adventures found their way to New York in this way. Stanley knew that if Bennett liked what he read, he would want more exciting copy about Livingstone to fill pages of his newspaper. But as each dispatch appeared in print, Stanley had no idea how his work was being received by Bennett and his *New York Herald* readers. Stanley knew his articles were major scoops, but he feared that nobody else shared his opinion and his words might be treated as little more than small page fillers once they arrived on Bennett's desk at Broadway and Ann Street.

Nothing could have been further from the truth.

Stanley's dispatches were critical of Livingstone's former expedition companion, Dr John Kirk, the man charged by the Royal Geographical Society with ensuring that the doctor had adequate supplies within reach. Stanley's articles described Kirk as Livingstone's 'quondam companion . . . a sad student of human nature . . . a most malicious person', who had acted in 'gross ignorance' for failing to know the doctor's whereabouts during Stanley's time in Zanzibar. Readers were told how Kirk had failed correctly to monitor the progress of supplies and letters sent to Livingstone by the Society from Zanzibar, how unsupervised porters carrying the goods had been lazing in Bagamoyo for three and a half months and how the *New York Herald* expedition had taken charge of the goods at Unyanyembe. According to Stanley, Kirk preferred to spend his time big game hunting instead of looking after British interests.

There was no love lost between the arrogant Stanley and the aloof Kirk and the reporter's dispatches were designed to discredit the Acting British Consul. If Kirk had been more cooperative towards Stanley in Zanzibar, he might have appeared in a better light in the pages of the *New York Herald*. Instead, Kirk figured as the worst type of British buffoon, lording it over his little Zanzibar fiefdom while the world's best-loved missionary-explorer suffered hardships in darkest Africa. Even Livingstone openly expressed disappointment in his former friend and was quoted as calling him 'lazy and indifferent' and 'no longer a companion'.

Under the headline 'Dr. Kirk's Neglect' Stanley hinted that Kirk should be recalled to London and, on behalf of all British people, be reprimanded for his indifference towards Livingstone. 'It is the case of the British public vs. Dr. John Kirk, Her Britannic Majesty's Consul at Zanzibar', wrote Stanley, implying that if such an issue were further publicly aired, Kirk would be branded the guilty party.

According to Stanley, Livingstone was 'not an angel; but he approaches to that being as near as the nature of a living man will allow'. As to the rumour that Livingstone had married an African princess, 'it is unnecessary to say more than that it is untrue and it is utterly beneath a gentleman even to hint at such a thing in connection with the name of Dr. Livingstone'. He told *New York Herald* readers:

> You may take any point in Livingstone's character and analyse it carefully and I would challenge any man to find a fault in it. . . . His gentleness never forsakes him; his hopefulness never deserts him. No harassing anxieties, distraction of mind, long separation of home and kindred, can make him complain. He thinks 'all will come out right at last'; he has such faith in the goodness of Providence. . . . To the stern dictates of duty, alone, he has sacrificed his home and ease, the pleasures, refinements, and luxuries of a civilised life. His is the Spartan heroism, the inflexibility of the Roman, the enduring resolution of the Anglo-Saxon – never to relinquish his work, though his heart yearns for home; never to surrender his obligations until he can write *Finis* to his work. . . . Each Sunday morning he gathers his little flock around

him, and reads prayers and a chapter from the Bible in a natural, unaffected, and sincere tone; and afterwards delivers a short address in the Kisawahili language, about the subject read to them, which is listened to with evident interest and attention.

According to Stanley, Livingstone was of a breed of men who rarely came along and, when they did, were forced to endure hardship and torment in God's name – in other words, a living, breathing, walking, talking, travelling saint from the same mould as the Apostles and St Christopher. And Stanley felt it his duty to set about Livingstone's beatification through the pages of his newspaper.

Thanks to Stanley's care and attention, Livingstone soon felt strong enough to travel again. The young reporter made sure that the doctor ate four balanced square meals daily and even made butter for his new friend from milk produced by cattle in the Ujiji marketplace. The travellers agreed to join forces to explore the northern end of Lake Tanganyika in order to discover if the lake had an outlet. Using 'nothing more than a cranky canoe hollowed out of a noble mvule tree of Ugoma', the travellers – plus sixteen rowers, a cook and two local guides – were hoping to discover a possible waterway for boats travelling along the Nile and onwards down the lake to Ujiji.

For a week, the expedition moved across the calm water of the lake, past fishing villages, islands and peaceful coves. They arrived at a point further north than that reached by Burton and Speke, where they discovered that a river called the Lusize ran into the lake – and not out of it, disproving the theory that the Tanganyika and a second lake, known to the natives as Muta Nzige (Lake Albert) were linked by the watercourse. It was a minor discovery, but sufficient to rekindle Livingstone's enthusiasm for travel once again and an opportunity for Stanley to observe the doctor in exploring mode. During the latter part of the expedition, they were attacked by tribes who thought they were slavers come for new captives. It was Livingstone's calm and reasoning behaviour – and his ability to speak their language – which saved the day and impressed Stanley.

On the ninth day, Stanley was stricken with fever, his first illness since leaving Unyanyembe. 'During the intervals of agony and unconsciousness, I saw, or I fancied I saw, Livingstone's form moving towards me, and felt, or fancied I felt, Livingstone's hand tenderly feeling my hot head and limbs,' Stanley reported. 'But though this fever, having enjoyed immunity from it for three months, was more severe than usual, I did not much regret its occurrence, since I became the recipient of the very tender and fatherly kindness of the good man whose companion I now found myself.'

In a short time, a special bond developed between Stanley and Livingstone, similar to the relationship between father and son. One day when Stanley was still partly delirious from the huge doses of quinine he had taken, he scolded a cook for failing to clean pots properly. The cook had the temerity to answer back and Stanley clouted the man. At the point where a major fight was about to break out between the two men, Livingstone appeared and calmly settled the dispute, reasoning with the cook, telling him he should be thankful that the 'little master' (Stanley) had come to the aid of the 'big master' (Livingstone), put food into their bellies and clothes on their back. The cook then apologised and wanted to kiss Stanley's feet, but the reporter would not allow it. By nightfall, Stanley and the cook had shaken hands and, thanks to Livingstone's paternal influence, the incident was forgotten.

Stanley was comfortable with Livingstone and the doctor found the American reporter serious, intelligent and the kind of stimulating company he had not enjoyed for so long. In the weeks spent together, they discussed many different subjects. Neither records if Stanley confessed his true identity and background to Livingstone or if the doctor spoke of his wife's alcoholism or his failure as a father. If Stanley had unburdened himself to anyone, it would have been to the man he had learned to trust and confide in while sitting on a mud verandah under the hot African sun hundreds of miles away from civilisation.

Livingstone's 'tembe' at Ujiji – a house
constructed from mud, wood, palms and
other native materials.

Chapter 22

'ON STANLEY, ON!'

Requests from the American Consul in Zanzibar to honour huge loans taken out by Stanley in the name of the *New York Herald* began arriving on James Gordon Bennett's desk before Stanley's dispatches. Bennett ignored them all. The fact that Stanley had been instructed to take as much money as was needed to find Livingstone had conveniently been forgotten. Instead, Bennett demanded to know from editorial staff what his reporter thought he was playing at, allowing months to pass without sending word of his progress. Nobody in the newsroom could answer the question.

It must have crossed Bennett's mind that Stanley had duped him and run off with large sums of money borrowed in the newspaper's name. He may have imagined that Stanley was living in the lap of luxury somewhere in the sun and if his competitors got to hear of it, Bennett would never again be able to show his face inside the fashionable New York clubs he loved to frequent.

Stanley had kept in touch with his editor as best he could. Because no direct telegraphic services were available from Zanzibar, communications had to be written and sent via ship to Bombay or Suez before being transmitted to London and on to New York. But Bennett judged the worth of his correspondents by the frequency of their dispatches and ability to get copy to him from the world's remotest regions. He was not interested in how hostile the terrain might be or how far a reporter might find himself from a telegraph station – Bennett wanted copy quickly even if the correspondent had to swim up waterfalls, run barefoot across burning deserts or dig a hole through the earth's crust. He wanted it fast and first.

Bennett was accustomed to receiving regular dispatches from Stanley as he made his way through assignments the editor had given him from his Paris hotel suite. When Stanley's communications dried up and there was silence, Bennett imagined the worst. Stanley had either jumped ship, joined a rival news organisation, absconded with a box full of money – or was dead.

It had been over three months since Stanley's short dispatch announcing 'receipt of positive intelligence of the safety of Dr. Livingstone' had arrived. Everyone at the *New York Herald* was now holding their collective breath for Stanley's next dispatch, having no idea of whether it might appear the following day, week, month – or year. Desperate to keep the scoop alive and the *Herald*'s role in the discovery prominent, Bennett reprinted a letter from Dr John Kirk that had already appeared in a British newspaper. Published on 11 December 1871, it mentioned that war between Mirambo, warlord chief of the Ruga-Ruga and Unyanyembe's Arabs had caused the road from Unyanyembe to Ujiji to be closed and that 'Mr. Stanley, an American gentleman' (the first time he had been identified by his name in the paper) had sent word to the American Consul that Livingstone might try to find his way back to civilisation via an alternative route. Kirk's letter provided no new information, but was enough to remind readers that the *New York Herald* still played an important part in the story.

Finally, on 21 December, a member of Bennett's news staff burst into the editor's office to announce that a long dispatch had arrived from Africa. They pored over the contents and read how the reporter had undertaken the business of recruiting and equipping his caravan and begun his march towards Ujiji. He described the trials and tribulations of trading with native tribes, horrors of the Makata swamp, sickness and desertions encountered on the journey and reports from fellow travellers about Livingstone. Bennett discarded editorial copy originally scheduled for page 3 and gave it over entirely to Stanley's dispatch, which he published in full the following day.

Bennett was ecstatic. This was just the exclusive the *New York Herald* needed in the run-up to Christmas and he ordered editorial staff to prepare follow-up pieces designed to keep the story alive until receipt of Stanley's next dispatch – whenever that might be. Stanley was, once again, the golden boy of American journalism and there was no further newsroom talk of him absconding with Bennett's money, working for a rival or failing to communicate with his boss. Instead, he was held up as a shining example of a loyal reporter who kept his eye on only one thing – the story.

The next day's paper included a tribute to 'our experienced Oriental traveller charged with the bold enterprise of an expedition into the heart of Eastern Equatorial Africa in search of Dr. Livingstone'. It added that an

African expedition was something new in modern journalism and in this, as in other great achievements of 'the third estate', the credit of the first bold adventure in the cause of humanity, civilisation and science belonged to the *New York Herald*. It praised Stanley (but not by name), as 'a traveller of varied and extensive experience in whom we were satisfied was the very man to detail on the perilous search in the wild of Africa for Dr. Livingstone'. The editorial rounded on the British government as

> too slow and too penurious in its feeble attempts on behalf of Dr. Livingstone. From what our representative in this African journey has already accomplished with his small force we are sure that a properly equipped exploring expedition of five hundred men from the British government could traverse without difficulty the whole breadth of Equatorial Africa from sea to sea. . . . It may be months before we hear again from our courageous African traveller, but we are strong in the hope not only shall we hear from him again, but that we shall hear of the complete success of this great undertaking, both in regard to Dr. Livingstone and the outlet of Lake Tanganyika. And so, from year to year, we gather in the bounteous harvest for our readers 'from the rivers to the ends of the earth'.

Bennett then sat back and permitted competitors across America to trumpet their praise for the *New York Herald*, which he reproduced in his own newspaper:

> The *New York Herald* has just given another evidence of journalistic enterprise that throws in the shade any of its former great achievements – *Trenton Gazette* (New Jersey)

> It will put to shame the British government and the enterprise of British people that an American newspaper should be left to organise and carry out an expedition into the heart of Africa, to ascertain the whereabouts of the celebrated Dr. Livingstone – *New Bedford Standard (Mass.)*

> The most extraordinary enterprise ever dreamed of is that which the *New York Herald* has undertaken in fitting out an expedition to penetrate the interior regions of Africa, where Dr. Livingstone is supposed to be detained by the natives, either to rescue the great explorer if possible,

or clear up the mystery of his fate. . . . If the expedition should succeed in bringing back Dr. Livingstone, or determining the fact of his death if he has perished, the tremendous celebrity that it will give to the *Herald* will no doubt be worth all the cost – *Buffalo Express*

One of the most remarkable journalistic enterprises the world has known – *Cincinnati Enquirer*

There seems to be no limit to the wonderful activity of the *Herald* in gathering news. It spares no pains or expense and overcomes the greatest obstacles – *Indianapolis News*

To control public opinion has, hitherto, been the mission of the press, but now we have the great newspaper of America entering a new field of enterprise, that commercial and geographical facts may be ascertained and defined. The *Herald* stands aloof from the press of the country. It defies men, parties, news associations and political combinations – and now supplants governments and enters upon a task as novel as its conception was daring and original – *Memphis Beagle*

The latest marvel is in the newspaper world, and the organising and equipping at an enormous outlay by a single newspaper establishment, an expedition to search out in the interests of science and humanity, the great African explorer Dr. Livingstone. The honour of creating this epoch belongs to a leading American journal – the *New York Herald*. It is nothing new in the history of this remarkable paper, for a gigantic journalistic idea to be developed and carried out, but of its later masterstrokes none is so positively startling in the idealistic breadth and grandeur than its Livingstone expedition, under the command of the gifted and courageous Stanley. It is the crowning point of the *Herald*'s enterprise. Had Livingstone been an American, the world would have marvelled at the expeditionary idea; but being a British subject, we are lost in admiration at the sweeping spirit of liberality made in the matter. . . . A fitting motto for the *Herald*'s Livingstone search expedition is found in the last words of [Sir Walter Scott's] *Marmion* – 'On Stanley, On!' – *Newark Journal*

Covered in embarrassment 'because bold American enterprise had succeeded in doing something British interests should have achieved two years before', the Royal Geographical Society announced in January 1872 that it was sending an expedition of its own to rescue Livingstone.

The Society stated that while Stanley had sent back positive news about Livingstone, the war between Mirambo's mercenaries and Arabs at Unyanyembe had obviously rendered it impossible for his expedition to reach Ujiji. The Society had, therefore, approached Her Majesty's Treasury for funds, promising to match pound for pound any sum donated by the government, stating that Livingstone's achievements belonged to the nation, which must now do its bit to bring the missionary-traveller safely home. It took the Treasury two weeks to respond: 'My Lords are of the opinion that the direction of the expedition is too doubtful to warrant the expense.' So the Society called for public subscriptions and £1,700 was raised with a promise of £1,500 more.

Daily Telegraph readers were told that Britain's 'national honour is at stake' and that expedition members handpicked to sail to Africa, walk halfway across the continent and rescue Livingstone included Lieutenant Llewellyn Dawson, RN, a naval officer with experience in China, Lieutenant William Henn, RN, Oswald Livingstone, the doctor's twenty-year-old son and Charles New, a missionary from Mombasa with knowledge of local native languages. They sailed from Southampton to Zanzibar on the steamer *Aydos* – just as Stanley and Livingstone were walking back together in the direction of Unyanyembe, where Stanley planned to equip the doctor with fresh supplies. The *Telegraph* added:

An American newspaper shamed the British people into this effort, not by high-sounding editorial verbiage, but by quiet and effective action. Actions do, indeed, speak louder than words, as is herein so thoroughly demonstrated by our contemporary's active triumph. If nothing more than is already known should come of the *Herald*'s expedition, enough has already been accomplished to command for our contemporary the proudest position yet achieved by any newspaper in what is called 'the fourth estate', but which is fast becoming the first. All honour to the journal whose founder and proprietor is justly entitled to be called the father of American journalism – and that means of the world. What the venerable Morse has accomplished for the electric telegraph, the white-haired septuagenarian Bennett has for a newspaper press.

In a lighter vein, and with tongue firmly in cheek, a letter published in the *New York Herald* on 5 May 1872 asked,

Sir – can't you 'let up' a little, on Livingstone? Has he any relatives 'on' the *Herald* that expect to become his heirs? Do you really wish to 'discover' him? Take my advice. Let the doctor alone (and if alive, he'll come home like Little Bo Peep), that is, if taking another view of the case, he hasn't gone off on the tail of a comet to see a running match on the Milky Way Race Track; in which case, with its usual enterprise, the *Herald* will have to establish an observatory to 'discover' him. Yours truly in the interest of Science . . . *(author not identified!)*.

And from *The Times*, London, 14 May 1872:

The RGS met on this date. . . . The organisation is 'very embarrassed' that they have not announced the discovery of Livingstone. There was good reason to believe that Mr. Stanley and Dr. Livingstone would meet at the beginning of the year, most probably on Lake Tanganyika. There was, however, one point upon which it might be well to set the public right. It has been generally inferred from the intelligence that Mr. Stanley had discovered and relieved Dr. Livingstone; but if there had been any discovery and relief it was *Dr. Livingstone who had discovered and relieved Mr. Stanley*. Dr. Livingstone, indeed, is in clover while Mr. Stanley is nearly destitute. It was known that he was without supplies and must have undergone much hardship and privation before he had reached Ujiji . . . where Dr. Livingstone had large stores and he was consequently in a position to assist Mr. Stanley on reaching that place. The President said he did not by any means desire to undervalue the exertions of Mr. Stanley and he thought it highly creditable to him to have penetrated so far and to have accomplished such a journey. He hoped that the expedition, which had left England, would discover and relieve them both and enable them to continue and complete their explorations. . . . He wished to say that never from the commencement since they had heard from Dr. Livingstone, had the council of the Geographic Society given countenance to the suspicion that Dr. Livingstone was no more. Dr. Livingstone was so well known in that part of Africa that if anything untoward had happened to him, intelligence would have reached the coast with great rapidity.

In June, pages of the *New York Herald* suddenly appeared with heavy black borders in solemn tribute to James Gordon Bennett 'the Elder', the paper's founder, editor and proprietor, who had died, aged seventy-seven, after an illness. Bennett Jr used the opportunity to divert reader's attention from the fact that nothing new had been received from Stanley since September. For days afterwards, the paper's pages were filled with tributes from the great, the good and rival newspapers. As the old man was buried in New York's Greenwood Cemetery, his large fortune passed into the hands of his son.

On 14 June 1872, the *New York Herald* informed its readers:

Mr. Oswald Livingstone, son of the explorer, writing from Zanzibar in the later days of April last, says: 'A caravan has arrived from Unyanyembe and we have seen some of the leading men who say that Stanley has reached Ujiji where he has met my father who has received the supplies sent up to him. There are no letters from them at this moment. I am inclined to think that some supplies have reached Ujiji and there is little doubt that Stanley has left.

On the eve of American Independence Day 1872, the *New York Herald* was again reflective – and desperate to receive another dispatch from Stanley. The article, headlined 'Review of the Progress of Geographical Discovery', likened Stanley and Livingstone to Ulysses, Ptolemy, Marco Polo, Bartholomeu Diaz, Vasco da Gama, Christopher Columbus, Cortez, Pizarro, Magellan, Captain Cook, Sebastian Cabot, Sir John Franklin, General Freemont, Burke and Wills, 'names with which we are all enthusiastically familiar along with their toil, suffering, courage and perseverance. . . . We can regard the wonderful triumph of Stanley, the *Herald*'s explorer, in his successful search for Livingstone, as a splendid triumph for the whole of the American press. Henceforth, the great discoveries of the world, scientific and geographical, are to be heralded not by the slow and ineffectual reams of books and through the ordinary agencies of publication, but by the press of the land.'

By now, Stanley was on his way back to the coast, but his dispatch announcing his meeting with Livingstone had still to appear in the outside world. Actual news of his return to Zanzibar preceded his remaining dispatches. On 4 July 1872 the *New York Herald* published a special report from London:

Copious information regarding the safety of Dr. Livingstone and the success of his explorations in equatorial Africa, is the great sensation of the day. The *Herald*'s dispatches have been quoted in all evening papers published in the city and large placards have been copiously posted in every quarter of London calling to attention news of the great explorer. These are surrounded by citizens who discuss the *Herald*'s feat. Leading London publishers have thronged the London Bureau of the *New York Herald* in Fleet Street. They profess the greatest anxiety to get into communication with the Commander of the *Herald*'s expedition. Their intentions are to anticipate the American publishers by bidding for a record of his experiences outside that which he will furnish exclusively to the *Herald*. Competition is keen between representatives of book publications here and they are prepared to offer large sums. Several of the best artists of illustrated journals have also called with the objective of securing a likeness of Mr. Stanley and to bid for the publication in their sheets of any sketches he may have made on the road to Ujiji and return to the sea coast. Next to Livingstone and Stanley, Mirambo . . . is among the prime favourites for pencil engrave treatment. It may be judged from the foregoing evidences how high the excitement runs among the entire people of Great Britain. The glorious news has been flushed far and wide and is the subject of universal and admiring comment on the *Herald*'s great success.

On the same day the *London News* published a letter which no one was expecting:

From R.O. Abergele – Your paper of the 18th instance states that Mr. Stanley, the representative of the *New York Herald*, which has proceeded to Africa in search of Dr. Livingstone is a Mr. John Thomas, a native of Denbigh, whose mother, at the present time, keeps a public house in St. Asaph. May I beg of you to correct the above statement in your next impression? Mr. Stanley's proper name is John Rowlands and his mother, at the present time, keeps a public house called The Castle Arms close to St. Hilary's Church, Denbigh, and not a house at St. Asaph as above stated. His grandfather on the paternal side was the late Mr. John Rowlands and on the maternal side, the late Mr. Moses Parry. Yours obediently.

An eagle-eyed reporter on the *Carnarvon and Denbigh Herald* was soon on the story and reported:

> Mr. Stanley, by discovering the hero of Africa, has himself become the hero of the hour. The discoverer of the 'African lion' has himself been lionised as no man ever was in this country perhaps since Livingstone himself paid us a visit a few years ago. All heroes move in a halo of mystery, so does Mr. Stanley. He has cleared up the Livingstone mystery only to create a Stanley mystery. To the geographers he is a sore puzzle and to the genealogists he seems to be no less a puzzle . . . he has left a deeper mystery still to hang over two important things – the source of the Nile and his own origin, especially the latter. What country has had the honour of giving him birth? This is the vexed question that has been asked again and again and to which no satisfactory answer has yet been given. 'He is a Welshman.' 'No, he is an American.' 'Denbigh is his native town.' 'No, Missouri, and not Wales, is his birthplace.' These are the conflicting replies that have been given to the puzzling question. Livingstone was lost to the world for years and the great question used to be 'Who will find him for us?' Stanley gloriously answered the question. Now Stanley's nationality is lost, and the great question for some time has been 'Who will find it for us?'

Catching the spirit of the intrepid traveller, a reporter went out in search of Stanley's 'lost' nationality and, to settle the question, located Stanley's mother at the Cross Foxes Inn, where he asked her to confirm or deny her relationship with Stanley. She replied, 'that she was, and that it would be impossible for her to deny it, even if she wished' that Henry Morton Stanley was her son, reported the journalist. Betsy produced four photographs of her famous son, taken at different times in America, Asia and Africa plus books he had sent as presents inscribed 'from Henry Morton Stanley'.

Betsy enjoyed the attention she was receiving from the reporter and confirmed that Stanley's real name was John Rowlands, now thirty-two years old, who had gone to New Orleans fifteen years before. She revealed that he was employed there by a gentleman 'and it was after him that he adopted the name of Stanley'. She spoke of his job as 'a special correspondent' for the *Missouri Democrat*, of his work for the *New York Herald* and how he visited his proud mother whenever he was back in the country. There was no mention of Stanley's 'real' father or why Betsy had allowed her boy to spend his formative years in the local workhouse. 'We were also told that there is no question but that he will in due time come out and declare that he is a native of Wales', the paper proudly announced.

Pagazi porters from the *New York Herald* expedition carry supplies across a swollen river on the march back to the coast.

Chapter 23

MISSION ACCOMPLISHED

Stanley and Livingstone's voyage on Lake Tanganyika – Livingstone called it 'our little picnic', Stanley referred to it as 'our cruise' – lasted twenty-eight days and covered over 300 miles of water. It was now time for Stanley to return to the coast and civilisation. During their Tanganyika expedition, Livingstone had agreed to accompany Stanley as far as Unyanyembe to collect any stores from Kirk's caravans that might be waiting. Livingstone drew up a list of additional supplies he needed for his expedition to find the source of the Nile. He asked Stanley – not Dr Kirk – to send them, along with fifty porters, each 'a reliable and free man'. Stanley selected a route to Unyanyembe avoiding tribal lands in which chiefs of Mirambo's Ruga-Ruga might delay them.

On returning to Ujiji, Livingstone began writing in earnest. One of his first letters was to James Gordon Bennett and after showing the letter to Stanley, the American reporter urged him to add the word 'Junior' after the editor's name 'as it was young Mr. Bennett to whom he was indebted'. Stanley hoped his editor would be delighted with the contents and publish it in full in the *New York Herald*. His diary states: 'The feelings of his heart had fond expression in the grateful words he had written; and if I judged Mr. Bennett rightly, I knew he would be satisfied with it. For it was not the geographical news he cared so much about, as the grand fact of Livingstone being alive or dead.' To James Gordon Bennett, Livingstone wrote:

It is in general somewhat difficult to write to one we have never seen . . . but the presence of your representative, Mr. Stanley, in this distant region takes away the strangeness I should otherwise have felt, and in writing to thank you for the extreme kindness that prompted you to send him, I feel quite at home . . . I am as cold and non-demonstrative as we islanders are reputed to be, but your kindness made my frame thrill. It was, indeed, overwhelming, and I said in my soul, 'Let the richest blessings descend from the Highest on you and yours!' . . . If my disclosures regarding the terrible Ujijian slavery should lead to the suppression of the east coast slave trade, I shall regard that as a greater matter by far than the discovery of all the Nile sources together. Now that you have done with domestic slavery all forever, lend us your powerful aid towards this great object. This fine country is blighted as with a curse from above . . . thanking you most cordially for your great generosity, I am gratefully yours. . . .

Livingstone wrote other letters to his children, the Royal Geographical Society, the Foreign Secretary and to personal friends. In total, twenty letters were addressed to Great Britain, six to Bombay, two to New York and two to Zanzibar – one an angry letter of complaint addressed to Dr John Kirk about his failure to send supplies into the interior and a second to Zanzibar's Sultan Barghash bin Sayid about the slave trade at Unyanyembe and Ujiji. Stanley even persuaded the doctor to write some exclusive pieces for the *New York Herald*, providing yet another scoop and allowing Bennett to extend the life of the story that had turned the journal into the Western world's most talked about newspaper.

To his daughter Agnes he described the events leading up to the time when Stanley appeared at Ujiji:

. . . An American flag at the head of a large caravan showed the nationality of the stranger. Baths, tents, saddles, big kettles, showed that he was not a poor Lazarus like me. He turned out to be Henry Morland Stanley,* travelling correspondent to the *New York Herald* sent specially to find out if I were really alive, and if dead, to bring home my bones. He had brought an abundance of goods at great expense. . . . To all he had I was made free. . . . He laid all he had at my service, divided his clothes into two heaps, and pressed one heap upon me; then his medicine chest;

---

* In his letter to Agnes Livingstone, the doctor referred to Henry 'Morland' Stanley, long after Stanley had ceased using it as an experimental middle name. Possibly, Stanley was considering replacing 'Morton' with 'Moreland' on returning to civilisation, where he would introduce the name in the book he expected to write about Livingstone's discovery. Not that it mattered. Livingstone referred to Stanley throughout their time in Africa as 'Mr Stanley', while Stanley addressed Livingstone as 'Doctor'.

Henry Morton Stanley was born 'John Rowlands – Bastard' in a small whitewashed cottage called Castle Row in the shadow of Denbigh Castle in the Vale of Clwyd, North Wales, on 28 January 1841. His grandfather, Moses Parry, was a local butcher and owned the cottage.

Between the ages of six and fifteen, John Rowlands was an inmate at the St Asaph Poor Law Union Workhouse, built between 1839 and 1840, 6 miles east of Denbigh and south of the village of St Asaph. Today the building is known as the H.M. Stanley Hospital.

The first known photograph of John Rowlands taken in 1856 when he was aged fifteen and about to enter the National School at Holywell, run by his cousin, Moses Owen. He was engaged as a 'pupil-teacher' – a monitor or school helper – and is pictured wearing a new suit of clothes 'suitable for a young scholar' bought for him by his Aunt Mary to wear in his new job. A travelling photographer, 'J. Laing, Castle Street, Shrewsbury and Queen Street, Wellington, Salop', took the picture.

It was while serving on the Yankee warship *Minnesota* that Stanley became friends with a fifteen-year-old enlisted sailor from Sayville, Long Island, called Lewis Noe, who joined as a messenger at Hampton Road, Vermont in June 1864. *(Christie's Images)*

Stanley, pictured in the military officer's coat he bought in a Constantinople bazaar in 1866 and wore to impress friends and relatives – including his mother and inmates at the St Asaph Workhouse. Photographed by Abdullah Freres, Constantinople. *(Christie's Images)*

Stanley revisited the scene of his earliest childhood at Denbigh Castle on 14 December 1866 wearing his bogus military uniform coat and wrote the following lie in the Royal Denbigh Bowls Club visitors' book: 'John Rowlands formerly of this castle, now Ensign in the United States Navy in North America belonging to the US Ship *Ticonderoga* now at Constantinople, Turkey. Absent on furlough.' (*Reproduced courtesy of the Clwyd Family History Society*)

In August 1867, Stanley found time to write to Lewis Noe: 'I am with Hancock's Command hunting Indians. . . . I am a Special Correspondent. Copies of my articles will be sent to you. When in Liverpool, I promised you any curiosities I could get as I always think of you and I have already succeeded in getting a bow and twenty arrows from a Comanche Chief . . . I will send anything else I get as soon as I reach St Louis. You need not write to me, as we are moving into the interior of the territories and are on "the war path".' My deep respect for all and in the meantime, God bless you. Your brother, Henry.'

James Gordon Bennett Jr, the flamboyant proprietor and editor of the *New York Herald* who summoned Stanley to his Paris hotel room in October 1869 and ordered him to go and 'Find Livingstone!!'. The image was drawn by Constantine von Grimm – 'Nemo' – for *Vanity Fair* in November 1884.

A study of Dr David Livingstone, commissioned by publisher John Murray to illustrate *The Last Journals of David Livingstone in Central Africa* (1874).

The famous meeting between Stanley and Livingstone at Ujiji, Lake Tanganyika, on 3 November 1871 – although Stanley mistakenly recorded the date as 10 November. It appeared in his book *How I Found Livingstone* and was widely used in newspapers and magazines. Stanley wrote: 'This engraving, for which I supplied the materials . . . is as correct as if the scene had been photographed.'

'The Main Stream Came Up to Susi's Mouth' – an illustration from *The Last Journals of David Livingstone* published in 1874 – showing an enfeebled doctor carried across a swollen river on the shoulders of his loyal servant, Susi, rain falling in torrents and other natives up to their necks in water. In reviewing the book, *The Times* stated that the image was an emblem of Livingstone's martyrdom.

The biggest scoop of the nineteenth century – 1872 headlines from the *New York Herald* exclusively announcing Stanley's successful discovery of Livingstone in the African interior.

LIVINGSTONE FOUND.

Herald Special Report from Zanzibar.

Detailed News of the Herald African Exploring Expedition.

CONFIRMATION OF THE FORMER REPORTS.

Livingstone and Stanley Together at Ujiji.

HOW THE WELCOME TIDINGS CAME.

THE SLAVE COURIER, SA'EED.

Story of Seyd ben Majid, the Arab Chief.

Difficulties and Pluck of the Herald Explorer.

THE NATIVE WAR NEAR UNYANYEMBE.

A LONG DETOUR NECESSARY.

The Herald Forces Waiting at Ujiji.

Face to Face with Livingstone at Last.

What Must Have Been a Happy Meeting.

Livingstone's Explorations Among the Great Lakes.

Impressive Triumph of Herald Enterprise.

TELEGRAM TO THE NEW YORK HERALD.

LONDON, May 20, 1872.

The following special despatch concerning the safety of Dr. Livingstone was received to-day at the Bureau of the NEW YORK HERALD here from the resident HERALD correspondent at Zanzibar. It was telegraphed direct from Aden, having reached there by the regular mail steamer from Zanzibar:—

THE GLORIOUS CONFIRMATION.

I have just received the following detailed confirmation of the rumor which formerly reached here, and which I sent on to you, that Stanley had found Livingstone, and that the

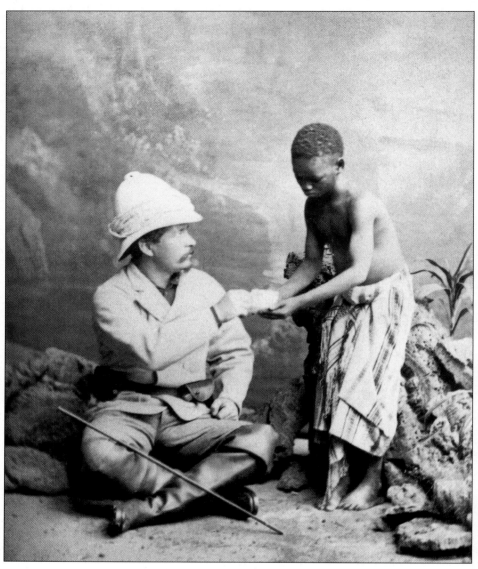

In a simulation of an African scene, Stanley, wearing the same clothes he wore when he met Livingstone for the first time, was photographed with his young companion, Kalulu – where master and servant re-enacted their roles for the camera.

Livingstone and Stanley meet again in London in the October 1872 issue of *Tailor and Cutter*, in a fanciful scene predicting the fashionable clothing they might have worn for the encounter.

The only picture in existence of Stanley's mother, Mrs Elizabeth Jones – the former Betsy Parry – landlady of the Cross Foxes public house at Glascoed, near Denbigh. In middle age, Mrs Jones had become a respectable member of the Glascoed community, with no scandalous evidence of illegitimate children to be found anywhere. The sketch was made in 1872 after she admitted to a reporter that she was Stanley's mother. By this time she had become plump and matronly and the artist sketched her standing in the gateway of her garden, her dark hair tied into a bun, wearing spectacles, a long apron and holding a nearly completed woollen sock hanging from a knitting needle. (*Hel Achau, Journal of the Clwyd Family Historical Society*).

Following its capture, Coomassie was burned to the ground, King Coffi's stone palace blown up and Sir Garnet Wolseley's men ordered to fall in and return to the coast. The Anglo-Ashanti campaign was a total success for England and another African adventure for Henry Morton Stanley.

The first photograph ever to travel down the Congo River – a *carte de visite* portrait of Alice Pike, Stanley's second great love, given to him in 1874 on the eve of his attempt to finish Livingstone's exploration work. Alice was seventeen when she met Stanley at the Langham Hotel. He was thirty-three. Alice accepted Stanley's marriage proposal, but her mother insisted they wait for his return from Africa. Alice later married the industrialist, Albert Barney. (*Christie's Images*)

A pair of 'eager, courageous, devoted and adventurous lads' called Edward 'Ted' Pocock (left) and Francis 'Frank' John Pocock, from Lower Upnor, Kent were engaged as Stanley's assistants on the Anglo-American Expedition. The Pocock brothers were sons of a fisherman and experienced boatmen, having spent their entire lives on the River Medway. Ted died of smallpox in January 1875 and his brother was drowned in the Congo in June 1877.

H.M. Stanley after the 1874 expedition.

Hamed bin Mohammed, better known as Tippu-Tib, was one of Africa's most notorious slavers.

King Leopold II of Belgium, told by his father to 'file his brain on other people's' and owner of a brain so large 'that one might wonder whether it didn't usurp the place of the heart'. With Stanley's help, Leopold was to acquire an African kingdom the size of Western Europe.

German-born physician and naturalist, Eduard Schnitzer, better known to the people of Equatoria as Mohammed Emin Pasha.

Stanley in the custom-made
uniform and hat he wore during
the Emin Pasha Relief Expedition.

UNITED
KINGDOM
TEA COMPANY'S
TEAS.

USED ALL OVER THE
WORLD!

NOTHING LIKE THEM
ANYWHERE!!!

1/3, 1/6, 1/9, & 2/- a lb.

First Hand,
Direct from the Mincing Lane Market.

Supplied to the
House of Commons.

7, 10, 14, and 20 lbs. packed in
Canisters without extra charge.

Delivered to any Address
Carriage Paid.

STANLEY : " Well, Emin, old fellow, this Cup of the United Kingdom Tea Company's Tea makes us forget all our troubles."
EMIN : " So it does, my boy."

UNITED KINGDOM TEA COMPANY, Limited.

Offices, 21, MINCING LANE, LONDON. Duty Paid Stores, Imperial Warehouse, Leman Street, London.

Stanley and Emin Pasha are the 'stars' of a magazine advertisement for the United
Kingdom Tea Company. Stanley: 'Well, Emin, old fellow, this cup of the United Kingdom
Tea Company's tea makes us forget all our troubles.' Emin: 'So it does my boy.'

THE GRAPHIC

AN ILLUSTRATED WEEKLY NEWSPAPER

No. 1,067.—Vol. XLI.] EDITION
Registered as a Newspaper] DE LUXE

SATURDAY, MAY 10, 1890

WITH EXTRA SUPPLEMENT [PRICE NINEPENCE
By Post 9½d.

MR. STANLEY AT THE ALBERT HALL
THE EXPLORER LECTURING BEFORE THE ROYAL GEOGRAPHICAL SOCIETY

The Royal Geographical Society honoured Stanley on 5 May 1890, by hiring London's Royal Albert Hall and filling it to the rafters with thousands of people wanting to witness the world's best-known explorer receive a special gold medal. Standing under a giant map of the Congo basin, Stanley told an audience of royalty, the peerage, politicians, scientists, writers and 'all classes of society' that this was by far the grandest assembly he had ever seen. He kept his audience in raptures telling the story of Emin's Pasha's rescue.

Dorothy Tennant turned down Stanley's first marriage proposal. She later told him that if he asked her again, she would accept.

PERSEVERANDO

EX LIBRIS

SIR·HENRY·M·STANLEY
FVRZE·HILL·SVRREY

A. Marchi   inv. del.

Furze Hill, Pirbright, Surrey – Stanley's country estate and a place where he could be happy with Dorothy and his son, Denzil.

then his goods and everything he had, and to coax my appetite, often cooked dainty dishes with his own hand. He came with the true American characteristic generosity. The tears often started into my eyes on every fresh proof of kindness. My appetite returned and I ate three or four times a day, instead of scanty meals morning and evening.

Livingstone also entrusted his personal journals to Stanley's care. The journal, carefully written into the pages of a Letts Diary, along with letters and other personal papers, was wrapped in a waterproof canvas cover and the words: 'Positively not to be opened' written across the front. Stanley gave the doctor his assurance that all letters would be posted within twenty-four hours of his arrival in London.

On 28 December 1871, Stanley, Livingstone and their caravan left Ujiji, the doctor and reporter travelling in a pair of large canoes, Mrs Webb's stars and stripes fluttering at the stern of Stanley's and the Union Jack at the stern of Livingstone's. Bombay led the rest of the caravan, including little Kalulu, herds of goats, sheep and donkeys, along the bank. They left the lake on 7 January 1872 and continued the rest of the way on foot, arriving at Unyanyembe fifty-three days later, on 18 February.

During the journey they passed through a deep forest where they came across the bleached skull of a fellow traveller. It was here that Livingstone confided to Stanley: 'I could never pass through an African forest, with its solemn stillness and serenity, without wishing to be buried quietly under the dead leaves. . . . In England there is no elbow room, the graves are often desecrated and ever since my wife was buried in the woods of Shupanga I have sighed for just such a spot, where my weary bones will receive the eternal rest they covet.'

Waiting at Unyanyembe were Livingstone's stores from the Royal Geographical Society which Dr Kirk had dispatched from the coast over a year before and Stanley had placed in safekeeping. That night the doctor insisted that Stanley be a guest at his table and they should feast together on his supplies.

Like hungry schoolboys, Stanley and Livingstone broke open one of the wooden crates containing the doctor's supplies. Inside were three tins of broken biscuits and six tins of potted ham – 'tiny things, not much larger than thimbles, which, when opened, proved to be nothing more than a table-spoonful of minced meat plentifully seasoned with pepper'. Stanley commented that supplies purchased by Kirk 'fell five hundred degrees below zero in my estimation'. Other crates held stone pots of jam, each containing a little over a teaspoonful of preserve. There was a Dutch cheese 'hard as a brick' and two sugar loaves. Another box revealed candles, salt, various sauces, essence of anchovies, pepper and mustard – hardly suitable fare for hungry travellers hundreds of miles from civilisation. There were potted meats, tinned soup and a box containing shirts, shoes, shoelaces and socks for the doctor, the only things of value to the missionary-traveller.

Stanley's own supplies left at Unyanyembe had been tampered with, including the bales of cloth and tools. Fortunately, it was easy to buy fresh food at Unyanyembe and Stanley purchased the ingredients for the Christmas dinner they had been unable to enjoy two months earlier. This time, the meal was a great success, washed down with some champagne and brandy, which the thief had failed to discover among Stanley's provisions.

Before leaving Livingstone, Stanley examined his own goods and turned half of them over to Livingstone, sufficient to last him until his return to Ujiji and onwards in search of the source of the Nile – enough for four years. They included over 2,000 yards of cloth, sacks of beads, 300lb of brass wire, a waterproof tent, an airbed, a canvas boat, tools, barrels of tar, sheets of ship's copper, rifles and a revolver plus ammunition, cooking utensils, a medicine chest, books, a sextant and clothes. The goods were packed into forty loads. Stanley promised he would 'hurry to the coast as if on a matter of life or death' and, after arriving in Zanzibar, enlist fifty men, arm each with a gun and hatchet and send them to Livingstone at Ujiji to follow him wherever he wanted to go. Without help from strong and trusty men, all the supplies in the world were useless to Livingstone.

By 13 March 1872, Stanley had spent four months and four days in Livingstone's company. He recorded:

This is the last day of my stay with dear old Livingstone; the last night we shall be together is present, and I cannot evade the morrow. I feel as though I should like to rebel against the necessity of departure. The minutes beat fast, and grow into hours. Our door is closed and we are both of us busy with our own thoughts. What his thoughts are I know not. Mine are sad . . . I have received the thanks that he had repressed all these months in the secrecy of his heart, uttered with no mincing phrases, but poured out, as it were, at the last moment, until I was so affected that I sobbed, as one only can in uncommon grief. The hour of the night and the crisis . . . his sudden outburst of gratitude, with that kind of praise that steals into one and touches the softer parts of the ever-veiled nature, all had their influence; and, for a time, I was a sensitive child of eight or so, and yielded to such bursts of tears that only such a scene as this could have forced.

Stanley told Livingstone he expected to reach the coast in forty days, 'if not in 40, I will in 50 – certain. The thought that I am doing you an important service will spur me on.'

On the day the expedition departed from Unyanyembe, Livingstone accompanied Stanley for a few miles. Earlier they had shared 'a sad breakfast together. I could not eat, my heart was too full; neither did my companion seem to have an appetite'. On the pathway out of town, Stanley turned to Livingstone and told him he should walk no further. Livingstone said: 'Well, I will say this to you, you have done what few men could do. And for what you have done for me, I am most grateful. God guide you safe home and bless you, my friend.'

'And may God bring you safe back to us all, my dear friend. Farewell!'

They wrung each other's hands, their faces flushed with emotion. Stanley recalled: 'At the moment of parting, the old man's noble face slightly paled, which I knew to be from suppressed emotion, while, when I looked into his eyes, I saw there was a kind of warning, the look well-nigh unmanned me . . . a little longer and I should have utterly collapsed. We both, however, preferred dry eyes and outward calm.' Stanley fought 'an audacious desire' to embrace Livingstone, but instead turned away and 'assumed a gruff voice and ordered the expedition to march'.

From time to time he turned back to see the doctor walking away in the company of his faithful servants, Susi, Chuma and Hamoydah, a 'deserted figure of an old man in grey clothes, who with bended head and slow steps was returning to his solitude, the very picture of melancholy, and each time I saw him – as the plain was wide and clear of obstructions – I felt my eyes stream, and my head swell with a vague, indefinable feeling of foreboding and sorrow . . . I took one more look at him; he was standing . . . with his servants near him. I waved a handkerchief to him, as a final token of farewell, and he responded to it by lifting his cap. It was the last opportunity, for soon we surmounted the crest of a land-wave and began the descent into the depression on the other side – and I *never* saw him more.'

It took fifty-four days to march back through the interior to Bagamoyo and sail across the channel to Zanzibar (although in his book *How I Found Livingstone*, published later the same year, Stanley claims the journey was completed in twenty-four days – which is true; twenty-four days marching and thirty days sheltering from torrential rains, crossing the notorious Makata swamplands once again, avoiding red ants, boas, scorpions, razor sharp cacti, dense jungle and fever which all played their part in slowing down the expedition's progress).

While Stanley's caravan avoided further encounters with Mirambo's warring mercenaries, they had endless battles with swarms of black mosquitoes and bad weather. They came to a deep river and, at its narrowest point, cut down a tree to act as a bridge. Most of Stanley's *pagazi* porters moved their bales and boxes over the tree trunk, but one over-zealous young man carrying Livingstone's tin box containing his letters and journal, placed the load on his head and began wading into the river. Suddenly he fell into a deep hole somewhere in mid-river and the man and his precious box were suddenly lost from sight. Fortunately, man and box resurfaced and Stanley called to him 'with a loaded revolver pointed at his head, "Look out! Drop that box and I'll shoot you."' Terrified, the young man slowly made his way to the bank and was pulled out, the contents still dry within the tin box.

Three days from the coast Stanley sent men ahead with letters addressed to the American Consul announcing their imminent arrival and carrying final dispatches for the *New York Herald*. A few days out of Bagamoyo, Stanley received word that something called the Livingstone Search and Relief Expedition had been formed to rescue both Livingstone and himself. The search party was assembled at Bagamoyo, about to set out into the interior.

On 6 May 1872, Stanley's caravan announced their arrival at Bagamoyo by firing rifles into the air. As they passed through the small town, Stanley noticed a young European wearing immaculately pressed flannels and a helmet similar to his own standing on the steps of a white building. He invited Stanley in, offered him a beer and said in an English accent, 'Eh, by George, I congratulate you on your splendid success.' This was Lieutenant William Henn RN, head of the Livingstone Search and

Rescue Expedition. He told Stanley that when word arrived that the doctor had been found, the expedition's leader, Lieutenant Llewellyn Dawson had resigned and returned to Zanzibar. The young Lieutenant said that Charles New, the missionary travelling with them had also resigned, leaving Livingstone's son, Oswell and himself the only members left. Lieutenant Henn informed Stanley that he did not think it worthwhile to continue the rescue mission because 'you have taken the wind out of our sails completely. If you have relieved him, I don't see the use of my going. Do you?' A young man entered the room and was introduced as Oswell Livingstone. Stanley shook his hand and said that whether Henn went or not, young Livingstone should go to his father. He promised to furnish him with men and stores.

It was settled. Henn decided he was surplus to requirements and would return to Zanzibar with Stanley to discuss his position with Dr Kirk while Oswell Livingstone would remain at Bagamoyo until men and supplies could be delivered. Finally, at 2 a.m. Stanley collapsed onto a comfortable bed with new cotton sheets and told his diary: 'Thank God, my marching has ended.'

In the morning, Stanley caught sight of himself in a mirror for the first time in over a year and noticed that 'I was terribly emaciated and changed . . . I was much older in my appearance and that my hair had become grey . . . I was so different that identity was almost lost, even during the short period of thirteen months; that is from March 23rd, 1871 to May 7th, 1872'. He estimated that when he had originally left Zanzibar he had weighed 170lb; thirteen months later, his weight was down to 110lb.

Volley after volley announced the caravan's return to Zanzibar. The Webbs were waiting to greet Stanley, standing in the same spot from which they had watched the American reporter's departure thirteen months before. A celebration dinner was held in Stanley's honour at their home at which the Reverend Charles New and Lieutenant Dawson were present. In a loud and positive voice designed to be overheard by others, Lieutenant Dawson said: 'Mr Stanley – let me congratulate you, Sir.' And then in more confidential tones intended only for Stanley's ears, he added: 'I envy your success.' As soon as word arrived with one of Stanley's messenger-couriers that Livingstone had been found, he had resigned on the spot. 'With bitter disappointment, I gave up the idea of attempting to encroach on what Dr. Livingstone had gone so far with and

evidently went on to finish. I felt that my presence in the country . . .
would be highly irritating to Livingstone,' he said. 'My instructions . . .
were to endeavour to procure from him copies of the geographical
information he had obtained. Also, I considered that I might cause him
annoyance, and probably prevent his disclosing what his movements had
been.'

Stanley records that Dr Kirk also paid him a courtesy call and he
'warmly congratulated me upon my success', but refused to have anything
further to do with sending supplies to Livingstone. Kirk had yet to read
articles in which Stanley was critical of the tawdry fashion in which the
British Consul had dealt with his old colleague. Stanley says nothing else
of their meeting, although it is certain that a great deal more was
exchanged between the two men and not recorded.

Stanley handed Dr Kirk a letter from his old friend, Livingstone. It was
headed 'A Complaint', which was underlined twice. Instead of fraternal
greetings, it began curtly: 'Sir . . .' and went on to state that prior to
Stanley's arrival in Ujiji he had been 'thoroughly jaded in body and mind'.
At the settlement he had discovered that £600 worth of supplies, paid for
by the Royal Geographical Society and sent from the coast, had been 'sold
off' by Sherif Bosher, who had been expressly charged by Kirk to transport
and care for the goods. Sherif Bosher had used the money to buy ivory
and slaves for himself, despite protestations from other Arabs. The letter
accused Kirk of employing slaves and a slaver to carry the goods into the
interior and his former friend of deserting him 'while I have received
nothing but friendship from Mr. Stanley'. It ends abruptly: 'Yours very
truly – David Livingstone, H. M. Consul, Inner Africa'.

Kirk had no alternative but to forward the letter to the Foreign Office in
London. The timing of its arrival could not have been worse, coinciding as
it did with publication of Stanley's articles criticising Kirk's tardiness
regarding the latter's care of Livingstone's supplies and efforts to ascertain
his whereabouts.

Questions were asked in Whitehall's corridors of power. A note from the
Foreign Secretary pinned to the correspondence file states: 'Let me know
anything you can find out about this attack on Dr. Kirk – Lord Granville.'
An anonymous Whitehall adviser wrote to Lord Granville:

Livingstone accuses Dr. Kirk of employing slaves to carry the goods
forwarded to him in the interior of Africa, when he ought to have

employed Arabs. It lays on Dr. Kirk's shoulders the blame of the failure of the goods not reaching him. Considerable allowance must be made for the quarrelsome tone of Dr. Livingstone's letter. We are aware of the hardships he must have undergone, particularly when he learned that the provisions and stores forwarded to him had been plundered. Dr. Kirk had done his best to send goods to Dr. Livingstone but it is no easy matter to find trustworthy men to entrust their lives in the interior. . . . I feel confident that Dr. Kirk will come out of the charges in light colours when they have been fully and dispassionately investigated, but cannot help thinking that Mr. Stanley, the American, may for his own purposes, have prejudiced Dr. Livingstone against Dr. Kirk and others who did their best to him. Sir Henry Rawlinson of the Royal Geographical Society should investigate the whole affair and we should leave the matter safely in his hands.*

Stanley formally discharged his men only to immediately re-engage twenty of them to return to Livingstone, along with a further thirty-seven *Wagwana* ('free men') natives. He began preparations for another expedition, to be led by Oswell Livingstone. What the Royal Geographical Society expedition lacked, Stanley purchased from the Zanzibar market. On 19 May 1872, Livingstone's son resigned from the expedition 'for reasons he thought just and sufficient'. Young Livingstone was not in the best of health. He was inexperienced, lacked confidence and Kirk advised him not to expose himself to needless risk in Africa's interior. Instead, a young Arab, who came highly recommended, was chosen to lead the new expedition to Unyanyembe.

Before leaving Zanzibar, Stanley shook hands with every member of the party. As they picked up their loads, he marched them along the street to the beach where a dhow was waiting to carry them across the channel to Bagamoyo. He watched them board and depart across the water. 'I felt strange and lonely, somehow,' he recalled. 'My dark friends, who had travelled over so many hundreds of miles and shared so many dangers with me, were gone and I was left behind. How many of their friendly faces shall I see again?'

---

* Following a thorough Foreign Office investigation and inquiry, Dr Kirk was later cleared of all charges of neglecting or failing Livingstone.

On 29 May, Stanley, Henn, New, Oswell Livingstone and a surprise
passenger, little Kalulu, boarded the steamer *Afrika*, chartered from the
German Consulate, and set sail for Europe. Lieutenant Dawson returned
home on a cargo ship travelling via Cape Town. In a letter to his father, he
explained that he did not begrudge Stanley his well-earned success but 'it
would be distasteful to me, if not both of us, to travel in company'. He
said he felt 'personally pained that Dr Livingstone had forwarded his
correspondence through an American agent, and at having avoided
making known his discoveries to an old friend like Dr Kirk, a fact which
augured ill for the reception of the English expedition'. Dawson was later
reprimanded by the Royal Geographical Society for his 'lamentable error of
judgement' in disbanding the expedition. He was said to have 'retired from
the field owing to a wrong impression of Dr. Livingstone's character'. Or
had he simply spent too much time in Dr Kirk's company?

The voyage entailed an enforced month-long stay in the Seychelles
while they awaited onward transport. At Aden, a cable was handed to
Stanley. It was from James Gordon Bennett, who told his star reporter:
'You are now as famous as Livingstone having discovered the discoverer.
Accept my thanks, and whole world.'

They sailed onwards to Marseilles in the mail steamer *Meikong*; there
Stanley discovered what Bennett had meant in his telegram. By 24 July,
George Hosmer, European manager of the *New York Herald*, and a
representative from the *Daily Telegraph* had been waiting two days on the
Marseilles quay for the *Meikong* to arrive. Hosmer had cabled Suez
informing Stanley he would be at the port, but rough weather had
detained the steamer and the shipping line had no idea when it would
dock. The newspapermen returned to their hotel, leaving a message that if
the steamer arrived during the night, Stanley should contact them –
failing to state where they were staying.

At 2 a.m. the newsmen were woken from their beds by knocking on
their hotel room doors. It was Stanley, wide awake, rested and eager to
talk about his African adventures. The *Meikong* had crept into port after
midnight and Stanley had disembarked, leaving the rest of his party on
board until daylight when they planned to travel to Paris by rail. He had
tramped the streets of Marseilles, calling at every hotel asking if a
Mr Hosmer was staying as a guest.

The *Daily Telegraph* reported that all thoughts of further sleep for the
night were abandoned while the newsmen sat up until morning listening

to Stanley's tale of 'the marvellous adventures and discoveries of Livingstone, and the not much less wonderful adventures and escapes of Mr. Stanley himself'. The *Telegraph* reporter told readers 'with some regret that . . . Mr Stanley is not an Englishman or rather a Welshman – as was recently reported in some journals – but an American citizen . . . a comparatively young man, having scarcely concluded his third decade. He stands about five feet seven inches high; he has a very broad chest and powerful-looking frame and a most intelligent expression of countenance; his hair naturally curling and once light in colour, has turned quite grey during his expedition, through exposure to the weather and the severe and repeated attacks of fever which he underwent.'

Stanley and Kalulu boarded a Paris-bound train on 26 July. For the eight-year-old African orphan, the experience of being part of a white man's retinue for the past ten months had been overwhelming. Kalulu had been loyal to his master, acting as his personal servant, gun-carrier and guardian of his tent, where he performed the same duties as Stanley's much-missed dog, Omar. He was quick in his work and soon learned Stanley's personal likes and dislikes, when to be close to his master and when to make himself scarce.

Stanley had originally planned to leave Kalulu in Unyanyembe when he returned with Livingstone. But the boy was an orphan with nowhere to go, and Stanley was afraid that the little fellow might end up as an Arab slave, so he brought the boy to the east coast and on to Zanzibar, hoping all the time to find someone trustworthy prepared to adopt Kalulu. By the time the *New York Herald*'s expedition was completed, Stanley had become attached to the boy and decided to take him to England and America as a living souvenir of darkest Africa.

At first the boy had been afraid of the ocean swell and sound of the engines when the *Afrika* headed out of Zanzibar, but he soon settled into shipboard life. During the Seychelles stop-over, Kalulu also learned something new – how to play. For his entire eight years, he had been required to perform tasks for other people, and as his master rested in his room or wrote on his balcony overlooking the sea, Kalulu swam and made friends with other children. The boy quickly began to pick up English words and phrases and by the time the 'Livingstone' expedition had completed its march, Stanley himself had acquired more than a smattering of an understanding of native dialects, including Kiswahili.

Using a combination of each other's languages, Stanley and Kalulu could communicate and during their long sea voyage to Europe and their time together in the Seychelles, the boy told his master stories from his homeland and of the things he had witnessed in the dark interior. Stanley listened carefully to these tales and formulated a plan to turn some of them into stories, perhaps for children, once his post-Livingstone work was completed. This would also include expanding his *New York Herald* dispatches and expedition journals into a book, which he planned to call *How I Found Livingstone in Central Africa*. By the time Stanley sailed from the Seychelles, he had completed the first draft, for which London publishers Sampson Low, Marston & Company would pay a fee of $50,000, a record sum for a travel book in the 1870s.

The train journey to Paris was both an adventure and nightmare for Kalulu. Once he had become used to the rocking of the carriage, the boy enjoyed gazing out of the window while strange-looking towns, villages and countryside flashed past. Whenever the train blew its whistle or rushed into a tunnel, the boy screamed and dived under the seat, refusing to come out until daylight filled the carriage again.

A hero's welcome awaited them in the French capital, where they checked into the luxurious Hotel d'Helder. The *New York Herald*'s Paris correspondent informed his readers that Stanley was

> today the lion of the great city of Paris . . . sought after, honoured, feted and talked about in a way that will turn his head if he has a head capable of being turned. . . . He has been in Paris now about a week and during the whole of that time he has had scarcely a moment's rest. All sorts of people call and ask to be presented to him. He is overwhelmed with invitations, a tithe of which he would not be able to accept were he to remain here a year. He is interrupted by newspaper reporters, importuned by correspondents of the pictorials for sketches and scenes from his travels, and generally lionized to an extent that has astonished him beyond measure. For the poor man did not know he had done anything so extraordinary until he got out of the wilds of Africa and found that the whole civilized world was ringing with his exploits.

Before departing, Stanley called on the British ambassador to hand over Livingstone's letters and papers for urgent delivery to London in diplomatic mailbags. He had promised to send them by the fastest possible means once his articles had appeared in the *New York Herald*. Now that most of his news from the interior had been published, Stanley was honouring his word. However, he insisted on personally handing Livingstone's journals to a member of the doctor's family. Stanley did not have sufficient confidence in Oswell Livingstone to pass the material to him at Zanzibar or on the homeward voyage. He preferred to entrust the valuable journal to Tom or Agnes Livingstone whom he expected to meet in London.

While in Paris, Stanley had seen copies of American, British and French newspapers openly casting doubt on his discovery, stating that the letters and journals brought out of Africa were forgeries, stolen from a courier on the way back to the coast. He read reports that 'Dr. Livingstone had discovered and relieved Mr. Stanley' and of Dr Kirk's responses to Stanley's criticisms of his actions which were misinterpreted as American attacks on a respected British diplomat. In an attempt to hang on to his comfortable job in Zanzibar and at the insistence of the Foreign Office, Kirk was now fighting back with letters of his own to newspapers denying charges of negligence.

The Paris daily, *Le Temps*, wrote:

We are inclined to doubt the authority of the Livingstone letters. The German geographer, Kiebert, has discovered various geographical blunders in the letters. He thinks that parts of the narrative were invented by Stanley and that they are valueless. He says it is possible that Stanley never even saw Livingstone.

Livingstone's son, Oswell, wrote to *The Times* on 27 July 1872 (giving the Royal Geographical Society's offices in Saville Row, London as his address):

The extreme joy afforded to me during my sojourn in Zanzibar by the news of my father's safety was painfully marred by the sad, and I am thoroughly convinced, erroneous, opinions prevalent in his mind during Mr. Stanley's travels with him in respect of his old and trusty friend, Dr. John Kirk. Before leaving Zanzibar I did my utmost, by writing to Dr. Livingstone, to place him in possession of that which I devoutly hope may neutralise influences under which he laboured, and also tend to reunite those old bonds of friendship, which should never have been imperilled by misconceptions. I live in hopes that my letters,

now half way to him, may convince him of what I have said regarding
the exertions made by Dr. Kirk during the time in which . . . he strove
to relieve my father through the agency of the Arabs at Zanzibar and,
likewise as to the affection always held towards him. Such publicity is
being given to statements made respecting Dr. Kirk that I beg the favour
of your inserting these few lines about him as soon as you possibly can.

Livingstone would doubtless have been embarrassed and angered by
such public airing of his feelings towards Kirk. He would have been
thrilled, however, to read *The Times* report about the Royal Speech on
12 August 1872, following the prorogation of Parliament, in which
Queen Victoria announced: 'My government has taken steps intended
to prepare the way for dealing more effectively with the slave trade on
the east coast of Africa.' The newspaper reported that 'this is the most
significant part of the throne's speech and we suppose it is not an error
to connect the announcement which has just been made by Her
Majesty to the recent discovery of Dr. Livingstone and dispatches
brought to the Foreign Office by Mr. Stanley of the *New York Herald*
from the great traveller'.

In a letter to the *Daily Telegraph*, Sir Henry Rawlinson thundered that he
had received nothing from Dr. Livingstone. He stated that the only
correspondence he had seen related to the 'bad conduct of those charged
with transmitting or conveying his supplies – a matter with which this
society does not wish to meddle. Therefore we are waiting to see if the
communications, which Mr. Stanley brings to London with him, will
contain any fresh geographical or personal facts. If they do, a meeting of
the geographical section of the British Association in Brighton, held in the
course of the next fortnight, will furnish an opportunity to communicate
such intelligence to the public.'

For Stanley, a new battle was just beginning.

Chapter 24

'WHAT HAD I TO DO WITH MY BIRTH IN WALES?'

America saves England – mighty Child
Of mighty Mother, it is nobly done!
Join your two strong right hands for evermore,
And swear that none shall sever them anew!
The tremble, crowned oppressors of mankind!
England, America, on your free soil
The slave may kneel; but only kneel to God!
Thou, gallant Stanley, scorning toil, alert,
Stern battling with they formidable foes,
Hast won the brilliant prize; and Europe turns
Her enviously grateful eyes on thee.

Roden Noel, 'Livingstone in Africa' (extract)

Stanley and Kalulu arrived at Dover on the boat train from Calais on 1 August 1872. Waiting on the dockside pier was Stanley's half-brother, Robert Parry and a cousin, both tipsy after a few drinks too many in a pub. Stanley had hoped to slip into the country unnoticed, which was not easy when travelling in the company of an eight-year-old African boy unhappy at wearing trousers, boots and socks for the first time. Not only were his relatives drawing attention to themselves with their drunken antics, but also to Stanley and Kalulu.

The half-brother and cousin insisted on sharing their famous relative's railway carriage back to London, where their drunken activities continued to annoy and embarrass Stanley and confuse Kalulu. At Victoria Station, the Foreign Secretary, Lord Granville, had sent a carriage to collect Stanley and take him to the Langham Hotel. He bade farewell to his relatives on the platform and they staggered off to the nearest pub.

Later that night Stanley recorded in his journal:

What a welcome! Had those stupid newspapers not mentioned my name, the vanity of my poor relations would not have been so kindled. Thus has my presentiment been realised on my first setting foot in England. They had already, of course, gained considerable *éclat* on the pier by their revelation of their relationship with me and a large crowd of quidnuncs, railway porters and others assembled to witness our meeting. I have never felt so ashamed, and would have given all I was worth to have been back in Central Africa. What little Kalulu must have thought of my drunken relatives I do not know. There is no reason in the world why I should recognise them in public. They only bring to my mind too vividly my treatment, when I deserved something else than the scorn they gave me as a child, and any charity that they might have shown me then, might today have been remembered and returned with interest.

A journalist from the *Scotsman* called on Stanley at the Langham on 2 August 1872, and attempted to interview him:

I had intended to see Mr. Stanley yesterday; but as he had to attend to an invitation to breakfast in the morning and an invitation to dinner in the evening, I did not succeed in catching sight of him. Today I called at the house of a mutual friend and there I was fortunate enough to meet Mr. Stanley. But even now I had not fully secured him, for before many minutes he rushed out on some business, telling me he would be glad to see me an hour or two further on in the day. About twelve-o'-clock I was able for the first time to get a few minutes of quiet conversation in a room in the Langham Hotel. Even here, however, we were not left undisturbed for many minutes. Firstly, there were many American acquaintances of Mr. Stanley staying at the hotel, and then the boy Kalulu called for some attention on the part of Mr. Stanley. The housekeeper had presented the lad with a pair of stockings, but he did not relish the gift and it was only by the intervention of Mr. Stanley that he could be induced to don those habiliments.

Much of Stanley's time in London was spent at the Fetter Lane offices of publishers, Sampson Low, Marston & Company. There he discussed his 700-page manuscript of *How I Found Livingstone; Travels, Adventures and Discoveries in Central Africa, including Four Months' Residence with*

Dr. Livingstone and illustrations to be included with his text. While Stanley was a proficient amateur pencil artist, he was not a great one and sketches made during his African crossing were handed to professional artist J.D. Cooper to work up into finished wood engravings.

For his return to London, Stanley had trimmed his shaggy beard, leaving just the moustache and a roguish goatee on his chin. A photograph of Stanley wearing a fashionable bow tie was taken by the London Stereoscopic Company and issued as a postcard sold in London shops for 1*d*. Stanley's face was now as well known alike to London's fashionable elite and its street urchins as those of Queen Victoria, Prince Albert and Henry Irving. As he travelled around the city, strangers tipped their hats and greeted him with a variation of the expression they had all read in his newspaper articles, enquiring: 'Mr Stanley, I presume?' He found them amusing at first, then intensely annoying. The phrase dogged Stanley for the rest of his life and there must have been times when he bitterly regretted ever having uttered the now historic remark. Over a century later, the phrase, 'Dr. Livingstone, I presume?' even turned up in the lyrics of a 1968 pop song by the Moody Blues.

Accusations that Livingstone's letters and journals were forgeries were still appearing in London newspapers. The *Standard* demanded that Stanley's dispatches be examined word-by-word by experts because 'we cannot resist some suspicions and misgivings . . . there is something inexplicable and mysterious in the business'. The *Spectator* said there 'is something of the comic in the newspaper correspondent who, in the regular exercise of his profession, moved neither by pity, nor love of knowledge, nor by desire of adventure, but by an order from Mr. Bennett, coolly plunges into the unknown continent to interview a lost geographer'.

On his second day in London, Stanley met Tom Livingstone to hand over his father's journal. Tom then scribbled a note stating his family 'have not the slightest reason to doubt that this is my father's journal and I certify that the letters he had brought home are my father's letters, and no others'. Lord Granville, the Foreign Secretary also wrote to Stanley and circulated a copy of his letter to leading newspapers: 'I have not the slightest doubt as to the genuineness of the papers', he wrote. 'I cannot omit this opportunity of expressing to you my admiration of the qualities which have enabled you to achieve the object of your mission and to attain a result which has been hailed with so much enthusiasm both in the United States and in this country.'

Despite these and other confirmations that Livingstone's handwritten communications were genuine, Stanley was still bitter that anyone could possibly doubt the word of a reporter from the *New York Herald*. He felt no better when he read in the 17 August 1872 issue of *Punch*: 'There is certainly one claim of immense amount which may be advanced by the United States and is incontestable; the claim of Mr. Stanley to have discovered Dr. Livingstone.'

A flood of inquisitive letters from strangers and early acquaintances began arriving at the Langham Hotel. Many begged for money. Others demanded to know if Stanley was really the American reporter he claimed to be. Mr Charles Ollivant, from Sale, Cheshire, a town close to where both Henry and Frances Stanley originated, wrote enclosing a press clipping from the *Rhyl Journal*, which claimed Stanley's real name was either Thomas or Rowlands. The newspaper wrote that Stanley was not American but Welsh-born and that Ollivant 'was happy to be in a position to give an authoritative denial to the statement, believing it to be utterly devoid of truth and dictated by a spirit of envy and malice'. Ollivant enquired if there was foundation in the story.

Stanley's reply contained more of the lies he used to cover details about his early life. He sent Mr Ollivant 'a thousand thanks for his letter and clippings' and stated that if he were to answer all letters received about his nationality he 'should certainly be called an idiot, and deservedly so'. He 'cared not what anybody wrote about me, nor do I intend to notice them. If English and Welsh folks are so gullible as to believe all the "rot" they read about me, I cannot help it; nor have I a desire to help it in any way. But for you and such kind friends *I say that I am an American* and can prove it with over 10,000 friends in the United States. The letter in the *Rhyl Journal* is all bosh . . . I have never sung a Welsh song – not knowing anything of the language. My name is neither Thomas nor Rowlands, Smith, Jones nor Robinson, but that which I have borne all my life – plain Henry M. Stanley. At 16 I was in Missouri, at 17 in Arkansas, at 18 in New Orleans, at 19 in Europe travelling, at 20 in the war and so on.'

Stanley chose not to fill in the gaps between his birth date and his sixteenth year, 'but in the public's great interest' Ollivant forwarded copies of his correspondence to the letters page of the *Daily Telegraph* inviting the newspaper to reproduce them. They did, printing both Ollivant's letter to Stanley and the reply he had received.

Vanity Fair described Stanley as of

a touchy and combative nature . . . contrived to quarrel with most of those with whom he has been brought into contact, and being a man of plain and blunt speech, he has said various things to which undue importance has been given through their being measured by the English rather than by the American standard of good manners and propriety. He is plucky, has proved himself an admiral newspaper correspondent and will have far more than earned the large sum of money, which he has told us was expended by the *New York Herald* upon his adventure to Africa. That is less than has been said for him and less than he evidently thinks of himself, but it is about as much as there is to say or to think.

Stanley was still out of humour when *Punch* printed a cartoon showing Livingstone relaxing in a hammock made from the Stars and Stripes alongside a 'private and confidential letter from Dr. Livingstone to Dr. Punch' saying that 'Stanley is an excellent fellow, a real good plucked 'un, and you are to make much of him, while he's with you, for his own sake as well as mine'.

While the worthies of the Royal Geographical Society continued to ignore the American who had found their man in Africa, its members demanded that a platform be made available for him to relate his story. The Society President, Sir Henry Rawlinson, was forced to write to Stanley sending 'our best thanks for the transmission of direct intelligence from Dr. Livingstone to several members of the Council of this society. This was the very earliest opportunity at which it was possible to convey their thanks, as the letters in question did not reach their destination until the end of last week. I take this opportunity of begging you, in the name of the committee, to accept our most cordial acknowledgements for the timely succour rendered to Dr. Livingstone in his great need and the expression of our admiration of the energy, perseverance and courage with which you conducted your expedition.' The letter invited Stanley to address a meeting in Brighton of the geographical section of the British Association on 18 August 1872, at which he was called on to present an account of his visit to Lake Tanganyika with Livingstone and the 'new route from Unyanyembe to Ujiji'. It would be followed by readings of extracts from Livingstone's journal. Around '1,500 distinguished persons' were expected to attend and although Stanley had never before addressed such a large and formal gathering of academic and intellectual geographers, he accepted the invitation and set about drafting a speech.

On 18 August, 3,000 people attempted to push their way through the doors of the Brighton Concert Hall in Middle Street when they opened at 9 a.m. Proceedings were not scheduled to begin for another two hours. The conference was a 'ticket only' affair, but once word got out that Stanley would be making a personal appearance, people who had never before been to a stuffy geographical meeting began to demand admission, including Emperor Napoleon III and Empress Eugenie of France, now living in comfortable exile in southern England, MPs, lords, ladies, military officials, geographers and Victorian society celebrity spotters. The media was out in force, too. For many this was their first opportunity to hear Stanley speak on the record, even if it was only about exploring an obscure lake thousands of miles away from Brighton.

The *Daily News* reported that the audience expressed its 'vociferous welcome, the Emperor and Empress applauding as heartily as the rest, causing Mr. Stanley to rise more than once to bow his acknowledgements'. The paper observed that 'determination and pluck are written upon the young traveller's face in characters which are unmistakeable, and if ever a man "looked the part" he has been called upon to play, it is the intrepid discoverer of Livingstone'.

The *Brighton Herald* provided readers with a unique word sketch of Stanley that day. In just a few sentences, the article managed to describe the appearance, voice, excuses and lies used by the man deliberately to mislead anyone prying too closely into his humble origins:

He is what we in England would call a short man, rather under than over five feet six inches. He is thick set and sturdy in make, conveying the idea that he possesses great powers of endurance; and his features, though not otherwise remarkable, have an air of great resolution. He is of dark complexion, wearing a small moustache, an imperial, and though stated to be only 28 years of age [Stanley was, in fact, thirty-one], his hair is here and there turning grey. He has not the look of a Yankee, as we in England understand that look, nor does he speak with an American accent – not, at least, in ordinary conversation, though, when he warms, there is the unmistakable twang. The report that

Mr. Stanley is an Englishman is unfounded. He is a native of one of the native states of the American Union, Missouri, and his father (as he himself informed us) was an American by birth, although, he added, 'my mother was an Englishwoman'. But to his distinction of birth between Englishmen and Americans, he seemed to attach very little importance, and expressed his wonder that people should trouble themselves about the matter. 'We all spring,' he remarked to us, 'from the same source.'

Sir Henry Rawlinson invited Stanley up onto the platform and the auditorium erupted to its feet, clapping and calling his name. Stanley was not prepared for this. He had expected polite applause – not a standing ovation. The applause lasted a full two minutes and Stanley allowed the audience to regain its composure before starting his speech. The *Daily News* said his address was 'triumphal' and the *Daily Telegraph* described him speaking 'with entire self-possession, composure, with a natural and effective oratory . . . with the evident purpose to speak his mind to everybody, without the slightest deference or hesitation'.

They were being kind. Stanley recorded in his journal that his stage fright was so extreme that it took him three attempts to begin speaking. When he was finally able to stammer out his words, he told the audience that he had been asked to present a brief paper dealing with exploration of the northern end of Lake Tanganyika – but at the last minute was called on to give an account of the whole expedition. The audience was delighted.

Without notes, Stanley launched into his story:

Ladies and gentlemen, I consider myself in the light of a troubadour, to relate to you the tale of an old man who is tramping onward to discover the source of the Nile – to tell you that I found that old man at Ujiji and to tell you of his woes and sufferings and how he bore his misfortunes with the Christian patience and endurance of a hero. . . .

He told the audience that, prior to being summoned to James Gordon Bennett's hotel room in Paris and instructed to 'Find Livingstone!' he knew nothing about Africa. Stanley admitted he had no idea where or how to begin his search after arriving in Zanzibar and how he relied on information in books by other explorers. He spoke about borrowing cash to put his caravan together, fit it out with supplies, of his men, their journey together, the trials and hardships of tramping through hostile territory and bits of information picked up along the way about an old white man at Ujiji. He described entering the settlement and seeing a 'grey bearded old man, dressed in a red shirt, with a gold band around his cap, an old tweed pair of pants, his shoes looking the worse for wear. Who is this old man, I ask myself. Is it Livingstone? Yes it is. No, it is not. Yes it is. "Dr Livingstone, I presume?" "Yes."' The audience erupted into loud cheers again. Hundreds in the audience repeated the famous phrase along with Stanley – the phrase he had given to the world.

All thoughts about lies, forgeries and falsehoods were now forgotten as Stanley steered his talk towards the point where he joined Livingstone on their 'little picnic' to the northern end of the Tanganyika. At this point Stanley picked up the formal text he had prepared a few days before. There were questions from eminent geographers in the audience and Stanley answered them in detail before taking his seat again. His appearance was a triumph.

It was now the turn of the Royal Geographical Society to eat humble pie in front of an audience of eminent geographers. Sir Henry Rawlinson mildly rebuked Stanley for the 'sensational' style of his retelling of the story of his discovery to his learned audience and called on both Livingstone and Stanley to produce 'hard facts' about their geographic claims. Having got that out of the way, Sir Henry then expressed his organisation's high opinion of Stanley's merits as a traveller 'and that his achievement in finding Livingstone reflected the greatest credit upon the country with which you are connected. As there have been some misconceptions on the subject, I take this opportunity of disclaiming on the part of the Royal Geographical Society, the slightest feeling of jealousy.'

The *Daily News* reported that 'Mr. Stanley is essentially a man for a platform and a popular assembly and if he could be induced to deliver a lecture and illustrate it with drawings, diagrams and maps he will furnish the public with an extremely attractive and instructive entertainment. Meanwhile people are asking what public honour is to be paid to him and when it will be announced. His achievement is not one which England can pass by, and some mark of recognition by the government would never seem more grateful than now. . . .'

Things turned sour the following evening when Stanley was a guest at a Royal Pavilion banquet given by the Brighton and Sussex Medi-Chirurgical Society in honour of the British Association's visit to the town. At midnight and following a convivial dinner at which wine, champagne and liqueurs had flowed freely, Stanley was called upon to respond to a toast 'to the visitors'. The toast was proposed by Mr Jardine Murray, who expressed 'deep regret that the rise of Mr. Stanley should have been the fall of Dr. Kirk', a gentleman whom he greatly respected and had been an old college friend. On rising to return the thanks, Stanley was greeted with warm applause and began speaking in what, according to the *Brighton Daily News*, was

> a most humorous vein, asserting that for the life of him he could not make out why he had been selected to respond, as they had doubtless heard enough of him the day before. However, he accepted the compliment as a token that they would like to hear some words regarding their great and illustrious associate (cheers and applause). Mr. Stanley then went on to point out there were few medical men who had had such a wide range of practical experience in the healing art as Dr. Livingstone, who had to deal with a number of strange and incongruous patients, giving pills to the natives of one district, potions, plaisters and ointment to others.

At this point, according to the newspaper, a member of the audience

> gave utterance to what Mr. Stanley apparently regarded as a derisive laugh, either at something he had said or his manner of saying it. This appeared to annoy Mr. Stanley exceedingly; and at once, quitting the humorous and cheerful style in which he had been speaking, he adopted a stern, emphatic and impassioned tone; protesting that he had not come there to be laughed at, and that he had had quite enough gratuitous sneering of late, without their adding to it. Alluding to the insinuations which had been made against him at the meeting of the Geographical Section on the previous day, that he indulged rather too much in 'sensationalism', he assured them that it was not to get the thanks of England or the English people that he had gone out to discover Livingstone, but as a matter of professional duty. They might call it what they liked; but if the finding of Livingstone in the heart of Africa after he had been given up for lost had not something of the 'sensational' then he did not know the meaning of the word. But why was it that his statements were questioned?

The Royal Pavilion fell silent, as Stanley sternly demanded: 'Is it because I am an American that you reward me with gratuitous sneering? Do you think that America would have enquired after the nationality of the man who might have prevented the assassination of President Lincoln before thanking him for the act? Why, then, should I be sneered at because I succeeded in discovering Livingstone? If that was to be the way in which I am to be treated, I will at once withdraw from your company.' And with that, Stanley strode out of the room, leaving guests in stunned silence. 'His departure was so sudden and unexpected that the meeting was quite taken by surprise and seemed uncertain what to do', the paper reported. The Mayor was first to speak and expressed 'very deep regret that anything should have occurred to annoy Mr. Stanley, and he must certainly say that it was a very unmannerly thing for the gentleman, whoever he was, to have laughed out in the manner he did.'

An offended Stanley returned to London early the following morning, but was persuaded to return to Brighton a few days later to attend the Mayor's 'farewell dejeuner' for the President and Executive of the British Association 'and other distinguished visitors' in the Royal Pavilion's banqueting room. Stanley was seated at the top table and agreed to say a few more words to the 200 guests. To everyone's delight he spoke at length about the ill-fated Livingstone Search Expedition, abandoned when they heard about the *New York Herald*'s success. While thanking Stanley for returning to Brighton, the Society's president, Francis Galton, used the occasion to take a final public dig at Stanley. He told guests: 'I cannot conclude without asking Mr. Stanley one question. I have read a paragraph in the papers, which gives me some hope that we may claim him as an Englishman or a Welshman. I hope he will tell whether the rumour is founded on fact.'

Stanley was not expecting this question. Had he known he would be asked to confirm his true nationality in front of 200 strangers, he would never have agreed to return to Brighton. He stood up slowly and the crowd cheered. He remained silent until the room was so quiet guests could have heard a feather drop. He told them:

Before I went to Central Africa, it was supposed that Livingstone was the most interesting topic of the day. Mr. Galton now wishes me to understand that the most interesting topic here is my most humble biography. Permit me to say that when I received my instructions from

Mr. James Gordon Bennett, he told me not to discover myself, but to go and discover Livingstone. [*Cheers*] As to myself, it is sheer idle curiosity; it is sheer nonsense. Why, I am hardly thirty years old and I have done nothing to justify demand for my biography. But let me say that I am going to write a book, and if Mr. Galton wishes to know my biography, let me advise him to look into it. [*Laughter*] He will find in it, also, many other interesting subjects [*laughter*] concerning the geographies of England and America, concerning adventurers, concerning travels, new geographical facts; and nothing shall be 'sensational', I vow.

With cheers ringing in his ears, Stanley sat down, having skilfully avoided the question while still providing Galton with an answer. That night he recorded in his journal:

A person like myself with such a miserable, unfortunate past cannot possibly find pleasure in speaking before people who have wined, and rather to the full, about his poverty-stricken childhood and indulge in maudlin grief over circumstances that were utterly beyond his control? What had I to do with my birth in Wales? It was only an accident that my mother did not prefer to stay in London when her pains informed her of the approaching event. Denbigh is only a day's journey for a pedestrian from the English border, and here these people are perpetually talking about Welshmen and Scotsmen and Irishmen as though these nationalities were foreigners to the English.

By 28 August Stanley was in better spirits thanks to a letter and package hand-delivered to his suite at the Langham. The envelope bore an official royal seal and the contents read:

Sir – I have great satisfaction in conveying to you, by command of the Queen, Her Majesty's high appreciation of the prudence and zeal which you have displayed in opening a communication with Dr. Livingstone and relieving Her Majesty from the anxiety which, in common with her subjects, she had felt in regard to the fate of that distinguished traveller. The Queen desires me to express her thanks for the service you have thus rendered, together with her Majesty's congratulations on your having so successfully carried on the mission, which you fearlessly undertook. Her Majesty also desires me to request your acceptance of the memorial, which accompanies this letter. I am, sir, your most obedient humble servant – Granville.

The 'memorial' referred to was 'a beautiful and valuable gold snuff-box set with brilliants' (more than sixty diamonds) which, Stanley said, 'will be treasured by me as among the pleasantest results of my undertaking'.

Punch used the occasion to spin one of its famous rhymes containing a message for the man who had found Livingstone:

> Her Majesty sends you a snuff-box, brave Stanley.
> The gift holds a hint which my Majesty adds:
> 'Tis that you, the undaunted, successful and manly,
> Should turn up your Nose at all cavilling cads.

On 10 September 1872, Stanley was summoned to meet Queen Victoria at Dunrobin Castle, the most distant of Scotland's great houses and set in the northern Highlands. He travelled north in the company of Sir Henry Rawlinson, who spent half the train journey trying to make amends for the Royal Geographical Society's initial doubts about Stanley's discovery of Livingstone and the other half instructing him how to behave in front of the Queen. Rawlinson had added: 'Of course, you are not to talk or write about what you should see or hear.' At midday, the Queen entered and the gathered assembly

> bowed most profoundly, and the Queen advancing, Sir Henry introduced me in a short sentence. I regarded her with many feelings, first as the greatest lady in the land . . . and lastly, as that mysterious personage whom I had always heard spoken of, ever since I could understand anything, as *The Queen*. And poor blind Sir Henry, to think that I would venture to speak or write about this lady, whom in my heart of hearts, next to God, I worshipped. Besides, only of late, she has honoured me with a memorial, which is the more priceless that it was given when so few believed me.

The Queen and the former workhouse boy spoke about Livingstone and Africa and Victoria reminded her guest that in 1858 she had met the doctor, who had named the Victoria Falls in her honour. Later that evening, as was her custom, Victoria sat at her desk to write to members of her family, married to various other royal personages across Europe. In a letter to her daughter, Princess Victoria, Crown Princess of Prussia, the Queen described Stanley as 'a determined, ugly little man – with a strong American twang'.

Drawing of H.M. Stanley by Constantine von Grimm – 'Nemo' – for *Vanity Fair*, November 1884.

Chapter 25

'THE MOST GIGANTIC HOAX EVER ATTEMPTED ON THE CREDULITY OF MANKIND'

While scepticism surrounding Stanley's claims began to evaporate in England, controversy still raged on the other side of the Atlantic thanks to an unlikely source – Lewis Noe.

Like everyone else living in the eastern states, Noe had read Stanley's dispatches in the *New York Herald*; and he decided to use his knowledge of the author to attack his former friend's character – and earn himself a few dollars. On 16 August 1872, he penned a long letter to the editor of the *Herald*'s rival broadsheet, the *Sun*, from his home in Sayville, Long Island, expressing 'a little incredulity to the story of Henry Stanley, Dr. Livingstone's alleged discoverer. I know the man. I know his fertile powers of invention, and more than once I have seen his ingenuity impose upon men and imposed most successfully. But, as I do not desire to throw discredit upon his alleged discoveries without at least showing a fair reason for my convictions, I will tell his story as I heard it from his own lips, from the lips of his relatives, and from irrefragable proofs which shall be forthcoming when desired.' The letter prompted the *Sun*'s editor to call Stanley's discovery of Livingstone: 'the most gigantic hoax ever attempted on the credulity of mankind'.

Noe's letter told the story of his meeting with Stanley when, at age fifteen, he had joined the navy during the closing months of the Civil War. He revealed that Stanley had encouraged him to desert, jump ship and travel to New York before exploring Europe and Asia. Noe claimed that Stanley had left him destitute in the city while he went off to become a reporter on the American frontier. On his return 'his winning manners and gentlemanly bearing, and his seeming attachment for me' impressed Noe's parents into allowing their son to join Stanley on his adventure. For his part, Noe admitted that his 'admiration of Stanley amounted to a youthful enthusiasm, and I longed to go with him in search of romance and adventure'. Stanley was to cover Noe's travel costs but once on board the ship *E.H. Yarrington* and in the company of Stanley's fellow reporter, Harlow Cook, Noe discovered he was expected to work his passage to Turkey.

He admitted how 'in boyish sport' he had set fire to some bushes next to where Cook was dozing in the sunshine, how the fire had spread causing him to run for his life, leaving Stanley and Cook behind to be arrested. When reunited with Stanley, 'I found that I was to be a slave and a beggar, and a slave, too, of a remorseless master'. He wrote about how Stanley had tied him to a tree, pulled the shirt from his back, whipped him 'until the blood ran from my wounds', persuaded him to help steal horses from a passing traveller, how the robbery had gone wrong, they had fled, were captured by Turkish bandits who bound and tortured them and 'treated me in a shocking manner'.

The letter recalled how they had arrived penniless in Constantinople, where Stanley had borrowed money to purchase clothing from the US Consul and sailed to England, where Noe stayed with Stanley's relatives while his friend, wearing a naval coat purchased in a Turkish bazaar, took off for Wales to visit his mother. The letter's contents were deliberately designed to shame Stanley, whom Noe described as

a daring adventurer, bold and unscrupulous, but intelligent and specious. . . . In disclosing his infamy to the world, I have but a single object and purpose, and that is, as far as I can, to prevent the subjection of others to the outrage and wrong I was compelled to submit to at his hands. More than once he has threatened to kill me if I expose him. With his cruel and revengeful nature, I believe he would not hesitate to carry his threat into execution, if a favourable opportunity occurred in which he could do it with impunity. And I am not without my fears of assassination. Indeed, I should confidently expect it were we to meet without the bounds of civilisation or in a sparsely settled country where crimes would not be quickly discovered or where the avenues of escape were open.

Noe added his own name to those who claimed Welsh roots for Stanley, stating that his former friend lived in Wales until the age of fifteen when he came to America. 'His real name was John Rowland [*sic*] and he was so called by his relatives [Uncle Tom and Aunt Maria in Liverpool] in my presence.' The *Sun* published the letter in full on 24 August 1872 and followed it up by sending a reporter to the house where Noe, now aged twenty-three, lived with his wife and her parents on their small farm. The interview, containing yet more 'revelations' about Stanley, appeared on 29 August 1872.

The *New York Herald* was accused of having been 'duped' into believing that letters sent by Livingstone to Bennett were genuine. Correspondents accused Stanley of forging the letters or of telling Livingstone what to write in communications to Bennett. In the interests of keeping the story alive for a few days longer, and safe in the knowledge that the letters were genuine, the *New York Herald* reproduced a facsimile of the first page of Livingstone's letter of thanks to Bennett, claiming two reasons for so doing – 'to present the public a specimen of how the great explorer writes in the wilds of Central Africa, with what firmness he grasps his pen and how he writes his mind without the afterthought usually visible in erasures and interpolations. The second is in exhibiting to the few doubting Thomas's in this continent, who may yet hold out against indisputable evidence, a sign whereby they can learn to enter the ranks of the millions of true believers.'

In response, the *Sun* obtained two letters written by Stanley to Noe five years earlier, reproduced facsimile copies and invited readers to compare his handwriting to that of Livingstone's in the previous day's *Herald*, claiming they had all been written by the same hand – Stanley's. The dispute was settled by eminent New York handwriting expert, Madame Fiat Justitia to whom Bennett paid a large sum to disprove the claim – so providing yet another article to keep the story on the boil for another day. Justitia's conclusion was that she 'must confess my inability to discover any resemblance whatever . . . I, for one, do not feel at all impressed with the belief that one hand wrote both letters.'

To finally silence its rivals, Bennett threw down a challenge in the columns of his newspaper. He said that now proof had been produced that Stanley had found Livingstone and that the doctor's letters were genuine, he would put up half the funds for another expedition to seek out Livingstone again and settle the affair. Other newspapers were to pay the balance and could send along as many correspondents as they wished. There were no takers.

In return for upholding his reporter's reputation and defending his claims, Bennett now expected a response from Stanley. His felt his correspondent, who was living in London on full pay and all expenses covered, ought to be filing stories to New York instead of fulfilling speaking engagements. Privately, Bennett knew that every time Stanley made an appearance, whether before Queen Victoria or any large distinguished group, the name of the *New York Herald* was favourably mentioned and his newspaper's reputation further advanced among the British intelligentsia.

Bennett sent Stanley copies of the *Sun*'s articles containing Lewis Noe's letters and interviews and asked for an 'on the record' response. Stanley replied on 18 September 1872, stating that the articles had triggered off 'conflicting emotions' when he read them.

> My first feelings were those of profound astonishment at the discovery of so debased a character as this wretched young man, Noe, turns out to be. He proclaims himself the victim of a foul and unnatural outrage, gives his name in full, with his present address; he dwells fondly on the disgusting details which unmanned him; offers himself up voluntarily to public scorn and contempt, and deliberately stamps himself as the greatest moral idiot in existence. I then felt regret at discovering the fact that there was a newspaper in the city of New York which could lend itself for the publication of such a disgusting, immoral letter as the one purporting to be written by Lewis H. Noe and exhibit a morbid delight in every circumstance and detail of this most shameful story.

Stanley said that to enter 'upon a detailed refutation of the various charges and accusations falsely levelled at me by this eccentric youth would be undignified and unworthy of me'. However, he gave a brief account of his experiences with Noe, avoiding any mention of deserting from the navy, stating only that in the summer of 1866 he 'took this boy as a kind of companion, who was to make himself generally useful'. Stanley blamed 'the young rascal' for setting fire to the bushes in Turkey, saying, 'I punished the young villain with a few strokes of a switch, a far lighter punishment than he deserved, as any sensible man will at once admit'. He added: 'The indignities and outrages which the ruffians subsequently visited upon a member of our party need not be repeated here, but I may mention that I was the one who was instrumental in relieving my party from all apprehensions of a worse fate.'

As far as instructing Livingstone what to write in letters to Bennett, Stanley averred 'that to neither of these letters have I put pen or pencil;

that I neither interpolated nor suggested one word, phrase or quotation to Dr. Livingstone while he was writing them and handed them to me, asking me "Will these do?" . . . As for the authenticity of the other letters I brought with me . . . [all recipients] have one and all come forward to testify to their authenticity.'

While Stanley's response provided Bennett with satisfactory answers – 'Our correspondent is simply a native American. Missouri and not Wales is his birthplace', thundered an editorial – the newspaper proprietor was unhappy that the early life of a *New York Herald* correspondent should have so much mystery surrounding it. After all, Livingstone's discovery had been an 'all-American' venture using an American newspaper's funds with an American 'commander' at its head. How could it be an American triumph, therefore, if the man in charge was from . . . Wales?

Chapter 26

NEW YORK TRIUMPH AND DISASTER

How I Found Livingstone in Central Africa became the book everyone wanted to read at the end of 1872. It was an immediate best-seller, making Stanley a rich man. Although the *New York Herald* did not benefit directly from sales of the book, it did no harm to the newspaper's reputation as a crusading, daring publication that spared no expense to deliver truth and excitement to its readers. Stanley dedicated the book to

> James Gordon Bennett, Esq., (Proprietor of the 'New York Herald'). This Record of the Expedition Sent in Search of Doctor Livingstone and of Travels, Adventures and Discoveries in Central Africa, is Respectfully Dedicated as a tribute to the generosity and the liberality which originated, sustained and crowned the enterprise, by his Grateful Special Correspondent – Henry M. Stanley, Late Commander 'New York Herald' Expedition.

Once the book was published, all England wanted to hear Henry Morton Stanley personally tell the thrilling story of his search for Livingstone. Audiences fell into two categories: people with a genuine interest in geography and exploration and those eager to be under the same roof as a famous personality and expecting to be entertained. Stanley was aware of this, and devised a programme that catered for all tastes. He delivered hard facts and told his story, but lightened things up by bringing on Kalulu from time to time to do what little boys do best – sing songs, dance and perform imitations, the only difference being that Kalulu's songs were sung in Kiswahili, his dances were tribal and his impressions were of a Muslim at prayer. The audience loved it, and Kalulu, who liked life in England, enjoyed it, too.

When Stanley was invited to dine at homes of his new friends, Kalulu was occasionally also invited, to be fussed over by great ladies in their equally great homes. The boy was polite, well mannered and spoke only when spoken to. He looked smart in the tailor-made suits, shirts and ties Stanley had bought for him, although he never did get the hang of wearing boots and shoes. When Stanley sent regrets that he was unable to dine due to other engagements, hosts would ask him to send Kalulu instead. A hansom cab would be sent to the Langham Hotel and Kalulu dispatched to a fashionable house in Kensington or Belgravia where he would meet other well-dressed children and take tea. He generally returned to the hotel with a sovereign in his pocket. His hosts usually reported to Stanley that Kalulu 'was a little charmer, and no mistake'.

In between speaking engagements in large venues across the country, Stanley travelled to Hamilton, Scotland, to meet remaining members of Livingstone's family and talk to them about the time he had spent with their father. Stanley was already acquainted with sons Oswell and Tom, but the meeting would be his first with Livingstone's daughters, Janet and Agnes.

Oswell was cool towards Stanley. He had just received a stern letter from his father expressing how shocked he was that his son had turned his back on him and not ventured into the interior with Stanley's caravan from Zanzibar. In a separate letter to his daughter, Agnes, the doctor said that Oswell should 'have had the sense to come with me and gain a little credit that may enable him to hold up his head among men and not be merely Livingstone's son'. Livingstone accused Oswell of cowardice and duplicity and said he was 'as poor a specimen of a son as Africa ever produced . . . a person who does not think of supporting himself by his own labour but runs away home calling loudly for more money'. Livingstone believed his family – including his sisters – wanted him home to write another best-selling book, go on the lucrative public-speaking trail again and provide them all with a comfortable income.

Janet Livingstone gave Stanley a Bible inscribed: 'Presented to Henry M. Stanley by Miss Janet Livingstone, 5th November 1872, Hamilton, Scotland.' Later Agnes Livingstone would give Stanley her father's sextant 'in grateful acknowledgement of his invaluable services rendered to my father in Africa'. Stanley was also granted the freedom of the Burgh of Hamilton 'in acknowledgement of his noble service in relieving Dr. David

Livingstone, when deserted and destitute in Central Africa'. The freedom scroll was placed in a Scottish silver casket, the first of many accolades given to Stanley in towns and cities around the world.

When Stanley and Kalulu arrived in Manchester to talk at the Free Trade Hall, a young married couple sat near the speaker's podium. The young woman was five months pregnant and known to her Manchester neighbours as Mrs Katherine Bradshaw – the former Katie Gough-Roberts from Denbigh, once Stanley's 'betrothed'. On returning to London after his discovery of Livingstone, Stanley had contacted Katie, care of her father, asking her to return correspondence he had sent her – especially the fifteen-page confessional letter penned in 1870. Katie replied that she was happy to return the letters, provided she could hand them over in person. Stanley declined, either because a face-to-face meeting with the girl who had rejected him was too painful, or because his love for Katie had turned to disgust.

Following the Manchester lecture, Katie and Urban Bradshaw followed Stanley to the home of the president of Manchester's Chamber of Commerce, where he was staying, and rang the doorbell. Katie scribbled a note asking Stanley to come to the door and passed it to one of the servants to deliver. But Stanley refused to come in person and Katie and her husband left without returning the letters or talking to Stanley. They would hold on to the letters for another thirty-five years.

Daily Telegraph, 20 September 1872:

America is more anxious to hear about Stanley and Livingstone than is England. Mr. Stanley has accepted an engagement to deliver in the United States a series of lectures on his explorations in Africa, and his discovery of the great father of all explorers, the Marco Polo of the Unknown Continent. The terms of his contract – to use an American word – are 'lucrative'. The number of lectures is specified, the time is limited and the 'remuneration' is fixed at £10,000 and all expenses paid. Now £10,000 represents more than £300 a year for life – the average income for an Oxford or Cambridge fellow of a college – and is beyond all doubt a very comfortable sum to realise in the period of some few weeks. Cynics, of course, will sneer and declare that the correspondent of the *New York Herald* commenced life as a flaneur, grew into a charlatan and has ended by becoming a professional mountebank.

While Bennett had granted Stanley permission to lecture in American cities – providing the *New York Herald* with another publicity coup – the proprietor did not want his newspaper to be associated with the venture. Bennett was now uncertain how to use the reporter whose name was better known than his own. *Herald* reporters quietly claimed that although Bennett was deliriously happy with Stanley's Livingstone scoop, he was resentful of his correspondent's success, reminding everyone that although his man had got the story, he himself had paid handsomely for the privilege. Bennett decided to let the hullabaloo quieten down before determining how best to use Stanley in future. After all, he could hardly send the world's best-known journalist out on routine stories. In future, all of Stanley's assignments needed to be important, significant and carry gravitas – otherwise he might become bored and go and work for a rival newspaper. Bennett decided to have a private meeting with Stanley when he called at head office on Broadway and Ann Street, where 'the boys' on the *Herald*'s news staff were planning a reception in their colleague's honour on the editorial floor.

Stanley and Kalulu sailed into New York on the *Cuba* on 20 November 1872 to be greeted by a battery of press colleagues from the *New York Herald* and competing newspapers. Kalulu was whisked off to the Fifth Avenue Hotel while Stanley was marched to the *Herald*'s offices to meet the boss. All work on the following day's edition stopped as Stanley swept into the building to the sound of cheers from his fellow newspapermen, most of whom he hardly knew, never having worked directly from the paper's head office. He was ushered into Bennett's presence and the door was firmly closed behind them. The conversation that took place was never disclosed and is said to have lasted just ten minutes. When the door opened again, Bennett and Stanley shook hands and parted – the boss to his desk to continue working and his star reporter to lunch with fellow newsmen.

To attract as large an audience as possible, Stanley's lecture series at New York's Steinway Hall was promoted with all the razzmatazz of a Broadway entertainment. Advertisements were taken out in theatre and vaudeville columns announcing:

STEINWAY HALL   STANLEY'S LECTURES
HENRY M. STANLEY'S
AMERICAN LECTURES ON THE DISCOVERY OF
THE REV. DR. LIVINGSTONE
DECEMBER 3/4/6/10/11/13 – MATINEES DECEMBER 7 & 14
SALE OF SEATS FOR THE COURSE, EIGHT LECTURES,
WILL BEGIN AT STEINWAY HALL, ON TUESDAY NOVEMBER 26.
COURSE TICKETS: $10.00

STEINWAY HALL   H.M. STANLEY
STANLEY'S MARCH INTO AFRICA!
(THIS WEDNESDAY EVENING)
MR. HENRY M. STANLEY'S THRILLING LECTURE
WILL BE GIVEN AT STEINWAY HALL
SUBJECT: 'THE MARCH OF THE STANLEY–LIVINGSTONE
EXPEDITION'
SPECIAL ANNOUNCEMENT! ON THIS OCCASION MR. STANLEY WILL
APPEAR BEFORE THE AUDIENCE COSTUMED, ARMED & EQUIPPED AS
HE WAS WHEN PURSUING HIS ARDUOUS JOURNEY INTO AFRICA
AND ACCOMPANIED BY THE LITTLE NATIVE AFRICAN – KALULU!
HE WILL ALSO DISPLAY THE FLAGS, SPEARS AND OTHER
ACCOUTREMENTS WORN BY THE NATIVES OF CENTRAL AFRICA
WHO FORMED A PART OF HIS EXPEDITION IN SEARCH OF DR.
LIVINGSTONE
THESE RARE CURIOSITIES WILL REMAIN ON EXHIBITION DURING
THE EVENING AT THE HALL. GENERAL ADMISSION: $1.00

Advertising was bold to attract a wide selection of the ticket-buying public, including those frightened of the word 'lecture' and more used to popular entertainments. For the first time, Stanley learned he was competing with himself for an audience. Two shows were playing in New York with identical themes that season – the 'sensation drama "Africa!!! Or Livingstone and Stanley"' starring the comedy duo Harrigan and Hart at the Theatre Comique and 'Dan Bryant's Burlesque Lecture "Stanley & Kalulu", introducing Stanley's Casyembra Negro boy, Kalulu' at the Opera House.

Conquering a tough New York audience would be his hardest assignment yet. . . .

Kalulu fascinated New Yorkers and Stanley had long since recognised his potential as a crowd-puller. On 21 November 1872, he invited some *New York Herald* colleagues to his suite at the Fifth Avenue Hotel to meet the little fellow who, according to a reporter was 'clothed yesterday after the manner of an English page of the nineteenth century, whose status is better expressed in the word "buttons".' Under the headline 'Stanley and Kalulu – Interesting Interview with the Negro Boy – An Amoozin' Little Cuss', the *New York Herald* told readers:

Although eleven years of age, his education must have been neglected in early youth, for he is very honest, although not much more than a year in the hands of civilisation. He was a little shy on being first introduced. When, however, he was addressed in Kiswahili, the language of his tribe . . . he talked with considerable fluency and a certain pertinence of reply. [Kalulu was shown a photograph and asked to name the person in the picture.] 'Lifinston,' replied the boy beaming with intelligence. [Stanley then asked Kalulu to run through some of his set party pieces.] A devotional look overcast the dusky features of the untutored lad, and he forthwith proceeded to imitate the praying of Arabs at sunset with the perfection of mimicry. . . . He also proved how the musical instinct of the children of Africa was strong within him. He rocked his body, rolled his eyes and burst forth in Kiswahili song. . . . In reply to further questions in his native tongue, he stated that he was at present in a country called London. He finds it hard to see the difference between slaves and freemen yet. In Africa people were owned by other people, and here, so far as he had looked into politics and business, he found it much the same thing. This boy has evidently a lot to learn from the bird of freedom. The coloured boys at the hotel he called pagans, and his white admirers he admitted to being brothers. At this stage in the proceedings he remembered some chestnuts in his pockets and all further efforts to draw out this interesting little African lion had as much effect as attempting to interview the lion at Central Park when polishing a bone.

On 25 November 1872, the *New York Herald* carried a curious headline: 'Livingstone Finds Stanley'. Underneath was a report about how John Livingstone, the doctor's older brother (by two years), had travelled to New York from his Canadian home to pay his respects to the man who had found his sibling. John Livingstone was invited to Stanley's hotel suite and went up to the room with a reporter. The reporter was hoping to witness Stanley opening his door with the words: 'Mr Livingstone, I presume?' but was disappointed when he said: 'I see a good deal of the Livingstone characteristic about your face, sir.' To which John Livingstone replied: 'Yes, I believe there is quite a resemblance between the doctor and myself – at least there was when we were young.' He explained that he was unable to go to Africa to see his brother so had done the next best thing – travelled to New York to see the man who had found him.

Stanley agreed to address the American Geographical Association, but the continual round of official lunches, dinners and speaking engagements took its toll and he was forced to cancel at the last minute when fever packed him off to bed. At one stage he attempted to get up and get dressed but John Livingstone was on hand to restrain him.

On 3 December 1872, Stanley gave his first lecture at the Steinway Hall on the subject of 'Life in Central Africa and the Horrors of the Slave Trade'. The auditorium was crowded with what the *New York Herald* described as 'a select and intellectual audience'. There were a number of empty seats, too. On display was a large map of Central Africa showing the regions through which both Livingstone and Stanley had crossed and some of the weapons Stanley had picked up from villages razed by Mirambo's men. The Stars and Stripes, which had been held aloft when Stanley marched toward Livingstone at Ujiji, was also prominently displayed.

John Livingstone and Kalulu sat in the front row and applauded enthusiastically when Stanley mounted the podium. James Gordon Bennett declined to attend, preferring to send along his chief drama critic, George O. Seilhammer to 'review' Stanley's 'performance' in the same way as he would cover a theatrical play.

Seilhammer felt that 'the earnest manner of the lecturer showed a degree of enthusiasm in his subject that was not lost on the audience'. He praised Stanley's 'admirable ability to photograph, as it were, in the minds of his hearers, the strange, eventful scenes through which he so triumphantly passed, which made even dry details attractive. As he warmed to his subject his descriptions became more interesting and his audience more deeply impressed. Rarely has a lecturer been called upon to handle a subject so difficult and abstruse, and rarely have efforts on the rostrum been crowned with similar success.'

Seilhammer told Bennett privately that he – and most of the audience – had found the lecture dull and Stanley's delivery lacking in drama. Bennett ordered Seilhammer to be more critical of Stanley's second 'performance' about the march from Zanzibar to Unyanyembe, delivered to an auditorium one-third full of 'attentive and intelligent' people. Seilhammer said the evening was 'more interesting, both in treatment and delivery, than the previous effort. But it was far from being a marked success. Mr. Stanley's elocution is bad, though it improves as he gets into his discourse and might be made acceptable if his manner of treating his subjects was such as to ensure a partial forgetfulness of his failure of oratory. Unfortunately this is not the case.'

Seilhammer found parts of the lecture 'intolerably dry and dull' and added: 'Though not enlivened by the orator's skill, his narrative of the way in which he was sent on his perilous journey was well received, because it had in it some of the personal spice which the public always demanded.' He criticised Stanley for failing to utilise the large map on show and use the African props properly 'to make his hearers interested by making them illustrative of his subject. In everything he overlooks the personal and the peculiar and treats only of the geographical and the commonplace.' Seilhammer said that the audience were hoping for 'a personal talk about strange people and sights. Instead Mr. Stanley is giving only geography and natural history and his anecdotes are spoiled in the telling. All this is unnecessary and it would be cruel to Mr Stanley not to say so.' Stanley was advised to 'forgo his manuscript and, forgetting the sing-song and doleful monotone in which his voice is too often pitched and simply talk to his audience of what he saw, heard and suffered while doing his duty so nobly for the *Herald*'.

Advance bookings for remaining lectures were poor and the organisers switched the venue to a smaller hall attached to the Plymouth Church without warning the public of the change. When ticket holders arrived at the Steinway Hall they were told by the janitor at the door: 'Stanley's played out; there will be no lecture tonight or any other night as Mr. Stanley's receipts do not meet expenses.'

According to Seilhammer, the third lecture, describing Stanley's discovery of Livingstone, was 'a marked improvement upon his last effort upon the platform'. The reviewer noted that Stanley appeared to have 'acted upon our counsel, discarded his manuscript and simply talked to his audience instead of disclaiming to them'. Stanley's 'style and manner

. . . was [*sic*] somewhat wanting, although his personal friends know well that when the occasion inspires him, he is a vivid and magnetic speaker'.

Bad reviews by his own newspaper and its competitors caused Stanley's lecture tour to collapse after the third night. With no new assignment for the *Herald* in the offing, Stanley had to think hard about where to direct his energy. Money was not a problem. Royalties for *How I Found Livingstone* came pouring in from England and America and he was still on full salary from the newspaper. So Stanley did what every good writer with energy to burn does – he wrote. Stanley turned his hand to fiction, one of only two occasions in his life when he wrote about subjects in which he was not the main player.

My Kalulu – Prince, King and Slave was 'written for boys . . . those clever, bright-eyed, intelligent boys, of all classes, who have begun to be interested in romantic literature, with whom educated fathers may talk without fear of misapprehension, and of whom friends are already talking as boys who have a promising future before them. These boys are the guests for whom I have provided a true Afric feast.'

The book was inspired by Kalulu himself, who had related stories about his African life to Stanley during their travels together. A fictitious Kalulu, several years older than Stanley's young companion, became the central character in a fanciful story about a boy born into slavery who becomes a courageous king, encounters wild animals, explores the dark interior, participates in tribal battles, witnesses a kidnapping, engineers a heroic rescue and observes secret ceremonies.

My Kalulu was written to be read in cliff-hanging episodes, one thrilling chapter leading effortlessly to the next. It was based on incidents collected by Stanley as he walked across Africa in search of Livingstone and tales related by Kalulu. It was intended to be a blend of fact and fiction and 'something lighter, fresher' than his previous book. In his introduction, Stanley assures 'those interested in Kalulu that some day, if I live, I shall attempt to take him back to his own country, through numberless adventures, incidents and scenes, in the hope that he shall enjoy his own again'. In the meantime, Stanley and Kalulu returned to England to await further instructions from Bennett.

Weeks passed without word from the boss, but Stanley kept busy completing *My Kalulu* and making occasional visits to his mother in Wales, often taking a gift of an African curio or artefact to decorate her pub. In April 1873, he was again summoned to meet Bennett in Paris –

the same city where the editor had famously given him the Livingstone mission. There was to be no repeat assignment of the same magnitude. At the Hotel des Deux Mondes, where Bennett had taken up residence, the editor ordered Stanley back to Spain on temporary cover until a story of importance broke. He informed Stanley that he was carefully monitoring events on Africa's Gold Coast, where a despot king threatened to invade a neighbouring British protectorate. Bennett told Stanley that if the situation deteriorated and the British government decided to send military aid, the job was his. Stanley returned to London, put Kalulu into a boarding school run by an Anglican minister in Wandsworth and returned to Spain, its routine riots and revolutions – and waited.

An illustration from Stanley's 1873 boy's adventure book, *My Kalulu – Prince, King and Slave*.

Chapter 27

COOMASSIE

It was November 1873 before events in Africa took a turn for the worse and Bennett kept his promise, pulling Stanley out of Spain and sending him to London to prepare for his next major story. Stanley was excited about returning to report another 'small British war' against tribesmen from the West African Kingdom of Ashanti (Ghana), who had invaded the territory of the neighbouring Fanti, a tribe living in a 2,000 square mile area under British protection on the mineral-rich Gold Coast. Like Emperor Theodorus before him, King Coffi of the Ashanti had taken European missionaries hostage – and the British decided to demonstrate superiority by striking hard to show who was boss in land over which the Union Jack fluttered.

As usual, there was another motive for a military rescue expedition to West Africa. Britain already controlled the Gold Coast but wanted to penetrate the interior for strategic, political and economic reasons. King Coffi's latest actions were nothing more than an excuse for Britain to attempt to increase their area of domination in this important and little developed part of Africa.

Stanley had plenty of time to ponder the possible outcome of the conflict as he sailed on the *Benin* from Liverpool to Sierra Leone. He considered the best result would be outright victory over the Ashanti, deposing their king and 'opening up the whole of Central Africa to trade and commerce and the beneficent influences of civilisation. . . . Two thousand Ashanti, under the leadership of an intelligent British officer, would soon extend the power of the English from Cape Coast Castle across the Thogoshi mountains to Timbuktu, and from the Mandingo land to Benin.' The *New York Herald* had again allocated Stanley generous funds, from which he purchased a small steam-driven launch, the *Dauntless*, to travel up and down West Africa's maze of rivers. The craft was carried as cargo on the deck of the *Benin* until needed.

In Sierra Leone, Stanley found that the bulk of the British army travelling out to quash the Ashanti were still on the high seas and he quickly became bored without a story to cover. He filed several dispatches about what might happen once the army arrived, but found British officers in the area unhelpful – even to the man who had found Livingstone. He decided to go in search of news, chugging down the coast in the *Dauntless*, hoping to discover stories among a small military advance party and interview its commander. He engaged an engineer to ensure the steamer remained in prime condition throughout the voyage.

Before setting out, Stanley offered space on his little steamer to fellow correspondents covering the conflict. Three accepted his invitation, but two backed out pleading fear of seasickness and expressing doubts about the safety of the vessel. This left Stanley with one other correspondent for company and they headed off in an easterly direction following the shore at a speed of 9 knots, 'the little yacht throbbing through every beam in her, the steam sizzed and swished vigorously, the funnel roared in concert, while the fan kicked up a foaming wake behind in quite an exhilarating style'.

The *Dauntless* sped along for over 70 miles, arriving off the coast of Accra. The reporters went in search of Captain Glover, formerly of the Royal Navy and now a senior civil servant charged with sending intelligence reports back to London about warring Ashanti tribes. Glover told the newsmen that the forthcoming campaign would be based on the inland settlement of Coomassie, which was surrounded by a deadly swamp and 'jungle so dense that even the strongest fell victim to the malaria it cherished . . . and through which the British army will have to march 140 miles, leaving numbers behind sick of fever and dysentery'.

Four thousand men would participate in the campaign, including soldiers from the Rifle Brigade, the 23rd Fusiliers and the 42nd Highlanders – the Black Watch – plus sailors, marines and members of the Royal Engineers supported by battalions of West Indians, Hausas and 'native allies'. This information provided one piece of decent copy which the restless Stanley could send to his newspaper. Otherwise, he told his journal, 'there is really nothing to write about, nor hardly anything to talk about'.

Days passed with still no sign of any troopships. Stanley became concerned about the *Dauntless* bobbing about under the blistering sun out in the lagoon. It was time to take her on another news hunt and again Stanley invited fellow correspondents to join him. His old friend from the Magdala campaign, George A. Henty of the *Evening Standard*, had just arrived, keen to send a dispatch to his paper as early as possible and agreed to join the voyage. Stanley had already scooped Henty once before in Africa and the newsman was determined not to let it happen again.

They set off at midnight and 'steamed down the coast at a rattling rate, heedless of the burden and forebodings which had been heaped on the heads of her passengers'. Two days later they arrived at a military camp where an advance party were making preparations to venture into the interior to battle with the Ashanti. Captain Glover was also there and invited Stanley and Henty to travel on his own vessel, *Lady of the Lake*, steaming up the 2-mile wide River Volta with a cargo of ammunition.

They travelled for several hours before reaching a bank where nearly three thousand 'armed, equipped and organised' native soldiers were encamped at a tented riverside barracks. Ashanti warriors were housed on the opposite bank and, despite being told that the battle would not commence until the rest of the army arrived, Stanley began to be excited about his assignment again.

By the time Stanley and Henty returned to join fellow correspondents, troopships had finally brought English soldiers. They spent Christmas Day in camp before the big push towards Coomassie began on 26 December 1873.

To Stanley's disappointment, the first two weeks of the march were uneventful, but on 8 January 1874 they had word that 'there were some strange people, probably Ashanti, skulking behind trees at some distance beyond'. One of them claimed to be an official messenger from the Ashanti capital carrying a letter from King Coffi 'to the English Chief', Major-General Sir Garnet Wolseley. The letter's contents were shared with news-hungry correspondents to turn into copy that could be sent back to the coast. The King claimed he had always loved white people and always been friendly towards them – so why were they marching on his capital? Wolseley composed a reply to be sent back with the messenger: 'Surrender or die'.

The Major-General treated the messengers to a demonstration of the newly invented Gatling gun, with its four barrels and ability to fire 400 rounds of ammunition. He told them that the white man's army had many such weapons and he would have no hesitation in ordering their use on any Ashanti daring to make war with Fanti. Looking worried, they quickly left to take Wolseley's reply to their King and tell him about the magical weapon they had seen.

A week later 'the apparition of a pale-faced captive – a shadow of a man suffering from pulmonary consumption, one who had lingered in compulsory detention at the capital of Ashanti for the last five years', stumbled into camp. He was a Swiss missionary who had been released by King Coffi as a goodwill gesture. Stanley was first in line with notebook in hand to interview him and learned that the King 'was aged around 35, arrogant, vain and cruel beyond measure . . . possessing about 300 wives. . . . It is death for a man to look at female possessions of the monarch.' The missionary told Stanley that when the King and his entourage approached, onlookers were required to turn their backs and cover their faces so as not to set eyes on his wives.

He learned that Coomassie contained considerable quantities of gold hidden in hundreds of secret places. Before any battle took place, slaves guarding the gold were killed so they would be unable to reveal its whereabouts in the event of their King's defeat. Over 15,000 people lived in Coomassie and the entire Ashanti army was made up of 48,000 men. The missionary also told Stanley that word about the Gatling gun's terrifying firepower had spread fear among the tribesmen – just as Major-General Sir Garnet Wolseley had expected.

Several days later, six German and French captives appeared on the track with their Fanti servants and a message from King Coffi saying he wanted 'no palaver with white men' and wished only to fight for land he claimed was his and now occupied by Fanti. He desired to 'be a friend of the white people and to establish commerce with them', was even prepared to pay large sums in gold to make up for his transgressions but the army 'must stay where it is and not advance further'.

Sir Garnet Wolseley had no intention of staying where he was and advanced towards Coomassie, hell-bent on victory, glory, British supremacy – and plenty of gold booty to take back to England. As the soldiers neared the capital, increasingly desperate messages arrived from the King suing for peace, pleading for mercy and offering to deliver as much gold as the Major-General wanted. These messages met with the same reply: 'I will burn your capital to the ground if my terms are not acceded to at once.'

The Anglo-Ashanti campaign was becoming a better story by the day, allowing correspondents to send riveting tales about tribal warfare and white captives back to their newspapers. Stanley painstakingly collected names and ranks of scores of men engaged in the conflict and included them in his articles. His copy graphically described camp life, the exchange of messages between Wolseley and King Coffi, the promise of unlimited gold, high morale among the troops and interviews with hostages as they were released. Stanley's fears that the campaign might turn into a damp squib were unfounded and the assignment became the story of a brave British military adventure in the dark African jungle.

By 1 February, Stanley was writing about armed combat at Ashanti villages on the approach to Coomassie and how Wolseley's soldiers had razed the settlements to the ground. Battles were not easily won and Stanley recorded that British troops admired the courageous way the Ashanti had fought in the face of the Gatling guns. While the British lost three men in the battles for the villages, the Ashanti lost hundreds. There were wounded on both sides.

Three days later, British soldiers were marching towards Coomassie through thick and thorny jungle so dense that the sun rarely pierced the canopy above. All the time they were secretly observed by Ashanti spies, creeping silently on all fours through the undergrowth. Occasionally they would come across villages in which human sacrifices were found 'for the purposes of affrighting the conquerors . . . the head severed from the body, was turned to meet the advancing army, the body was evenly laid out with the feet towards Coomassie. This laying out meant no doubt: *"Regard this face, white men, you whose feet are hurrying on to our capital, and learn the fate awaiting you."'*

At Amoaful, a town close to Coomassie, the companies lined up, firing in succession according to order and retreating to reload while another group marched forward to fire. When the Black Watch advanced to the playing of bagpipes, the Ashanti fled in panic. Stanley described this as 'a new game of war which the white man inaugurated in Ashanti and which the Ashanti did not understand'.

Stanley makes no mention of whether he personally took up arms against the Ashanti. War correspondents were expected to be neutral and not use weapons against enemy forces. But thirty years after the Coomassie campaign, Sir Garnet Wolseley recollected in his memoirs, *Story of a Soldier's Life*:

Not twenty yards off were several newspaper correspondents . . . one soon attracted my attention by his remarkable coolness. It was Henry Stanley, the famous traveller. A thoroughly good man, no noise, no danger ruffled his nerve, and he looked as cool and self-possessed as if he had been at target practice. Time after time, as I turned in his direction, I saw him go down to a kneeling position to steady his rifle, as he plied the most daring of the enemy with a never-failing aim . . . I can still see before me the close shut lips, and determined expression of his manly face, which, when he looked in my direction, told plainly I had near me an Englishman in plain clothes, whom no danger could appal. Had I felt inclined to run away, the cool, unflinching manliness of that face would have given me fresh courage. I had previously been somewhat prejudiced against him, but all such feelings were slain and buried at Amoaful.

Following a shaky start to their relationship, Stanley and Sir Garnet later became close friends.

After the battle, Sir Garnet Wolseley rode victoriously into the fallen city of Coomassie and immediately sent a message to King Coffi, who had gone into hiding, informing him that 'now you have seen the power of England you should give yourself up and be treated with all royal dignity'. To demonstrate to citizens of Coomassie that the British meant business, a young man found stealing from a food store was publicly hanged from a tree and his body left swinging for all to see. There was no further plundering or resistance offered by the Ashanti.

The correspondents decided to explore the captured African city. They entered wattle and mud dwellings, storehouses, barns and market stalls and were impressed by their neatness and cleanliness. The city was three and a half miles in circumference with a central road a mile and a half in length running down the centre. At the end of the road, correspondents experienced 'foul smells so suffocating that we were glad to produce our handkerchiefs to prevent the intolerable and almost palpable odour from mounting into the brain and overpowering us'. In a grove they 'found 30 or 40 decapitated bodies in the last stages of corruption and countless skulls which lay piled in heaps and scattered over a wide extent. The stoutest heart and the most stoical mind might have been appalled.'

From this 'Golgotha' they proceeded to the royal palace, described as 'a number of houses with steep thatched roofs, clustered together and fenced around with split bamboo stakes occupying an area 400 or 500 feet square, at one corner of which rose a square two-storey stone building'. They passed through deserted courtyards where lay 'war drums stained with blood . . . and decorated with human skulls' as they made their way towards the stone structure, which had been King Coffi's private residence. 'The upper storey contained much valuable plunder,' Stanley related and he feverishly scribbled an inventory of everything on display: golden masks, toys, bracelets, Persian rugs, British-made carpets, leopard skins, silken umbrellas, silver tankards, copies of *The Times* and *Bristol Courier*; valuable, curious and worthless things all heaped together in every room. 'An old curiosity shop could not exhibit a more miscellaneous variety of things than this King's bedchambers, private apartments and storerooms contained,' Stanley reported. The goods later fetched £5,000 at auction.

Sir Garnet Wolseley sent word to King Coffi that he expected him to honour a peace treaty which included clauses stipulating that there would be 'perpetual peace between the Queen of England and the King of Ashanti'; that the King would pay 50,000 ounces of gold dust to cover the cost 'of the expenses he has occasioned to her Majesty the Queen of England by the war'; and that he would renounce all right or title to Fanti lands. Coomassie was then burned to the ground, King Coffi's stone palace blown up and Wolseley's men ordered to fall in and return to the coast. The Anglo-Ashanti campaign had been a total success for Britain and Sir Garnet Wolseley and another African adventure for Henry Morton Stanley.

On 25 February 1874, Stanley was on his way back to England in the steamship *Dromedary*, sailing via the Cape Verde Islands. After going ashore there he was told that Livingstone had died at Ilala, near Lake Bangweolo, nine and a half months before. His body was on its way back to England on board the *Malwa* sailing out of Aden.

Stanley's journal entry that night took on an uncharacteristically pious tone:

Dear Livingstone – another sacrifice to Africa! His mission, however, must not be allowed to cease; others must go forward and fill the gap. Close up, boys! Close up! Death must find us everywhere. May I be selected to succeed him in opening up Africa to the shining light of Christianity! My methods, however, will not be Livingstone's. Each man has his own way. His, I think, had its defects, though the old man, personally, has been almost Christ-like for goodness, patience, and self-sacrifice. The selfish and wooden-headed world requires mastering, as well as loving charity; for man is a composite of the spiritual and earthly. May Livingstone's God be with me, as He was with Livingstone in all his loneliness. May God direct me as He wills. I can only vow to be obedient – and not to slacken.

Chapter 28

A LIVING-STONE

Open the Abbey doors, and bear him in
To sleep with king and counsellor, chief and sage,
The Missionary, come of weaver-kin,
But great by work that brooks no lower wage.
He needs no epitaph to guard a name
Which men shall prize while worthy work is known;
He lived and died for good – be this his fame –
Marbles decay; this is a Living-stone.

Punch, 25 April 1874

After Stanley had left Livingstone near Unyanyembe on 14 March 1872, the old doctor had nothing better to do than sit it out, waiting for men and supplies his young American friend would send from Zanzibar. On 19 March – Livingstone's fifty-ninth birthday – he recorded in his journal: 'My Jesus, my King, my Life, my All; I again dedicate my whole self to Thee. Accept me, and grant, O gracious Father, that ere this year is gone I may finish my task. In Jesus' name I ask it. Amen. So let it be.'

Livingstone also contemplated how he might cause further harm to Africa's barbaric slave trade. On 1 May he completed an article for the *New York Herald* which included the phrase which would eventually find its way onto his tombstone in Westminster Abbey: 'All I can say in my loneliness is, may heaven's rich blessing come down on every one – American, English, Turk – who will help to heal this open sore of the world.' Exactly one year later, Livingstone was dead.

Livingstone had plenty of time to consider his next enterprise, attempting to prove that the River Lualaba was the source of the Nile. He planned to head south, marching around Lake Tanganyika, crossing the Zambezi and following the southern portion of Lake Bangweolo before travelling west along its southern shore.

Stanley's fifty-six handpicked men arrived in Unyanyembe on 8 August and Livingstone was overjoyed. The men joined five others, the only remainder of Livingstone's original followers. He wrote: 'How thankful I am, I cannot confess.' The men were employed at salaries of up to $30 a year for a period of two years, paid in advance by the *New York Herald*, and their contracts stipulated that should the doctor wish to continue working after that time, they should remain until new porters were engaged.

The men also brought a letter from Stanley, written at Zanzibar, in which he told Livingstone that 'very few amongst men have I found I so much got to love as yourself'. He said that both England and America expected their people to do their duty. 'Do yours as persistently as heretofore & come back to your friends and country to be crowned with the laurel, and I will go forth to do mine.' Stanley reminded the doctor: 'Do not forget the *Herald*, please. The *Herald* will be grateful to me for securing you as a Correspondent.' Livingstone was true to his word.

The final journey began on 25 August 1872. By 8 October, he had reached Lake Tanganyika where the expedition rested. Livingstone's dysentery and bowel disorder had returned. He continued losing blood and several of his men were also sick. As the season advanced, the rain returned, swelling rivers and streams and turning the ground into a quagmire. It was still raining incessantly in January 1873. Their path lay across flooded rivers and Livingstone often had to be carried on the shoulders of his men.

By 19 September, Livingstone had taken no food for a week. Tribes were unfriendly and unwilling to sell food. They continued for the next four months on rations. The doctor wrote:

Carrying me across one of the broad, deep, sedgy rivers is really a very difficult task. One we crossed was 2,000 feet broad. The first part, the main stream, came up to Susi's mouth, and wetted my seat and legs. One held up my pistol behind, then one after another took a turn, and when he sank deep into an elephant's footprint he required two to lift him, so as to gain a footing on the level, which was over waist deep. It took us a full hour and a half to cross over. The water was cold, and so was the wind. We are anxious about food. The lake is near, but we are not sure of provisions. Our progress is distressingly slow. Wet, wet, wet; sloppy weather, truly.

The end of April marked the final days of Livingstone's travels. When he awoke on the 28th, he found it difficult to walk, so his men carried him across rivers and swamps until they came to Chitambo's village – named after the local chief – in Ilala (now Zambia), where they built a primitive shelter in which the doctor could rest until he was well enough to travel. The men laid him on a rough bed in the shelter, where he spent the night.

When his men peered through the doorway the following morning, they found Livingstone still asleep and left him undisturbed. Later his mind seemed to wander as he asked vague questions about the country they were in and sighed in pain, 'Oh dear, dear', and drifted back into sleep. Later he awoke and asked Susi to boil water and bring his medicine chest, from which he took calomel to calm his fever.

At daybreak the next morning, Majwara, the sixteen-year-old Ugandan boy who acted as Livingstone's gun carrier and slept close to his master's doorway, called in alarm to Susi: 'Come to master, I am afraid; I don't know if he is alive.' Worried his master might be dead, Susi roused Chuma and three others and the party carefully entered the hut. By the light of a candle still burning by his bed, they saw the doctor kneeling in prayer, his back to them, his body stretched forward and head buried in his hands on the pillow. They were afraid to approach him, not wishing to disturb their master at prayer. Seeing no movement, they drew closer and one of them touched his cheek. It was cold. David Livingstone had died several hours before, alone and in the act of prayer.

What should now be done with their master's body? The men conferred; he must be taken home on a final journey to the distant land over the seas from where he had originally come to Africa thirty years before. They agreed they must carry him to Zanzibar from where they knew large ships sailed to a place called England where Queen Victoria lived.

The undertaking was fraught with danger. They ran the risk of encountering tribes deeply superstitious of a dead body passing through their territory, who would confiscate the corpse if it were discovered and use it at witchcraft rituals. Livingstone's attendants, Susi and Chuma, were elected to lead the caravan. One of the men, Farijala, knew how to prepare a body. A hut was constructed without a roof and open to the skies as Jacob Wainwright, who had been educated at a missionary school, uttered Christian prayers. The doctor's skin and bone corpse was laid on the ground, Farijala cut the body open and had the heart, intestines and internal organs removed, placed in a tin box and buried. While removing the organs, Susi and Chuma saw a blood clot several inches in diameter obstructing Livingstone's lower intestines, confirming that the doctor had almost certainly died in excruciating pain. Salt was placed inside the body and the corpse exposed to the sun. No other means were taken to preserve it, apart from placing a small amount of brandy in the mouth and hair.

When the body was completely dry two weeks later, Livingstone's legs were folded underneath his knees. It was wrapped in calico, slid into a cylinder of tree bark and stitched in sailcloth. Finally, this strange 'coffin' was tarred to make it waterproof. It was now ready to begin its journey to Zanzibar, lashed to a pole and carried by two men.

Jacob Wainwright carved an inscription on the Mpundu tree under which the body had rested and where the tin box was buried. The tree remained standing on the site of Chitambo's camp at Lake Bangweolo for twenty-six years, until it became diseased and was cut down. The inscribed section was removed and sent to London where it is today part of a collection owned by the Royal Geographical Society.

It took nine months for the men to carry their master's body, clothes, papers, instruments and personal possessions to the coast. Ten men died of fever on the way. As expected, they encountered unfriendly tribes on their journey, but told them their 'cargo' contained supplies. At one village the chief was unhappy with this explanation and Livingstone's loyal men had to fight their way out with their precious consignment.

In Unyanyembe the men were met by another Royal Geographical Society-funded expedition, unaware of the doctor's death and, according to the Society, bringing 'the best equipped expedition which ever left Zanzibar for the purpose of exploration'. Its leader, Lieutenant Lovett Cameron, RN insisted that Livingstone's body be buried there and then, but the men were determined to take it to the coast. Cameron demanded to examine the contents of the crates and tin boxes containing Livingstone's possessions and told the men he was commandeering them on behalf of the British Consul. Susi, Chuma and Jacob Wainwright protested, but Cameron insisted on removing Livingstone's geographical instruments for his own use.

Chuma was sent ahead to prepare the British authorities in Zanzibar for the arrival of their master's body. Dr Kirk was on leave in England and naval attaché Captain William Prideaux, acting in his absence, was informed on 24 February 1874 that a group of weary men had arrived at the mission in Bagamoyo carrying a strange load. They claimed its contents was 'mwilli wa Daudi' – 'the body of David'. Prideaux sent a warship to collect the corpse. Uncertain what to do with the brave and loyal men who had carried Livingstone through the interior for the last nine months and concerned about how his actions might be interpreted by Kirk when he returned, Prideaux paid them from his own pocket, dismissed them and sent them home.

Devoted men who had risked their lives to walk hundreds of miles with the remains of their master, facing numerous perils along the way, were treated like ordinary porters. Their devotion to the white man who had never beaten them or bound them in chains but had shown only kindness, was later rewarded by the Society which struck a medal for every man who had helped to bring Livingstone's body to the coast. By the time the medals reached Zanzibar, the group had broken up and gone their separate ways. Most of them never received their decoration. Susi and Chuma pleaded to be allowed to travel to England to accompany their master's coffin, but only a single African sailed with the body, Jacob Wainwright – the man who had carved Livingstone's name on the tree at Chitambo's camp. He had been with Livingstone for only a year, but because he had attended a Church Missionary Society school, was considered 'civilised' and his passage to England and the cost of a new suit were funded by a Zanzibar church hoping he might raise funds on his travels.

Livingstone's body was removed from the cylinder, placed in a conventional coffin and stowed on the hold of the P & O steamship Malwa travelling to Southampton. Stanley was part of a reception committee waiting on the quayside on 15 April 1874 to witness the arrival of the coffin. Crowds looked on silently as it was lifted from the cargo hold and settled onto the deck. Jacob Wainwright sat on one of Livingstone's tin trunks and rested his elbow on his master's coffin as one of the ship's passengers took his photograph looking forlorn and awkward in his new suit. He had written some words in an unsteady hand on a piece of card: 'To the memory of Dr. Livingstone, friend of the African'.

The flag-draped coffin was conveyed by a black horse-drawn hearse through Southampton's silent streets to the station and so transferred to London. The city came to a standstill as another hearse and mourning coaches took the coffin to the Savile Row headquarters of the Royal

Geographical Society. There the remains were 'positively identified' by
Sir William Ferguson and a small number of Livingstone's Society
colleagues, including Dr Kirk.

When the coffin was opened and the body unwrapped from its primitive
coverings, it was unrecognisable. Nearly one year after his death, the only
thing proving the decaying corpse on the table was that of Dr David
Livingstone was a lump on the bone of the left humerus, damaged by the
lion that had attacked him thirty years before. Thanks to the doctor's own
account of this incident in his book on missionary travels, this was the
only proof needed by the learned gentlemen that what lay before them
was all that remained of Dr David Livingstone.

Inside one of Livingstone's trunks was an undated letter (probably
written after Christmas 1872) addressed to Stanley. Again it expressed the
old man's gratitude to his young friend for 'finding him' and stated:

I am . . . devoutly thankful to the loving Father above for helping you
through all your manifold *Masika* [rainy season] toils, and bringing you
safely to Zanzibar, with your energies unimpaired, and with a desire to
exert yourself to the utmost in securing all the men and goods needed
for this my concluding trip. I am perpetually reminded that I owe a
great deal to you for the drilling of the men you sent . . . I keep most of
your handsome presents of champagne for a special occasion. . . .
I thank you very much and very sincerely for all your kind generosity.

Over the next few days, thousands filed past Livingstone's coffin where
it lay in the Royal Geographical Society map room at Savile Row.
A nationwide appeal was launched by Livingstone's friends 'for means to
support the family of the traveller'. On 18 April, the funeral took place at
Westminster Abbey. Stanley led the eight pallbearers, who also included
Dr Kirk, William Cotton Oswell, William Webb and Jacob Wainwright. The
Daily Telegraph reported:

Most notable among the throng as they carry the coffin to the grave,
are the African travellers who constitute such a natural guard of
honour for this dead man. Foremost among them in right of gallant
special service and nearest to Livingstone's head, stands Stanley –
suntanned anew from Ashanti. . . . But for Stanley, Livingstone would
have died long back, without aid or news from us.

The polished oaken coffin was carried to its last resting place, a dark cavity in the Abbey floor in the centre of the western part of the nave, halfway between the western doors and the choir. The coffin contained a brass plate with the inscription: 'David Livingstone, born at Blantyre, Lanarkshire, Scotland, 19th March 1813, died at Ilala, Central Africa, 4 May, 1873.' The newspaper noted:

> the solemn dusky faces of the two Africans, Wainwright and little Kalulu, Mr. Stanley's boy, who are standing among the nearest, and the mind reverts to the widely different scene a year ago, when Livingstone, after much pain, which is not spared to the best and kindliest, gave up his gallant, loving, pious spirit to his Master and Maker, and when yonder Negro [Joseph Wainwright] had read over him the very service which has now again been so grandly celebrated for him with pomp and rolling music, like a King. The African – a simple-looking, quiet, honest lad – attracts many eyes as he stands by the grave; he knows alone of all present the aspect of that other burial spot, and to him more than all this one must be impressive. But he takes his wonder, like his duty, stolidly – his thoughts appear to be lost in his master's memory.

Wreath upon wreath was dropped into the tomb and Stanley and Kalulu took 'a long parting glance at the great traveller's resting place' before leaving 'the good, great-hearted, loving, fearless and faithful David Livingstone' for the final time. As they rode through London's streets, Stanley was fired with a resolution to complete Livingstone's work and 'to be, if God willed it, the next martyr to geographical science, or, if my life was to be spared, to clear up . . . the secrets of the Great River throughout its course'.

Chapter 29

LADY ALICE

The *New York Herald*'s London bureau in Fleet Street was almost next door to the headquarters of the *Daily Telegraph*, the newspaper that had been first to break Stanley's Livingstone scoop to British readers thanks to its agreement with James Gordon Bennett.

A few days after Livingstone's funeral, Stanley strolled over to the *Telegraph*'s offices and 'while I was discussing journalistic enterprise in general with one of the staff, the editor [Edwin Arnold] entered. We spoke of Livingstone and the unfinished task remaining behind him. In reply to an earlier remark, which I made, he asked: "Could you, and would you, complete the work? And what is there to do?" I answered: "The outlet of Lake Tanganyika is undiscovered. We know nothing scarcely of Lake Victoria; we do not even know whether it consists of one or many lakes and therefore the sources of the Nile are still unknown. Moreover, the western half of the African continent is still a white blank."' Arnold, who secretly admired Bennett's bold style of journalism and aspired to replicate it in the *Daily Telegraph*, asked: 'Do you think you can settle all this if we commission you?' – which seemed unlikely as Bennett still had prior claims to Stanley's services.

Secretly, *Telegraph* publisher Edward Lawson dispatched a telegram to his fellow publisher in New York: 'Would you consider joining the *Daily Telegraph* in sending Stanley out to Africa, to complete the discoveries of Speke, Burton and Livingstone?' and within twenty-four hours a one-word reply came back from Bennett: 'Yes.'

News of the jointly funded *Herald–Telegraph* expedition was released simultaneously in London and New York on 17 July 1874, announcing that the proprietors had joined forces in organising

an expedition of African discovery, under the command of Mr. Henry M. Stanley. The purpose of the enterprise is to complete the work left unfinished by the lamented death of Dr. Livingstone; to solve, if possible, the remaining problems of the geography of Central Africa; and to investigate and report upon the haunts of the slave traders. Mr. Stanley will represent the interests of the two nations whose common interest in the regeneration of Africa was so well illustrated when the lost explorer was rediscovered by the energetic American correspondent . . . and it may be hoped that very important results will accrue from this undertaking to the advantage of science, humanity and civilisation.

The public was informed that Stanley would return to Africa 'as the ambassador of two great powers, representing the journalism of England and America, and in command of an expedition more numerous and better appointed than any that has ever entered Africa'. The announcement continued that the joint venture would be an example for other nations to follow – 'they send armies to conquer while the press sends armies of peace and light'.

During the summer of 1874 and in between making preparations for his return to Africa, Stanley found time to fall in love. American-born Alice Pike was barely seventeen years old when she met Stanley at the Langham Hotel during a visit to London with her mother, Ellen. Mrs Pike, wealthy widow of a property tycoon, was taking her three daughters – Alice, Nettie and Hessie – on a grand tour of Europe and was thrilled to hear that the famous 'fellow-American', Henry Morton Stanley, was staying at the same hotel. She had also heard that he was London's most eligible bachelor.

Stanley was immediately attracted to Alice, whom he preferred out of the three daughters. At thirty-three, Stanley was nearly twice her age, but he told his journal that while Alice was 'elegant, she wore too many diamonds'. Over dinner with Mrs Pike and her daughters, he had spoken about Africa and confessed to his journal that he found the sisters 'very ignorant of African geography and, I fear, of everything else'. Alice's own first impressions of Stanley, whom she called Morton, were of a man with a 'rugged, bronzed face. . . . It was easy to see he wasn't a man given to light laughter or things of play. . . . There was not a man nor a woman in all London who did not know of Stanley, *the* Stanley. His name was on every tongue; it was *his* name that was mentioned at dinner; everyone, everywhere heard it.' Within days of meeting the Pikes, Stanley recorded that if Miss Alice 'gives me encouragements, I shall fall in love with her'.

He admitted that this might not be conducive to his happiness 'for she is the very opposite of my ideal wife'.

Alice and Stanley were seen together each day, walking in the park, boating on the Serpentine, dining at fashionable restaurants, attending plays and recitals and taking out-of-town railway excursions.

The Pikes returned to London for a few days following their European tour and Stanley accompanied them to Liverpool where they would board a steamer back to New York. Miss Alice and her Morton swore undying fidelity to each other and Stanley described their parting at the foot of the gangplank as 'tender'.

Stanley relished the challenge of returning to Africa and entered into a flurry of activity planning everything in detail, ordering equipment, guns, ammunition, ropes, saddles, medical supplies and provisions, purchasing scientific instruments and a portable boat of his own design to explore Central Africa's lakes. The boat would be built from durable Spanish cedar in five separate sections, each of which would be 8ft long. The sections would be constructed in two halves allowing them to be carried with greater ease by porters. The finished boat would be 40ft long with a 6ft beam and 30in deep.

Edwin Arnold recommended the services of a custom boat builder from Teddington called James Arthur Messenger, whose Water Lane premises stood on a 2-mile open stretch of the Thames where Queen Victoria's royal barge was stored. Messenger was a champion sculler who had been appointed the Queen's barge master in 1862. He employed thirty men in Teddington to build boats and was thrilled to receive a letter from Stanley asking if he could come and discuss a most unusual boat-building project.

Over lunch at the Angler's Hotel next to the Teddington boatyard, Stanley laid his own sketch plans before Messenger. Although the boat was long, it had to be light and durable in order to be carried overland. And it had to be built quickly and shipped out to Zanzibar in time for the expedition's departure date in November. Messenger assured Stanley that the boat would be built, tested and shipped by the agreed date. It was named the *Lady Alice* in honour of Alice Pike.

Stanley began recruiting a small number of English personnel prepared to travel into the unknown with no guarantee of returning. Once announcements about the expedition became public, Stanley received 1,200 letters from all kinds of people begging to travel to Africa with the famous Henry Morton Stanley. He rejected them all.

While staying at the Langham Hotel, Stanley had become friendly with its young desk clerk, Frederick Barker 'who, smitten with a desire to go to Africa, was not to be dissuaded by reports of its unhealthy climate, its dangerous fevers, or the uncompromising views of exploring life given to him'. Despite having no experience of foreign travel, Barker's mother gave her son permission to join the expedition as its accountant, keeping careful check on expenditure.

Edwin Arnold suggested the expedition should include 'one or more young English boatmen of good character' whose navigation skills would be useful when taking the *Lady Alice* upriver. Arnold took Stanley to Kent, where he moored his private yacht on the River Medway for weekend sailing. At Lower Upnor, they met a fisherman called Henry Pocock

who had fine stalwart sons, who bore the reputation of being honest and trustworthy. Two of these young men volunteered at once. Both Mr. Arnold and myself warned the Pocock family repeatedly that Africa had a cruel character, that the sudden change from the daily comforts of English life and the rigorous one of an explorer would try the most perfect constitution; would most likely be fatal to the uninitiated and unacclimatised. But I permitted myself to be overborne by the eager courage and devotion of these adventurous lads, and Francis 'Frank' John Pocock and Edward 'Ted' Pocock, two very likely-looking young men, were accordingly engaged as my assistants.

Henry Pocock urged his sons to stick by their new employer in Africa 'through thick and thin' – advice that they were to follow to the full measure.

Before departing for Africa, Stanley made a quick Atlantic crossing to New York to brief Bennett on his proposed journey – and to propose marriage to Alice Pike. She accepted at once, although her mother insisted the wedding must wait for Stanley's safe return from Africa. Alice gave Stanley a carte-de-visite photograph of herself to carry on his travels. They promised to write to each other, both realising the difficulties of maintaining regular correspondence while Stanley was deep in Africa's interior. However, they agreed that their letters could always be read on returning to Zanzibar or forwarded to him with messengers.

In London Stanley was given 'a magnificent prize mastiff called "Caster"' by Baroness Burdett-Coutts, the English philanthropist and socialite. He later bought three more dogs, a retriever, a bulldog and a bull terrier, from Battersea Dogs' Home, called respectively Nero, Bull and Jack by the Pocock brothers. An English officer gave Stanley a second mastiff known as 'Captain'.

On 15 August 1874, 'having shipped the Europeans, boats, dogs and general property of the expedition' to Zanzibar, Stanley left England for Africa 'to begin my explorations'. At the same time, he also fulfilled his wish to take Kalulu home to Africa.

Stanley returned to Zanzibar on 21 September 1874, twenty-eight months after he had previously left the island following the Livingstone assignment. He found suitable accommodation for himself, Kalulu, the Englishmen, dogs and tons of equipment at the home of Augustus Sparhawk, an American trader based in Zanzibar.

Little had changed apart from the market where Stanley had once witnessed slaves being sold. He noted: 'Happily, there is no such market now, Zanzibar's slave trade having been abolished by the Sultan Barghash bin Sayid', following gentle coercion by the British government responding to Livingstone's influence and anti-slavery articles by the *New York Herald*. It was later discovered that Sultan Barghash continued to trade in slaves in secret and was himself one of the main beneficiaries of the traffic.

The expedition members bartered for cloth, beads, coils of brass wire and tools in the bazaars and sent it back to Sparhawk's house to be rolled into bales, poured into sacks and packed. They then began enlisting over three hundred men for the expedition. Stanley had been told the best men for the job were the Wagwana, the name given to sons of former slaves who had bought their freedom or inherited it on the death of their masters. Wagwana had been successfully used by Burton, Speke and Grant and were from the same group from which Stanley had sent men to Livingstone on his return to Zanzibar.

Word quickly spread that Stanley was hiring able-bodied men willing to carry a load. Hundreds asked to be considered – 'almost all the cripples, the palsied, the consumptive and the superannuated . . . all the roughs, rowdies, and ruffians of the island' were rejected. Twenty men who had remained loyal to Stanley on the 1872 Livingstone expedition were re-hired. Over two hundred more were recruited (plus another hundred on the mainland) and Stanley admitted that 'many were engaged of whose character I had not the least conception until, months afterwards, I learned from their quarrels in the camp how I had been misled by the clever rogues'. Each man was paid between $2 and $10 per month plus rations depending on their strength and intelligence and enlisted for up to two years. On signing, each adult received a $20 dollar advance – or four months pay – and each junior member of the party $10. Advance ration money was also paid to each man and the *Daily Telegraph* was sent a bill for £1,300 to cover early expenses.

Stanley drew up an expedition charter, which was read out to each man in his native language. It stated that they would be treated with kindness and patience. In the event of sickness, they would be given medicine and if unable to proceed, they would not be abandoned but conveyed 'to such places as should be considered safe for their persons and their freedom'. Those remaining behind would be given cloth or beads 'to pay the native practitioner for his professional attendance and for the support of the patient'. Stanley also agreed 'to act like a father and mother' to them and resist all violence 'by savage natives and roving and lawless bandits'. In return, Wagwana promised to undertake duties like men, to honour and respect instructions, be good and faithful servants – and never to desert.

Stanley recruited 'a native detective' called Kacheche, whose job it was, with assistants, to track deserters and bring them back to camp. The 'detectives' would often travel a day's journey behind the rest of the expedition and receive instructions via a messenger when anyone absconded. They would be ordered to watch for him along the path and at local villages in the expectation of capture.

In the middle of this activity, the steamer arrived carrying the sections of Stanley's exploring boat *Lady Alice*. Anxious to ensure that the pieces could be carried easily, he had each weighed 'and great was my vexation and astonishment when I discovered that four of the sections weighed 280 lbs each and that one weighed 310 lbs. She was, it is true, a marvel of workmanship . . . but in her present condition her carriage through the jungles would necessitate a pioneer force a 100 strong to clear the impediments and obstacles on the road'. A ship's carpenter was recruited who, with the aid of the Pocock brothers, cut each subsection in half, producing pieces that could be carried along narrow paths of the interior with greater ease.

The entire cargo weighed over 8 tons, divided as nearly as possible between the 300 men into 60lb loads. Their departure, on 17 November 1874, was timed to coincide with the ending of Ramadan and Stanley was relying on the men's goodwill to turn up and be ready on that day. True to their promise, 224 of them were sitting on the quayside ready for work at sunrise.

Expedition members and their goods were loaded on board Arab dhows that would transport them across the channel to Bagamoyo. As fast as each dhow was reported filled, off it went in a westward direction 'and into the arms of fortune . . . as we glide away through the dying light towards the dark continent'.

Stanley recruited extra men at Bagamoyo from among those recently arrived at the coastal town with incoming caravans from the interior. On the morning of 17 November 1874, Ted Pocock sounded a bugle to wake the expedition and signal that they would shortly be on their way. Stanley noted that the 'boat carriers are Herculean in figure and strength, for they are practised bearers of loads . . . and will carry sections of the first European-made boat that ever floated on Lakes Victoria and Tanganyika and the extreme sources of the Nile. To each section of the boat there are four men, to relieve one another in couples. They get higher pay than even the chiefs . . . and besides receiving double rations, have the privilege of taking their wives and children along with them.' Six asses were also taken along – one each for Stanley and the Englishmen and two for the sick. Three net hammocks would also support anyone injuring themselves or falling ill, with six men acting as a walking ambulance party.

At 9 a.m., 356 souls headed out of town, 4 native chiefs in front followed by 12 guides clad in red robes and carrying wire coils, then a long line of 270 men carrying cloth, wire, beads and sections of the *Lady Alice*, followed by 36 women and children of the chiefs. Towards the rear rode the Englishmen on their asses followed by their gun bearers – including Kalulu, now happily back in his old job – and 16 chiefs acting as a rearguard. The procession stretched for over half a mile from end to end. The heat was intense, reaching 140 degrees and seemed to burn through the Englishmen's sun helmets. Even the Wagwana appeared to be suffering. Before the day was out, the mastiff 'Castor' would be dead from heat exhaustion and the other dogs showing signs that they were also in distress.

The Pocock brothers travelled ahead with the boat carriers so they could quickly assemble the craft on the banks of the first major hurdle, the Kingani River. Stanley's journal records that the *Lady Alice* 'did admirable service in the ferriage . . . the entire expedition crossed the river in her within two hours'. However, within a week of their having set out, by 23 November, porters were suffering from sore shoulders, blistered feet, sickness, lung disease, spitting up blood and generally complaining. Stanley noted: 'White men behave very well.' On 28 November, the mastiff 'Captain' died.

The journey continued through 'lion country' full of game. Stanley shot a zebra for a group of Wagwana asking for a change in their diet 'much against my wish, for I think zebras were created for better purpose than to be eaten'. By mid-December, desertions were frequent. At first detective Kacheche and his gang of assistants had been following a day's journey behind, resulting in the capture of sixteen men. The Wagwana soon became wise to this and later deserters struck out in other directions to avoid detection. Stanley ordered detectives to go into the bush before dawn and hide until the expedition had begun the day's march. This measure deterred many from escaping but nevertheless during the first five weeks of the march over fifty men absconded, taking their advance pay and weapons with them.

The rainy season began in earnest on 23 December. Both Ted and Frank Pocock fell ill with fever. On 25 December, Stanley told his journal: 'A more cheerless Christmas was seldom passed by me, and I venture to say that none of the other European members of the expedition ever experienced such a dull, gloomy misery . . . besides, our men suffered from sore famine – as two yards of cloth purchased here only as much as a palm's breadth of cloth would have procured elsewhere'. On the same day Stanley wrote to Alice:

I am in a centre-pole tent, seven by eight. As it rained all day yesterday, the tent was set over wet ground, which, by the passing in and out of the servants, was soon trampled into a thick pasty mud bearing traces of toes, heels, shoe nails and dog's paws. The tent corners hang down limp and languid, and there is such an air of forlornness and misery about that it increases my own misery. . . . Outside, the people obviously have a fellow feeling, for they appear to me like beings with strong suicidal intentions or perhaps they mean to lie still, inert until death relieves them . . . I have not had a piece of meat for ten days. My food is boiled rice, tea and coffee, and soon I shall be reduced to eating native porridge, like my own people. I weighed 180 lbs when I left Zanzibar, but under this diet I have been reduced to 134 lbs within 38 days. The young

Englishmen are in the same impoverished condition of body, and unless we reach some more flourishing country . . . we must soon become mere skeletons. . . . Besides the terribly wet weather and the scarcity of food from which we suffer, we are compelled to undergo the tedious and wearisome task of haggling with extortionate chiefs over the amount of blackmail which they demand, and which we must pay. . . . Another of my dogs, 'Nero' the retriever, is dead. Alas! All [the dogs] will die.

As they trudged through the rain, Stanley spent time 'from morning until night' taking solar observations, making ethnological notes, negotiating with local chiefs seeking payment for permission to pass through their land and tending to the sick. He noted: 'In addition to all this strain on my own physical powers, I was myself frequently sick from fever and wasted from lack of proper, nourishing food; and if the chief of an expedition be thus distressed, it may readily be believed that the poor fellows depending on him suffer also.'

The path climbed to 4,000ft as 'the floodgates of heaven' opened, drenching the camp and men. When Stanley awoke in his tent, he discovered 'that my bed was an island in a shallow river, which, if it increased in depth and current, would assuredly carry me off . . . but the most comical sight was presented by "Jack" and "Bull" perched back to back on top of an ammunition box, butting each other rearward, and snarling and growling for that scant portion of comfort'.

With lives hanging in the balance and no sign of game in the area, Stanley decided to dispatch forty trustworthy men ahead in the hope of finding friendly tribes prepared to trade for food. They were instructed to buy what they could and hurry back with supplies. Meanwhile, Wagwana roamed the forest searching for edible roots or berries – anything to stem the bitter pangs of hunger. 'Some found a putrid elephant, on which they gorged themselves, and were punished with nausea and sickness.' The supplies produced sufficient oatmeal to provide each member of the party with two cupfuls of gruel, brewed in a 'Torquay dress trunk' emptied of its contents and filled with 25 gallons of water, 10lb of oatmeal and four tins of 'Revalenta Arabica'. Those sent to buy food returned next day with 'a supply of millet seed just sufficient to give all hands a small meal'.

By 16 January 1875, the party had arrived in the district of Suna where Stanley recorded that of the 347 who had left Bagamoyo, 89 had deserted, 20 had died and 8 had been left behind in villages after falling ill – leaving

230 expedition members capable of continuing. With one-third of his workforce gone and 7,000 miles still to cover, Stanley reduced the amount of baggage carried by the men, discarding and burning everything superfluous. Personal items, luxuries, books, cloth, beads, wire, extra tents were sacrificed.

On the same date Stanley recorded: 'Ted Pocock has been seriously ill since we arrived here, whether it is smallpox, typhus or African fever that he is suffering from I know not. He has been wandering in his head for the last two days, but I hope sincerely that he will recover, as he has been very useful to the expedition. He is a young man of such cheerful disposition that his loss would be seriously felt.' Next day Stanley noticed hundreds of red pimples with white tops scattered over Ted's chest and arms – smallpox pustules.

Ted Pocock died the same day. Stanley's journal describes him as 'a gentle, amiable creature, of medium stature, shy blue eyes and light coloured, silky hair. He was excessively fond of his brother, and did his duty in my employ well and efficiently and was always civil. His brother Frank possesses these virtues perhaps in greater degree than Ted, but it would have been difficult to elect two better young men for the expedition than Francis and Edward Pocock.' Ted was buried under an acacia tree, marked with a cross. Standing over the grave, Stanley said: 'May he rest in peace in this grave, having lived to drink of the extreme southern sources of the Nile.' Fred Barker was also 'feeling feeble' at the service and Stanley confessed, 'I have a fever, but I performed the burial service over my departed companion.'

In a letter to Ted's father in England, sent by a messenger who was also carrying a newspaper dispatch from the shores of Lake Victoria Nyanza, Stanley wrote: 'Poor Ted deserved a better fate than dying in Africa, but it was impossible that he could have died easier. I wish that my end might be as peaceful and painless as his. . . . Be consoled, for Frank still lives, and from present appearance is likely to come home to you with honour and glory such as he and you may well be proud of.' Henry Pocock did not receive Stanley's letter until October, ten months after his son's death.

Conditions improved. There had been skirmishes with savage tribesmen along the way, but Stanley's hunger-driven men had won the day and cattle and contents of villages were eagerly seized by the party. Many were killed on the journey and others wounded, further reducing the expedition's size and increasing the number of injured or of those suffering from dysentery, rheumatism, asthma, skin diseases, malaria and typhoid. At the end of January 1875 they passed through villages willing to trade and Stanley was able to record that 'the voice of the gaunt monster – hunger – was finally hushed'. Fresh porters were hired to replace those too weak to proceed.

On 27 February, the 104th day of the march, the expedition was ascending a long gradual slope with Frank Pocock at its head. At the brow of the hill, Stanley noticed Frank madly waving his hat in the air and then running towards the rest of the expedition 'his face beaming with joy as he shouted enthusiastically, "I have seen the lake, sir, and it is grand."' They had arrived at Lake Victoria Nyanza, sixteen years and seven months after Speke had first set eyes on the water in an attempt to prove – misguidedly – that it was the Nile's source.

A camp was built to house the expedition for several weeks while Stanley went exploring in the *Lady Alice*. Before bolting the sections together and equipping the boat for a long voyage, Stanley wrote a letter to Alice and articles for his newspapers. He had already dispatched five pieces from Zanzibar and another during the early part of the march relating the expedition's progress to date. The latest dispatch would contain the story of their journey through the rain, their hunger, tribal battles, Ted Pocock's death, desertions, sicknesses, privations and their struggle to the shores of Victoria Nyanza. It would take seven months for the article to travel along the path and by ship to Aden, from where it was telegraphed to both newspapers, appearing in print on 11 October 1875.

On 8 March 1875, the *Lady Alice* was ready to explore the lake and with Frank Pocock and Fred Barker remaining, Stanley called for volunteers to crew her. No one came forward, claiming they knew nothing of life on the water, secretly afraid the boat might send them to a watery grave. Stanley ordered one of his men to appoint a crew of ten strong Wagwana. The boat was launched with plenty of supplies and goods for trading. They explored rivers, islands, coves, encountered friendly tribes willing to trade and hostile groups who threw spears at them, forbidding them to land. On 28 March they encountered thirteen native canoes conveying lake pirates over the water. Stanley hoped to engage them in conversation but they surrounded the *Lady Alice* and attempted to board her. Stanley and his crew managed to beat them off and an elephant rifle was used to kill four raiders. There were further adventures in store for the *Lady Alice* and her crew across the water.

Chapter 30

MTESA AND MIRAMBO

They now entered the kingdom of Emperor Mtesa of Uganda, 'the Great Potentate of Equatorial Africa', ruler of 3 million people and husband to 300 wives. Stanley sent a messenger asking permission to visit his court. It would generate wonderful copy for his newspapers and at the same time help establish relations between Britain and Mtesa's empire. Permission was granted and the Emperor sent six large canoes paddled by 182 men to escort the *Lady Alice* to his large lakeside settlement. On shore, 2,000 natives waited in two lines to greet the white visitor, drums beating, musketry firing.

Stanley recalled Speke writing that Mtesa was 'a youthful prince, vain and heartless, and a wholesale murderer and tyrant delighting in fat women who have been made thus unctuous by being fed on milk'. When pages arrived to escort Stanley into the Emperor's presence, he found 'a tall, clean-faced, large-eyed, nervous looking thin man clad in a tarbush black robe, with a white shirt belted with gold' who shook Stanley's hand warmly and invited him to sit on an iron stool. Stanley observed: 'When he blows his nose, the three greatest chiefs rush down on their knees and implore the honour of brushing or drying the mucus from the napkin. If he smiles, the whole court smiles. If he frowns, instantly all wear submissive patient looks. If he storms, all fall prone to the ground and swear to clutch the moon for him should he desire.'

Speaking through interpreters, Stanley and Mtesa discussed many things, 'principally about Europe and heaven – the inhabitants of the latter place he was very anxious about, and was specially interested in the nature of angels'. Drawing on pictures seen in Bibles and copies of Milton's *Paradise Lost*, Stanley described them as best he could. 'Led away by my enthusiasm, I may have exaggerated somewhat,' he later confessed. Mtesa, however, appeared to absorb everything his white guest was saying.

Ever since his encounter with Livingstone, Stanley had inwardly become a more spiritual person and sometimes attempted – and failed – to emulate the late doctor. In Mtesa, Stanley saw a man with great influence over his neighbours, someone who, if converted to Christianity, would be a powerful force for good. With a touch of Livingstone in his pen, Stanley wrote in his journal: 'I shall destroy his faith in Islam, and teach the doctrines of Jesus of Nazareth.'

The Emperor staged a boat race on the lake in 'Stamlee's' honour, involving 40 canoes and 1,200 rowers. Mtesa asked his new white friend to demonstrate his proficiency with a rifle and pointed to a sleeping crocodile 200 yards away on a rock. Stanley took aim and fired – fortunately hitting the crocodile with the first shot. Stanley quickly developed an admiration for the Emperor, particularly when he learned that Mtesa aspired to 'imitate, as much as lies in his power, the ways of the white man'.

At their meetings Stanley gently introduced the subject of Christianity to Mtesa and spoke about how God had sent his Son to the world, had lived life as an ordinary man and 'was seized and crucified by wicked people who scorned His divinity, and yet out of His great love for them, while yet suffering on the cross, He asked His great father to forgive them. I showed the difference in character between Him whom white men love and adore and Mohammed, whom the Arabs revere; how Jesus endeavoured to teach mankind that we should love all men, excepting none, while Mohammed taught his followers that slaying of the pagan and the unbeliever was an act that merited Paradise. I left it to Mtesa and his chiefs to decide which was the worthier character. . . . I also began to translate the Ten Commandments.'

At Ulagalla, Mtesa's inland capital, Stanley recorded on 11 April: 'I have been again fortunate in meeting a white man in the heart of Africa for Monsieur Linant de Bellefonds . . . in the service of the Khedive [of Egypt] arrived in the capital today with 40 [Sudanese] soldiers. He came in great state which gave Mtesa much delight to see the discipline and order of his advance towards the capital.'

Ernest Linant de Bellefonds was a Franco-Belgian member of the Egyptian service, dispatched by Colonel (later General) Gordon to visit Mtesa to negotiate a treaty of commerce between him and the Egyptian government. Stanley and de Bellefonds enjoyed each other's company and in his next newspaper dispatch, he described the Frenchman as 'a gentleman extremely well informed, energetic and a great traveller . . . in

Colonel Bellefonds I also perceived great good fortune, for now I had the means to despatch my reports of geographical discoveries and my long delayed letters'.

Colonel de Bellefonds agreed to wait an extra day while Stanley composed a long dispatch to his newspapers describing his encounter with Mtesa and the need for Christian missions to be established in the Emperor's country. He told readers:

> I have undermined Islamism so much here that Mtesa has determined henceforth, until he is better informed, to observe the Christian Sabbath as well as the Moslem Sabbath . . . he has caused the ten commandments of Moses to be written on a board for his daily perusal, as Mtesa can read Arabic, as well as the Lord's Prayer and the golden commandment of our saviour: 'Thou shalt love thy neighbour as thyself.' This is great progress for the few days that I have remained with him, and, though I am no missionary, I shall begin to think that I shall become one if such success is so feasible. . . . But, O, that some pious, practical missionary would come here! What a field and harvest ripe for the sickle of the Gospel. . . . He must be tied to no church or sect, but profess God and His son. . . . He must belong to no nation in particular, but the entire white race. . . . Such a man or men, Mtesa invites to come to him. He has begged me to tell the white men that if they will only come to him he will give them all they want.

To make it easier for religious societies to consider establishing stations in Uganda, Stanley's article suggested that missionaries thinking of coming to Africa should bring Mtesa a present of 'three or four suits of military clothes, decorated freely with gold embroidery, with half a dozen French *kepis*, a sabre, a brace of pistols with suitable ammunition; a good fowling piece and rifle of good quality, as the Emperor is not a barbarian; a cheap dinner service of Britannia ware, an iron bedstead and counterpanes, a few pieces of cotton print, boots, &c.' He suggested types of cloth, military buttons, gold braid, silk cord, red blankets 'and a few chairs and tables' which the missionaries should also bring to sell to members of Mtesa's court. Missionaries were instructed what tools, seeds and grain to take to Uganda, along with 'a few volumes of illustrated journals, gaudy prints, a magic lantern, rockets and photographic apparatus. The total cost of the whole need not exceed £5,000.'

De Bellefonds carried Stanley's dispatches and letters to Gordon's headquarters at Khartoum, from where they travelled on to Cairo in a diplomatic pouch and were forwarded to London. Later that year, de Bellefonds and thirty-six soldiers were massacred by Sudanese tribesmen, creating a popular Victorian myth that the former was still carrying Stanley's articles concealed in one of his boots when he perished. Legend had it that they were forwarded to England covered in the unfortunate man's blood.

It was time for Stanley to return to his men. Before leaving Mtesa's country, the Emperor made Stanley promise he would return to continue their discussions about Christianity. He ordered thirty canoes and rowers to transport his new white friend's entire expedition to the other side of the lake. When Stanley reached the shore he found that the canoes were not forthcoming. He was assured by one of Mtesa's senior aides that they would be delivered to his camp in a few days and the *Lady Alice* took to the waters again.

Thirty-six hours after departing, the crew of the *Lady Alice* had not found any lakeside settlements prepared to trade for fresh food. They sighted an island dominated by a high plateau, known as the island of Bumbireh. What occurred when they landed became the subject of one of Stanley's most famous and fantastic articles, a story straight out of the pages of a Victorian adventure book. The incident was carefully recorded in his private journal, a diary not intended for publication but used by Stanley as an *aide-mémoire* for his later dispatches and books. It is a tale of one of the most daring escapes from death ever to occur in Victorian Africa and took place on 28 April 1875:

At 9 a.m. came to a small cove . . . the precautions and prudence which had formerly governed us in our intercourse with unknown tribes were in this instance omitted, as we had nothing whatever in our boat except a little coffee and fruit-food. . . . As we entered the cove we saw the plateau's summit lined with men and heard shouts like war cries, yet necessity and imminent starvation compelled us to ground our boat and endeavour to entice the people to part with some food for us for cloth or beads. As soon as we grounded our boat the men rushed down from the plateau, and as I saw their hostile demeanour I loaded my two guns and revolvers, and told my men to push the boat off, but my people either deemed I was too suspicious, or else their dread of starvation got the better of their fear of man, for they did not stir a hand to obey me, but began to make friendly speeches to the natives who now numbered several score, to say that they were Wagwana, friends of Mtesa come to purchase food.

On hearing this, the natives lowered their spears and advanced towards the boat with smiles and friendly gestures. They then grabbed the boat and dragged it from the lake onto dry land. Stanley produced two revolvers and fired them into the air, but more armed natives arrived on the scene chanting terrible war cries. They snatched the boat's oars and ran away to a safe distance, leaving the passengers of the *Lady Alice* high and dry on the beach. Half an hour later a native delegation demanded five cloths and five pieces of wire. The boat had no wire on board, but Stanley offered twenty cloths in exchange for the return of his oars.

He takes up the story again:

Upon this they shouted to prepare for war and the people began to descend with drawn bows. I told my men to push the boat into the water and I began the action with my elephant gun, killing one of the foremost and wounding another. Before I could lay my hands on my second gun, the boat was in deep water, the men clinging to her sides. Assisting one in, I told him to assist the others while I kept the enemy off with my shotgun loaded with buckshot. This did good service, for they withdrew in haste back to the hills, while my men tore up the boards and seats and used them as paddles with which we got out of the cove then hoisted sail and sailed away still firing at the wretches.

Stanley related this tale in print on other occasions. In each case he slightly altered the story, elaborating certain details, increasing the number of natives waiting on shore and making the incident more exciting, dramatic and dangerous (as if this hair-raising incident needed any elaboration). Stanley was a storyteller who knew what readers expected from him – thrilling tales about daring deeds with their hero struggling against all odds against heathen natives in darkest Africa. No harm was done if he tinkered with the truth, providing the incident itself actually took place. Stanley did not invent his African stories – he did not

need to. On occasions, however, he embellished them to make them more
stirring and give readers better value, a task he performed admirably.

Eight months had elapsed since the *New York Herald* and *Daily Telegraph*
had received a dispatch from Stanley. Rumours circulated that the
expedition had been slaughtered by cannibals. Bennett was now
accustomed to long periods of silence from Stanley and he ordered a
reassuring editorial to be written stating: 'For our part, we have no doubt
of Stanley's safety. His courage, coolness, energy and judgement have
been so signally displayed that he merits supreme confidence. Such a man
will triumph when any other explorer would be baffled and defeated.'

The *Lady Alice* arrived back at camp on 5 May 1875, fifty-seven days and
1,000 miles after setting out to cross Lake Victoria Nyanza. During the
latter days they had existed on wild bananas and little else, rowing the boat
with poles cut from the forest and lashed to planks from the *Lady Alice*.
    Sad news awaited them. Fred Barker, the former Langham Hotel desk
clerk who had been so desperate to leave his job and visit Africa with
Stanley, had died on 23 April of a congestive chill. His health began to
suffer a month before and he had grown weaker by the day. Despite the
heat outside his tent, Fred's body was ice cold to the touch. Frank Pocock
gave him brandy, heaped bedclothes on him, but he never warmed. He
was buried near the lake and a wall of stones surrounding his grave
marked his last resting place. Four other men had also died of dysentery.
    Writing to Fred's mother, Mrs Charlotte Barker, in London, Stanley
described her son as 'a rare young man, mettlesome, manly, and
thoroughly English in his good qualities'.

Mtesa's canoes had still not materialised, forcing Stanley to call on
another tribal Emperor for help, Lukongeh of Ukerewe. Lukongeh was
delighted to assist in return for Stanley imparting 'some of the secrets of
Europe, such as medicine to make lions and leopards, to cause the rain
winds to come when called, to cause his women to be fruitful, and to give
himself more virility. These demands are commonly made by the most
ignorant and superstitious African chiefs.' A compromise was reached: in
return for 'promising to send two suits of English cloth (of crimson and
blue flannel), medicine for rheumatism and headache, a revolver and
ammunition, a bale of cloth, beads, a cap, an English rug, two ivory tusks,

iron and brass wire', Stanley was given 23 canoes to transport 150 men and the expedition's supplies from the great lake's south-eastern shore to its north-western extremity. From there Stanley planned to travel overland to explore Lake Albert Nyanza.

The journey began on 19 June, with most of the canoes paddled by inexperienced men who could not swim, let alone row. Five canoes sank during the first day, the hapless occupants rescued by the *Lady Alice*, 'now up to her gunwale with 22 men and 30 loads, and if a breeze rose, she would, unless we lightened her of property, inevitably sink'.

Their route exposed them to more savage tribes, including another skirmish with the population on the island of Bumbireh. Stanley was prepared for them this time and before they could attack his flotilla, he was ready with loaded guns, to retaliate and take prisoners. He seized many of the islanders' own canoes and won back the *Lady Alice*'s stolen oars. By the time Stanley felt he had repaid the people of Bumbireh for his previous inhospitable reception, many of the island's men lay dead on the beach.

On 29 July Stanley recorded that his expedition had joined forces with the Waganda tribe with a collective fleet of '37 canoes capable of carrying 548 men for such was now the actual number of the Anglo-American Expedition'. Stanley lost another important member of his team the following month – Jack the bull terrier bought from the Battersea Dog's Home in London, killed after an altercation with a wild cow that gored it to death. Stanley was now left with just one dog out of the five brought on the expedition, Bull.

By 22 August Stanley had circumnavigated Lake Victoria Nyanza and 'can state positively that there is but one outlet from the lake – the Ripon Falls'. Strangely, he makes no reference to Livingstone in his entry and the doctor's desire to produce this same proof for the Royal Geographical Society. The discovery would finally confirm John Hanning Speke's claim sixteen years earlier that the lake had a single outlet at the Ripon Falls (named after former Society president, the Marquess of Ripon), but never proven due to Speke's inability to produce the geographical data demanded by the Royal Geographical Society. Thanks to meticulous notes, map references, solar observations and ethnological records, Stanley would not fall into the same trap. He always acknowledged that the source of the Nile was identified by Speke, disputed by Burton, supported by Livingstone and confirmed by himself.* Stanley's voyage around the lake also proved that Victoria Nyanza was a single lake and not several, as was originally thought.

It was time to revisit Mtesa and Stanley 'was received with joy and honour by Emperor and chiefs'. Thousands lined the route to Mtesa's throne, covered in a golden cloth and standing on a leopard rug, where he promised to supply Stanley with a small army to escort the expedition overland from his country to Lake Albert Nyanza. However, because Mtesa was currently engaged in a war with the neighbouring Wavuma tribe, he would not allow Stanley to proceed any further. Instead, he gave assurances that his war would soon be over and suggested that Stanley should march with his people to a new camp in the company of 150,000 warriors, 50,000 women and 50,000 slaves. A further 400 large canoes carrying 10,000 men followed along the shoreline. For the journey 'Mtesa's face was covered with a whitish paste, his head was uncovered and he wore a blue check dress'.

At this point Stanley could have abandoned the remainder of the expedition. After all, he was confident he had identified the source of the Nile, had succeeded in gathering new and valuable geographical information, sent back a raft of fascinating dispatches and almost converted a heathen African emperor to Christianity. He could return safe in the knowledge that his assignment was complete, marry Alice Pike and settle down. 'But being again assured that the war would not last long, I resolved to stay and witness it as a novelty, and to take advantage of the time to acquire information about the country and its people,' he told his journal.

By sunset, Mtesa's army was comfortably ensconced in a city of 30,000 dome-like houses. 'Stamlee', as Mtesa's people called him, and his expedition were assigned 'commodious quarters' near the Emperor's imperial lodging. It was here that 'the good work I had commenced resumed' – talking with Mtesa about Christianity and the Gospels. For assistance Stanley called on a fifteen-year-old boy called Dallington, a student from the Universities Mission at Zanzibar, who was travelling with

---

* This was not true. The Victorian explorers all played an important part in locating the source of the Nile, but it was thanks to twentieth-century satellite technology that the source was finally identified as springs surfacing in a mountainous region in Burundi located midway between Lakes Victoria and Tanganyika.

the expedition as a companion for Kalulu. This 'bright and intelligent' boy was tasked with translating sections of the Bible into the Emperor's language and acting as Stanley's 'gospel' interpreter. Thanks to Dallington, Mtesa eventually received 'an abridged Protestant Bible . . . embracing all the principal events from the creation to crucifixion of Christ. St. Luke's Gospel was translated entire, as giving a more complete history of the Saviour's life.' When it was complete, Mtesa called his chiefs together and asked: 'Now I want you, my chiefs and soldiers, to tell me what we shall do. Shall we believe in Jesus or in Mohammed?'

The chiefs were divided, not knowing which path to suggest in case it angered Mtesa. The Emperor announced that 'the white man's book must be the true book' basing his opinion on the difference in conduct he had noted between Arabs and Europeans. 'The comparisons he so eloquently drew for them were in all points so favourable to the whites, that the chiefs unanimously gave their promise to accept the Christians' Bible, and to conform, as they were taught, to the Christian religion.' Stanley later reflected:

Flattering as it may be to me to have had the honour of converting the pagan Emperor of Uganda to Christianity, I cannot hide from myself the fact that the conversion is only nominal. . . . A few months talk about Christ and His blessed work on earth, though sufficiently attractive to Mtesa, is not enough to eradicate the evils which 35 years of brutal, sensuous indulgence have stamped on the mind; this, only the unflagging zeal . . . of a sincerely pious pastor can effect. And it is because I am conscious of the insufficiency of my work and his strong evil propensities, that I have not hesitated to describe the real character of my 'convert'.

To ensure Mtesa kept his faith, Stanley released Dallington to act as the Emperor's personal 'chaplain' until Stanley's appeal for missionaries was answered. His article in the *Daily Telegraph* eventually generated £14,000 in donations to equip and send members of the Church Missionary Society to Uganda. Stanley personally supervised the laying of foundations for the Emperor's first church on the summit of a hill adjoining Mtesa's palace at Ulagalla and plans were made for a cathedral to be constructed in Rubaga, his new capital. British missionaries did not find their task as simple as Stanley's newspaper article might have suggested, but the mission station ultimately prospered and in 1908, the *Manchester Guardian* could write that it was one of 'the most successful and modern missions' in Africa.

Meanwhile, the warring Wavuma tribesmen were preparing for battle with Mtesa's forces on the lake. They were said to command 300 war canoes and 6,000 expert sailors compared to Mtesa's 190 canoes and 3,000 sailors. To pacify the enemy, Mtesa sent a young boy soldier to the Wavuma with a peace treaty. They tore his body to pieces and threw them into the lake. Enemy canoes were floated and weeks of fighting followed. Stanley began bitterly to regret returning to Uganda.

Peace between tribes was declared in October, with Mtesa named the victor. The Anglo-American expedition could now continue its journey – reinforced by an armed escort of 2,300 local tribespeople.

Before leaving, Mtesa ordered that his entire lakeside settlement be burned to the ground – without first warning his people. Inflammable materials used to build the dome-like dwellings erupted into leaping flames which rolled over roads between the houses. Stanley recalled:

There was only one way left and that was to run before the flames up the mountain of Nakaranga, and thus make a wide detour. We were not alone . . . there were at least 60,000 human beings struggling in a solid body in the same direction, trampling down the weak, aged and sick in their devouring haste to be away from the sea of fire below. It was a grand scene but a cruel one – for hundreds of sick, little ones and witless men and women perished in it. The flames almost took my breath away, they seemed to lick the air before it entered my lungs, but with heads held low we charged on blindly, knowing no guide but saving self-interest and self-preservation. I kept my people together by dint of severity, as several were more than half inclined to give up. We had an hour of such work for the camp was three miles long . . . by 7 p.m. I had the entire satisfaction to see my people all about me, separate, in a well selected camp, thankful that we were out of that heedless, reckless rush of human beings.

The enlarged expedition marched out of friendly Uganda into hostile Wanyoro territory in January 1876 and nine days later they sighted Lake Albert Nyanza. The Wanyoro were uncomfortable with such a large party of men from another territory, led by a white man, in their country and the expedition was forced back to the Victoria Nyanza. The trip was not unsuccessful. It provided Stanley with an opportunity to record Albert Nyanza's astronomical position, calculate that it covered an area of 21,500 square miles, explore land and chart rivers flowing into the lakes, discover a new snow-capped mountain which natives called Gambaragara – but Stanley renamed Mount Gordon Bennett 'in honour of my American chief' – and a 'lofty hump' which he named Mount Edwin Arnold after the *Daily Telegraph*'s editor.

Stanley headed south towards Lake Tanganyika and Ujiji, the place where he had met Livingstone four years before. On the journey, Bull, the last of Stanley's faithful canine companions, died of exhaustion. For days the dog had been lagging behind the rest of the expedition, but Stanley assured readers of his articles that Bull died 'eyes to the last looking *forward* along the track he had so bravely tried to follow'.

On 18 April word arrived at a large settlement called Serombo, some two and a half miles in circumference and containing over a thousand native dwellings, 'that the phantom, the bugbear, the terror whose name silences children and makes women's hearts bound with fear; that Mirambo himself was coming, that he was only two camps away and that he had an immense army of Ruga-Ruga mercenaries with him'. This was the same Mirambo who had caused Stanley to take the great southerly diversion to Ujiji in 1872 to avoid his murderous men. Now the chief with the dreaded name was coming to meet the white man he had heard so much about.

A scouting party, sent to monitor the warlord's arrival, reported that they had sighted 'the African Bonaparte' with 1,500 of his armed bandits, clothed in crimson cloth and white shirts. He was described as 'a young man, a very nice man, well dressed. He wears the turban, fez and cloth coat of an Arab, and carries a scimitar. He also wears slippers. He has three young men carrying guns for him. Truly, Mirambo is a great man!' Three Ruga-Ruga arrived requesting to see the white man to give him salaams from Mirambo. Their master wished to see him and enquired whether he sent words of peace back to Mirambo. Stanley had no alternative but to say that he 'would be glad to shake hands with so great a man . . . and make strong friendship with him'.

Torn between fear and excitement over the next scoop about to happen, Stanley steeled himself to receive Mirambo, who, thanks to *New York*

Herald dispatches, was as famous in America and Europe as he was in Central Africa. He arrived at Serombo on 21 April to the sound of drums and gunfire, 'so different from all I ever conceived of such a redoubtable chieftain and a bandit of such terrible reputation'. Mirambo was

a man 5 feet 11 inches in height, about 35 years old, well-made but with not an ounce of superfluous flesh about him; handsome, regular featured, mild, soft spoken, with what you would call a meek demeanour, generous, open-handed with nothing of the small cent ideas of narrow-minded men. Indeed I did not let myself readily believe that this could possibly be the ferocious Chief of the terrible Ruga-Ruga . . . I had expected something of the Mtesa type . . . but this unpresuming quiet-eyed man of inoffensive meek exterior . . . indicated nothing of the Napoleonic genius which he has for five years displayed in the heart of Africa to the injury of Arabs and commerce and nearly trebling the price of ivory.

Stanley remained silent but met Mirambo's eyes 'which were composed and a steady calm gaze. And unlike all other Africans I have met, they met your own and steadily and calmly confronted them. Thus I have seen Mirambo.'

That night Stanley was summoned to the warlord's tent 'where we made brotherhood by an incision in each other's right leg above the knee until a couple of drops of blood were drawn; which interchanged and [the wound] rubbed with butter' and one of Mirambo's men repeated a solemn curse should Stanley prove faithless to the friendship. Stanley later presented 'his new brother' with a pistol and a box of 100 cartridges, while Mirambo sent three milk cows to the white man and his men. The blood brothers who were once at war with each other now parted as friends.

On 27 May, Stanley marched into Ujiji for the second time, 'but neither white man nor letters from Europe greet me this time. . . . The sun shines as bright, the sky is blue, but from the fact that the imposing central figure of the human group drawn together to meet me in 1871 is absent, Ujiji in spite of the beauty of its lake and the greenness of its palms, seems strangely forlorn and uninteresting.'

Stanley's next task was to circumnavigate 800 miles of Lake Tanganyika in the *Lady Alice* to prove that no waterway connected it with the Albert Nyanza. This he accomplished in fifty-one days, with the usual interruptions from unfriendly tribes and he returned to his men at the end of July. By carefully following the shoreline of both lakes, Stanley was able to solve numerous geographical problems concerning both stretches of water.

The final hurdle now beckoned: an attempt to prove or disprove that the mighty River Lualaba, whose course Livingstone had traced for 1,300 miles, was the same stretch of water as the Nile, the Niger or the Congo. So far, the Anglo-American expedition had followed the footpaths of others. This part of the journey would take them into uncharted territory to identify the Lualaba from its source and follow it to its end – wherever that might be.

The attempt did not begin well. A messenger sent from Unyanyembe to collect letters brought from the coast by caravan returned with plenty of mail for Stanley and Frank Pocock – but there was nothing from Alice Pike. Stanley's party was ferried across to Lake Tanganyika's western shore in two groups. While the first party was paddled across, thirty-eight men absconded. Frank Pocock and Kacheche were sent to bring them back. They returned with four deserters, who had told them that everyone lived in fear of the next part of the expedition – the prospect of being eaten by cannibals and never returning. When Stanley attempted to reassure them that there was nothing more to fear than they had already encountered, they accused him of being a slave driver.

The expedition was now in danger of being abandoned. Stanley himself became ill with fever as temperatures soared to 138 degrees. On 14 September, Stanley's journal states simply: 'Kalulu deserted today for no known reason. . . .' The following day Kacheche found the boy, along with four others, trying to negotiate a passage back across the lake to Ujiji. Kalulu and his fellow deserters 'received merited punishments, which put an end to misconduct and faithlessness, and prevented the wreck of the expedition'. They were manacled in slave chains.

They marched 220 miles to the Lualaba, 'about 1,400 yards wide, a broad river of pale grey colour, winding slowly from south and by east'. It reminded Stanley of the Mississippi and he confessed that 'a secret rapture filled my soul as I gazed upon the majestic stream. The great mystery that for all these centuries nature had kept hidden away from the world of science was waiting to be solved . . . and now before me lay the superb river itself! My task was to follow it to the ocean.'

At an Arab settlement, Stanley hoped to find an escort prepared to guide the expedition through the great rain forest that lay ahead. The best known Arab in the district was Hamed bin Mohammed, better known as Tippu-Tib, 'a tall, black-bearded man of Negroid complexion, in the prime of life, straight and quick in his movements, a picture of energy and strength. He had a fine intelligent face. . . . After regarding him for a few minutes, I came to the conclusion that this Arab was . . . the most remarkable man I had met among Arabs.' This notorious ivory and slave trader 'was neat in his person, his clothes were of a spotless white, and his fez-cap brand new, his dagger was splendid with silver filigree'.

Tippu-Tib had escorted other explorers along the Lualaba, but fear of strangers by cannibalistic tribes and a shortage of good canoes had dissuaded them from progressing further downriver. Stanley was confident that 'a heavy fee' might entice Tippu-Tib to provide an escort. Tippu-Tib was unsure. 'If you white people are fools enough to throw away your lives, that is no reason why Arabs should,' he said.

One of Tippu-Tib's aides claimed that the country along the Lualaba's banks was full of man-eating snakes, leopards, gorillas, cannibals and treacherous waterfalls. Stanley was hesitant about marching into the unknown. He consulted Frank Pocock who assured Stanley he would stick by him whatever decision was made. They would toss a coin, the best out of three falls – heads they would venture up the Lualaba, tails they would return to Zanzibar. They tossed the coin, which landed 'tails up' six times consecutively. Despite the omen of the coin, Stanley and Frank resolved to cling to the Lualaba.

Tippu-Tib agreed to allow his men to remain with the expedition 'for 60 camps', moving in any direction of Stanley's choosing over a period of three months, in return for which he would receive $5,000 as payment for the services of 140 men assigned to the expedition plus their food. Tippu-Tib himself, along with 700 of his people, planned to travel with Stanley for part of the way, visiting various settlements within the great forest, relieving them of their ivory and acquiring new slaves. 'Slaves cost nothing – they only require to be gathered,' Tippu-Tib told Stanley.

'Few tribes will dare to question our passage now,' Stanley noted in his journal. On 24 October, the expedition struck out into the unknown region – a hitherto large and empty space on the map of Africa.

Two days later, Kalulu, who since his recapture had been better behaved, met with an accident. Contrary to orders, a porter had retained a cartridge in his rifle, carelessly left it lying around on stacked goods where it had accidentally been knocked over causing it to explode. Kalulu, who was resting on his mat near the fire, was wounded in eight places, the bullet passing through the outer part of his lower leg, the upper part of his thigh and, glancing over his right ribs, through the muscles of his left arm. Stanley recorded: 'Though the accident had caused severe wounds, there was no danger and by applying a little arnica, lint and bandages, we soon restored him to a hopeful view of his case.'

It was as humid as a Turkish bath as they penetrated the primeval forest, a region Stanley described as 'filled with invisible savage enemies; out of every bush glared eyes gleaming with hate; in the stream lurked crocodiles to feed upon the unfortunates; the air seemed impregnated with the seeds of death'. They entered a village whose sole street was adorned with 186 skulls, laid out in two parallel lines. The natives declared them to be the skulls of gorillas but Stanley believed they were human.

When they next sighted the Lualaba, Stanley ordered the *Lady Alice* to be assembled and while he sailed downriver with thirty-six men and the injured Kalulu, the rest followed on land with Tippu-Tib. The river propelled the boat through the water faster than men could walk with heavy loads and it was three days before they met up with the land party again, many of whom were now suffering from smallpox. Six people had died in the three days since Stanley had left them, the number rising to eight two days later.

The going was slower due to tribal attacks in which poisoned arrows and spears were used to pick off the men. Occasionally Stanley's men responded with rifle fire, but all too often the enemy was unseen, laying in wait for an opportunity to kill the strangers. Expedition members became dispirited – especially Tippu-Tib who warned Stanley that judging by the speed of the river current, rapids would be ahead along with more 'natives hostile, cannibalism rampant and smallpox raging'.

Remaining canoes carried through the forest were now turned into 'hospital canoes' for the sick. Canopies fashioned from forest vegetation were built over them to protect the sick from the vicious sun beating down on forest and river.

On 22 December Tippu-Tib declared that he had had enough and was pulling out, taking his men and slaves with him, but permitting porters contracted to Stanley to remain. He was paid a banker's draft of $2,600, half of the original price agreed.

At dawn Stanley, his men, their women and children, '143 souls in all, and the riding asses of the expedition' were ready to float downriver. New canoes had been purchased from friendly tribes and others 'acquired' at gunpoint from hostile natives to join the *Lady Alice*. Once the party was waterborne, Stanley hoped there would be less fatigue now everyone was a passenger with no loads to carry. On 30 December, two top-heavy canoes capsized in crocodile-infested waters, drowning two men and losing four rifles. Stanley wrote: 'I hope to God that there are no tremendous cataracts ahead, with steep hills on each side of the river. Such a place would indeed be a chasm.'

Dense forest covered the river banks and islands in its stream. Natives were unfriendly, dispatching their best warriors to the water's edge to hurl poisoned missiles in the expedition's direction. A few shots from one of Stanley's rifles was usually sufficient to send them scurrying off, but it was unnerving not knowing what lay around the next bend. One tribe even attempted to capture the *Lady Alice* and her canoes with nets because 'they considered us as game to be trapped, shot or bagged at sight'.

By 3 January 1877, the river was running even faster, a sign that dangerous rapids were directly ahead. Canoes were taken from the water and the *Lady Alice* dismantled and carried down sloping banks at the side of roaring waterfalls. One consisted of seven major cataracts stretching for over 50 miles which, at Frank Pocock's insistence, was named the Stanley Falls. A survey of the top cataract revealed that the next few days would be difficult for the Anglo-American expedition. The rapids were too dangerous to float the canoes, so Stanley ordered men to cut a wide pathway down through dense jungle over which boats and supplies could be hauled.

On one calm stretch, six canoes were successfully floated downriver, but a seventh capsized in a turbulent stretch and disintegrated. Most of the rowers managed to swim ashore but a man called Zaidi, clinging to a piece of wreckage, found himself hurtled at speed towards a raging waterfall. Stanley's journal records:

Providence interposed to save him even on the bank of Eternity. The great falls . . . was split by a single pointed rock, on which the fragment of canoe was driven, the lower end got jammed below, and Zaidi found himself perched in the centre of the falls, with about 50 yards of falling water and furious black-brown waves on either side of him. . . . The solitary man seated on the pointed rock with the brown waves rising up to his knees seemed to be much calmer than any of us who gazed upon him in his terrible position. We then cast about for means to save him.

Creepers were cut and thrown to Zaidi, but the force of the water snapped them like thread. Stanley then called for a pair of volunteers to climb into a canoe lashed with tent rope, which paddled into mid-stream allowing Zaidi to grasp the rope and pull himself to safety. But the rope knocked the man into the river and he disappeared under raging waters – only to re-emerge seconds later clinging to the canoe, which was carried by the current to a small island in mid-river, marooning the men. Canes were cut from the forest, which, when lashed together, created long poles which they fed across the river to the island. Using creepers, the stranded men secured the poles on their island prison and climbed into the water, grasping a pole in each hand. 'The cheers we gave were heard far above the roar of the waters . . . and the three most gallant lads of the expedition had been saved.'

It took twenty-two days to descend the waterfalls and cataracts of the Stanley Falls and reach a calm section of river again. Here they encountered 'a frantic host of feathered warriors' paddling a fleet of fifty-four canoes, twenty-five of them 'monstrous canoes . . . about ten of which contained probably 500 men'. The war party had been observing the expedition's progress down the falls and was ready to do battle with the white man and his people. They 'lifted their voices in a vengeful chorus . . . the instinct of most of our party is to fly . . . the rifles of our boat are directed against the fugitives. The shields that have been our booty from many a fight are lifted to bulwark the non-combatants, the women and children and every rifleman takes aim waiting for the word.'

The leading canoe was 'a Leviathan among native craft. It has 80 paddlers, standing in two rows, with spears poised for stabbing, their paddles knobbed with ivory and the blades carved. There are eight steersmen at the stern, a group of prime young warriors at the bow, capering gleefully, with shield and spear; every arm is ringed with broad ivory bracelets, their heads gay with parrot-feathers.'

The Leviathan bore down on Stanley's canoes at racing speed and a storm of spears was hurled at the same time as the expedition's rifles were fired. Canoes rushed past each other and Stanley confessed, 'my blood is up – it's a murderous world, and I have begun to hate the filthy, vulturous shoals who inhabit it. I pursue them upstream, up to their villages; I skirmish in their streets, drive them pell-mell into the woods beyond, and level their ivory temples; with frantic haste I fire the huts, and end the scene by towing the canoes into mid-stream and setting them adrift.'

Native drums carried news downriver that a murderous white man was coming in their direction. Stanley tried to avoid conflict but there were more attacks which he 'answered with the energy of despair and tore through them with blazing rifles, leaving them wondering and lamenting'.

The river curved westward and south-westward, it widened daily to between 5 and 8 miles and channels became numerous. On 7 February, they spotted three small canoes paddling towards them. Their occupants seemed to be peaceful and Stanley snatched up a handful of beads and wire indicating he was willing to trade. Expedition canoes remained in the river while Stanley steered the *Lady Alice* to the shore. A chief appeared, bringing a large quantity of bananas and fish. Using a mongrel mixture of native languages, Stanley asked the chief the name of the river they were floating down. The chief replied: 'Ikuta ya Kongo!' (the river of Congo). His journal records: 'There had really been no doubt in my mind since we had left the Stanley Falls that the terrible river would prove eventually to be . . . the Congo, but it was very agreeable to be told so.'

They arrived at an open lake-like expansion of river surrounded by sandy cliffs, which reminded Frank Pocock of the White Cliffs at Dover and which, with Stanley's approval, he christened Stanley Pool. It was calculated to be 1,235 miles from their starting point. The Congo continued over more cataracts which required the canoes to be lifted from the river and carried down steep and rocky pathways hacked through the jungle. When these were too steep to lower canoes, they sent empty vessels spinning over cataracts and retrieved them from calmer waters at the bottom. In places the water was so fierce that canoes were often smashed into matchwood or sucked into whirlpools never to be seen again.

Tragedy struck on 29 March. The expedition was passing along fast-moving waters with canoes floating through calmer sections near the bank. Stanley had instructed that under no circumstances should canoes move out towards the strong undertow for fear of being swept away. The longest canoe, carrying Kalulu and several others, was further out from the shore than was safe. Stanley called to him and 'he replied with a depreciating smile and an expostulating tone, "I can pull, sir; see!"' and satisfied that Kalulu and his fellow paddlers were in control, thought no more of it. The river was 450yds wide at this point, but soundings confirmed it was 138ft deep. Its course was rapid 'but not dangerous to people in possession of their wits'.

The canoe carrying Kalulu and his companions was now gliding with the speed of an arrow towards the falls over the treacherous calm water. Expedition members watched it in agony. Soon it reached an island which divided the falls into two sections and was swept down the left branch. 'We saw it whirled around three or four times, then plunge down into the depths, out of which the stern presently emerged pointed upwards – and we knew then that Kalulu and his canoe-mates were no more,' wrote Stanley. Their bodies were never found. The falls were later christened the Kalulu Falls.

The boy slave whom Stanley had taken under his wing in the hope of finding him a family, who had become something of a son in the same way John Rowlands had been 'adopted' by Henry Hope Stanley, whom he had never intended to take to England and America but was loathe to leave in Africa, had become his mascot during lecture tours, captured the public imagination on both sides of the Atlantic, was now gone. Stanley had promised to bring him back to his homeland; now he lay dead at the bottom of a turbulent river in the same dark continent where he was born.

The expedition dug out a further 6 miles of track next to the cataracts. More canoes and supplies were lost. Stanley's journal records: 'No news of the lost men and I fear I must give them up for lost, poor fellows. My heart aches sorely for them especially for Kalulu. But it is such a dangerous career we now run, accidents are so numerous and daily and I myself run daily three or four startling adventures, that we have scarcely space or time to wail or sleep. Peace to them, and I pray we may have (for it is a sad life) when we die.'

The party was still following dangerous rapids in June. Stanley had positioned himself on high rocks to survey the surrounding land through field glasses when he noticed a canoe carrying eight men shooting down the river. It overturned, spilling its crew into the foaming water. He was unaware that the canoe was one of his own – and that one of the rowers, now feared drowned, was Frank Pocock.

Stanley learned later that in an uncharacteristic – and irresponsible – rush of boldness, Frank had suggested an attempt to shoot the rapids. Others protested that it would be dangerous but Frank challenged them 'saying we are afraid of death'. Reluctantly they entered the canoe and steered a course close to the shore, but undertow pulled them into mid-river and plunged them headlong to their deaths in a mass of foam and spray.

Stanley told his journal on 3 June:

Alas, my brave, honest, kindly-natured, good Frank, thy many faithful services to me have only found thee a grave in the wild waters of the Congo. . . . Would that I could have suffered instead of thee for I am weary. Oh so weary of this constant tale of woes and death; and thy cheerful society, the influence of thy brave smile, the utterance of thy courageous heart I shall lack, and because I lack, I shall weep for my dear lost friend . . . I feel utterly unable to express my feelings or describe the vastness of my loss.

Stanley's handwriting then becomes illegible, betraying his distress at the loss of his friend and the last of the three Englishmen who had travelled to Africa with him in search of adventure. Frank's body was later seen floating downriver by local natives, but they refused to recover it for fear it might bring a curse to their tribe. The canoe was discovered broken in two at the bottom of the falls.

Expedition members fell into deep gloom. Supplies were almost exhausted. The men became indolent and apathetic, moving slowly down the path. Some died from infection caused by ulcerous sores on their feet and legs while others suffered from a worm which ate its way into their toes, depositing eggs which formed ulcers. Stanley became despondent, remorseful and weighed down with anxiety. 'I have publicly expressed a desire to die a quick sharp death, which I think just now would be a mercy compared to what I endure daily,' he wrote. 'I am vexed each day by thieves, liars and unconquerable laziness of the Wagwana. I am surrounded by savages, who from some superstitious idea may rise to fight at a moment's notice. . . . Ah Frank! You are happy, my friend. Out of this dreadful mess. Out of this pit of misery in which I am plunged neck deep.'

Over the past nine months the expedition had been forced to defend itself from hostile tribes in 28 large settlements and nearly 40 villages, fought 32 battles on land and water, contended with 52 falls and rapids, constructed 30 miles of track through forests, hauled canoes and the *Lady Alice* 1,500ft up a mountain, then lowered them down the slope to the river. They had also 'obtained as booty in wars over $50,000 worth of ivory, 133 tusks and pieces of ivory, but with the loss of 12 canoes . . . and 13 lives. . . . Had I the least suspicion that such a terrible series of falls were before us, I should never have risked so many lives and such amount of money.'

Friendly natives offered to help carry canoes and sections of the *Lady Alice*, 'now in a wretched condition', past remaining falls in return for cloth. 'I must haste, haste away from this hateful region of death, terror and barbarism, to kinder lands lest death by starvation overtake us,' Stanley wrote.

The *Lady Alice* was now surplus to requirements and Stanley decided to abandon the boat named after the fiancée he had not heard from in three years. The fully assembled vessel was lifted from the water and carried to the summit of some rocks overlooking the Congo. She was only three years old. Two years before she had coasted around the shores of Lake Victoria, twelve months later she circumnavigated Lake Tanganyika and on 31 July 1877, after a journey of nearly 7,000 miles, 'she was consigned to her resting place above the Isangila cataract, to bleach and to rot to dust'.

On 4 August, tribesmen told Stanley that the European Trading Station furthest up-country from the Atlantic Ocean at Embomma was just six days away by water. Stanley's people were weak and tired and further falls still had to be negotiated – but the end of their journey was now just one week away. Stanley composed a letter addressed 'to any gentleman who speaks English at Embomma' stating he was six days' journey away with 115 souls, men, women and children. 'We are in a state of imminent starvation. We can buy nothing from the natives . . . there are no provisions that may be purchased. I, therefore, have made bold to despatch three of my young men with this letter craving relief from you. I do not know you; but I am told that there is an Englishman at Embomma, and as you are a Christian and a gentleman, I beg you not to disregard my request . . . we are in a state of the greatest distress, but if your supplies arrive in time, I may be able to reach Embomma within four days.' Stanley asked for rice, grain and cloth to barter for food and told them to hurry as 'starving people cannot wait. The supplies must arrive in two days, or I may have a fearful time of it among the dying. Of course I hold myself responsible for any expense you may incur in this business.' He added that 'if you have such little luxuries as tea, coffee, sugar and biscuits such as one man may carry' he would personally be grateful. It was signed 'H.M. Stanley – Commanding Anglo-American Expedition for Exploration of Africa' and he added a PS: 'You may not know me by name; I therefore add I am the person that discovered Livingstone in 1871 – H.M.S.'

Stanley's messengers disappeared as fast as their weakened bodies would allow. The rest of the expedition slowly made its way in the same direction. The messengers returned on 7 August carrying rice, potatoes and fish 'plus five gallons of rum . . . and sundry small things for myself, such as tea, sugar, bread, butter, jam, fruit in a tin, tobacco and three bottles of India Pale Ale. The skeletonized men began to revive and this afternoon there is not a soul but is joyful. The long war against famine is over.'

The weary expedition party trudged into Embomma on 9 August and were met by a group of Europeans operating a trading post. It was the 1,000th day since the Anglo-American Expedition had set out from Zanzibar, their journey through the dark continent completed, their tasks fully accomplished.

Stanley was duty-bound to return his people to their homes and used his influence to persuade the Royal Navy to provide free passage for himself and his expedition to Zanzibar on HMS *Industry*, which was anchored at the mouth of the Congo. He completed five separate dispatches to his newspapers relating the full story of his Congo journey and paying a glowing tribute to Frank Pocock. The articles, along with personal letters to Alice, were brought to England in the care of a British trader returning on leave. He also wrote to Henry Pocock, Frank's father. The letter arrived at his home in Lower Upnor, Kent days after the story of his son's death had appeared in the *Daily Telegraph*. Stanley said he felt the loss 'as keenly as though he were my brother . . . there was not a finer, braver, better young man in the world than your son Frank'.

In Zanzibar, expedition members lined up to receive their wages. Thirteen women who had travelled with their men were also rewarded, along with children of the chiefs. Pay was allocated to the families of those who had died along the way and dozens turned up claiming to be relatives of the deceased and authorised to collect their pay.

Augustus Sparhawk, the Zanzibar-based American who had hosted Stanley at the start of his expedition, handed a parcel of letters and newspapers to his friend. Stanley was shocked to read in a newspaper cutting sent by James Gordon Bennett and headed 'Society News' that Alice Pike had married an American architect called Albert Barney over a year before. While he was battling across Africa, Alice's photograph carefully wrapped in oilskins never far from his reach and his boat named in her honour, his fiancée had met and married another man. Stanley fell into a deep depression.

When it was time to return to England on the P&O steamer *Pachumba*, Wagwana turned out in force to witness Stanley's departure. To Stanley's surprise they picked him up bodily and carried him over their heads to the pontoon boat travelling to the steamer. As the pontoon headed out of the harbour, Wagwana commandeered a large boat and rowed out to the steamer, shouting that they would continue to consider 'Stamlee' their master until they received news of his safe arrival in England.

In London there was a letter waiting from Alice. It is the only letter from Alice to Stanley which still exists and is today part of the Stanley collection at the British Library in London. In it, Alice congratulates 'Morton' on his success, telling him she had shed tears when she read his newspaper reports about the death of Kalulu and the fate of the *Lady Alice*. 'I had hoped she would have proven a truer friend than the Alice she was named after, for you must know, by this time, I have done what millions of women have done before me, not been true to my promise.' Alice craved Stanley's forgiveness and asked for her letters to be destroyed 'as I have burnt all yours'. She ended: 'Adieu, Morton, I will not say farewell, for I hope in some future time we may meet – shall it be as friends?' It was signed 'Alice Barney'.

The *Lady Alice*.

Chapter 31

LEOPOLD II

Rightly they call him Breaker of the Path,
Who was no cloistered spirit, remote and sage,
But a swift swordsman of our wrestling age,
Warm in his love – and sudden in his wrath.
From 'Henry Morton Stanley', Sidney Low, 1904

By the time Stanley arrived in Marseilles on the way back to England, thirty Anglo-American Expedition dispatches had been published in the *New York Herald* and *Daily Telegraph*. Newspaper readers from Denbigh to Denver had waited eagerly for Stanley's African articles and were not disappointed. Each was a thrilling combination of adventure story and geography lesson rolled into one. Stanley also commented on how the continent's landscape and mineral wealth were ripe for exploitation by forward-thinking governments seeking a toehold on this new part of Africa. His notebooks were crammed with information about flora, fauna, topography and people and about how rivers and corridors through the interior might be turned into routes of commerce. These notes were used while writing his epic account of the journey, *Through the Dark Continent*, which he began drafting in Zanzibar to divert his mind from Alice Pike.

One of the keenest readers of Stanley's journalism was Leopold II, King of the Belgians, whose father had attempted various colonising schemes in parts of the developing world and instructed his son to 'file his brains on other people's'. Leopold wanted to acquire a slice of Africa for Belgium, a country no larger than Wales – and Stanley was just the man to help him achieve his objective. Hearing that Stanley was visiting Marseilles to attend a banquet in his honour, Leopold dispatched a pair of emissaries to meet the explorer. They told him that the King welcomed an opportunity for a meeting in Brussels to examine ways and means of gaining his co-operation on 'a new African venture'. Stanley was flattered, but exhausted and depressed by Alice's unfaithfulness. He replied: 'I am so sick and weary. At present I cannot think of anything more than a long rest and sleep. Perhaps in six months time I shall see things differently.' Stanley did not turn the Belgians down flat and the emissaries sensed that he was interested, information which they conveyed to their king.

Stanley threw himself into a punishing work schedule. He completed *Through the Dark Continent*, which he delivered to Sampson Low, Marston & Company in April for publication to critical acclaim two months later. When not writing, Stanley gave talks to Royal Geographical Society members and to a capacity audience at London's St James's Hall, at which Edward, Prince of Wales was guest of honour. He visited Manchester, Liverpool and Leeds where he spoke about the grand opportunity now available to Britain to build roads, railways and river stations from the mouth of the Congo to its source in the interior to promote trade. Stanley spoke of the region's wealth in raw materials – copper, saltpetre, gold, palm oil, fibre for rope and paper, grasses for mats, nets and fishing lines, timber for shipbuilding and furniture. He likened the region to the Amazon and Mississippi and stressed that it was now open and ready to be claimed – and it should be Britain that must claim it, warning the country to act quickly or it would regret it.

There were no takers for the Congo to be found anywhere in the British Isles. Instead, humanitarian groups attacked Stanley's account of his treatment of Africans, accusing him of murder and brutality towards natives. The brickbats had begun to fly before Stanley had returned to England and following hard on the publication of his dispatch describing the battle at Bumbireh Island. The Anti-Slavery and Aborigines Protection Society urged the government to censure Stanley for 'his act of blind and ruthless vengeance'. They suggested he be taken back to Africa under a British flag and 'hanged with impartial justice as other murderers are'. The government replied that it was powerless to do anything as Stanley was an American citizen. The *New York Herald* sneered at 'those howling dervishes of civilization who, safe in London, dare attack American vigour and enterprise while Britain sits back and does nothing to further the cause of African exploration'.

Quietly, the Foreign Office instructed Dr Kirk in Zanzibar to mount his own investigation into Stanley's conduct following complaints by a British missionary about murder, brutality, cruelty, plunder and the use of guns against 'defenceless' natives during the Anglo-American expedition. Kirk was delighted with the opportunity to discredit Stanley and pay him back for disparaging remarks made in articles penned during the search for Livingstone. He interviewed Wagwana who had travelled with the expedition 'and from these men and from statements of others, I have been led to form the opinion that the doings of Mr. Stanley in this expedition were a disgrace to humanity and that his proceedings will prove one of the principal obstacles that future explorers and missionaries will have to meet when following his track'.

In documents now housed at the National Archive, Kirk accused Stanley of using women slaves for his personal concubines before passing them on to his men. He stated that Wagwana had informed him that during one attack on a native village, Frank Pocock had 'seized and carried off' a young native girl who had been 'used by Pocock as his mistress'. The report added: 'Soon after his death, she had a child of which it is said he was the father', and that the girl was later given to his native detective, Kacheche, 'who now lives in Zanzibar with the woman and Pocock's half-caste child, which he is desirous to get rid of as Mr. Stanley left nothing out of Pocock's wages for its maintenance'.

Kirk alleged that Stanley had kicked and beaten a man to death during the expedition and that 'the chain gang was seldom empty on the march'. He concluded: 'If the story of this expedition were known it would stand on the annals of African discovery unequalled for the reckless use of power that modern weapons placed in his hands over natives who never before had heard a gun fired.'

In his defence, Stanley included the following in his preface to *Through the Dark Continent*:

The rule of my conduct in Africa has not been understood by all, I know to my bitter cost; but with my conscience at ease and the simple record of my daily actions . . . to speak for me, this misunderstanding on the part of a few presents itself to me only as one more harsh experience of life. And those who read my book will know that I have indeed had a 'sharp apprehension and keen intelligence' of many such experiences.

Matters were not helped by graphic illustrations produced by John Shoenberg from Stanley's own sketches for *Through the Dark Continent* which found their way into the *Illustrated London News*, showing Stanley firing at spear-wielding savages in their great canoe, some lying injured with gunshot wounds at the bottom of their boat. These and other 'action' pictures helped make the book a best-seller and establish Stanley's reputation as a man not prepared to be overrun by savages.

A Belgian politician once said that the brain of Leopold II was so large 'that one might wonder whether it didn't usurp the place of the heart'. He was a king who surrounded himself with brilliant and trustworthy advisers, including those prepared to pave the way for Belgian colonisation of potentially rich parts of the globe which did not currently appear on any map. In 1876, just as Stanley was preparing for the final part of his Congo expedition, Leopold initiated an international conference in Brussels to examine the 'propagation of civilisation among the peoples of the Congo region by means of scientific exploration, legal trade and war against Arabic slave traders'. It would explore ways and means of 'healing the sore' of Africa's slave trade, building 'scientific stations' in strategic locations that could also be used to generate trade and seek ways of colonising the region with Europeans. With great understatement and considerable disingenuity, Leopold informed delegates that 'the idea of a future partition of Africa underlies the scheme' but that Belgium did 'not aspire to the direction of it' because 'Belgium is small; it is happy in its lot; it nurses no other ambition than to serve humanity and civilisation in peril in the heart of Africa'.

The conference was attended by eminent geographers, scientists, diplomats, soldiers, engineers, officials and a handful of explorers. Its outcome was the creation of the Association Internationale Africaine, or AIA, under the presidency of Leopold II who led an international committee comprising delegates from eleven countries. It even had its own flag – and it was under the protection of this flag of convenience that the head of one of Europe's smallest monarchies was able to begin creating a personal empire the size of Western Europe. The Belgian government had no part to play in the AIA's affairs and Leopold was keen to distance the new organisation from his country's politicians.

After six months spent in futile attempts to convince Disraeli's Conservative administration and British business leaders of the commercial opportunities along the Congo, in the summer of 1878 Stanley visited Paris and Brussels for meetings with Leopold and his representatives. At the age of thirty-seven, Stanley had become disillusioned with journalism and the negative and damning press coverage he had received in Britain and the United States. Stanley was ready for new challenges. His *New York Herald* salary for the three years he had been away with the Anglo-American Expedition plus royalties from books and lectures were sufficient to keep him comfortable for life. He could have retired, but felt he still had more to offer – and if an ungrateful Britain did not care to listen to what he had to say about opening up Africa, then he would talk to someone who would.

By this time, Leopold had read *Through the Dark Continent* from cover to cover and told the 'able and enterprising American' that he had learned more about Africa from this book than from any other. As far as Leopold was concerned, no Belgian could achieve his personal aspirations for Africa. Only two men were equipped to win 800,000 square miles of the dark continent, 76 times the size of Belgium, for its ambitious monarch: Henry Morton Stanley and a 26-year-old French-Italian naval officer and explorer called Count Pietro Francois Camille Savorgnan de Brazza, who had also been following African rivers hoping to find the Congo. When Brazza returned to Europe at the same time as Stanley, he learned from *Daily Telegraph* articles that while following the course of a small river called the Alima, he had been less than five days away from reaching the Congo's main artery.

De Brazza had secured some funding for his expedition from the AIA and was invited to Brussels by Leopold, decorated, kissed on both cheeks and asked hundreds of questions. But Brazza wanted to create an African empire for France, not Belgium, and politely refused to entertain ideas from another government – leaving Stanley as the only avenue left open to Leopold.

At an audience in Brussels, Stanley told the King that the Congo could only become a commercial proposition if a railway was built to link the river stations with the Atlantic port. To achieve this, agreements must be reached with tribal chiefs prepared to allow Europeans to exploit, mine and harvest their land 'for scientific and technical' purposes, build roads and plant farms – actions which would change for ever the way tribes had lived in riverside settlements for thousands of years. The river also needed to be exploited by steamers able to navigate their way along safer parts of the riverine system, particularly the upper section, which stretched for 1,250 miles before arriving at the cataracts, from where a tramway would be carved out of the jungle for the rest of its course.

In November 1878, a commercial syndicate was formed by 'various persons of more or less note in the commercial and monetary world from England, Germany, France and Holland', and, with a start-up capital of 1 million gold francs, was named the Comité d'Etudes de Haut-Congo (CEHC). Stanley was offered a contract to supervise construction of three river stations, launch a steamer on the Upper Congo and maintain communications with the sea. It looked simple on paper. In reality it would require all of Stanley's energy and spirit to accomplish. A sum of $100,000 was allocated to equip the expedition and Stanley offered a salary of $5,000 a year, to be paid out of Leopold's personal account. He immediately cabled his resignation to James Gordon Bennett in New York, who must have received it with relief, once again not knowing what to do with Stanley after his return from his latest African assignment.

Stanley would be taking orders directly from two people: Leopold and Colonel Maximilien Strauch, General Secretary of the AIA, a career soldier in the Belgian infantry who had been appointed the CEHC's chief administrative officer. Strauch would be responsible for selecting Stanley's European assistants – mostly Belgian military personnel – and be his principal point of contact for the next five and a half years.

Stanley was ordered to remain silent about the expedition. Leopold was concerned that foreign powers would object if they learned that Stanley was returning to the Congo, possibly to plant an American flag on African soil. Or they might draw their own conclusions if they heard he was employed by a king trying to acquire a large slice of Africa for his empire. There would definitely be no dispatches to the *New York Herald* or *Daily Telegraph* on this expedition.

When Stanley boarded the Zanzibar-bound steamer *Albion* under a veil of secrecy at Marseilles in January 1879, he knew that while the CEHC and the AIA might be international organisations, the sole object of his mission was to help win the Congo for Leopold II. He noted: 'Now I am equipped by a foreign people to try and obtain the Congo for it [Belgium]. Well, so be it. We shall see what we can do. . . .' A letter from Leopold later spelled out his expectations from Stanley: to 'purchase for the Comité d'Etudes as much land as you will be able to obtain, and that you should place successfully under the suzerainty of the Comité as soon as possible and without losing one minute, all the chiefs from the mouth of the Congo to the Stanley Falls'. Strauch pointed out that the King had no intention of creating a new Belgian colony but rather a new State, as large as possible, and running it. It is clearly understood that in this project there is no question of granting the slightest political power to Negroes. That would be absurd. The white men, heads of stations, retain all the powers. They are the absolute heads of stations made up of free and freed Negroes. Every station would regard itself as a little republic. Its head, the white man in control, would himself be responsible to the Director General of stations, who in turn would be responsible to the President of the Confederation [Leopold].

Stanley's departure remained a secret and he crossed the Channel unnoticed before making his way to Marseilles. Because Stanley was accustomed to vanishing for years on end for his work as a reporter, his disappearance from Europe would go equally unnoticed. If anyone at the AIA enquired of his whereabouts, it was agreed they should be told he had accepted royal support for 'a scientific and humanitarian undertaking, to be made public in the fullness of time'.

While the *Albion* nosed its way towards Zanzibar, the Belgian freighter *Barga* was taking on supplies and equipment for the mission at the port of Antwerp – a collection of paddle boats, wooden screw-propeller steam launches and a twin-screw steel steamer called respectively the *Royal*, *Belgique*, *Esperance* and the *Jeune Afrique*. Prefabricated buildings, tons of tools and food were loaded into the ship's hold. The *Barga* slipped quietly out of Antwerp unannounced and under cover of darkness.

At Zanzibar Stanley recruited men who had travelled with him previously and then sailed with them through the Suez Canal and down Africa's west coast to Banana Point near the mouth of the Congo, where they joined other Europeans on the CEHC payroll. Men recruited included sixty-eight Zanzibaris and Somalis, forty of whom had crossed Africa with Stanley two years before. Former slaves from the Lower Congo would be hired locally to reinforce numbers once the party arrived in West Africa. Despite Dr Kirk's accusations that men working for the Anglo-American Expedition had been mistreated, Stanley encountered few problems hiring porters. Kirk and Stanley did not meet each other and people known to Stanley guessed he was passing through Zanzibar on his way to another adventure on the mainland. Questions were only asked when they learned that the boat carrying Stanley and his men out of Zanzibar was not bound for Bagamoyo, but a destination thousands of miles away on the other side of the continent. By then it was too late to get any answers.

Chapter 32

BRAZZA

As Stanley and his men steamed towards Aden, the Suez Canal, Alexandria and Gibraltar before turning south into the Atlantic, Count Brazza was writing to the government of the French Republic:

The mouth of the Congo does not belong to any other European power. A little way beyond is the Portuguese colony of Angola and to the north the French colony of Gabon. . . . French explorers have already planted the national flag on two affluents of the river where it flows to the east of Gabon. Struck by the commercial advantages this great artery presents, various nations are seeking to take possession of it. The Belgian government, in particular, have just sent Stanley there with considerable equipment and unlimited resources. Alone, France, whose rights are greater than those of any other power . . . cannot keep aloof from this pacific contest. To reserve our rights and without prejudice to the future, it would suffice to go and hoist the French flag at Stanley Pool before the Belgian expedition can get there. That would be possible. While Stanley is forced to clear a way for himself through difficult country, slowed down by equipment and numerous obstacles, Brazza, who knows the country, can set out from the French colony without baggage and arrive above the falls after a rapid march. . . . This mission must be kept secret and put into execution in the event of its arriving before Stanley. In the opposite case, it would appear simply to be engaged in geographical exploration.

The French Republic agreed that their honour was at stake and authorised Brazza to waste no time in leaving for Gabon with the sole purpose of unfurling the Tricolor over Stanley Pool and claiming as much of the Congo as possible for France.

Stanley was unaware of it, but the race for Africa was under way.

On 15 August 1879, Stanley's ship reached the Congo estuary. He wrote: 'Two years have passed since I was here before, after my descent of the great river in 1877. Now, having been the first to explore it, I am to be the first who shall prove its utility to the world. I now debark my 70 Zanzibaris and Somalis for the purpose of beginning to civilise the Congo Basin.'

The entire force making their way up the Congo in steamers brought from Belgium now consisted of 210 natives selected by Stanley and 14 Europeans appointed by Strauch. Within a week of arriving, they were making their way 110 miles upriver past trading posts that had been operating for years to Vivi, where the first station was to be established. The first of scores of treaties with local chiefs was settled easily; for the ceremony Chief Mavungu donned 'a blue lackey's coat, a knit Phrygian cap of vari-coloured cotton' while the sub-chiefs clothed themselves in a combination of second-hand military tunics, hats and coats obtained at trading posts downriver. Stanley wore clothes of his own design which had been custom-made by a first-class London tailor – a high-buttoned Ruritanian-style grey tunic with decorative piping on the front and sleeves, topped with a matching peaked cap with studded air holes around the crown and a linen handkerchief at the back to protect his neck from the sun.

Native chiefs and Europeans were invited to a banquet under the stars at which the first toast was to 'His Majesty the King of the Belgians, the prime mover and best supporter of the Expedition du Haut Congo'. The next was to 'Her Majesty Queen Victoria and the President of the United States' and the last to 'the contributors who have supported the expedition'. Stanley noted that the natives seemed to appreciate fine European wines – but ensured that discreet control was kept over the bottles.

Stanley's American friend in Zanzibar, Augustus Sparhawk, who had run an import–export agency on the island and rendered assistance to the explorer before and after previous expeditions, was appointed head of the first station at Vivi. Sparhawk understood Africa and Africans and spoke Kiswahili. His job would be to receive all goods and mail sent to Vivi from Europe, dispatch them to new stations scheduled to be opened further upriver, organise caravans and generally supervise future expedition networks.

British-built prefabricated wooden huts were pieced together for the station buildings, a road was laid, fruit trees planted and everything went according to plan. Only Stanley and the men who had travelled with him down the Congo in the opposite direction knew what lay ahead – a high plateau of rapids, rocks, marshes, ravines over which the men would have to carry the four boats before the second station could be established at Isangila 52 miles away. Boat interiors had to be gutted, engines and boilers removed and carried separately over steep terrain using manpower and wagons.

In March 1880, Stanley wrote to Strauch and his fellow bureaucrats in Brussels – none of whom ventured outside Europe – attempting to explain the magnitude of the undertaking ahead of them.

As our task is to establish stations and means of communication between them, the difficult task must be performed. First, we have to make a road, then to return to Vivi to haul the *Royal* overland 52 miles with its boiler and machinery. Third to return with the wagons to Vivi and haul the steamer *En Avant*, boiler and machinery. Fourth, return to Vivi with the three wagons to haul the boats and heavy impedimenta. Fifth, to return to Vivi for the stores up river. The total mileage of all these journeys will be 520 English miles, exclusive of the journey cutting a road. All this distance and long mileage only covers our progress to Isangila.

At this rate it would take months to reach Stanley Pool.

In his reply, Strauch urged Stanley 'to act quickly regardless of all other considerations'. Leopold's spies had been keeping a close eye on Brazza's movements and had seen a copy of a letter from the Count to the Societé de Géographique of Paris confirming that he was now rushing down one of the Congo's tributaries towards the great river and Stanley Pool to claim it for France. The King told Stanley: 'The interest of the enterprise demands that you should not tarry in your first station. Rivals whom we cannot disregard threaten, in fact, to forestall us on the Upper Congo. Monsieur Brazza will try to follow the Alima down to its junction with the Congo, where he hopes to arrive before us. We have no time to lose.'

Count Brazza was making excellent progress on his commando assault towards Stanley Pool. In another dispatch intercepted by Leopold's spies, Brazza boasted that 'Stanley, I am told, at the present moment, [has] come up against obstacles I anticipated.' These included uncooperative tribes unwilling to trade at any price, difficulty in recruiting extra porterage along the route and tough terrain to be traversed by men hauling heavy loads that slowed down the journey. Brazza's intelligence was good. He reported that two of Stanley's Europeans had died and a third sent back to Banana, too ill to travel further.

Stanley replied stiffly:

> I beg leave to say that I am not a party in a race for the Stanley Pool, as I have already been in that locality just two and a half years ago and I do not intend to visit it again until I can arrive with my 50 tons of goods, boats and other property and after finishing the second station. If my mission simply consisted of marching to Stanley Pool, I might reach it in 15 days, but what would be the benefit for the expedition or the mission that I have undertaken? . . . Double our power and we will double our speed; treble the working power and our progress will be three times quicker. With sufficient men we could be at Stanley Pool within one month.

Instead of sending funds to pay for extra natives capable of building roads and carrying heavy loads through the gorges and precipices which passed the cataracts, Leopold sent four Belgians – an engineer and three officers – and instructions to Colonel Strauch to 'see from Stanley what's wanted. It would be a mistake to be stingy. We must equip Stanley from top to toe and give him staff and supplies in abundance, otherwise we are lost.' There was talk of buying scores of mules from Spain to help carry the loads, but Stanley calculated that he would need hundreds to do the job properly. Talk then shifted to sending out a large party of Chinese coolies to work as labourers, but nothing came of donkeys or Chinamen and Stanley's men continued the Herculean task of blasting through boulders and building their road through hostile terrain.

Occasionally Stanley would notice men who seemed unsure how to handle their tools properly. He would stop what he was doing to instruct them until he was satisfied they knew how to use the equipment correctly. The Zanzibaris were astonished by his energy and the way he demonstrated pickaxe, sledgehammer and 'fire sticks' (dynamite) to smash and blast his way through solid rock walls. As a mark of their admiration, they gave 'Stamlee' a new name – 'Bula Matari' or 'the breaker of rocks'. Stanley was delighted with his new name. He wrote: 'The name is merely a distinctive title, having no privileges to boast of – but the "friend" or "son" or "brother" of Bula Matari will not be unkindly treated and that is something surely . . . ?'

The way to Isangila continued. Surviving on a diet of beans, goat's meat and sodden bananas, the men built three bridges, filled ravines and gorges with rock and earth and surveyed mountains. Still more cataracts and mountains lay ahead. And then one evening when work on the Isangila road had ended for the day and the men were ready to eat their meal, one of Stanley's assistants ran into camp waving a piece of paper. Stanley saw the signature at the foot of the page – 'Le Comte Savorgnan Brazza, Enseigne de Vaisseau'.

Stanley asked the assistant who had given him the paper and was told that a 'Francess' (Frenchman), a little distance away in the forest, had written words on the paper and told him to take it to his master. Moments later, a dignified white man wearing the blue uniform of a French naval officer and accompanied by a handful of Senegalese soldiers and interpreters, walked into camp, marched up to Stanley's tent and introduced himself as Count Brazza.

'At that time I may well be pardoned if I did not appreciate rightly the position of this gentleman,' Stanley recalled. 'When I departed for Africa in 1874 I had never heard of him, and in 1878, during all my travels in Europe, it had only been intimated to me in a casual manner that he had accompanied an earlier expedition to the region.' Acting as though he met French naval officers in the middle of the jungle every day, Stanley offered him a seat, gave him dinner and listened to the story of Brazza's earlier attempt to locate the Congo. Stanley admitted that he 'spoke French abominably and his [Brazza's] English is not of the best, but between us we contrived to understand each other'. Stanley learned that Brazza was making his way back to the Atlantic coast after visiting Stanley Pool, where he had established a guard post on the northern banks, under which the French flag now fluttered in the breeze. He had left the station in charge of Sergeant Malamine Kamara and two sailors and was on his way back to France – mission completed.

The Count failed to inform Stanley that he had entered into a treaty with King Makoko, whose territory covered the northern part of Stanley Pool. He had passed French flags to sub-chiefs at local settlements and ordered them to be flown from the highest point at each village in recognition of his possession of their territory in the name of France. Five local chiefs had made their mark on the treaty, signifying that they had ceded their territory in return for protection and assistance.

Stanley hosted Brazza for two days before his unexpected guest announced he had to leave. He wished Stanley 'bonne chance' and then glanced at the 1,500ft hurdle of quartz and sandstone rock confronting the road builders and said: 'It will take you six months to pass that mountain with those wagons. Your force is far too weak for such work as you are engaged in; you should have at least 500 men.' Stanley could only agree, but he swallowed his pride and smiled. His men had not called him Bula Matari for nothing and seven weeks later they had ploughed a wide furrow up the side of the mountain, across the top and down the opposite side. The road along the river was taking shape.

In February 1881, one year after leaving Vivi, the expedition opened the second station at Isangila after forging agreements with local chiefs. In total, going backwards and forwards to Vivi to fetch and carry equipment and supplies, they had covered a distance of 2,300 miles in order to lay 53 miles of road. By now 6 Europeans and 22 Africans had died and a further 13 Europeans had been struck by tropical fever and returned to the coast. There was still another 140 miles of roadway to construct before they reached Stanley Pool and the workforce now consisted of 110 men, transporting 50 tons of boats, equipment and supplies.

In response to a letter from Strauch asking why his men could not work faster, Stanley replied: 'I beg to inform you that if the whole talent and genius of Belgium were here to assist my progress with their advice, they would not increase my working force, but they might add to my burdens and sick list.' He said that his men performed their duties well 'and to expect they should do more would be criminal ingratitude in me'.

The road gang arrived at a river section that would allow them to float boats on the water for the next 88 miles. While one of Stanley's Europeans supervised building the Isangila station, 'Bula Matari' sailed upriver with a handpicked team of Europeans to prepare tribes for their arrival, hoping to come to some agreement for construction of a third station at Manyanga.

There was no trace of life anywhere on its banks, apart from empty and deserted settlements. The reason soon became clear. First one of Stanley's men came down with a fever, then others followed. After a few days, only Stanley and one other man were well enough to look after the remaining sick men. One of them, an engineer called Paul Neve, wrote to his parents saying that Stanley had taken great care of him 'during these bad days.

He brought to bear the sort of care a blacksmith applies to repair an implement that is most essential and that has broken down through too rough usage, one he is in dread of losing; teeth clenched in anger, he smites it again and again on the anvil, wondering whether he will have to scrap it or whether he will yet be able to use it as before.' Neve died at Isangila a few weeks later.

The sick were brought to Isangila to recover – and then Stanley recognised symptoms of malaria in his own body, and knew there was little he could do apart from take a dose of the same medicine he prescribed for his men – 60 grains of quinine, a few minims of hydrobromic acid in an ounce of Madeira wine. He passed in and out of consciousness for ten days. On one occasion he called his Europeans and Zanzibaris together and told them he was about to die. He bade each farewell and instructed one of his officers to inform Leopold 'that my strength has played me false and that I am sorry not to have been able to carry out to a finish the mission he entrusted to me'. He gave instructions that work constructing the road and stations should continue following his death. He then fell back into his coma, waking twenty-four hours later feeling 'a miserable, helpless wretch as though I was pressed down by a crate. The lower part of my back seemed to be palsied; large tumours and bed sores afflicted me. . . .'

Stanley did not die. He took days to recover and while he regained his strength, he read letters from Strauch demanding to know what was going on. He replied that 'despite minor setbacks', all was progressing well. Strauch asked for clarification about punishments meted out to Africans working on the road gang, especially those recruited locally. Stanley replied that it took a year to drill and discipline 'a body of raw negroes'. He said that punishment took two forms: the whip and irons.

The first is repulsive if inflicted with severity; it wounds, disfigures and renders disgusting the very person in whom you wish to plant self-respect and invest with a certain dignity and for whom you desire to entertain a certain degree of liking. . . . The best punishment is that of irons, because without wounding, disfiguring or torturing the body, it inflicts shame and discomfort. . . . The West Coast natives gave me great troubles the first year. They entered the stores at night, they killed all our chickens, they entered native villages and committed great depredations at night, they violated native women, even small children they attacked, they deserted by fours, sixes and tens. . . . I wish to adopt the most humane method – the least hurtful to the body, but which is a preventive without barbarity, which is a security against repeating abominable crimes against desertion . . . I want a method which will enable me to prove that though I am resolved to repress crime and desertion, the offender may perceive that I entertain no hate towards him.

Stanley's frustration came boiling to the surface in a letter to the Colonel in which he confessed that his health was 'so fearfully battered with the endless, wearisome tedious work, never forward – but it is much backward'. He complained that with every new delivery of mail he was expected to take on additional responsibilities, change plans, deal with the arrival of new and inexperienced officers, who

absolutely know nothing of practical life – who appear even never to have been instructed in the simplest camp duties, who are always weak and ailing in health, who have to be carried about and instructed like little children, but who have never-the-less stomachs to feed and are encumbered with baggage, who are jealous of their rank and each of whom wants a separate station, or post, or duties, apart from another's influence. All these tasks so utterly at variance with what should be my simple duty supplemented by entreaties that I should hurry to Stanley Pool, beat Brazza in speed and astonish the world by miracles as though I had 1,000 Zanzibaris to assist me in performing these marvellous feats. . . . The truth is – pardon me for saying so – that you do not comprehend the position here, and that my letters are misunderstood. . . .

In July 1881 Stanley returned to the place Frank Pocock had named in his honour – Stanley Pool. There he learned that Brazza had entered into a treaty with native chiefs on the northern shore and that villages in the district were now considered French protectorates, supervised by 'a Governor' appointed by Brazza to oversee matters until a formal delegation arrived from France. 'The Governor' was Sergeant Malamine Kamara, a simple but shrewd Senegalese sailor, now living in a wretched hut with nothing better to do than fend for himself and two colleagues until relieved from his post by the French. Hearing that Stanley's men were in the vicinity, he instructed the paramount chief, Makoko, to forbid other chiefs to provide 'Bula Matari' and his men with supplies 'or let intruders install themselves in their country'.

Fresh meat was scarce and Stanley's workers needed decent fare to generate enough energy to continue building their road under the burning sun. To get around the problem, Stanley made friends with Ngalyema, King of Ntamo who had resisted all overtures from Brazza to forfeit his territory and thus turn the whole of Stanley Pool over to France, closing the area to other nations.

Ngalyema told Stanley that Brazza had threatened to have him executed when he returned to Stanley Pool. To put Ngalyema into a good frame of mind, Stanley presented him with a pair of asses and a big black dog. In return, Stanley received gifts of pigs, goats, 200 rations of cassava bread and five gourds of palm wine. Over the next few weeks, Ngalyema turned hot and cold towards 'Bula Matari' but a deal was finally struck when Stanley agreed to write to Brussels requesting a circular sheet iron box be sent, painted black, 'something like a large and deep sponge bath with cover' which the King of Ntamo intended for use as his coffin. Stanley acceded to the request, allowing him to ask any favour from Ngalyema and his tribes in return. On this basis, the fourth station at Stanley Pool was built and 'Bula Matari' gained control of an area covering 400 square miles of the southern portion of Stanley Pool. He named the station Leopoldville in honour of the monarch in whose service he was employed. It included a block house, impregnable against gunfire, a village for his natives, each house complete with a garden for vegetables and bananas, with a main street running through the centre and a waterfront promenade where he imagined that Europeans would one day take Sunday strolls 'to survey the noble prospect of river, cataract, forests and mountain'.

Orders to buy or trade for ivory to export to Belgium for sale on the open market frequently appeared in Strauch's letters. Leopold instructed Stanley: 'I am desirous to see you purchase all the ivory which is to be found on the Congo, and let Colonel Strauch know the goods which he has to forward to you in order to pay for it and when.' Stanley protested that he could only purchase ivory if he was furnished with advance funds; the only goods he had to trade with were used on food. A letter dated 25 March 1882 stated that 50 tusks were at the station at Stanley Pool worth £1,125 in England with another 150 readily available from tribal chiefs. Natives demanded payment in the form of 2,500lb of brass wire, which Stanley estimated would cost £83, turning in a nice profit for Leopold. Later letters confirm that tens of thousands of pounds worth of ivory were eventually purchased for Leopold and exported to Belgium for sale.

Stanley's communications with Leopold and Strauch make frequent reference to who should take over his work once his contract came to an end. Neither the King nor the Colonel chose to comment on these remarks, urging Stanley to move ever onwards, buy more ivory and grab more land. Secretly Stanley was afraid that he would return home, his work incomplete or that he would be replaced by an inexperienced Belgian incapable of taking on the mantle of 'Bula Matari'. He confessed to Leopold: 'If I leave Africa dissatisfied with myself and my work, the approval of others will be worthless. I am like a cabinetmaker expected to make a splendid work for an Exposition Universelle but my tools break in my hands, are faithless, and I give up work in disgust. Were I to abandon your work today with no man fit to undertake it here, I should expect and deserve and obtain your contempt and entire condemnation.'

Finding a site for the fifth station was relatively easy. Stanley took one of his steamers upriver and located a likely spot at Mswata, a settlement flying the French flag. Stanley won the confidence of the local chief, became his blood brother and tore down the Tricolor flying over his village. Within days he sailed further upriver to procure a location for a sixth station, where, in a Congo tributary, a large open stretch of water was discovered which Stanley named Lake Leopold II.

Fever crept up on Stanley again, and he was brought back to Leopoldville unconscious. His European officers decided he should return to Europe. He was too ill to argue and was sent downriver, passing other stations he had created during the previous three years.

On hearing that Stanley was returning to Europe for rest and recuperation, Leopold told Strauch: 'I think it essential to send Stanley a letter of three or four lines stating, "In the event – which I hope will not arise – of Mr. Stanley's health obliging him to stay away from the Congo, he is authorised to pick an acting substitute from the personnel of his enterprise".'

When Brazza returned to Paris after claiming the northern shore of Stanley Pool for the French Republic, he had expected a hero's welcome. Instead, he had to remind people who he was and what he had achieved in the name of France. During two visits of exploration to Africa he had discovered the source of an important river, collected vital information on East Africa's mineral wealth, hoisted the Tricolor over the northern shore of Stanley Pool and proved that the area could be reached by routes other than along the Congo – the river he had narrowly missed discovering himself.

He arrived in France emaciated by fever. When he announced his return and achievements, French government ministers could not have been more uninterested. Brazza hoped for recognition and a grant allowing him to return to Africa to claim more land for France, but no one was prepared to listen. He complained to French geographers that Stanley had been employed for Belgium and Britain and together they planned to gobble up as much of Africa as they could hoist their flags over.

The King of the Belgians, however, felt he needed Brazza on his side as part of his Congo venture. He secretly invited Brazza to Brussels to assess his interest and assure him that the road-building project supervised by Stanley was not an exercise in land grabbing but 'an international humanitarian' project. Brazza rejected Leopold's advances, despite being offered an attractive salary to mastermind the construction of a railway around Stanley Pool to be built and operated by a French company.

Stanley arrived in Brussels to learn that the Comité d'Etudes de Haut-Congo no longer existed but had been replaced by a new organisation, the Association Internationale du Congo, with just one member – King Leopold. The King failed to admit that the change was for political reasons, disingenuously insisting that greater work could be performed under the banner of an international organisation.

Strauch was told that Stanley's successor, whoever that might be, must give the railway priority; a fast and effective transport system was the only way the expanding stations could communicate with each other. Strauch's surprised reaction was to enquire exactly what Stanley meant by 'a successor', reminding him that he had a five-year contract which still had two years left to run. With the possibility of Brazza returning to Africa, he was needed back in the Congo immediately. Stanley was under the impression that his contract had been renegotiated with the CEHC and besides, doctors had warned that it would be folly to return to the tropics, his health was in danger of collapsing and his workload too great for someone in his physical condition. Moreover, the CEHC no longer existed.

The information was conveyed to Leopold who expressed disappointment and asked: 'Surely, Mr Stanley, you cannot think of leaving me now, just when I most need you?' With that remark Stanley's powers of resistance failed 'and in a weak moment I assented to depart once more for the Congo, on or about November 1'.

Meanwhile, in Paris, Brazza was using every opportunity openly to denounce Stanley and bring the French government round to his way of thinking. In the pages of *Le Temps*, *Le Petit Journal* and *Voltaire*, he accused Stanley of having 'American designs' on Africa, claiming that the only countries equipped to govern Africa were France, Britain and Portugal. He wrote:

I never was in the habit of travelling on African soil in martial array like Mr. Stanley, always accompanied by a legion of armed men, and I never needed to resort to barter, because travelling as a friend – not as a conqueror – I everywhere found hospitable people. Mr. Stanley had adopted the practice of making himself respected by dint of gunfire; I myself travelled as a friend and not as a belligerent. That is why I was able to make this pacific conquest which has so surprised the American explorer in the service of the King of the Belgians.

Brazza's statements annoyed Leopold, who preferred not to comment on his true intentions for Africa. Stanley was outraged by the accusation that he had made 'himself respectable by dint of gunfire'. His last three years in Africa had been essentially peaceful and care was taken not to mistreat natives or spill blood, which Stanley claimed 'would be a bar to future peace and commerce. It would spread everywhere and disturb Africa and Europe.' Stanley also had Parisian newspaper friends and wrote articles addressing Brazza's accusations, pointing out that despite his claims of securing territory for the French Republic, the land in question was just 9 miles long, and hardly worth worrying about.

The *New York Herald*'s Paris bureau chief had formed an organisation called the Stanley Club and arranged a banquet in honour of its former star reporter scheduled to take place on 20 October. Stanley planned to use the occasion to state that Brazza's 'so-called treaty' with Makoko was not worth the paper it was written on and that France had no claim on land north of Stanley Pool. Although never proved, legend has it that on the day of the banquet Stanley met Brazza on a Paris boulevard and told him: 'Brazza, I am going to have the pleasure of giving you a bit of a mauling this evening.'

The banquet was a sell-out. Included among the guests were French, American and British correspondents who listened to Stanley accuse Brazza of failing to tell Makoko the significance of the scrap of paper containing words in a language the African king did not understand. He said that if Brazza succeeded in getting his government to put its seal to the deeds, Makoko would be in for a surprise when he learned what it meant to sign away his country to a foreign power. He claimed that Africa's people attached no more importance to the French flag than to an ordinary piece of cloth from which to make a waistcoat. Stanley spoke of his own African achievements, the continent's great future and closed by saying he could 'not join the chorus of the apostle Brazza, who has introduced an immoral diplomacy into a virgin continent. It is true that I have been and still am temporarily in the service of the Association Internationale Africaine; but I am an American, therefore free of all political leanings and interested in Africa solely as an unhappy continent. My only ambition is to leave there lasting traces of my work.'

On that note, the doors of the banqueting room burst open – and in strode Brazza. The room fell silent and the uninvited guest was offered a seat. He walked up to Stanley, shook his hand and in fractured English is reported to have said:

I felt bound to appear publicly among those who thus welcome him [Stanley], for it behoves me to declare that I see in Mr. Stanley not an antagonist, but simply a labourer in the same field. Although we represent different interests, we converge towards the same goal; the advance of civilisation in Africa. I am glad today that Mr. Stanley's expedition through the dark continent imposed on me, through painful and perhaps inevitable circumstances, the duty of myself setting to work in these regions. The flags which I distributed everywhere as a symbol of peace and friendship are borne from tribe to tribe and proclaim that a new era has begun for these populations. Gentlemen, I am French and a naval officer and I drink to the civilisation of Africa by the simultaneous efforts of all nations, each under its own flag.

Newspaper coverage of Brazza's dramatic entry into the banquet won him new friends in France. He was invited to address the Sorbonne and Société Historique to urge official ratification of his treaty, which was accepted by the French government the following month, along with the allocation of funds for a new expedition allowing him to consolidate France's new little empire on the banks of Stanley Pool. The encounter did Stanley no harm, either. The men were seen to shake hands and agree that they were brother explorers with a single objective in mind. A truce between the two men was declared, bringing public bickering to an end and the start of a strange friendship between the suave French naval officer and the former workhouse boy.

Stanley had been away from the Congo for just one month when Leopold wrote to Strauch: 'It is clear that things at Vivi are going badly.' In Stanley's absence, his duties had, rather bizarrely, been assigned to a German naturalist and geologist called Dr Peschuel-Loesche who spent most of his time examining Africa's plant life and rock formations instead of making sure that all was in order at the stations, where discipline had become lax, supplies were not forwarded and work on the road had ground to a halt. Dr Peschuel-Loesche soon fell out with his subordinates and Strauch rapidly dispatched the Herr Doktor back to Berlin. A group of Stanley's more capable men then took control but innumerable cracks began to appear in the staffing and day-to-day operations at the stations. They managed to upset local tribespeople, several villages were razed to the ground, fourteen natives were killed, with others taken prisoner and punished, leaving a chain of resentment and revenge from Vivi to beyond Stanley Pool.

Before returning to Africa in December 1882, Stanley made major demands on Leopold and Strauch – he wanted more Zanzibaris to help with the work, a better quality of European to run the stations (including British officers) to replace inexperienced 'flighty headed youngsters' on whom he had hitherto been obliged to rely, better weapons and more equipment to build stations and infrastructure surrounding them. 'Bula Matari' got everything he had asked for.

On his return journey upriver to Stanley Pool, he passed a mournful succession of neglected and blighted stations; Leopoldville, which he had left as a busy and thriving township, was now an overgrown, hungry waste. He spent the first few months plastering the administrative cracks that had appeared, restoring the network of stations to working order and making plans to open new ones upriver.

By the following October, Stanley was in command of 100 Europeans, 600 natives and a fleet of 8 steamers. To protect his men, Stanley was supplied with state-of-the-art Krupp guns to be mounted on the steamers, machine guns, 1,000 quick-firing rifles and 2 million cartridges. For the next eighteen months he would negotiate treaties with the chiefs, giving Leopold – and ultimately Belgium – political jurisdiction over the territory. It was not always easy to win over the natives and Stanley had to use all his powers of patience, tact and gentleness to accomplish his task. Assurances were given that full recompense would be made to native settlements and that their surrounding land and property rights would be respected. Over 400 chiefs were dealt with in this fashion, laying the foundations of what would become the Congo Free State. Many chiefs remembered Stanley from his previous visit to their district and their own first encounter with a white man, travelling with large canoes and a mixed group of men, women and children travelling in the opposite direction. Now he was back with strange-looking 'canoes' which belched black smoke into the humid air. They traded as they had done before – cloth, beads, brass wire and shells – but on this return visit they also become blood brothers with the man named 'Bula Matari'.

Further upriver, the steamers passed what had once been a large riverside settlement, which had been torched and abandoned, its crops destroyed, trees felled and livestock slaughtered. There was an eerie silence along the riverbank. Stanley ordered his steamers to steer to the bank, where they disembarked to investigate further. Later they came across 200 starving people huddled together. They had witnessed something terrible – and feared that the perpetrators had returned to dish out more of the same. Assurances were given that they came in peace. Through interpreters the party learned that the village had been attacked by Arab slavers only days before. They had carried off the strongest men, women and children and slaughtered the rest. The people said their village was one of hundreds visited by slavers and that thousands had been taken away – and thousands more slain or left to die along the riverbank. The people now cowering in fear were those who had managed to escape or had been away from the village when the raiders arrived.

Several miles further along the river, Stanley's flotilla encountered the Arab raiding party and witnessed hundreds of desolate captives 'in a state of utter and supreme wretchedness' chained together in groups of twenty, guarded, starving and lying in their own filth. He recalled that his first impulse was to turn the Krupp guns on the Arabs and liberate the slaves, feeling 'an almost overpowering urge to avenge these devastations and massacres of people'.

But he would not take the law into his own hands 'and mete out retribution . . . because I represented no constituted government, nor had I the shadow of authority to assume the role of censor, judge and executioner'.

He was greeted warmly by the slavers and learned that in less than a year they had plundered 35,000 square miles of territory. Other slaves were being marched either west, where they would be shipped by Portuguese traders to the Caribbean, or east for the long journey to Oman's slave markets. The slavers were part of a large and powerful group, but Stanley's party was similarly powerful thanks to their weapons and could easily have overpowered the Arabs with their firepower and liberated the slaves. But to do so would have triggered war with thousands of slavers operating over the full width of Central Africa, which would have put his stations, men and thousands of innocent people in danger. So he sailed onwards the following day 'being in a hurry to leave such scenes' in the direction of the Stanley Falls where another station was built and eventually became the town of Stanleyville.

In the summer of 1884, work on founding the new State of the Congo was virtually complete and a worthy successor was needed to carry on where Stanley would eventually leave off when he returned home. A main contender was General Charles Gordon, who as 'Gordon Pasha' would later become the Mahdi's slaughtered martyr at Khartoum, and who was prepared to give up his Sudan posting to become Governor of the Lower Congo. Gordon had distinguished himself in China, Egypt and India and was as keen to destroy the slave trade as Livingstone and Stanley. He accepted the position but the Egyptian government refused to release Gordon at any price and two years later he was murdered trying to defend Khartoum. Instead, the job went to Englishman Sir Francis de Winton, who was given the title of Administrator General on 8 June 1884 – the same day that Stanley sailed from Vivi to the sea to embark for his return to Europe.

He said farewell to his officers. Some were sorry to see him go, many were glad to know that he would not be returning. As for 'Bula Matari' himself, he would write: 'I know that many of my officers were inclined to regard me as "hard". I may now and then have deserved that character, but then it was only when nought but hardness availed. When I meet chronic stupidity, laziness and utter indifference to duty, expostulation ceases and coercion or hardness begins.'

Stanley travelled to Belgium to present his final report to Leopold. He estimated that it had cost 37 million gold francs to create the Congo Free

State. In five years he had opened 22 stations along the river, supervised the building of 235 miles of road through some of the dark continent's most hostile terrain, put steamboats on the river, secured treaties with 450 independent tribal chiefs along the length of the Congo and its tributaries, created opportunities for commercial trading and provided a firm foundation on which the fledgling country could build its future.

The United States was the first nation to recognise the new country – officially renamed the Congo Free State – following a major conference in Berlin held between November 1884 and February 1885 to discuss commercial freedom to trade in Africa. Stanley was appointed technical adviser to the American delegation headed by General Sandford, a former US Ambassador to Belgium.

It was while working with the Americans that Stanley quietly brought up the subject of his nationality. He confessed to Sandford that he was not the all-American citizen everyone supposed, but a British subject who for the last few years had been travelling on a diplomatic passport endorsed by Belgium. On his return to Washington, Sandford promised to put wheels in motion for official recognition of Stanley as an American citizen, which he finally became on 15 May 1885, twenty-six years after walking down the *Windermere*'s gangplank in New Orleans, penniless, unknown and alone in the world.

Other countries were quick to follow suit; among those to recognise the new country were Britain, Italy, Austria-Hungary, the Netherlands and Spain. In April 1885, Leopold, with the approval of his country's parliament, was pronounced Sovereign of the Congo Free State. It was made clear that the link between Belgium, its ruler and the new African nation was strictly personal and did not involve the small European country in any way.

As the Congo Free State began to win international recognition, Brazza was appointed Governor General of the French Congo in 1886 and spent the next decade establishing schools, clinics and job-training programmes. He insisted that European traders pay fair wages to African employees. He was awarded the Légion d'Honneur for his achievements, but disparagingly labelled a 'foreign negrophile' in some quarters. Brazza learned of his own dismissal as Governor General of the French Congo in 1898 when he read about it in a newspaper. Six years later he returned to Africa to lead an investigation into the execution of two soldiers accused of inflicting torture on natives. He discovered the entire Congo territory was riddled with corruption, with natives living in appalling conditions. As investigations continued, Brazza's health deteriorated. He died in Dakar, was given a full state funeral in Paris – and his report suppressed because it placed the French government in an embarrassing light. Brazza was a 'peaceful conqueror', an idealist and a man who admired Stanley, but viewed him as a colonial rival. The Congo metropolis of Brazzaville is one of only a few African cities still retaining its colonial name out of respect for the man.

In 1908, a year before his death, King Leopold was forced to sell the Congo to the Belgian state following Europe-wide indignation over the treatment of Congolese by his colonial regime. He never once visited his African kingdom. In the twenty years following Stanley's return to Europe, the Congo's population declined from 20 million to 8 million people. Congolese were murdered and forced into labour by Belgium's colonial military personnel. Lashings and the taking of hostages were techniques used to 'encourage' villages failing to meet their rubber or palm oil production quotas. Women were raped, hands were cut off for minor offences, settlements looted, villages burned and rebellions repressed in a period of history in which the fate of the Belgian-administered Congolese can be compared to that of the victims of the Nazi Holocaust, Stalin's purges and to passages from Joseph Conrad's *Heart of Darkness*.

Belgium's colonial past still remains a skeleton in its cupboard. Following independence in 1960, the Belgian Congo endured political upheavals and civil wars, causing its economy to collapse and making the Democratic Republic of Congo, as it is known today, one of the world's most politically unstable nations with one of Africa's highest crime rates. The civil war currently raging through the country has claimed tens of thousands of lives and shows little sign of ending.

Chapter 33

DOLLY TENNANT

Leopold intimated that following Stanley's period of rest and recuperation, he would be given the job of Director General of the Congo Free State, operating from Brussels and the Congo itself. Until that time, the King of the Belgians continued to pay Stanley a 'consultant's salary', taking advice as and when it was required.

Stanley kept himself occupied writing his two-volume work, *The Congo and the Founding of its Free State*. It was written with his usual speed and it appeared in London bookshops in May 1885 – less than one year after his return from Africa. It was not a grand adventure story on the scale of *How I Found Livingstone* and *Through the Dark Continent*, but it still sold well thanks to positive reviews and serialisation in newspapers and magazines in Britain and America. It was later translated into twenty languages and dedicated to 'the generous monarch who so nobly conceived, ably conducted, and munificently sustained the enterprise which has obtained the recognition of all the great powers of the world'.

There was also an opportunity for Stanley to enjoy the apartment he had leased a few years before but had hardly lived in. He was now forty-four, but following the hardships of life in Africa and recurring bouts of gastritis – a legacy of his travels and an illness that would plague him for the rest of his life – he appeared ten years older. A friend described him at this time: 'The rich, black hair had become tawny and tow-coloured, the bright, fresh complexion had become sallow and the skin was pitted almost as if from smallpox, but the eyes were still those of fiery youth and energy.'

Living at the Langham Hotel was comfortable and convenient, but Stanley needed a home of his own, somewhere to store the books, treasures and artefacts he had collected on his travels, a place to write and to entertain friends. The apartment was located at 30 Sackville Street, just off Piccadilly and close to London's amenities. He decorated it with Congolese knives and fighting axes, native spears, trophies, ornaments, paintings and photographs. He shared the house with a Congolese Basoko boy called Baruti – or 'Gunpowder' – who had been brought to England by Stanley's successor in the Congo, Sir Francis de Winton, 'with a view to impressing on him the superiority of civilised customs'. The boy found it difficult to adapt to life in London and Sir Francis asked Stanley to care for him in the same way as he had taken Kalulu under his wing years before. Like Kalulu, Baruti was sent to school and was often seen with Stanley on the platform at speaking engagements.

Stanley also employed a valet called William Hoffmann, a seventeen-year-old Londoner with a German father, who had been working as a bag maker when Stanley met him delivering an order to a guest at the Langham Hotel. Shortly after their meeting, Stanley is said to have placed his hands firmly on Hoffmann's shoulders, stared into his eyes and asked if he would like to come and look after him at his apartment – despite having no experience of domestic work. Hoffmann later said that the offer 'was too wonderful to be true'.

Whether William Hoffmann was another young man, who, like Lewis Noe, Fred Barker and Frank Pocock, stirred Stanley's longings for male companions is open to debate. In both adolescence and maturity, Stanley enjoyed the company of younger men, although this is no guarantee that he harboured sexual longings for them.

Dr John Kirk – who for the past three years had been ennobled as Sir John Kirk – was never invited to dine at Sackville Street. He had returned to Britain from Zanzibar to advise the Foreign Office on African colonial issues. Kirk had written to King Leopold praising Stanley's boldness as an explorer but pointing out that 'the American' did not have the trust of Britain's diplomatic service, intimating he knew too much about Stanley to find a good word to say in his favour. He was bold enough to suggest that Leopold appoint a better class of administrator to manage the Congo stations, in order to make 'room enough for a rough pioneer like Stanley'.

Kirk's disparaging remarks, along with others made by former European staff in the Congo, did little to speed Leopold's decision about how he might use Bula Matari in the future. Strauch informed Stanley that 'we do not know exactly when we shall need you' but he would let him know so he would have ample time to prepare. For what? Ample time was something Stanley now had in abundance. His book was written and published, his speaking engagements at an end; for the first time in years he now had time on his hands with few prospects of anything exciting on the horizon.

Although bold in his work as a reporter, explorer and leader of men, Stanley still remained timid in the face of the opposite sex. Polite conversation with women seated next to him at private dinner parties presented few problems, but taking things further was a difficulty. He was afraid to ask a lady out, fearing that she might decline his invitation. The fear of rejection – any kind of rejection – never left him.

Thanks to Edwin Arnold of the *Daily Telegraph*, romance returned to Stanley's life in the summer of 1885 while he was doing nothing in particular, still awaiting Leopold's call. Her name was Dorothy 'Dolly' Tennant, the London-born artist daughter of a wealthy landowner from Neath, North Wales, who had died fifteen years previously after serving as Member of Parliament for St Albans. Her mother, Gertrude – 'Gertie' – was one of London's best known *grandes dames*, a socialite whose exclusive and elegant Georgian home at 2 Richmond Terrace, Whitehall, provided the setting for a salon attended by the cream of Victorian artistic, literary and political society.

Dolly sometimes modelled for artists and had enjoyed their company since childhood. She had studied art in Paris and at the Slade School of Art in London and made a decent living illustrating magazines with pictures of London ragamuffins, chimney sweeps and assorted urchins. Not that Dolly needed to earn a living. Her father had left the family comfortably off with property interests in Wales and the palatial Georgian house in Richmond Terrace which on most evenings hummed with good conversation, music, and the sound of guests enjoying excellent food and wine.

Dolly was a tall, statuesque, handsome woman and, at the age of thirty-four, still unmarried. If she had received marriage proposals by the time she met Stanley, she had certainly turned them all down. There is no evidence to suggest that Dolly was even looking for a husband, even though she moved in a wide social circle in which eminent suitors were available at every turn.

The first meeting between Dolly and Stanley took place at one of Gertie's dinner parties at Richmond Terrace. The hostess had invited Edward Arnold and requested him to bring along his friend who had written the new Congo book her daughter was currently reading avidly. Other guests that night included William Gladstone and Joseph Chamberlain.

Gertie seated Dolly between Stanley and Gladstone, men with different opinions on every subject under the sun. The dinner party was a lively occasion with polite banter exchanged between the Liberal politician known as 'the Grand Old Man' and the brash American explorer. Later that evening, Dolly asked Stanley to sit for her while she painted his portrait. Over several long sessions, with Stanley sitting smoking in a comfortable chair and Dolly at her easel, their friendship grew. Dolly encouraged her new friend to talk about Africa, his vision for its future, and about Livingstone, while in turn he asked her about art and poetry. They had little in common, but there was chemistry between them.

Dolly had read all of Stanley's books and out of curiosity asked after whom the *Lady Alice* had been named. Stanley told her the story of Alice Pike, his engagement and her unfaithfulness. Dolly felt sorry for him, sensing the disappointment and loneliness surrounding his fame. Although Stanley had been too timid to declare love for Dolly, he felt ready to propose to her at an early stage in their relationship – but again, fear of rejection raised its head. He confessed to a friend that he was also more than a little afraid of the extrovert Gertie, concerned that she might be part of a marriage 'package'.

When Stanley became ill again with gastritis in March 1886, Dolly and Gertie were regular visitors at his bedside. He was too ill to travel to Bodelwyddan Churchyard near Denbigh on 3 April to attend his mother's burial service; Betsey had died the week before aged sixty-three. Local newspapers noted that she had long been the landlady of the Cross Foxes pub at Glascoed, where a fine collection of African curios, including native helmets, spears, shields, war clubs, photographs, books and signed letters from her famous son decorated the walls. A brass plate on her coffin was inscribed with the simple words: 'Elizabeth Parry – mother of H.M. Stanley the African explorer'. Stanley paid for the funeral and burial expenses and, as usual, paid no attention to the latest articles in Welsh newspapers reminding readers that the man who had found Livingstone and travelled the length of the Congo was really one of their own. He would tell his little secret to Dolly and Gertie in his own time.

When fit enough to travel again, Stanley's doctor sent him on a tour of European spa towns from where he wrote daily to Dolly, addressing her as 'My dear Miss Dorothy', signing his letters 'most faithfully yours, Henry M. Stanley'. The letters hinted that he missed her and that his pleasure would have been enhanced if she had been present to share the joys of his journey with him.

By June 1886 Stanley had come to terms with the fact that King Leopold was not going to keep his word and appoint him Director General of the Congo Free State. But 'Bula Matari' was not concerned. If the call came, he might have been prompted to propose to Dolly and take her along as the Director General's wife. Her intellect and social skills would have made her an ideal candidate for this role. Instead, he visited Richmond Terrace daily and each time he returned to Sackville Street frustrated that while Dolly had hinted how she felt about him, he had been too afraid to declare his own feelings in case she misconstrued his meaning.

After wrestling with his feelings for hours, he wrote a heartfelt letter to Dolly finally admitting that although he was 'woefully ignorant of women's ways' he was 'rich only in love of you'. He pleaded with her to 'end this exasperating doubt of mine', to reply as soon as possible – and if it was rejection, simply to return the letter. And that is exactly what Dolly did. Her reasons were not recorded. Perhaps she did not relish life as a traveller's wife spending long periods away from home. Africa was a long way from the comforts of Richmond Terrace, the social scene, her ragamuffins, artist's palette and the company of her mother. Or perhaps she did not love him.

Stanley was rejected again – this time both by a woman and by a king. He had spent the last year and a half awaiting a summons from Leopold and some indication from Dolly about her feelings towards him. The former was silent and the latter rejected his love. The future without either looked empty.

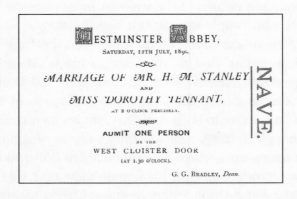

WESTMINSTER ABBEY.

SATURDAY, 12TH JULY, 1890.

MARRIAGE OF MR. H. M. STANLEY
AND
MISS DOROTHY TENNANT,

AT 2 O'CLOCK PRECISELY.

NAVE.

ADMIT ONE PERSON
BY THE
WEST CLOISTER DOOR
(AT 1.30 O'CLOCK).

G. G. BRADLEY, *Dean.*

Chapter 34

EMIN PASHA: MAN OF MYSTERY

What's become of Stanley
Since he gave us all the slip,
Started off, as gay as can be,
On his Equatorial trip,
Sworn on his returning track
To bring fame – and Emin – back?

Punch, 2 June 1888

In the event, Stanley did not have long to wait for his next challenge and when it presented itself, he pounced on it with enthusiasm and gratitude. It would mean a chance to return to Africa on a high-profile mission that would keep him fully occupied mentally and physically – and put Dolly Tennant out of his mind.

In January 1885, General Charles Gordon, the man Stanley had hoped would administer the Congo, was massacred with his Egyptian garrison in Khartoum. He had been sent to the Sudan by the Egyptian government, which ruled the country, to evacuate 60,000 Egyptian officials, soldiers and Christians of every nationality threatened by rebels led by the Muslim mystic known as the Mahdi. In his role as Governor General, the straight-backed British officer arrived in Khartoum as rebels were preparing to surround the city. He was slaughtered wearing full dress uniform and decorations attempting to defend Khartoum. His head was cut off, stuck on a pole and placed at the entrance to the Mahdi's tent. The rest of his body was thrown into the river. Over four thousand others were hacked to pieces and a further six thousand surrendered, later to be killed in cold blood. Almost instantly, Gordon became a martyred warrior-saint in the eyes of a British public prepared to lay the blame for failing to relieve the siege and avert the tragedy on the Marquess of Salisbury's government.

The only part of Sudan to escape disaster was the province of Equatoria, a green and fertile region in the southern part of the country on the left bank of the Nile, close to Lake Albert Nyanza. It was populated by 1,500 Egyptian and Sudanese native men and women. The governor of the province was a mysterious German-born physician and naturalist called Eduard Schnitzer, better known to his people as Mohammed Emin Pasha. Fearing he would be unable to offer resistance to the Mahdi's forces – to say nothing of tribesmen and raiding parties of slave traders – Emin began smuggling out letters to foreign governments, opinion formers and British friends pleading for assistance before his men suffered the same fate as General Gordon. He told the world that his province had been cut off from all communication with the outside world since May 1833. He claimed Equatoria had been 'forgotten and abandoned' by the Egyptian government, attacked by local tribes and was now on the brink of capitulation.

Emin's letters were secretly carried from Equatoria by members of Uganda's Church Missionary Society who took them to Zanzibar, from where they were posted to the outside world. One letter to an English friend in Edinburgh, Dr Robert Felkin, stated: 'I have certainly some glimmerings of hope, that as Egypt appears to be unable to send us aid, England may at some future day take advantage of the position in which we find ourselves, to remain true to her former traditions of a humanitarian and civilising mission.'

It was clear that any aid sent to Emin and his people would have to come from private enterprises who would profit from his stock of ivory, said to weigh 75 tons, which rescuers could claim as compensation. England had fought and won too many 'small wars' in the past in order to rescue and defend hostages. They had cost the country a fortune and the new cost-conscious Conservative government was unlikely to mount a rescue mission for a mysterious German with an oriental name and in charge of foreign nationals. The official line was that Equatoria was someone else's territory and they must take responsibility for it. If, however, funds were raised in England for a private relief expedition, the British government was prepared to use their good offices behind the scenes to help as much as possible – provided it did not cost the taxpayer a penny.

Through the pages of national newspapers, Dr Felkin suggested a small-scale expedition be mounted carrying clothing, ammunition and medical supplies to Emin. The idea was picked up by Stanley's friend, Scottish shipping tycoon Sir William Mackinnon, whose British India Steam Navigation Company operated profitable services around India, Burma, the Persian Gulf and the east coast of Africa and mail services between

Aden and Zanzibar. The millionaire Scotsman had his eyes set on introducing services along the Congo, and viewed the relief mission as a philanthropic way of gaining support for his company.

Mackinnon set about raising £9,000 using his influence in Zanzibar and the Congo Free State, providing the Egyptian government chipped in a further £10,000 towards the cost of relieving their governor and his people. Even the Royal Geographical Society managed to raise £1,000 from its members. The Society was aware that Emin had gathered together a huge library of geographical and scientific information from the region and hoped its small contribution would give them access to the material first, along with anything else new the rescue mission might come across. The end result was the creation of the Emin Relief Expedition, an organisation with funds in place, but no leader to utilise them.

In order to get away from England and thoughts of Dolly, Stanley accepted a £10,000 fee to give a lecture series in American cities at the end of 1886, opening in Boston on 9 December.

In London Stanley had been following the progress of the Emin Relief Expedition with interest. Before leaving for America, Mackinnon asked Stanley if he might be prepared to lead the rescue mission providing sufficient funds were raised. Stanley agreed but stated that if the relief committee preferred another leader, he would be happy to stand down and donate £500 from his own pocket towards the fund.

Stanley put an expedition plan together for Mackinnon to consider with his associates and potential backers. It contained a budget to cover the cost of everything required, including British personnel, the hire of local men, supplies, equipment, guns, ammunition, a 28ft long collapsible steel boat called the *Advance* and built along the same lines as the *Lady Alice*, plus goods with which to trade along the route. More than forty pack donkeys, ten riding asses and saddles would also have to be purchased.

Stanley suggested four feasible routes a rescue party might take to Equatoria – three of them fraught with danger from natives, presenting few prospects of collecting fresh food and water along the way or likely to anger France and Germany who would suspect the expedition of territorial ambitions as its ultimate goal. Stanley told Mackinnon that there was only one route safely open 'and that is the Congo'. Steamship traffic on the river was now thriving, the roadway was in full use along with the stations linking the entire network together. The only problem foreseen was a lack of transport vessels on the Congo's upper portion, meaning that supplies, ammunition and the collapsible boat would have to be carried for that part of the journey to within 200 miles of Albert Nyanza and Equatoria.

'There is one other thing, however, that must be done,' Stanley told Mackinnon. 'Obtain the sanction of King Leopold.' Thirteen days after disembarking in America a telegram arrived: 'Your plan and offer accepted. Authorities approve. Funds provided. Business urgent. Come promptly. Reply. Mackinnon.' Stanley cabled that he would cut his lecture tour short and return immediately. His American agent, James B. Pond, was left pulling his hair out, cancelling remaining lectures and forfeiting £8,000. By Christmas Eve Stanley was back in London and conferring with Mackinnon.

Meanwhile, Emin's situation appeared more serious by the day. He was trapped, surrounded, desperate, his people were ill, many were dying and they all faced starvation. Escape was impossible in any direction and besides he did not wish to put his people's lives at further risk. He had fulfilled his duties to General Gordon and the Egyptian government to the letter – what was now to be done for him? Whatever it was, could it please be done quickly? Stanley estimated it would take an expedition three months to reach Emin and when he was finally located, who knows what state he would be in – if, indeed he and his people were still alive when the rescue party arrived.

An appeal was launched for experienced military personnel and civilians with exceptional skills to join the expedition. Hundreds begged for a chance to travel with Stanley on a heroic rescue mission certain to bring fame and glory to everyone taking part. 'Had our means only been equal to our opportunities, we might have emptied the barracks, the colleges, the public schools – I might almost say the nurseries – so great was the number of applications to join our adventurous quest,' wrote Stanley.

From the host of applicants, seven handpicked volunteers were selected. They included Lieutenant William Grant Stairs, a Canadian serving with the Royal Engineers who obtained special unpaid leave to travel with Stanley. William Bonny, a former army sergeant, was engaged as a medical assistant after gaining experience in military hospitals in the Zulu and Nile campaigns. Lieutenant John Rose Troup, experienced at working with the police in the Congo and fluent in Kiswahili and other native dialects, was hired as the expedition's accountant. Next to be engaged were Major Edmund Musgrave Barttelot of the 7th Fusiliers who had served in Afghanistan and the Sudanese Nile and Captain Robert H. Nelson of Methuen's Mounted Horse Brigade, a Zulu wars veteran.

Two civilians were also accepted. Arthur Jermy Mounteney Jephson, a public-school-educated former officer with the Royal Irish rifles admitted he was 'quite unaccustomed to roughing it in the wilds', coming as he did from a wealthy family. The selection team considered him too high class for the job but a donation by his cousin of £1,000 towards the relief fund was 'an argument that the committee could not resist'. James Sligo Jameson, a rich big-game hunter and passionate ornithologist was also prepared to place £1,000 on the table in return for the privilege of travelling with Stanley. An army surgeon called Thomas Heazle Parke would be taken on in Cairo as the relief expedition's chief medical officer and Herbert Ward, an English employee of the Congo Free State, was engaged when the party arrived in Africa.

The expedition committee favoured a route from the east coast, journeying west inland, but Stanley insisted that the Congo route was the best; travelling inland via the Atlantic coast and the river network, road and stations would cut 500 miles from the journey. Secretly he visited Brussels and sought King Leopold's permission to travel through the Congo with an armed escort. At a meeting at the royal palace, Leopold carefully brought up the subject of his failure to appoint Stanley Director General of the Congo, blaming high politics as the reason. Stanley heard that the French – under the influence of Brazza – had objected to his appointment and Leopold had no intention of upsetting Belgium's larger neighbour.

Leopold gave the expedition permission to use the Congo route providing that Stanley agreed to accept 'one or two little commissions' on the side, using his influence to persuade Emin to remain in Equatoria with his troops, guns and ammunition and run the territory as part of the Congo Free State. Now that Egypt had lost its hold on the region, Leopold was ready to incorporate Equatoria as part of his expanding empire. He also urged Stanley to seek out Tippu-Tib and persuade him to work for the Congo Free State in return for opposing other Arab slave traders. For a salary of £30 per month, Tippu-Tib would be appointed a commissioner at Stanley Falls where he would control operations on that important section of the main route to the Nile watershed. Ever since Stanley's departure back to England, Stanley Falls had become the centre of Tippu-Tib's slaving realm. He had captured the station and turned it into a slave-raiding centre from where he now controlled his empire.

Unknown to Leopold, Mackinnon also had plans to employ Emin as a figurehead, in his case for the East African Association, the commercial trading arm of the British India Steam Navigation Company, to be located on the shores of the Victoria Nyanza. Mackinnon had read about Emin in the *Graphic* and felt that his knowledge of and influence in Africa would be valuable to the proposed company if it were profitably exploited.

On 7 January 1887 Leopold placed his fleet of Congo river steamboats at Stanley's disposal. Stanley sent a message to Emin advising that help was on its way and not to attempt escape without the firearms the expedition would bring. The world was told that the object of the expedition was 'the relief of Emin Pasha, the said relief consisting of ammunition in sufficient quantity to enable him to withdraw from his dangerous position in Central Africa in safety, or to hold his own if he decides to do so for such length of time as he may see fit'. Stanley's role was described as 'aiding a man who is fighting against fearful odds to uphold the banner of civilisation in the heart of Africa'.

Eduard Schnitzer, the man better known as Mohammed Emin Pasha, was what people today might call a bit of an oddball. He was born in Austrian Silesia (now Poland) in 1840 and after graduating from medical schools in Paris, Berlin and Vienna, joined the Turkish army as a medical officer. He used his time productively, learning Turkish, Arabic and Persian. By 1870 he was serving the Ottoman governor in northern Albania, having converted to Islam, adopted a Turkish mode of living and given himself the Islamic name of Mehmed or Mohammed. Six years later he joined General Gordon as a medical officer in Khartoum where he was known as Emin Effendi and called upon to undertake administrative duties and conduct diplomatic missions to Uganda and surrounding territories. Gordon was impressed by his commitment and ability to 'blend in' with his surroundings and promoted him to governor and chief medical officer to the outlying territory of Equatoria, with the title of 'bey' (honoured officer). He handled staff and natives with sensitivity and won their respect. He took an Abyssinian woman as his wife, although there is no record of any formal ceremony taking place, and fathered a daughter called Farida.

Emin Bey was good at his job and when not controlling his large province from the town of Lado, travelled throughout the district taking surveys, making extensive notes and sketches about flora and fauna and attempting to bring an end to slavery in the region – creating plenty of enemies along the way. He had a large house built constructed from reeds, domed and oval in shape, where he kept his library, scientific instruments, specimens and sketches. Emin obviously lived in a style befitting his status as a governor and behaved more like a benign emperor in his own little kingdom. He was responsible for over 200 Egyptian government employees assigned to Equatoria, including 10 officers and a further 15 non-commissioned personnel, over 300 white and black clerks employed to administer the region, 159 women and 100 children, the wives and offspring of the governor's staff.

Writing in the *Graphic*, Felkin described Emin as a tall thin man of military bearing.

The lower part of his face was hidden by a well-trimmed black beard, and a moustache of the same colour partially veiled his determined mouth. His eyes, though to some extent hidden by spectacles [Emin was short-sighted], were black, piercing and intelligent; his smile was pleasing and gracious; his action graceful and dignified; and his whole bearing that of a man keenly alive to everything passing around him. Courteous but somewhat reserved, he was distinguishable as a thorough gentleman . . . Emin Pasha is a remarkable linguist, having a knowledge of most European languages, of several of those spoken in Asia and of many African dialects.

He wore a white uniform and a fez. By total strangers he could have been mistaken for a dignified Turk, instead of a cultured German.

Now aged forty-seven, and elevated to the rank of 'pasha' (general) and seemingly abandoned by the Egyptian government following the Mahdist uprising, Emin became isolated from the rest of the country and smuggled out his pleading letters. The last thing he expected was a reply – but that is exactly what he received via an undercover courier. It was from H.M. Stanley, the man who had discovered Livingstone and followed the course of the Congo from its source to the sea, informing him that he had been hired to equip a rescue expedition and would soon be on his way in the company of British volunteers and 600 Zanzibari natives. He added that he would be travelling via the Congo to the head of its navigation, from where they would march to the southern end of Lake Albert and the neighbourhood of Kavalli, where he hoped a message would be waiting informing them of Emin's whereabouts.

When Emin read that help was on its way and who was responsible for bringing it, he feared the worst. He was aware of Stanley's determined reputation and from what he had read about the man, understood him to be arrogant and insensitive. Emin feared for his ivory deposits, certain they would be confiscated by rescuers to defray their enormous costs. Before Stanley's message had arrived, things had looked bleak. Now they looked worse. . . .

January 1887 ended with Stanley being made a Freeman of the City of London and travelling to Sandringham at the invitation of Edward, Prince of Wales, to give a short lecture on the route he proposed to take to rescue Emin Pasha. 'Had a very attentive audience,' Stanley later noted. Sir William Mackinnon organised 'a farewell banquet' for Stanley at Burlington House on 19 January and the following day the steamship *Navarino* set sail for Africa carrying the expedition's volunteers and supplies. Stanley travelled on another ship, arriving in Alexandria a week later.

Before departing, Stanley was introduced to Burrows Wellcome & Company, a British-based pharmaceutical manufacturing concern owned by American-born Henry Wellcome. The company offered Stanley the first of its famous travelling 'Tabloid' medicine chests, an elegant portable carrying case made from Morocco leather, containing compartments storing sixty phials of compressed medicines and pills, syringes, hypodermic needles and tubes of products suitable for tropical regions. Wellcome's scientists had conducted studies into the problems experienced by explorers and travellers needing to carry medical supplies to combat a multitude of tropical diseases. The 'Tabloid' was the result, a medicine chest in a case designed to withstand a variety of climatic conditions from hot African sun to Arctic chill. Each came with detailed instructions on how to diagnose a particular medical condition, correct medication and the dosage to be used.

John Edgington & Company of Duke Street, London, produced special tents for Stanley and his volunteers made from canvas dipped in a preservative of sulphate of copper, guaranteed to protect them for three years, allowing men to sleep in tents which prevented rain from seeping through. Fortnum & Mason of Piccadilly 'packed up 40 carrier loads of choicest provisions. Every article was superb, the tea retained its flavour to the last, the coffee was of the purest Mocha, the Liebig Company's Extract was of the choicest, and the packaging of all was excellent.' Other sponsors included Bovril, whose newspaper advertisements included a picture of Stanley wearing his now familiar peaked cap with aerated holes and holding a steaming cup of the beverage with the slogan: 'Stanley recruits his strength with Bovril'. The United Kingdom Tea Company – 'used all over the world, nothing like them anywhere!' – planned a major campaign once Stanley and Emin had met, showing them sipping tea and surrounded by happy-looking natives.

In Cairo Stanley met Khedive (the appointed head) Tewfik, who handed him a letter for Emin promoting him to rank of Lewa Pasha (Brigadier-General). The letter confirmed that 'the famous and experienced African explorer, whose reputation is well known throughout the world', was appointed to relieve the governor and his staff and bring them to Cairo by the most appropriate route. It stated that anyone wishing to stay in Equatoria could do so at their own risk but without further assistance from the government.

Stanley sailed on to Zanzibar, arriving on 22 February. Many recognised 'Bula Matari' as he walked through Zanzibar's teeming streets on his way to meet Tippu-Tib, 'a much greater man today than he was in 1877 when he escorted my caravan, preliminary to our descent down the Congo. He is now the uncrowned king of the region between Stanley Falls and Tanganyika Lake, commanding many thousands of men inured to fighting and wild equatorial life.' Stanley needed the slaver's men to convey ammunition and weapons to Emin Pasha – and ivory out of the interior.

Stanley and Africa's most feared slave trader reached an agreement whereby 600 of Tippu-Tib's men would work for £6 per loaded head carrying ammunition and ivory between Stanley Falls, Lake Albert and back, using £13,200 of the expedition's funds. Negotiations went so well that Stanley felt confident enough to broach the subject of Tippu-Tib taking on the Governor's job at Stanley Falls. His duties would be to hand back the station he had captured and defend it from Arabs raiding the region for slaves and natives trying to drive Europeans from the river.

Flattered that a European king had even heard about him, Tippu-Tib accepted the offer, including a clause stating that he must abstain from slave traffic below the Falls. A European would be appointed to ensure that the directive was carried out and Tippu-Tib's salary would be discontinued if he breached any article in the contract. In the space of a few hours, Stanley had managed to accomplish two of the expedition's most difficult tasks. If things continued along these lines, locating and rescuing Emin Pasha would be easy, thought Stanley.

By the time Stanley was ready to sail around the continent to the mouth of the Congo, 620 Zanzibaris and Sudanese soldiers, Tippu-Tib and his men had been enlisted and on 25 February 1887 they left Zanzibar in the *Madura*, travelling via the Cape of Good Hope, arriving on 18 March. Problems began hours out of port when Zanzibaris decided they did not care for their Sudanese brothers. A fight broke out below decks, Sudanese using spears and Zanzibaris tearing up floorboards to use as weapons. Stanley and his volunteers quashed the battle and medical men spent days fixing broken arms and serious wounds to heads, shoulders and ankles. To avoid further conflict, Stanley sent the Zanzibaris to the stern and Sudanese to the bow, with orders not to 'invade' each other's territory.

At the mouth of the Congo, the rescue mission learned that King Leopold's entire fleet of river steamers placed at Stanley's disposal were either broken down, grounded on sandbanks or lay as rusting hulks on the muddy shore. Not one steamer was fit for use, including one named the *Stanley*, described as 'a perfect ruin'. In the short time since Stanley had left the Congo, the area's Atlantic coast had become a thriving trading centre and other steamers were anchored offshore. They included the vessel *Peace* owned by the Baptist Mission and the *Henry Reed* owned by the Livingstone Island Mission. The Baptists were persuaded to loan their steamer for the mercy mission, but the Livingstone missionaries refused to lend their only means of travelling upriver. Stanley threatened to write to *The Times* accusing the missionaries of ingratitude for past services and unchristian behaviour towards the man who had saved the man after whom their organisation was named. The missionaries relented and chartered the *Henry Reed* to the expedition for £100 per month – which Stanley estimated to be 30 per cent per annum of its overall value.

Stanley inspected the steamer named in his honour and found its condition not as bad as he had been led to believe. He ordered work to commence around the clock to make it river-worthy again. He also discovered that the towing barge *En Avant*, used on his previous Congo trip, could be fixed and used to tow another vessel. The *Florida*, a steamer still being built for the Sanford Exploring Company and no more than a hull with floorboards, was commandeered. A canopy was erected overhead to protect passengers from the sun and the steamer went into service four months before it was originally due to be floated on the water.

The *Peace*, with Stanley on board, became the expedition's flagship, towing the steel boat *Advance*. The *Stanley* pulled the *Florida* while the *En Avant* transported Tippu-Tib plus ninety-six relatives and followers travelling with the new Governor to Stanley Falls. The boats were still not large enough for all the men and their supplies and arrangements were made for the *Stanley* to return at various intervals to collect anyone and anything not needed on the first stage of the expedition. The flotilla, carrying three-quarters of the party, set sail upriver on 1 May.

During the river journey, Stanley had his first opportunity to observe his handpicked officers and civilian volunteers at work as one steamer boiler developed a fault, then another, slowing progress and quickening tempers. First to feel their leader's wrath were Stairs and Jameson, who failed to show Stanley the respect he felt he deserved. At age forty-six, some of Stanley's men considered their commander too old for the task – and at every opportunity Stanley went out of his way to prove he was fitter, stronger, brighter and more alert than the former public schoolboys he had hired. At one stage, Stanley and Jameson nearly came to blows over the former big-game hunter's inability to manage porters. Stanley yelled abuse from the deck of the *Peace* moored some distance from the bank on which Jameson was standing. It was only the distance between steamer and shore that prevented physical contact following what Jameson described as 'a most disgraceful row'. A pair of missionaries who overheard the altercation were shocked by Stanley's language, reminiscent of Nelson, the sadistic second mate of the *Windermere* which had taken Stanley to America thirty years before. The volunteers became outraged, offended and resentful – but kept their feelings to themselves.

When the flotilla arrived at the Bolobo native settlement 400 miles inland, Stanley planned to remove 200 sick men plus others not immediately needed and leave them in the care of an officer. They would later be collected by one of the *Stanley*'s return visits to deliver supplies not loaded on the outward journey. He selected Barttelot for the job, but the young officer protested and Ward and Bonny were assigned the task when Bolobo was sighted on 8 May.

The next port of call was Yambuya, a desolate spot near Stanley Falls, close to where Tippu-Tib had built his Manyuema slaving stronghold on a fortified island in mid-river and where 600 men promised to help carry the expedition's goods and ammunition were expected to be waiting. But there was no sign of the slaver's promised forces and assurances were given that they would arrive in nine days.

Stanley had no intention of waiting for extra men to appear. He ordered the *Stanley* back downriver to collect remaining supplies, announcing that he would be pressing ahead overland with some volunteers and porters, cutting a pathway through the uncharted Ituri rain forest until they arrived at Lake Albert. There, he expected news of Emin Pasha's whereabouts to await him. Someone had to remain behind to ensure Tippu-Tib kept his promise and produced the 600 men, who instead of carrying Emin's weapons and ammunition would now haul supplies the flotilla had left behind and brought to Yambuya when the *Stanley* returned weeks later.

None of the volunteers wanted to remain with Tippu-Tib and his Manyuema forces, knowing from Stanley's account of his character in *Through the Dark Continent* that he was both dangerous and untrustworthy. Barttelot was told that he was selected to remain with Sudanese soldiers until Tippu-Tib's reinforcements arrived. The rest of the party would continue through the forest as an advance column. When the extra men materialised, Barttelot was to lead them along the same route carrying supplies from the *Stanley*, estimated to be 500 loads, which would be used as barter. Stanley assured Barttelot that markers would be made in the forest by blazing trees and cutting saplings to leave traces of the route to be followed. The orders added that if Tippu-Tib sent insufficient men to bear the loads, Barttelot was to use discretion as to what could be discarded to enable a successful march by his rear column. The young officer and his Sudanese soldiers would be joined by '40 to 50 supernumeraries', including the Irishman James Jameson. Troup, Ward and Bonny would travel back on the *Stanley* to collect supplies and travel back to Yambuya on the steamer. On returning, Barttelot would assume the role of officer in charge and direct the rear column in the same direction as the advance party.

Before leaving to hack their way through the forest, Stanley suggested that Barttelot go through the ceremony of blood brotherhood with Yambuya's local chief to win him over and prevent attack by his natives. Stanley witnessed the ceremony, which Barttelot found 'particularly disgusting. . . . On the flowing blood a pinch of dirty salt was placed, and this had to be licked. The chief performed his part as though he loved it. The Major looked up and saw the cynical faces of his friends and was mortified.'

At sunrise on 28 June, Stanley, 5 volunteers and 380 natives prepared to leave Yambuya and enter the Ituri rain forest for the 540-mile march to the Albert Nyanza. He told Barttelot: 'Now Major, my dear fellow, we are in for it. Neck or nothing! Remember your promise and we shall meet before many months.' Barttelot replied: 'I vow to goodness, I shall be after you sharp.' Stanley urged Barttelot and Jameson 'to keep a stout heart'. Those were the last words Stanley would ever say to the two British volunteers remaining at Yambuya in charge of the rear column.

The forest force was divided into four companies commanded respectively by Stairs, Nelson, Jephson and Parke. Each used men experienced in handling bill hooks, axes and machetes to clear a pathway through the ancient forest, which was indicated on maps as nothing more than a vast empty space, an undiscovered country known only to hostile natives, wild animals, reptiles and birds. The forest was filled with mist during early morning hours. The expedition would start at six each day and hack, hew, tunnel and crawl through swamps and jungle for five hours before stopping for rest and food. They would then continue for a further four hours before making a clearing for an overnight camp in which hundreds of fires lit the thick darkness covering the seemingly limitless world of trees all around.

After a month the men began to lose their courage. Hard work and scant rations left everyone experiencing hunger pangs for most of the day and night. The absence of sunshine and the gloomy environment made everyone depressed. Mosquito bites, cuts from thorns and infections from poisoned skewers hidden in the ground by natives as traps for their enemies, produced ulcers on their skin and the sick list became 'alarmingly large'. Men began to die, while others threw their baggage into the bush and ran off with their rifles, never to be seen again.

Three Zanzibaris who had deserted were recaptured and brought to camp. Stanley called his men together and asked them what they would do if natives came and stole their weapons. Everyone agreed that if they were captured they would be condemned to death by hanging. Pointing to the three deserters, Stanley said: 'Very well then, you have condemned them to death. One shall die today, and from this day forward, every thief and deserter who leaves his duty and imperils his comrades' lives shall die.' Lots were cast and the deserter drawing the shortest straw was first to be hanged from a rattan noose thrown over a stout branch. 'The signal was given and the man was hoisted up. Before the last struggles were over, the expedition had filed out of camp.'

At dawn, arrangements were begun to execute a second man. Another noose was thrown over a branch and the men silently gathered around to watch the second of their fellows punished by hanging. Stanley could see that the executions were getting the message across that deserters and thieves paid with their lives. Before the hanging, Stanley arrived at a secret agreement with Rashid, one of the Zanzibari leaders. As soon as the noose was placed around the man's neck, a group of handpicked men would throw themselves on Stanley's mercy and plead for the deserter's pardon. It worked. The men promised never to steal or desert from Bula Matari again. The reprieved prisoner wept, threw himself at Stanley's feet and 'never was there such a number of warmed hearts in the forests of the Congo as on that day'.

Starvation claimed its victims. Occasionally wild berries and plantains were discovered, but there was no fresh meat in the forest. Some 108 men were lost through death and desertion on the march. It took 137 days to reach the native settlement of Ibwiri, later known as Fort Bodo, where fresh meat, fruit and vegetables helped the men regain their strength.

Twelve days further march into the forest eventually brought them to open grasslands and a place where they could at last see the sky and breathe fresh air. On 13 December, 169 days from Yambuya, the expedition stood on a high cliff overlooking the Albert Nyanza 2,700ft below, where 'the white man's smoke boats' were said to be constantly plying the lake and visiting ports in his province. But there was no sign of Emin Pasha or his steamers. Stanley's party returned to Ibwiri to await Barttelot, Jameson and the rear column. Lieutenant Stairs and twenty Zanzibaris were ordered back to the forest to hunt for the men, whom Stanley expected to be following some days behind.

While awaiting the arrival of the volunteers and Tippu-Tib's men, Captain Nelson supervised the building of a fort at Ibwiri and Stanley, accompanied by Jephson, Parke and a detachment of carriers, returned to the lake with sections of their steel boat, *Advance*. At the lakeside settlement of Kavalli, Stanley found a message waiting from the white man known to natives as 'Malleju – the bearded man'. It was from Emin

Pasha, stating he had heard rumours of a white man appearing on the south shore. If it was him they were seeking, they should remain where they were, send a messenger stating they had returned to the lake, and he would join them later in his steamer.

The *Advance* was bolted together and Jephson, with a handful of native guides, travelled up the lake, where two days later they expected to find Emin Pasha. They carried a letter from Stanley suggesting that Emin send

> rations sufficient to subsist us while we await your removal, say about 12,000 or 15,000 lbs of grain, millet or Indian corn, which if your steamer has any capacity, you can easily bring. If you are already resolved on leaving Africa, I would suggest that you should bring with you all your cattle and every native willing to follow you. . . . I hear you have an abundance of cattle with you; three or four milk cows would be very grateful to us if you could bring them in your steamer and boats. . . . We shall have to forage far and near for food while we await your attendance, but we shall endeavour to stay here until we see you. All with me join in sending you our best wishes and are thankful that you are safe and well. Believe me, dear Pasha, your most obedient servant, Henry M. Stanley, Commanding Relief Expedition.

It looked to Stanley as if another African triumph was now just a few days away from his reach. Looks, however, can often be deceptive.

H.M. Stanley meeting Emin Pasha.

Chapter 35

THE REAR COLUMN

Ichabod, Ichabod!
To Emin he's departed.
Does he travel up the Congo?
Or hobnobs he with some Pongo
Of a native Afric chief,
Some slave-dealing royal thief,
Whom he marvellously teaches
To be honest and wear breeches?
How he tames the cruel hearted
Millions there, who now revere
Colt's revolvers, home-brewed beer?
And – just as 'twere Livingstone –
Lifts his hat, holds out his hand –
'Emin Pasha, I believe?'
Do such flattering thoughts deceive?
Shall we greet his well-known face
Once more in the market place?

Punch, 2 June 1888

Jephson located His Excellency Emin Pasha, Governor of Equatorial Province at the lakeside port of M'swa. The *Advance* was spotted through a telescope by one of Emin's officers and a guard of honour, wearing their Ruritanian-style blue uniform tunics, gold epaulettes, cherry-coloured trousers, shiny black boots and fezzes on their heads, was sent to the jetty to welcome Jephson and his men. A comfortable bed, a spacious bath, a cold beer and excellent food awaited the young volunteer.

Emin was not there to greet him, but word of Jephson's arrival was carried further up the lake and the Governor sent a message back saying he would return in two days. Jephson was glad of an opportunity to rest in comfort, eat good food and spend time away from Stanley's prickly company.

Strangely, life at M'swa was not conducted under the siege conditions Jephson had expected. There was an abundance of food and Emin's military personnel went about daily duties seemingly oblivious to the fact that they could be attacked and mutilated by a multitude of enemies at any moment.

Emin returned on his steamer, the *Khedive*, on 27 April and welcomed the young Irishman. Jephson was expecting 'a tall man, of a military appearance, but instead I saw a small, wiry, neat, but most unmilitary-looking man, with unmistakable German politeness of manner'. Emin asked Jephson what he needed. Jephson said that a notebook, a little oil and a bar of soap would be appreciated, 'all of which he wrote down, grumbling all the time at the smallness of my demands. He enumerated several things he could give me, and seemed to take the greatest pleasure in being able to give them. His kindness was overwhelming. . . . It was a pleasure to me to get someone quite new to talk to, especially such a clever, intelligent man, whose conversation must at all times be deeply interesting.'

Jephson handed Emin the letter Stanley had written before his departure. As he read it, Emin wondered why the famous man who had come to relieve him and his people from their plight was begging for food. But he fulfilled the request. The *Khedive* was loaded with cows, goats, sheep, chickens and grain. By late afternoon of 29 April, Stanley looked out of his tent and observed a dark object on the lake's distant horizon. He reached for binoculars and saw a plume of smoke through the heat haze. An hour later, a large steamer was visible heading in their direction. At last, the Pasha was on his way.

Stanley's men gathered on the shore, firing guns and waving flags in the evening air as the steamer drew closer. Bula Matari himself had been considering how to greet the man he had come to rescue, deliver in triumph, the person on whose behalf the expedition party had suffered.

It was dark by the time the *Khedive* had birthed and after repeated salutes from rifles, Emin Pasha himself walked into camp accompanied by Captain Casati, his Italian-born deputy, and Jephson. Stanley shook hands with them all and asked which was Emin Pasha. A slight figure, wearing glasses and a fez said in excellent English: 'I owe you a thousand thanks, Mr Stanley – I really do not know how to express my thanks to you.'

Stanley recalled: 'I expected to see a tall, thin military looking figure, in faded Egyptian uniform, but instead of it I saw a small spare figure in a well-kept fez and clean suit of snowy cotton drilling, well ironed and of perfect fit. A dark grizzled beard bordered a face of Magyar cast, though a pair of spectacles lent it a somewhat Italian or Spanish appearance. There was not a trace of ill health or anxiety; it rather indicated good condition of body and peace of mind.' This, then, was Stanley's first impression of the beleaguered man he had come to snatch from the jaws of death, the same who only a month earlier had written a letter pleading, 'If Stanley does not come soon, we are lost.'

They talked for two hours and consumed five half bottles of champagne. Stanley gave Emin a new pair of trousers purchased in Cairo – and arranged for 6ins to be cut from the leg so they would fit. Like everyone else, Stanley had been expecting a man 6ft tall, 'but in reality Emin Pasha does not exceed 5ft 7ins in height' – 2ins taller than Stanley.

The next day, Stanley and Emin sat down together for a lengthy conversation. Afterwards, Stanley admitted to his journal: 'I am unable to gather in the least what his intentions may be.' Nor did things improve in the ten days that followed. Emin would remain if his people remained. Emin would go if his people went – despite the fact that his province totalled 10,000 people, including thousands of women and children, all of whom were, apparently, in danger of being slaughtered by rebels. Stanley boldly suggested it might be possible to evacuate the entire population if sufficient donkeys, cows and sheep were assembled to help carry and feed the exodus. He suddenly saw himself in the role of a Moses, with Emin as his Aaron, leading the captive 'children of Equatoria' from danger to the new Promised Land at Victoria Nyanza. There the Pasha would become a living legend and Moses/Stanley his deliverer from evil. It was an undertaking too ambitious, vast and difficult to consider. Or was it?

Stanley outlined the options open to Emin: travel to Egypt with the rescue mission; remain in Equatoria as King Leopold's representative; or escape to the Victoria Nyanza and command the East African Association on behalf of Sir William Mackinnon. Emin repeated he would only evacuate the province if his people decided to leave. He refused to consider the second option, stating that Equatoria belonged to Egypt. But he agreed to consider the third alternative.

It was accepted that Emin would return to Equatoria to consult his people and Jephson would accompany him, while Stanley backtracked through the forest to find Barttelot, Jameson and the rear column, now seriously overdue. Stanley selected 107 men, equipped each with twenty-five days' rations and headed into the dark, humid equatorial forest. The original nightmare journey from Yambuya to the lake had taken 129 days to complete. The march in the reverse direction was accomplished in 62 days, each new day starting in the hope that men from the rear column would be sighted and ending with no sign of them.

The first European they encountered in camp at Banalya was William Bonny, who stared at Stanley as if he were looking at a dead man who had miraculously been brought back to life. Pressing his hand, Stanley said: 'Well, Bonny, how are you? Where is the Major? Sick, I suppose?'

Bonny replied: 'The Major is dead, sir.'

'Dead? Good God! How dead? Fever?'

'No sir, he was shot.'

'By whom?'

'By the Manyuema – Tippu-Tib's people.'

'Good heavens! Well, where is Jameson?'

'At Stanley Falls.'

'What is he doing there, in the name of goodness?'

'He went to obtain more carriers.'

'Well, where are the others?' Bonny stated that Ward had travelled downriver to Bangala while Troup had been invalided home months before. 'These queries, rapidly put . . . prepared me to hear as deplorable a story as could be rendered of one of the most remarkable series of derangements that an organised body of men could possibly be plunged into,' wrote Stanley.

When Stanley's advance guard left Yambuya to enter the forest, Barttelot and Jameson were left with 600 loads and 200 carriers too ill to march further. To follow Stanley's route, the volunteers depended on Tippu-Tib keeping his word and producing 600 men to carry the goods. Barttelot and Jameson distrusted Tippu-Tib and were apprehensive about his ability to muster an army prepared to enter an unknown region with no guarantee of safe return. Barttelot was under the impression that Stanley had assigned him the role of commander of the rear column as a means of being rid of him for a while. As he watched Stanley march out of Yambuya, he began to regret volunteering for this foolish mission.

The *Stanley* arrived on 14 August with Bonny, Ward, Troup plus stores and the men who had been left at Bolobo. There was silence from Tippu-Tib. Pleading, cajoling or threatening produced no results. The volunteers considered taking 80 Zanzibaris and following Stanley, but the jungle had

grown so quickly that vines and foliage obliterated the markers intended
to indicate their route. They would have to sit it out in this desolate place,
await Stanley's return and expect a reprimand for failing to follow him.

Loads in their care contained tinned meat and jams, but Stanley had
forbidden volunteers to touch the food until they had crossed the forest
and arrived at the lake. Gentlemen did not break promises even if they
were starving and, once their rations were consumed, the volunteers had
to forage, trade and sometimes beg for food from the Manyuema in a
district now facing a famine. They resorted to digging up the bitter
manioc (cassava), the only thing that grew abundantly in the parched
fields. When boiled for hours, the vegetable – poisonous when consumed
raw – could be eaten like a potato. After soaking in water for days it could
be dried, pounded into flour, made into bread, dumplings, porridge and
tapioca. But the volunteers did not know this and became ill after eating
manioc that had been incorrectly prepared.

Months passed and there was still no sign of Tippu-Tib's men. The
volunteers resorted to kidnapping native women and children and holding
them ransom in exchange for food. The natives retaliated, raided the
Englishmen's huts seeking their women and children and stealing
anything else they could lay their hands on. Tippu-Tib occasionally
helped. On the occasions that volunteers were obliged to call on him at
Stanley Falls to ask when his men were coming, he provided goats, sheep
and rice to take back to Yambuya. But no men, only excuses.

On one miserable day at Yambuya, firing was heard on the opposite bank
of the river and the volunteers could see through field glasses that Tippu-
Tib's slavers were rounding up natives. Ward and Bonny pleaded with the
Arabs and brought one back to camp who told them that 500 of the 600
promised men had been attacked by natives on their way to Yambuya and
were lost, absconding and going off in every direction. The Arab had been
in charge of one of the groups. Tippu-Tib later confirmed the story and,
smiling, told the volunteers that it would take a few days to round them up.
To ensure the Arab slaver kept his word, Jameson announced he would
remain with Tippu-Tib to insist he carry out his side of the bargain. A
month later, Jameson was still waiting for the slaver to fulfil his promise.

It was while Jameson was travelling with Tippu-Tib that the young
amateur ornithologist witnessed a ritual of the sort he and fellow
volunteers might have experienced in one of their hunger-induced
nightmares. They visited the native settlement at Riba-Riba where

traditional dances were arranged for the Arab guests. Drummers and performers caked their bodies in white clay, sang wierd chants and contorted themselves.

Tippu-Tib told Jameson that the natives were known to be cannibals and years before he himself had witnessed human fat, produced from boiling bodies in a large pot, floating down the river. Jameson disbelieved the story and Tippu-Tib turned to an Arab companion and asked for a handkerchief to be brought. A man holding the hand of a small native girl appeared, accepted the handkerchief, produced a knife and stabbed the girl to death. Three men came forward and began cutting up the child's body, each taking away a limb to clean off blood in the river before dropping it into a cooking pot. The child had not uttered a sound.

Jameson was disturbed that he was somehow responsible for the cannibalistic murder he had witnessed at Riba-Riba. If he had believed Tippu-Tib's story in the first place, the girl might still have been alive. He excused himself, found a quiet place and searched for his sketchpad in an attempt to draw the terrible scenes he had witnessed in case evidence needed to be produced at some future inquiry.

It was now Barttelot's turn to confront Tippu-Tib, who announced he would be unable to round up all the men from his district and would have to visit a neighbouring region – forty-two days' march away – to recruit the rest. Amazingly, Barttelot believed him. He had no other choice. Meanwhile, volunteers became thinner by the day, their spirits broken.

Ward wrote to his family in England, telling them about the eternal waiting. 'Day after day passes; we see no strange faces, we hear no news; our men are growing daily thinner and weaker.' Barttelot was on the edge of a nervous breakdown. He hated Africa, Africans, the heat, the filth, the lack of decent food – and most of all he hated Stanley. He suffered one tropical fever after another and rambled for hours on end. When he was well, he behaved irrationally, ordering natives to be flogged for reasons that existed only in his head.

Rumours circulated that Stanley and his men had perished in the great forest. The demoralised volunteers discussed returning to the coast, but they knew that without someone to carry supplies, they would be dead in days. They decided that one of them should attempt to get back to civilisation and Ward was elected to use any means possible to reach one of the stations and cable England, telling the world of their plight. Otherwise they would die together at Yambuya.

Unexpectedly, 400 Manyuema carriers suddenly turned up ready for the march to join Bula Matari. They were expecting 600, but 400 were enough to get them on their way to rejoin the advance column. They were an undisciplined and cantankerous rabble. Loads that could not be carried, including eight boxes of Stanley's reserve clothing, medicines, provisions, charts and bottles of Madeira wine, were sent downriver. Ammunition for Tippu-Tib took precedence and there were enough Manyuema men to carry Emin Pasha's ivory back.

Troup was too ill to walk and it was agreed he should return to England. The remaining volunteers, recharged with hope now they knew they would soon be on their way, awaited Tippu-Tib who arrived demanding to examine loads his men were expected to carry. He was shown the regulation 60lb packs and objected, stating his men could not possibly carry anything heavier than 40lb. The next three days were spent unpacking loads, repacking them and sending the surplus downriver. Before leaving, Tippu-Tib demanded £1,000 of his total payment plus forty-seven bales of cloth, ammunition and gunpowder. Barttelot was authorised to draw up the necessary bank draft and handed it to the slaver.

On 11 June, one year after Stanley's advance column had marched into the forest, the rear column left Yambuya. Out of the 271 Zanzibaris left at the settlement, only 139 were now alive, of whom 101 were fit enough to walk. The remainder of the column comprised Manyuema men with wives and children, a dangerous, savage and cannibalistic group. There were daily desertions and Barttelot was concerned there would be insufficient porters to carry Emin's supplies and ammunition. He told colleagues that the only solution lay in buying slaves from Tippu-Tib to supplement the depleting column. He returned to Stanley Falls to negotiate with the slaver, leaving Jameson in charge advancing through the forest. The porters rebelled, throwing the rear column into chaos that Jameson was unable to control.

Barttelot returned to find the column in disarray, porters firing indiscriminately into the air and no sign of any discipline to be seen. He found Jameson and Bonny desperately appealing to the men to calm down and stop firing. No one was listening. Barttelot said he had been unable to buy slaves from Tippu-Tib but had a letter authorising him to purchase them from the headman of a nearby village, who refused to part with his men. The rear column trudged on, a ragged, disobedient and disagreeable army that threatened to turn on its leaders at any time.

At the slightest hint of trouble, Barttelot flew into a rage, shouting at the men and beating those unfortunate enough to get in his way. Indiscriminate gunfire at night prevented him from sleeping and on the following days he was unable to think clearly and decisively. Early one morning he was woken by the sound of drumming, a daily ceremony performed by Manyuema women to greet the dawn. He knew it would eventually stop, but on this particular day he climbed from his camp bed, reached for his pistol and headed in the direction of the noise. When he found the woman responsible, he screamed at her to stop. She refused. He yelled his order again and she continued. A shot rang out and a bullet hit Barttelot below the heart and he fell dead.

There was confusion everywhere. Men stampeded into the forest, afraid that the remaining volunteers might seek revenge or wrongly accuse them of Barttelot's murder. Bonny was woken and ran through the camp to find out what had happened. He was confronted by an armed mob marching in the direction of the volunteers' tents. 'I had no arms. I walked up to him [the head man] and asked him if he was leading his men to fight me. He replied, "No." I said: "Then take your men quietly to their houses and bring all the headmen to me, for I wish to speak to them,"' he later testified. Many headmen had vanished into the bush and those remaining were told by Bonny that they would be held responsible for the Major's death and loss of goods. Nearly all of the Manyuema had fled, taking fifty loads with them.

Barttelot's murderer was named as Sanga, husband of the woman the Major had been screaming at. Sanga had fled in terror, frightened he would be shot on the spot by the volunteers or slaughtered by his own people. The body of Major Edmund Musgrave Barttelot, described by Stanley as 'a generous, frank and chivalrous young English officer', who had left his privileged English life to volunteer for the expedition without pay, expecting adventure with a great explorer, was wrapped in a blanket and buried in the forest.

It was decided that Jameson would travel to Stanley Falls to inform Tippu-Tib of what had happened. There, he learned that the murderous Sanga was in hiding, telling anyone prepared to listen that he thought the Major was going to beat his wife in the same way he had seen him beat men on a previous day. He was tried before Jameson and Tippu-Tib, found guilty, shot and his body thrown into the Congo.

On his way back to the rear column, James Sligo Jameson, the wealthy young civilian and amateur ornithologist who had witnessed the dark cannibalistic ritual in the jungle weeks before, was struck down with fever and died at the village of Bangala, grief-stricken for Barttelot and worn out by his efforts to join up with the advance column. On the same day as his death, Stanley returned to Banalya to discover for himself the fate of the rear column.

Hundreds begged for a chance to travel with Stanley on the Emin Pasha Relief Expedition. From the host of applicants, a handful of volunteers were selected. Two of them were Arthur Jermy Mounteney Jephson (left) and Major Edmund Musgrave Barttelot of the 7th Fusiliers.

Chapter 36

THE ESCAPE FROM EQUATORIA

> He strode o'er streams and mountains
> To free the leaguered band:
> He stood by Nile's far fountains,
> Lord of the Old Dark Land!
> Where death the forest haunted,
> And never dawned the day,
> He pierced the gloom undaunted –
> For that was Stanley's way.
>
> Gerald Massey, 1889

When Stanley heard Bonny's story, 'my first fear was that I had become insane'. Volunteers were required to complete daily reports in Stanley's absence, even if there was little to write about. Stanley examined these with a growing sense of incredulity as he read about 'darksome shades in the vicinity of Stanley Falls or along the course of the Upper Congo'. He read of shocking cannibalistic rituals observed by the men and references to 'quantities of human bones . . . discovered by some reconnoitring party, human limbs . . . found in cooking pots, sketches made by an amateur artist [Jameson] are reported to have been made of whole families indulging in cannibal repasts; it is more than hinted that Englishmen are implicated in raids, murder and cannibalism, that they have been making targets of native fugitives. . . . Each in his turn becomes possessed with an insane desire to say or write something which overwhelms common sense and exceeds ordinary belief.'

Stanley went on an inspection tour of the camp to which Bonny had limped back with 102 of the original 260 men – 42 of whom now lay on the ground close to death. 'Pen cannot picture, nor tongue relate the full horrors witnessed within that dreadful post-hold,' he wrote. 'The nameless scourge of barbarians was visible in the faces and bodies of many a hideous looking human being . . . disfigured, bloated, marred and scarred.'

Flyblown corpses lay unburied. Others, barely living, lay motionless, their bodies covered with festering ulcers. 'I scarcely know how I endured the first few hours, the ceaseless story of calamity vexed my ears, a deadly stench of disease hung in the air, and the most repellent sights moved and surged before my dazed eyes. . . . If I were to record all that I saw at Banalya in its deep intensity of unqualified misery, it would be like stripping the bandages off a vast sloughing ulcer, striated with bleeding arteries, to the public gaze, with no earthly purpose than to shock and disgust.'

Despite the death and dirt surrounding him, Stanley found time to bemoan the fact that Barttelot had dispatched his commander's personal possessions upriver. He noted: 'He reduces me to absolute nakedness. I am so poor as to be compelled to beg a pair of pants from Mr. Bonny, cut another pair from an old white blanket in the possession of a deserter, and another from a curtain in my tent.' The reserve boxes of clothing and tasty Fortnum & Mason delicacies, which would have sustained the volunteers at Banalya for many weeks if they had dared open them, were never seen again.

Rear column survivors were removed from the Banalya 'pest house' and taken to an island in the middle of the river to regain their strength. Stanley had no intention of wasting time. His feet were itching to get back to Albert Nyanza and surmount the final hurdle – leading Emin Pasha and his people to freedom. The sick would be carried in canoes travelling along the river while the main body would march along the parallel track over which Stanley was about to march for the third time. He dismissed all but 60 Manyuema and combined the remaining forces with the men he had brought from the lake, totalling 283 porters for 275 loads.

About one month away from Ibwiri, now renamed Fort Bodo by Stanley, they abandoned the canoes and struck out overland, carrying the sick over a shorter route. This took them across the territory of the pygmies, who were quick to pick off several carriers with spears before realising that strangers passing through their land meant them no harm. The rest of the march was just as tough as previous journeys through the forest. One camp was named 'Starvation Camp' because it offered absolutely nothing in the way of food. By the time they burst out of the great forest and reached Fort Bodo on 20 December, 106 men had died from illness, starvation, pygmy attacks, poisoned arrow wounds or had ended up in the cooking pots of cannibals encountered en route.

It had been 188 days since Stanley had left the settlement in search of the rear column and he was expecting a message to be waiting from Emin and Jephson giving their location. There was nothing. Stanley cursed both men, unaware that they were now prisoners of Emin's mutinous officers and that Mahdist rebels had seized control of half of Equatoria.

Arthur Mounteney Jephson was enjoying a life of luxury as the guest of the Governor of Equatoria. They had travelled up the lake to Wadelai, a large fortified station of neat bamboo huts set either side of a wide street. Emin's hut was the largest, decorated with European furnishings including a dining table and chairs, a pair of divans and bookcases filled with volumes about plants and insects. This was the house Emin shared with his pretty little six-year-old daughter Farida, who wore Arab costume. Jephson found her delightful and realised that living in such a comfortable home, eating good food and with uniformed soldiers at his beck and call, Emin had carved out a Ruritanian empire for his daughter and himself. No wonder he appeared reluctant to leave.

It was true that Emin worked hard. In his role as a doctor, he visited the hospital each day before returning to tackle a mountain of paperwork, although Jephson was never sure who would ever read the reports and letters written by the Governor. Emin also visited parts of his province, travelling on one of his two steamers, on horseback or wagon. The only time he stopped working or travelling was when he peered into his microscope with his one good eye to examine insect specimens brought to his collection.

Jephson was assigned his own hut in the shade of lime, orange and pomegranate trees and settled down to a comfortable and leisurely existence, occasionally travelling with Emin on official business. At each place soldiers from the local garrison greeted them with full military honours. The soldiers were referred to as Sudanese, but were drawn from surrounding tribes and few had ever been to the Sudan. Some soldiers took Jephson into their confidence and voiced concern that if Emin left Equatoria, their traditional customs would be sacrificed. Others said they wanted to remain where they were or be relocated to a coastal settlement. It became apparent that Emin exercised little control over his people, who were happy to smile, bow and let him continue on his way. This Pasha was not their leader or saviour, simply a figurehead whom they tolerated while getting on with their lives. Most worrying of all was a rumour that a rebel battalion of Emin's own soldiers was in mutinous mood and planning to overthrow him.

Jephson was troubled by his conscience. He was enjoying comfort and good food while his fellow volunteers were probably suffering privations attempting to rescue a man possibly not worth rescuing. To control events before they turned nasty, Jephson suggested that Wadelai should be evacuated. Emin stated that before leaving, he needed to know what people living in other parts of the province wanted to do. Until then, they would remain and continue living as before.

After several weeks, Emin suffered a mild heart attack and Jephson was left to his own devices. It was a strange and unreal existence with everything tranquil on the surface and a hotbed of rebellion lurking beneath. Everyone seemed aware of it except one person – Emin Pasha. Jephson wondered what Stanley would have made of the situation.

Emin and Jephson went on another tour to let Equatoria's people know their Governor was still alive. A tribal dance was arranged in a settlement known as Dufile and as the performance began, Emin was handed a letter from an officer stating that the rebellious battalion planned to arrest him. Emin and Jephson made preparations to leave – but to where? Other garrisons were likely to include soldiers happy to see the back of Emin Pasha and their safety could not be guaranteed.

Emin ordered Dufile's ammunition store to be emptied and the contents taken to Wadelai, but when they arrived at the arsenal, they discovered rebel troops had beaten them to it. Jephson urged Emin to do what Stanley would have done – return and exert his authority. But Emin Pasha was not Henry Morton Stanley and he ran like a frightened rabbit. Jephson recorded: 'From that day I lost faith in Emin's advice and assurances with regard to his people; I felt that a heavy cloud was gathering over us, and that serious trouble was impending.'

Rebels began attacking other settlements, capturing their arsenals and taking prisoners. Emin sought Jephson's advice and the younger man suggested that messages be sent to rebel areas stating that those wishing to leave with the Pasha must be allowed to depart, while those preferring to stay could do so. The message was sent back down the road.

At Dufile, Emin and Jephson were arrested by drunken soldiers from the rebel battalion and taken to a prison compound where a list of Emin's 'crimes' was read out. He was told he would be executed – slowly and painfully.

Jephson managed to smuggle a letter out to Stanley in secret, informing him of their situation and warning that rebels planned to travel down the lake, trap the rescue expedition and slaughter them all. It ended: 'If we are not able to get out of the country, please remember me to my friends.' A second secret letter written by Emin requested Stanley to take care of his daughter in the event of his death.

Rebel leaders were given a triumphant entry into Dufile and commandeered Emin's house. They sent for Jephson and, lounging on Emin's divans, demanded that the young man give an account of himself. They wanted to see the letters the Khedive had sent to Emin and which Jephson was carrying. They tore them up and threw the pieces on the floor claiming they were forgeries. With nothing to lose, Jephson rounded on his captors, accusing them of treachery and abusing the good intentions of someone who had come to rescue them. This last point struck their Muslim sensibilities and, to Jephson's surprise, he was released. Shortly afterwards, Emin, too, was allowed out of the stockade, to collect his daughter and return to Wadelai where he was reunited with his books, insects and microscope as if nothing had happened.

A great deal had happened and Emin had witnessed it from the confines of his prison stockade. He had seen a revolution by rebels who had no idea how to control a country once they came to power, afraid of what might happen if Emin evacuated the province. When their revolution collapsed after only a few weeks, the people begged Emin to become their Governor again and protect them from advancing Mahdist rebels. He refused, telling them he was now a private citizen, no longer prepared to lead people who had attempted to oust him. As an ordinary citizen he could do as he pleased. He knew it was only a matter of days before he was arrested again by the approaching mob – and probably beheaded in the street. It was time to get out of Equatoria and he began preparing for his escape, ordering scores of bearers to carry his store of ivory tusks to the lake.

On the night before their departure, Emin's soldiers deserted. Before daybreak, nearly six hundred of his people – men, women, children, cattle and dogs – turned out to follow him. They no longer felt secure in Equatoria and knew their Pasha would look after them. Wherever he went, they were going, too.

It was now Jephson's turn to take on the role of Moses, leading hundreds of frightened and bemused people to freedom. A large assembly gathered outside Emin's house waiting for him to give the word. Emin was too busy taking care of his daughter and left the job to his young friend. As they set off towards the lake, a straggling line of refugees stretched back for 3 miles. Some fell by the wayside, too ill or old to cover the distance. There was shouting, crying, bleating. It was uproar – but a moving one and by nightfall they had arrived at the lake and made camp from whatever materials could be found.

Hours after they had departed, the rebels rode in. They looted, raped, burned the settlement to the ground and passed the death sentence on Emin and Jephson.

Instead of parting the waters of the Albert Nyanza, Jephson sailed across it on the *Khedive*, which had yet to be seized by the Mahdist rebels. He needed to alert Stanley that Emin and hundreds of his people were waiting to cross over. On his arrival, Jephson recalled that Stanley 'received me in his usual calm manner, tempered, however, by a smile. I think he was pleased to see me again. I know I was glad to see him.' Stanley wanted to know what Emin planned to do once he and his people landed safely on their side of the lake. Jephson was forced to admit that after eight months with the Pasha, he had no idea.

On 16 February, the *Khedive* brought Emin and the first group of sixty-five of his people across the water. Stanley was determined to let Emin know the lengths to which he and his men had gone to arrive at this moment. Jephson was sent to the water's edge to greet Emin while Stanley remained in his tent watching carriers haul crates, chests, boxes and trunks into camp. Stanley counted 104 carriers hauling 60 loads full of Emin's goods and made up his mind to insist that Emin discard two-thirds of his boxes and crates. Then came the sick and elderly, followed by mothers with babies and small children. Stanley worried how his men were going to carry everything and lead everybody back to the coast.

Stanley and Emin exchanged polite greetings. There was no time for long discussions that day. The *Khedive* had to return to transport another group of people and their cattle and Stanley was determined to let Emin supervise the operation. It was therefore agreed that the *Khedive* would make as many journeys back as was safe and necessary until everyone wishing to taste freedom with Emin had been rescued from the rebel stronghold. The operation took six weeks. As the numbers at the camp swelled to over five hundred, Emin's followers were reminded that English people had heard about their plight and need for ammunition to defend themselves. The Khedive had asked Bula Matari to bring as many who wished to travel to Egypt to return with him. Those who wanted to stay could do so.

Lieutenant Stairs and William Bonny were dispatched to lakeside tribal settlements with instructions to hire men prepared to travel 1,400 miles to the sea. Those completing the journey would be guaranteed safe passage back to their villages. Stairs and Bonny returned with 312 carriers, a mixture of dwarfs, men 7ft tall and an assortment of tribes-people considered trustworthy.

There was no doubt who was in charge of the camp, which grew in size each day – and it was not Emin Pasha. As usual, Stanley rose early and began issuing orders immediately. Emin spent his days pottering about making scientific observations, catching insects and butterflies. He fell into deep depression when Stanley lost his temper, informing Emin that every day they lingered by the lake cost the relief committee £400. Emin was alarmed by the number of his men who snapped to attention when Stanley appeared. It seemed they would do anything for Bula Matari. He retreated into a dignified silence nursing his bitterness and resentment towards the man who had come to rescue him.

At sunrise on 10 April, Stanley blew the whistle to signify that it was time for 1,510 people – expedition members, remaining Manyuema, local natives and Emin's people – to pick up their children, baggage, supplies and ivory and begin marching towards the southern shore of the Albert Nyanza. The journey was not without its hardships and interruptions. Stanley was the cause of the first difficulty when he fell ill with gastritis. Dr Parke and the contents of Henry Wellcome's 'Tabloid' medicine chest soon had him back on his feet. Men deserted, their ringleaders were hunted down, dragged back, tried by the rest of the porters, found guilty and hanged.

As the march progressed, many of Emin's people transferred allegiance from the Pasha to Bula Matari. Stanley enrolled Emin's fittest men into a new company, issued them with guns, gave them special rations and told them only to take orders from himself or the British volunteers. They included Emin's personal guards and orderlies. When Emin heard what Stanley had done, he stood outside Bula Matari's tent and shouted: 'Mr. Stanley, I am sorry that I ever agreed to go with you.' It was too late. Stanley was telling his volunteers that Emin was small-minded, an outcast, a Governor with no one to govern, rejected by his people and saved by brave Englishmen.

On the journey to the coast, the expedition came within sight of snow-capped peaks the natives called the Ruwenzori Mountains, peaks which the ancient Greek astronomer and geographer Ptolemy had named the 'Mountains of the Moon'. For most of the year the peaks were obscured by cloud, but for three successive days there were clear skies and Stanley 'saw them, spell-bound'. There were other discoveries, too. Stanley and Emin disagreed on many things, but concurred that the Semliki River linked together the Albert Nyanza with a new lake which Stanley named Albert Edward Nyanza – after the Prince of Wales – thus settling the few remaining doubtful geographic points regarding the sources of the Nile for the benefit of the Royal Geographical Society.

The expedition reached the Victoria Nyanza in September and headed east throughout October and November towards Bagamoyo, the coast, Zanzibar – and home. As they drew to the end of their long march, word was sent down the pathway to coastal settlements that Stanley's rescue party was approaching. On 28 November, a 170-man expedition from the Imperial British East African Company arrived with supplies of rice, European provisions – including champagne – clothing and footwear.

The sound of the noon cannon at Zanzibar signalled that they were nearing journey's end. Zanzibaris in the group were ecstatic. The return journey had taken seven and a half months. Stanley and his men had been travelling for the last two and a half years, covering a distance of 6,032 miles. Out of the original group of 620 Zanzibaris who had travelled with Stanley, only 225 returned to their island home. Of the 60 Sudanese, only 12 survived. Of the 570 refugees who had followed Emin out of Equatoria, 290 completed the journey; around 80 had died on the march, the rest had gone missing along the way.

They stumbled into Bagamoyo, part of German East Africa, on 4 December, where the authorities provided emergency shelter for the carriers and Emin's people. The Imperial German Commissioner gave a banquet in honour of Stanley, Emin and the volunteers that same evening. It was a crowded occasion to which Zanzibar's diplomatic community were invited along with elite British and German naval personnel and Mackinnon's local representatives. In the street, the Zanzibaris had a party of their own, singing, dancing and feasting. Emin was invited to sit at the Commissioner's right hand on the top table. He politely declined, insisting that Stanley take the seat of honour. He had learned that he could invoke Stanley's displeasure quickly and did not want to upset him one last time.

Guests noted that Emin's eyesight, which had never been good, appeared to have deteriorated. He had to place the special menu produced for the evening at the end of his nose in order to read it and hold his face only inches over his food in order to see what was on his plate.

When it was time for speeches, Stanley was the first to rise to his feet. Speaking in what one guest described as 'a sonorous voice, using fine, dramatic, rolling phrases full of religious references, such as many a Welsh preacher might use', Stanley reflected that it had been proved by previous expeditions 'that success was only gained by hearty goodwill, unwearied effort, and uttermost striving. My companions and myself, like men animated with one mind, have devoted every fibre and all our strength, morally and physically, to accomplish the purpose for which we set out.'

Emin could have used his reply to complain about Stanley, the way he had been treated and his position undermined during the march to the sea. Instead, he gave voice to an eloquent outpouring of gratitude 'to the generous English people' who had rescued him and his people.

After dinner and with a German band playing, guests mingled. Stanley described Emin as 'gay and happy' as he made his way from one end of the table to the other, chatting with guests. Stanley remained in his seat listening to a long political story related by the German Commissioner. Later in the evening a steward whispered in Stanley's ear that 'Pasha has fallen down'. Stanley took this to mean he had stumbled over a chair, but the steward added: 'He has fallen over the verandah wall and into the street and is dangerously hurt.'

Stanley flew downstairs into the street where two pools of blood soaked the ground. There was no sign of Emin, who had been rushed to the German Hospital. It appeared that the Pasha had wandered onto the balcony for fresh air and because of his failing eyesight had not noticed a low wall overlooking the street 20ft below. He had lost his balance, fallen over, sliding down the verandah's sloping roof and crashed to the ground. He was unconscious when a member of the Imperial German Commissioner's staff found him and arranged to take him to hospital.

At the hospital, Emin lay on a bed, still unconscious, his head covered in soaking red bandages. Stanley sent Dr Parke to the hospital to examine Emin. Although his injuries were serious, the doctor found no fractures. As well as damage to his head, Emin's right side and back were also severely bruised. Stanley later visited Emin's bedside. He was now fully conscious although dangerously ill. 'Well, Pasha,' said Stanley, 'I hope you don't mean to admit the possibility that you are to die here, do you?' Emin said his accident was not as bad as that.

Dr Parke was ordered to remain with Emin and send daily reports about the patient's progress. Emin instructed his German orderlies to bar Stanley from the hospital. He dismissed Parke, refused to see other British volunteers and made it known that he wanted nothing further to do with the Emin Pasha Relief Expedition (whose final bill for the venture amounted to nearly £28,000) or any commercial organisation interested in employing him for highly paid jobs in their service. Stanley was informed that once he had recovered from his injuries, Emin would accept a position with the German government service in East Africa.

Angrily, Stanley strode to the shelters where Emin's people were camping. He explained they were going to Zanzibar. Anyone refusing would be put in chains and dragged there. From the island they were taken to Egypt. Emin claimed he was prevented from communicating with them.

Once in Zanzibar, Stanley stayed at the home of the British Consul, Colonel Euan Smith. In a letter to Lord Salisbury the Consul noted:

His [Stanley's] hair is as white as snow. When I first saw him he looked dreadfully done up; but the rest and good living have worked a wonderful change for the better in his appearance. His experiences and sufferings have been beyond anything that it would enter the mind of man to conceive, and he has a frightful tale to tell of the inhumanities and cruelties of the Arabs in Central Africa, which will, I am convinced, make all England ring with indignation. He is thoroughly in earnest in his belief that to him has been confided the mission of rescuing the natives of Central Africa from their present desperate situation.

Stanley's four English officers . . . are certainly a splendid quartet of Englishmen; but there is no love lost between them and Stanley, who, I fancy, though an unqualified leader of natives, does not understand how to treat Englishmen. They all, however, unanimously acknowledge that no other leader could have successfully extricated the expedition from the hideous difficulties in which it found itself entangled. . . .

It is easy to see that Stanley has neither liking nor admiration for Emin Pasha; and he openly expresses his opinion that the estimation in which [he] was held in England, as an heroic figure holding his post against overwhelming odds, is entirely false and unsatisfactory. He declares the Pasha to be a weak-minded, sweet natured, pleasant-

mannered *savant* but to be wholly incapable of ruling or leading men.
. . . Stanley hardly cares to disguise the contempt with which he
speaks of the Pasha, and he hints that a very great deal of curious
matter will see the light before long. In the meantime, the poor Pasha
is something of a prisoner in the hands of the Germans, whose tender
mercies are perhaps not without a tinge of unintentional cruelty.

Referring to the expedition's Zanzibaris, Smith noted: 'It is melancholy to
reflect that, as Stanley informs me, when pay day came, and they were
paraded to receive nearly three years wages, their Arab owners assembled
at the pay office and seized from each the entire sum he received. I am
told that the largest proportion of the sum so received went to the Sultan
as being the largest slave-owner. . . .'

There was one more task for Stanley to address before he left Africa. He
brought a legal action against Tippu-Tib in the Zanzibar Consular Court
for breach of agreement, claiming £10,000 in damages for failure to
furnish the expedition with the 600 carriers he had promised and for
other crimes against his volunteers. Stanley knew the money lay in gold
in the slaver's Zanzibar bank account from the sale of ivory. The result of
the action was never made public.

Letter from Queen Victoria to H.M. Stanley, Windsor Castle, 10 December:

My thoughts are often with you and your brave followers, whose
dangers and hardships are now at an end. Once more, I heartily
congratulate all, including the survivors of the gallant Zanzibaris, who
displayed such devotion and fortitude during your marvellous
expedition. Trust Emin Pasha progresses favourably.

Telegram from H.M. Stanley to Queen Victoria, Zanzibar, 12 December:

Your Majesty's most humble and devoted servant Stanley thanks you
from the bottom of his heart on behalf of his English officers, his
Zanzibari and Sudanese followers, for your Majesty's most gracious
message received yesterday. Your Majesty's words have elicited the
most profound and respectful loyalty, gratitude and enthusiasm. The
thought that the Queen was interested in us all often encouraged us
in our darkest moments of incertitude and depression; and the

assurance that you now so graciously send, that your Majesty is satisfied with our work has more than re-paid us for what we have passed through. Stanley.

Letter from Queen Victoria to the Marquess of Salisbury, Osborne, 23 December:

> The Queen was immensely relieved, as Lord Salisbury was, at poor Stanley's and Emin Bey's safety, and thinks it has been a source of great satisfaction and rejoicing in this country.

Stanley did not return to London directly, claiming the city was in the grip of influenza. He wanted time gently to reacquaint himself with European society and take stock of his life. At the age of forty-nine, he also needed time to consider what he might do next.

In January 1890, Stanley checked into Cairo's fashionable Shepherd's Hotel, where other guests found him a curiosity and crowded around him every time he came out to stroll in the gardens. In order to find peace and quiet, he fled to the seclusion of the Villa Victoria to begin writing the story of the Emin Pasha relief expedition. He called it *In Darkest Africa* and wrote at a furious pace, drafting 8,000 words daily for fifty consecutive days starting at 6 a.m. and ending at midnight. He concluded the book with these memorable paragraphs:

> Good-night, Pasha . . . you will know better when you have read these pages, what the saving of you cost in human life and suffering. . . .
>
> Good-night, Gentlemen of the Relief Committee! Three years are passed since your benevolence commissioned us to relieve the distressed and rescue the weak. Two hundred and sixty all told have been returned to their homes; about 150 more are in safety. . . .
>
> Good-night, oh! My Companions! May honours such as you deserve be showered upon you. To the warm hearts of your countrymen I consign you. Should one doubt be thrown upon your manhood, or upon your loyalty or honour, within these pages, the record of your faithfulness during a period which I doubt will ever be excelled for its gloom and hopelessness, will be found to show with what noble fortitude you bore all. Good-night Stairs, Jephson, Nelson, Parke, and you Bonny, a long good-night to you all!

Stanley had achieved everything expected of him, apart from one thing. He had been commissioned to rescue Emin Pasha, which he had done successfully, delivering the Pasha's people from possible slaughter at the same time. But he had failed to secure Emin for either Mackinnon or Leopold. The rescue mission had succeeded – but at what cost? Stanley would soon find out.

The front-page drawing from the *Illustrated London News* of Stanley with a Maxim gun.

Chapter 37

MARRIAGE AND CONTROVERSY

> . . . And when the heat of Afric's sun
> Grew quite too enervating,
> Some bloodshed with the Maxim gun
> Was most exhilarating!
> He found the sport a sweet relief,
> And nothing if not 'manly' –
> The ever-joking, mirth-provoking, brandy-soaking robber chief,
> The coming Viscount Stanley.
>
> From *Funny Folks*, a satirical journal, 1890

Stanley returned to Europe with his volunteers, travelling to Brussels where they were afforded a triumphal welcome at the Gare du Midi. A pair of the city's burgomasters argued over who should be first to greet the heroes of Africa. The station was decorated with the colours of Belgium, the Congo and the United States. VIPs were admitted free while members of the public were charged 2*d* to stand on the station platform. Stanley's party, in official carriages, passed through streets full of cheering people. The Belgians had obviously changed their attitude towards their monarch's dominance of the Congo. Leopold was now 'the great benefactor of the nation', and royal, government and geographical hosts in Brussels expressed enthusiasm 'for the grand Africa' now ruled over by their king. Stanley was awarded gold and silver medals, the Grand Cross of the Order of Leopold and the Grand Cross of the Congo. The volunteers each received medals from the Royal Brussels Geographical Society.

Leopold and Stanley spent days locked in discussion about the Congo's commercial prospects and the part Stanley might play in its future. There was talk of him returning to Africa to create and train a Congo army. A large fee was mentioned and Stanley said he would consider the offer, pleading for time to recover from three years of hard work and illness. He returned to England on 26 April 1890, where a special train was waiting to take him to London. Another large crowd of enthusiastic admirers awaited his arrival at Victoria Station.

Stanley had surrendered the lease to his Sackville Street home before leaving for Africa. He stayed in 'comfortable rooms at DeVere Gardens' which had been rented and made ready for him by Sir Frances and Lady de Winton. A mountain of letters greeted him on his return – and one of them was addressed in familiar handwriting. It was a short note from Dolly Tennant, addressed to 'Dear Mr. Stanley' saying that she would be pleased to see him again, not because he had achieved great things, but because he had returned safely and she had feared she might not see him again. He declined to answer.

On 6 May, Stanley travelled to Windsor Castle to be presented to Queen Victoria for the second time. This time the Queen was more enthusiastic about receiving the 'determined, ugly little man – with a strong American twang', whom she had first met eighteen years previously. Her journal records that on this occasion he was 'the wonderful traveller and explorer, Mr. Stanley, who has been absent for so many years and so long in search of Emin Pasha'. The Queen wanted to offer Stanley an official honour, but first needed to ascertain his true nationality. Was he the American he had always claimed to be, British, or, perhaps, Welsh? The Queen records:

Saw Lord Salisbury afterwards. We spoke of many things, of Stanley, and what he could do, of his not wishing to have an order offered him, etc. . . . After dinner spoke to Mr. Stanley, who said that the part of the country he had explored was very healthy, and would be a splendid place of emigration. Then we went to the White Drawing Room where we were joined by the ladies and gentlemen and Mr Stanley gave us a most interesting lecture.

It is not known if Stanley admitted details of his birth to the Queen,* but he must have confessed to taking American citizenship in 1885 so forcing the withdrawal of the offer of a knighthood, an honour the workhouse

---

* It is unlikely that Stanley admitted to Queen Victoria that he was a bastard, born in Wales. The Queen recorded the minutest details in her daily journal and would almost certainly have included this snippet of information if it had been offered.

boy, Civil War prisoner, frontier reporter, African explorer and 'breaker of rocks', would have loved.

The Royal Geographical Society was not slow to honour Stanley. On 5 May 1890, they hired the Royal Albert Hall and filled it to the rafters with thousands of people wanting to witness the world's best-known explorer receive a special gold medal. Standing under a giant map of the Congo basin, Stanley told an audience of royalty, the peerage, politicians, scientists, writers and 'all classes of society' that this was by far the grandest assembly he had ever seen. He kept his audience in raptures as he recounted the story of Emin Pasha's rescue.

At a subsequent reception, Dolly was one of scores of people lining up to shake Stanley's hand. She urged him to call on her at Richmond Terrace. He said he would consider it, but made no attempt to get in touch with the lady who had rejected him four years previously.

Dolly wrote again wishing Stanley well and saying goodbye, promising she would avoid going anywhere where they might meet by chance. Stanley sent back a stern reply, telling her how her rejection had wounded him and that he still felt the pain. Despite the offer to avoid Stanley, Dolly turned up at a reception in his honour that same evening. She chose her moment carefully and when there was a suitable gap among the crowd of admirers flocking to his elbow, she planted herself next to him and softly whispered that he if were to propose again, she would accept.

That night she wrote to him, addressing him as 'Bula Matari' and admitting that rejecting his proposal had been a mistake, which she had made because she had 'felt afraid'. She told him that he was a man who knew more about life and love, while she was just a girl, 'unacquainted with affairs of the heart'. The letter did the trick and days later, an official announcement of their engagement appeared in *The Times*. They would be married in Westminster Abbey on 12 July 1890.

Thousands flocked to the Victoria Gallery in London's Regent Street to view the *Stanley and Africa Exhibition* at which artefacts from the explorer's own travels were displayed alongside other pieces loaned by Stanley's volunteers. King Leopold agreed to be the exhibition's patron and visitors were drawn from all walks of life who had read about Stanley in books and newspapers and now had an opportunity to view spears, shields, knives, axes, paddles, beaded ornaments, stuffed animals, photographs, maps and books brought from the dark continent. The clothes that Stanley had worn when he greeted Livingstone in 1872 were on display together with rifles, revolvers and other equipment. It was the next best thing to actually being in Africa. The official catalogue stated: 'The collection is intended to illustrate all Africa between the tropics, graphically representing Central African life and scenery, and the development of commerce.' The centrepiece was a plaster bust of Stanley by Conrad Dressler, mounted on a rectangular plinth and inscribed 'Stanley Africanus'.

Once again, Stanley's image was everywhere. Newspapers produced special 'Stanley numbers' retelling the story of Emin's heroic rescue – providing excellent publicity for his forthcoming book. He was given the freedom of several British cities and even became the subject of a children's boxed game 'following his journey, players having to negotiate a route via Stanley Pool and the Congo Forest' before arriving at Lake Albert Nyanza. Minton produced chinaware figures of Stanley wearing his distinctive explorer's costume and cap while Royal Doulton manufactured a commemorative Emin Pasha Relief Expedition glazed pottery jug inscribed with the motto: 'Out of darkness into light', and the names of Stanley's volunteers. Music and popular songs were composed in his honour – 'The Stanley March', 'Welcome Stanley', 'Stanley's Rescue', 'The Source of the Nile Waltz' and 'The Banjo March: The Stanley'. Not for the first time was Stanley's name mentioned in London's music halls. A favourite joke went:

'I say, I say, why did Stanley take so long to find Emin Pasha?'
'I don't know. Why did it take Stanley so long to find Emin Pasha?'
'Because there's no "M" in Pasha!'

The first edition of Stanley's two-volume *In Darkest Africa* sold 150,000 copies in its first weeks of publication in June 1890. It was translated into French, German, Italian, Spanish and Dutch. The African-adventure hungry Victorian public could not read enough of Stanley's story of the search and rescue of Emin Pasha, encouraging his volunteers to pen their own accounts. Arthur Mounteney Jephson was first off the mark and his book *Emin Pasha and the Rebellion at the Equator* was published by Sampson Low, Marston, which had produced all of Stanley's books. Authorship was credited to 'A.J. Mounteney Jephson with the revision and co-operation of Henry M. Stanley'. Herbert Ward's version was entitled *My Life With Stanley's Rear Guard*, while Lieutenant John Rose Troup's story was called *With Stanley's Rear Column*, James Jameson's *The Story of the Rear Column* (edited by his widow using his diaries) and Dr Thomas Parke's *My Personal Experiences in Equatorial Africa*. Each account attempted to be impartial, but their leader did not always appear in the best light. The books depicted Stanley as a fair, yet stern and uncompromising expedition commander and they all sold well in British bookshops in 1890–91. William Bonny was the only surviving British member of the expedition not to have kept a diary or published an account of his time in Africa with Stanley.

From the *Illustrated London News*, 19 July 1890:

> The marriage of Miss Dorothy Tennant to Mr. H.M. Stanley was performed on Saturday July 12 in Westminster Abbey in the presence of a large congregation including many persons of high distinction, rank and fashion; but we sincerely regret to add that Mr Stanley was suffering from the effects of an acute attack of illness – gastritis – which had commenced on the preceding Thursday evening. It was considered by his medical attendant – namely Dr. T.H. Parke, army surgeon and one of his comrades in the Emin Pasha Relief Expedition – to be a renewal of the disease which so nearly proved fatal to his life in the African forest, two or three years ago; but they were enabled to subdue its virulence on this occasion in a few hours, permitting Mr Stanley, though in an enfeebled condition, to go through the wedding ceremony which was a matter of public as well as of private interest.

Magnificent floral bouquets sent by Stanley and his volunteers decorated the Abbey nave and others marked Livingstone's tomb. When Stanley entered at 2 p.m. thousands of onlookers waiting for a glimpse of the bridegroom, saw a 49-year-old white-haired man, looking ten years older, pale, stooped and leaning heavily on a stout stick. He was supported by his best man, the Comte D'Arochue, representing King Leopold. His groomsmen were Stairs, Parke, Jephson, Nelson and Bonny.

The bride arrived accompanied by her brother, Charles Tennant, two bridesmaids and her pageboy nephew. She wore a white satin dress embroidered with pearls, with a bodice and long train of white silk. Round her neck was a diamond necklace presented to her by Sir William

Mackinnon from which was suspended a miniature of Queen Victoria surrounded by gems, a gift from Her Majesty. Dolly placed her wedding bouquet on Livingstone's tomb as she passed by.

Stanley remained seated for much of the ceremony and it was with difficulty that he knelt at the high altar for the blessing. The most arduous part was standing upright and walking out of the Abbey towards the great west door. The going was slow and halfway down the aisle, the bridegroom was seized by stomach cramps and had to sit down. In order not to disappoint the crowds outside, the bride was led out of the Abbey and into her waiting carriage by Sir John Millais, whom the crowd mistook for Stanley. Stanley left in one of the rear carriages, the roaring crowd unaware that the man lying along the back seat, his eyes closed, his face contorted in agony, was the man who had found Livingstone, walked the length of the Congo, rescued Emin Pasha and married Dolly Tennant just moments before.

Gertie organised a fine reception for the couple at Richmond Terrace, but Stanley was too ill to participate and was advised to rest in a quiet room. Later he was able to stand and Mr and Mrs H.M. Stanley left the house in an open carriage in the company of Dr Parke and Jephson to travel to Waterloo Station, where they boarded a train to Melchet Court, near Romsey, Hampshire, which had been offered as a honeymoon destination by way of a wedding gift by Lady Louisa Ashburton, a Tennant family friend. That evening, Stanley managed to write in his journal:

Being sick from a severe attack of gastritis . . . I was too weak to experience anything save a calm delight at the fact that I was married, and that now I shall have a chance to rest. I feel as unimpressed as if I were a child taking its first view of the world . . . it is all so very unreal. During my long bachelorhood, I have often wished that I had but one tiny child to love; but now, unexpectedly as it seems to me, I possess a wife; my own wife – Dorothy Stanley now, Dorothy Tennant this morning.

Later the following week, Dr Parke was able to tell the *Illustrated London News* that Stanley was 'free from fever and progressing favourably, quietness being essential to his recovery'. He was said to be enjoying 'long drives in the New Forest'.

After a month at Melchet Court, the newlyweds visited France, Italy and Switzerland before travelling to Belgium where Stanley introduced his wife to King Leopold at the Chalet Royal residence in Ostend. Stanley took long walks with the King in the palace grounds, while Dolly remained inside fretting that Leopold was trying to tempt her husband back to Africa on a project he would find difficult to resist.

In England, Stanley toured the country collecting honorary doctorates from universities before returning to his new home at Richmond Terrace in October to pack for a long lecture tour of the United States. Dolly, her mother and Jephson, now acting as Stanley's secretary, joined him on the voyage.

Trouble was waiting in New York. While sailing across the Atlantic, a storm of protest had broken out in England over the fate of the rear column, mainly stirred up by the grieving families of Barttelot and Jameson, distressed by what they had discovered about the deaths of their sons in the pages of *In Darkest Africa*. The anti-slavery lobby raised its head, questioning Stanley's use of non-free men, parliamentarians voiced concerns about the 'little commissions' Stanley had undertaken for Leopold and Mackinnon while others openly criticised Stanley for cruelty towards natives.

From his hotel bedroom, Stanley fired off letters and telegrams to the newspapers that had printed the accusations. He said he regretted the death of the young volunteers but accused them of failing to follow orders properly. The relatives responded by stating that such young and inexperienced men should never have been left in charge of the rear column and at the mercy of the unscrupulous Tippu-Tib.

In response to the charges that Stanley had employed slaves during the Emin Pasha relief expedition, he commented: 'I employed English agents at Zanzibar to engage my people and every precaution was taken that no one was enlisted who could not swear he was a freeman. I was only four days in Zanzibar, but, before these men were accepted, they had to re-swear that declaration before the British Consul-General [Colonel Euan Smith] that they were free. The accusations made against me that I employed slaves are, therefore, most disgraceful.' The fact remains that many Zanzibaris travelling with Stanley on his last great journey across Africa were slaves, an unpalatable truth borne out by Colonel's Smith's letter from Zanzibar to Sir Henry Ponsonby on 28 December 1889, stating: 'It is melancholy to reflect that, as Stanley informs me, when pay day came, and they [the Zanzibaris] were paraded to receive nearly three years' wages, their Arab owners assembled at the pay office and seized from each the entire sum he received. I am told that the largest proportion of the sum so received went to the Sultan as being the largest slave-owner. . . .'

Addressing the accusation of cruelty, Stanley wrote:

I lay no claim to any exceptional fineness of nature; but I say, beginning life as a rough, ill-educated, impatient man, I have found my schooling in these very African experiences, which are now said by some to be in themselves detrimental to European character. I have learned by actual stress of imminent danger, in the first place, that self-control is more indispensable than gunpowder, and, in second place, that persistent self-control under the provocation of African travel is impossible without real, heartfelt sympathy for the natives with whom one has had to deal. If one regards these natives as mere brutes, then the annoyances that their follies and vices inflict are indeed intolerable. In order to rule them, and to keep one's life amongst them, it is needful to regard them as children, who require, indeed, different methods of rule from English or American citizens, but who must be ruled in precisely the same spirit, with the same absence of caprice and anger, the same essential respect to our fellow men.

Regarding the 'little commissions' Stanley chose to say nothing further than he had openly stated in the pages of *In Darkest Africa*.

The argument raged for days. The *St James's Gazette* came to the conclusion that 'the expensive and superfluous relief of Emin has brought no advantage either to the rescuers or to the rescued. . . . Although, perhaps, it may have been worthwhile to relieve Emin in order to afford Stanley an opportunity to still further add to his great deeds as an explorer, it was certainly not worthwhile to relieve him for the purpose of presenting the German government with a new and experienced leader of expeditions calculated to open a route to the centre of Africa.'

The Times carried a letter from the Reverend Wilmot Brooke stating that cannibalism had occurred at the Yambuya camp and adding: 'Eyewitnesses, both English and Arab, have assured me it was a common thing, which they themselves have seen on passing through the camp, to see human hands and feet sticking out of their cooking pots.' Responding to the charge, Stanley demanded: 'Who were the English who had seen this curious sight?' The Reverend Brooke chose not to reply.

Controversy rumbled on as Stanley's party travelled across the United States and Canada in a special Pullman carriage, named 'Henry M. Stanley', containing a kitchen with a cook, a dining car which converted into a dormitory at night, a drawing room with piano, three state bedrooms and a bathroom. Dolly was thrilled with the way her new husband was received 'by his countrymen' and Gertie also approved.

In April they returned to England. Stanley had earned a handsome $60,000 for his lectures and netted more when a few days later he took to the road again, lecturing throughout England and Scotland. Dolly remained at Richmond Terrace, joining him at weekends, when she brought letters from their London home. One was an invitation to preside over the Welsh National Eisteddfod – the highest honour extended to any Welshman active in the arts and literature. Dolly urged her husband to accept, if only to bury old ghosts from his past and publicly admit to the world that Wales was the land of his birth. Stanley was not so sure. He still harboured grudges against Wales, its people and the way he felt he had been treated as a child. In a letter to Dolly, he said: 'I feel that we, the people of Wales generally, and I, are not in such close sympathy as to enable me to say anything sufficiently pleasing to their ears.'

Stanley accepted the Eisteddfod invitation and an earlier one to lecture in Carnarvon, to which eight excursion trains transported people wanting to hear their native son talk about Africa. He told Dolly that 'crowds of hard-featured, homely creatures, rushed up, the crowd being enormous. . . . As I moved through the crowd, I felt hands touch my coat, then, getting bolder, they rubbed me on the back, stroked my hair, and, finally, thumped me hard, until I felt that the honours were getting so weighty I should die if they continued long. Verily, there were but few thumps between me and death! A flash of fierceness stole over me for a second, and I turned to the crowd; but they all smiled so broadly that, poor, dear, mad, creatures, I forgave them, or, at least, resolved to submit.'

The tour ended in July when Stanley and Dolly left for a holiday in Switzerland, where they walked in meadows, read aloud to each other and retired early as Stanley was still in the African habit of rising early. It was while strolling through a damp meadow in Mürren that the man who had marched across Africa three times, slipped on wet grass and broke his left ankle. He was taken to the hotel in pain, which brought on a malaria attack. He was ordered to remain in bed – and to cancel his Eisteddfod engagement.

On the eve of a lecture tour to Australia and New Zealand, Dolly became agitated when a letter addressed to Stanley, stamped with the official seal of the King of the Belgians, landed on the doormat at Richmond Terrace. She felt her husband was pining for Africa and was afraid that Leopold might offer Stanley a commission that was more attractive than London life, but which might finally wreck his health.

Jephson was asked to accompany Stanley to Leopold's seaside residence, take care of the ferry tickets, luggage and a myriad other minor details that surrounded the great traveller on the move. Stanley wrote to Dolly: 'After dinner, the King cautiously approached and sounded me out on the possibility of my resuming duties on the Congo. I pointed to my broken leg (left ankle), for I am still very lame. "Oh," he said, "not now, but when you return from Australia, sound in health and limb." "We shall see, Your Majesty," I said. "I have a big task on hand for you, when you are ready", were his last words.'

The wedding of Henry Morton Stanley and Dorothy Tennant at Westminster Abbey, London, 12 July 1890.

Chapter 38

THE MEMBER FOR NORTH LAMBETH

While accompanying her husband on his travels 'down under', Dolly broached the subject of Stanley renouncing the American citizenship he had taken in 1885 and reclaiming his British nationality once again. Throughout the tour, well-wishers had enquired why the Queen had not given Stanley any official recognition and he had patiently replied that as an American, he was unable to receive a knighthood or any other title bestowed by the Queen. But in his fiftieth year, Stanley began thinking that a title in front of his name would signify full recognition of his achievements and that it mattered not a jot whether those achievements had been gained by him as a Welshman, Englishman or an American. It would also be nice for Dolly to have a title, and Lady Dorothy Stanley had a pleasing ring to it.

Back in England, Stanley wrote to the Home Secretary asking to resume his British citizenship. A reply informed him that he would need to prove he had spent a total of five years residing in Britain and on checking his diaries, Stanley discovered he had been a resident for five years and ten months. On 20 May 1892, Henry Morton Stanley took the British Oath of Allegiance and became a British subject once again.

Dolly wrote:

Soon after our marriage, I thought of Parliament for Stanley. It seemed to me that one so full of energy, with such administrative power and political foresight, would find in the House of Commons an outlet for his pent-up energy. I also felt he needed men's society. . . . To be shut up in a London house was certainly no life for Stanley; also, at the back of my mind was the haunting fear of his returning to the Congo. I thought that, once in Parliament, he would be safely anchored. At first he would not hear of it, but his friend, Mr. Alexander Bruce, of Edinburgh, joined me in persuading Stanley to become a Liberal-Unionist candidate for the London constituency of North Lambeth. We went into the battle just ten days before polling day. We were quite ignorant of electioneering, and I must say we had a dreadful ten days of it.

North Lambeth was one of London's largest working-class constituencies, extending from York Road, directly opposite Richmond Terrace on the other side of the River Thames, to Crystal Palace.

On 20 June 1892, Stanley told his journal: 'Have consented to contest the constituency against Alderman Coldwells, Radical. I accepted because D. is so eager for me to be employed, lest I fly away to Africa.' In a printed address, Stanley informed the electorate:

I am, as you know, a man of the people. Whatever I have achieved in life has been achieved by my own hard work, with no help from privilege, or favour of any kind. My strongest sympathies are with the working classes . . . and if you will do me the honour to return me to parliament, I promise to be active and faithful in the discharge of my duties to my constituency.

On 27 June Stanley addressed voters from a cart in Lambeth High Street. Dolly was thrilled to see him attempting to get so close to the people he hoped to represent in Parliament. For his part, Stanley hated the experience and swore he would never again appear in such an undignified fashion.

Two days later he held an election meeting at Hawkeston Hall, Lambeth where the great explorer was howled down by an organised rabble of costermongers imported by Alderman Coldwells for the purpose of frightening off his political rival. A ringleader was stationed in the gallery where he used a folded newspaper to signal a new round of interruptions to his henchmen to make as much noise as possible. At one stage Dolly, who shared the platform with her husband, stood up and yelled at the rabble: 'When all of you and I are dead and forgotten, the name of Stanley will live, revered and loved.' Few people heard her. The platform was stormed and Stanley and Dolly fled from the hall. When they attempted to climb into their brougham and drive away, the mob held on to the door of the carriage and tore it off.

Stanley was shaken, having thought that the election would bring him a landslide victory based on his reputation and a few public appearances.

If this sort of disturbance had happened in Africa, he would have reached for his Winchester or his whip and fought his way out of trouble. But this was an altogether different – and dirtier – game and one totally unfamiliar to him. For once, Stanley was relieved to be beaten, even though the majority against him was only 130. 'I have been through some stiff scenes in my life, but I never fell so low in my estimation as I fell that day; to stand there being slighted, insulted by venomous tongues every second, and yet to feel how hopeless, nay impossible, retort was and to realise that I had voluntarily put myself in a position to be bespattered with as much foul reproaches as those ignorant fools chose to fling at me,' Stanley recalled.

Dolly persuaded him to remain a Liberal-Unionist candidate and he faint-heartedly agreed, thinking he would not have to face another election for a further four years. His only condition was that he would 'never ask for a vote, never do any silly personal canvassing in high streets or by-streets, never to address open-air meetings, cart or wagon work, or to put myself in any position where I can be baited like a bull in the ring. The honour of MP is not worth it.' At occasional meetings he spoke about Empire, duty, commerce, home rule in Ireland, the great opportunities offered to Britain by Africa and how railways would transform the dark continent. He took trouble with his speeches, even though Dolly often wished he had 'greater and better-educated audiences' to hear them.

In January 1893, Stanley wrote to Dolly from Cambridge where he was lecturing:

Having announced my intention of standing again as candidate for N. Lambeth, I propose doing so, of course, for your sake; but after my experience in North Lambeth you must not expect any enthusiasm, any of that perseverant energy, which I may have shown elsewhere, and which I still show in an honourable sphere. But this political work involves lying, back-biting, morally damaging your opponent in the eyes of the voters, giving and receiving wordy abuse, which reminds me of English village squabbles; and I cannot find the courage either to open my lips against my opponent or to put myself in a position to receive from him and his mindless myrmidons that filthy abuse they are only too eager to give. . . . Six or seven years ago I was a different man altogether, but this last expedition has sapped my delight in the rude enjoyment of life, though never at any time could I have looked upon electioneering as enjoyable. The whole business seems to be degrading.

To remain busy, Stanley spent time lecturing, producing a book of African short stories called *Tales from Africa* every bit as good as Kipling's *Jungle Book* and starting work on his memoirs, which he intended to be the only true account of his life. In its pages he planned to confess the full story of his birth in Wales, workhouse upbringing, childhood, escape to New Orleans, his meeting with Henry Hope Stanley, role in the Civil War, life as a frontier reporter and foreign correspondent, and to describe in detail the search for Livingstone and his subsequent adventures in Africa, ending with the relief of Emin Pasha and marriage to Dolly. But the prospect of going back over his life and recalling so much that was painful was gruelling and he found the work difficult, picking up his pen only occasionally to write when he could summon sufficient energy.

Parliament was dissolved in June 1895 and Stanley reluctantly prepared for another election battle, which he half hoped he would lose again. Dolly had other ideas. 'I realised that since usage and custom demanded that the Parliamentary candidate shall call on the voters, and that Stanley positively, and I think rightly, refused to do so, we were in danger of losing the constituency,' she wrote. 'I realised that whichever way the workingman means to vote, he likes to feel he has something you want, something he can give. He likes even to refuse you, and oblige you to listen to his views and his principles. So, if you do not choose to go and kow-tow before him, he puts you down as "no good" or, at any rate, "not my sort". After our defeat, therefore, in 1892, I resolved to "nurse" North Lambeth, since that is the accepted term, and to do so in my own way.'

Dolly threw herself into the election campaign, occasionally joined by her famous husband. They used committee rooms in Westminster Bridge Road as campaign headquarters and Dolly persuaded ladies from the Conservative Association to help with canvassing. On 10 July 1895, the *Evening Standard* reported: 'Mr. H.M. Stanley paid early visits to his committee rooms today and was met with a cordial greeting. The meetings on Mr. Stanley's behalf have so far been marked by great enthusiasm and have been very different from those of 1892, which were characterised by disgraceful radical rowdyism.'

On the eve of the election, a leading Liberal journal wrote that 'Mr. Stanley's course through Africa has been like that of a red hot poker drawn across a blanket and that he nightly sleeps on a pillow steeped in blood.' On election day itself the *Evening Standard* reported: 'There are no lack of canvassers for the Unionist candidate. There are several smart equipages in the district in the interests of Mr. Stanley and small trades people in Lambeth Walk and New Cut have brought out their traps and even coster barrows to convey voters to the poll. Mr. Stanley is assisted by a large and enthusiastic body of workers, amongst whom, by no means the least powerful ally, is Mrs. Stanley.'

When the polls closed, Stanley returned to Richmond Terrace while Dolly remained at the committee rooms as votes were counted. Late into the night she crept upstairs to a dark, empty attic, from where she could see the victory signal posted in the night sky from the returning office half a mile away – a red flash confirming they had won or a blue flash if the Radical candidate was returned.

'As I knelt by the low window, looking out on the confused mass of roofs and chimneys, hardly distinguishable against the dark sky, I thought passionately of how I had worked and striven for this day; that because Stanley had consented to stand again, I had vowed (if it were possible, by personal effort, to help towards it) that he should be returned. I felt how great he was and I prayed that he might not be defeated and might keep him from returning to Africa,' Dolly recalled.

The hours passed and Dolly began to doze. Suddenly 'the sky flushed pink over the roofs,' she recalled, 'to the west a rosy fog seemed gently to rise, and creep over the sky; and soon, a distant, tumultuous roar came rolling like an incoming tide and I went down to meet Stanley.' Stanley polled 2,878 votes while his opponent, C.P. Trevelyan (Labour) polled 2,473 – giving Stanley a majority of 405.

Downstairs, the committee rooms were starting to fill with cheering supporters. The door burst open and a group of men entered with Stanley in their midst 'looking white and very stern. . . . He was seized, and swung up like a feather, on men's shoulders and carried to a table at the further end of the room. As he passed me, I caught his hand; it was so cold, it seemed to freeze mine. He was called upon for a speech. "Speak to us Stanley," was shouted. Stanley merely drew himself up and with a steady look, very characteristic, said quietly, "Gentlemen, I thank you and now good night."'

Minutes later Stanley and Dolly were seated in a hansom cab making its way over Westminster Bridge towards Richmond Terrace. During the drive, they did not speak. In the hall of their home, Dolly thought he would say something about the victory, but he only smiled and said, 'I think we both need a rest; and now for a pipe.'

Dolly was exhausted. The election campaign had been the hardest work she had ever undertaken and she fled to France for a rest, leaving Stanley behind in London for the 12 August 1895 opening of the fourteenth Parliament of Queen Victoria's reign, with Arthur Balfour as its Prime Minister.

The journey from Richmond Terrace to the Houses of Parliament was less than three minutes by hansom cab, but Stanley decided that his new political role demanded purchase of a cab of his own to ferry him to and from the Palace of Westminster, across the river to his constituency and to the various clubs and institutions he had joined. The sophisticated black carriage, inscribed with the initials 'HMS' on the door, whisked Stanley around London in comfort as he sat back in the black leather, horsehair seat. He used the cab to make his parliamentary debut, arriving early to be met by a large crowd of well-wishers eager to cheer their new MP. On his way into the chamber, the doorkeeper greeted him with the words: 'Mr Stanley, I presume?'

Stanley hated life as an MP. At the end of his first week as the member for North Lambeth, he was writing that the atmosphere in the House during the summer 'is simply poisonous. I do not wonder, now, at the pasty, House of Commons complexion; 400 people breathing for ten or eleven hours the air of one room must vitiate it. Then my late hours, 2 and 3 a.m. simply torture to me. . . .' He despised parliamentary business conducted 'in a shilly-shally manner, which makes one groan at the waste of life. . . . It has become clearer to me, each day, that I am too old to change my open-air habits for the asphyxiating atmosphere of the House of Commons.' Constituency business was 'wearying', requiring him to correspond with 'hundreds of people I am unacquainted with, but who insist on receiving replies. This correspondence alone, entails a good three-hours' work each day. The demands of the constituents consume, on average, another two hours. The House opens at 3 p.m. and business continues to any hour between midnight and 3 a.m. It is therefore impossible to obtain air or exercise.'

Stanley had hoped that his African experience and knowledge might make him useful during debates, but confessed that 'I have, as a Member, less influence than the man in the street. On questions concerning Africa, someone wholly unacquainted with the continent, would be called upon to speak before me. I have far less influence than any writer in a daily newspaper; for he can make his living presence in the world felt, and, possibly, have some influence for good: whereas I, in common with other respectable fellows, are like dumb dogs. . . . Any illusions that I may have had, illusion that I could serve the Empire, advance Africa's interests, benefit this country, were quickly dispelled.'

Yet life had its compensations. By 1896 when Stanley was aged fifty-five and Dolly forty-five, they decided to adopt a baby. They agreed the child should be an orphaned boy from Denbigh; a child who would benefit from two things denied to Stanley as a boy – loving parents and a home. The child was named Denzil Morton Stanley and, according to Dolly, her husband was 'greatly rejoiced' at the arrival of the little boy. He rushed out and bought picture books and toys more suited to a four year old, so great was his happiness at having a child at Richmond Terrace. He was baptised using water from Lake Albert which Stanley had brought back in a bottle years before.

Later in 1896 when Stanley was stricken with gastritis complicated by malaria, he loved to have baby Denzil placed beside him on the bed. One day when the child was there, Stanley looked to Dolly and said: 'Ah, it is worthwhile now – to get well!' Bouts of illness arrived without warning and with such intensity that his breathing was impeded. During malaria attacks, shivering preceding the hot stage was so violent that the bed he lay on would shake and the glasses on his bedside table vibrate and ring. Sometimes on a hot day, Dolly would come into the house after taking Denzil for a walk and find Stanley not in his study. She would rush upstairs to discover him in bed, covered in blankets, quilts and overcoats, his teeth chattering and pleading for hot-water bottles. Such was Africa's legacy.

The pharmacist, Henry Wellcome, was a regular visitor to Richmond Terrace and brought quinine, instructing Dolly how to prepare 25 grains with a drop of Madeira – and then wait. At this time, Dolly wrote: 'I vowed in my heart that he should never return to the country which had taken so much of his splendid vitality.'

To recuperate, Stanley and Dolly journeyed to Spain, visiting scenes he had covered as a young correspondent. While travelling on a train from Madrid, Stanley again suffered an attack of gastritis. When they arrived at midnight, he was in pain and hardly conscious. Dolly spoke no Spanish and knew no one in Madrid, so checked him into the nearest hotel and went in search of a doctor – but there was little that could be done. Day by day he grew weaker and in desperation, Dolly decided to take him home to England. By the time they reached Paris, Stanley had begun to recover and for the next two days he was free of pain, but spasms returned with redoubled violence 'and it was with the greatest of difficulty that I succeeded in getting him back to our home in London'.

Dolly spent three months nursing Stanley. He accepted the pain and weakness, silently and stoically. Occasionally it returned – Dolly knew by the sound of Stanley's voice when he called in the dead of night that the pain had come back. He was placed on a starvation diet, enfeebling him to such an extent he was unable to sit up in bed. The doctor changed his treatment, arranged for a masseur to come to the house each day to stimulate his now wasted limbs and ordered him to eat properly. By the end of 1896, his health had returned.

Later, writing to Dolly from Brighton, Stanley told his wife:

Warmest greetings to darling little Denzil, our own cherub! Possibly, I think too much of him. If I were not busy with work and other things, I should undoubtedly dwell too much on him, for, as I take my constitutional, I really am scarce conscious that I am in Brighton. For, look where I may, his beautiful features, lightened up with a sunny smile, come before my eyes all the time! I see him in your arms and I marvel at my great happiness in possessing you two! Believe it or not, as you like, but my heart is full of thankfulness that I have been so blessed. Denzil is now inseparable from you – and you from him – and together you complete the once vague figure of what I wished; and now the secret of my inward thoughts is realised, a pre-natal vision, embodied in actual existence.

Stanley had made up his mind not to stand for a second term in Parliament. Apart from the occasional speech about the importance of railways in Africa, he had hardly uttered a word from the floor of the House and his views were rarely sought. He could have been vocal on a number of issues: African trade, slavery and workhouses, but he chose not to be. The energy such issues required was simply not there and when he left Parliament in May 1898, he was 'glad at the prospect of retiring and being quit of it all'.

Chapter 39

FURZE HILL AND HAPPINESS

In the autumn of 1898, Stanley decided to look for a country house where Dolly, Denzil and Gertie could flee from the London smog and enjoy the open-air life Stanley loved so much. They would retain the Richmond Terrace property, which belonged to Dolly's mother, and use it on social visits to the city. Stanley now planned the life of a country landowner, in a quiet place where he hoped to complete his memoirs, work on which had stopped during his four years as a Member of Parliament.

Stanley collected property information from scores of estate agents and he and Dolly visited twenty different houses in Kent, Buckinghamshire and Sussex over a two-week period in November. None was suitable. By mid-December they had viewed fifty-seven properties but only one merited a second viewing, Furze Hill, a 70-acre estate with a lake in the Surrey village of Pirbright, 30 miles from London on a direct railway line to Waterloo and situated in rolling green countryside and woodlands. Dolly thought it delightful and an ideal country home for family and visiting friends. 'The more we examined it, the more we liked it,' wrote Stanley, 'but there was much to improve and renovate. Therefore, as the place pleased me and my wife and her mother, I entered into serious negotiation for the purchase and by Christmas, I had secured the refusal of it; but as it was let, possession was deferred to June, 1899.'

On 17 April of that year, the boy born John Rowlands – bastard, and known to the world as Henry Morton Stanley and 'Bula Matari' – was made a Knight of the Grand Cross of Bath in the Queen's Birthday Honours list.

Furze Hill now gave newly ennobled Sir Henry energy and passion and he spent his days designing an extra wing to the house, installing electric lighting, a 'bathing house', improving grounds and garden, purchasing furniture for its many rooms – and a complete fire engine. He carefully measured every room, planning the move to Pirbright with the same precision he had used to plan his African expeditions. The move revitalised Stanley and put a fresh spring into his step. On 4 September, he recorded: 'We went with D. to our house at Furze Hill. Slept for the first time in our country home.' Dolly wrote: 'He now took an ever-increasing delight in the place. He planned walks, threw bridges across streams (one of which he named the Congo), planted trees, built a little farm from his own designs after reading every recent book on farm building and in very short time transformed the place.'

Everything was designed and built to last. He replaced wooden window frames with stone, fences were 'strongest and of the best description; even the ends of the gate and fence posts, he dipped in pitch and not merely in tar, that the portion in the ground might resist decay. It was his pride and joy that all should be well done.' Stanley bought a Broadwood piano, canoes for the lake and full-size billiard table – 'We could neither of us play, but he said, "I want those who come to stay here, to enjoy themselves",' Dolly recalled. An orchard was planned and scores of rose bushes planted in the garden. Together they purchased books for their library: classics and books about travel for him, popular novels and volumes on art for her. He stocked the storeroom cellars with food 'as for an expedition, or to stand a siege. There were great canisters of rice, tapioca, flour enough for a garrison, soap, cheese, groceries of all kinds, everything we could possibly require, and each jar and tin was neatly ticketed in his handwriting, besides careful lists written in a store book, so that I might know at a glance, the goodly contents of the room.'

This period marked the Indian summer of Stanley's life. At last, peace and enjoyment were his and he was quietly happy – something new to the man who had written: 'I was not sent into the world to be happy nor to search for happiness. I was sent for special work.'

By 1903, Stanley had supervised the rebuilding of Furze Hill. Dolly and Denzil had still to move in, although Stanley spent most of his time there overseeing building work. It was in March of that year that he complained of momentary attacks of giddiness. It made Dolly uneasy and she insisted on accompanying him whenever possible. She recalled: 'Just before Easter, we were walking near the Athenaeum Club, when he swayed and caught my arm. My anxiety, though still vague, oppressed me and I was very unwilling to let him go alone to Furze Hill; but he insisted, as he said there were yet a few "finishing touches to be put" before we came down for Easter. Great was my relief when we were summoned to Furze Hill; everything was ready at last!'

On the night of 17 April, Stanley woke in pain. He had suffered a stroke, lost the power of speech, and his body was paralysed down the left side. A doctor was called who made him comfortable. Despite falling in and out of consciousness, Stanley insisted on being shaved.

He lay immobile for months, calm, uncomplaining; the very embodiment of proud independence, now weak and helpless as a child. His health allowed him to sit in the garden in an invalid chair where he received occasional visitors. His friend, Henry Wellcome, came every week to spend the day with him. By September he could stand and walk a few steps, his speech had returned but anything too complicated fatigued him.

In April 1904 an attack of pleurisy knocked him down again and Dolly summoned an ambulance-carriage to take him back to Richmond Terrace. That same evening he asked Dolly: 'Where will you put me?' Seeing that she did not understand, he added: 'When I am – gone?' She replied: 'Stanley, I want to be near you; but they will put your body in Westminster Abbey.' He said: 'Yes, where we were married; they will put me beside Livingstone – because it is *right* to do so.'

A few days later he bade farewell to Dolly: 'Goodbye dear, I am going very soon, I have – done.' Denzil came into the room and he stroked the boy's cheek. 'Father, are you happy?' asked the boy. 'Always, when I see you, dear,' he replied.

On the night of 8 May 1904, Stanley's mind was wandering. He said: 'I have done all my work – I have – circumnavigated.' And then with a passionate, longing cry: 'Oh, I want to be free! I want to go – into the woods – to be free!' Towards dawn he turned to Dolly at his bedside and said: 'I want – I want – to go home.'

As Big Ben struck 4 a.m. he opened his eyes and asked: 'What's that?' Dolly told him that it was four o'clock. 'Four o'clock,' he slowly repeated. 'How strange! So that is Time!' And two hours later, as Big Ben was alerting Londoners that it would soon be time to get out of bed, Sir Henry Morton Stanley died. He was sixty-three.

The public had no idea that Stanley was seriously ill. He said that if his condition became known, 'people will remember me as an invalid'. The world was shocked when an official announcement issued through the Central News Agency informed newspaper readers that the great explorer had been in poor health for some time, but during the last fortnight his condition became gradually worse and despite the unremitting attention of two doctors and two male nurses and the devoted nursing of Lady Stanley, all hope of his recovery was abandoned soon after midnight. In addition to pleurisy Sir Henry's chances of recovery were complicated by an old disease of the heart. He was kept alive for some hours by frequent administrations of brandy and champagne. . . . Hundreds of people, ranging in rank from working men to MPs and members of the House of Lords, made anxious inquiries at Richmond Terrace on Monday night on his illness becoming known. Though unable to speak, he was conscious to the last and was able to recognise those around him.

Stanley's body was conveyed to Westminster Abbey and the coffin lay before the same altar where he and Dolly had been married fourteen years earlier. Dolly issued another statement through the Central News Agency: 'Lady Stanley wishes it to be known that Sir Henry would have liked to be buried in Westminster Abbey, near Livingstone. There is a general desire, shared by the daughter and grandson of Dr. Livingstone that Sir Henry should rest beside Dr. Livingstone in Westminster Abbey and it may be taken for granted that that will be so.' But the Reverend Joseph Armitage Robinson, Dean of Westminster, had other ideas. While permitting the funeral to take place at the Abbey, he refused to allow Stanley to take his final resting place next to Livingstone, 'because this was a man with blood on his hands'.

A large and distinguished congregation attended the funeral. Both King Edward VIII and Leopold, King of the Belgians sent representatives and the rest of the Abbey was filled with ambassadors, MPs, British and foreign government ministers, representatives from geographical and missionary societies, colleagues, friends, newspapermen and hundreds of Stanley's everyday admirers who had applied for tickets. Dr Kirk sent regrets that he was unable to attend 'as I have made arrangements elsewhere'. James Gordon Bennett, now based in Paris, was also absent.

Stanley's oak coffin travelled from Richmond Terrace in an open carriage-hearse pulled by four plumed black horses. Hundreds lined the streets, hats off in respectful sign of mourning. Dolly and her mother led the mourners, along with little Denzil, now aged eight, wearing a black sailor suit. Pallbearers included Livingstone Bruce, the doctor's grandson,

Henry Wellcome and a frail-looking Arthur Mounteney Jephson, now the only officer of the Emin Pasha Relief Expedition still alive. As the coffin was carried towards the altar, pallbearers paused for one minute at Livingstone's tomb.

Following the funeral, the coffin was carried on a special train to Brookwood Station in Surrey, from where it was taken to Pirbright churchyard, a short distance from Furze Hill. Weeks later a giant granite monolith, weighing 6 tons and measuring 6ft high by 4ft wide was brought from Dartmoor and erected over his final resting place. Its presence in the churchyard is impressive and easy to locate. The inscription on its face is simple:

Henry Morton Stanley
Bula Matari
1841–1904
Africa

The granite monolith erected over Stanley's grave.

Chapter 40

LOOSE ENDS (1904–2002)

Dolly received hundreds of letters and telegrams from around the world following Stanley's death. Most were sincere messages of condolence from people like Count de Brazza and others whose lives he had touched or those who felt they knew Stanley from his books, articles and lectures. Others were different.

One day a letter arrived bearing a Manchester postmark. On opening it, Dolly discovered it was from the former Katie Gough-Roberts, now Mrs Bradshaw, stating that she still possessed 'certain letters' written by her former fiancé in the 1870s. She said that a publisher, eager to capitalise on Stanley's death, wanted to produce an exploitative biography, which promised to take the lid off his early life. They had approached Katie offering to purchase any correspondence she may have kept from the great man – and she was being urged by her husband to sell them and give Dolly first refusal.

Stanley had completed writing the story of his life up to the point when he had been released from Camp Douglas in 1862. Dorothy planned to finish the book, using her husband's diaries, notes and articles to fill in the story of the rest of his life. The last thing she wanted was a scandalous, muck-raking book produced by a get-rich-quick outfit, ruining the lasting testimony to her husband she wanted to publish herself.

Dolly sought help from Henry Wellcome, who agreed to do everything in his power to obtain correspondence that might otherwise damage her husband's reputation. After pressure from Wellcome, Katie finally surrendered Stanley's correspondence, including the closely written fifteen-page 'confessional' letter, for the sum of £150.

Stanley's former servant, William Hoffmann, was also making loud noises about writing an account of life with Stanley, including his experiences travelling with the Emin Pasha Relief Expedition. Dolly mistrusted Hoffmann and instructed Wellcome to talk him out of exploiting his association with Stanley. He was paid to remain silent but was in desperate straits and continued to pester Dolly and Wellcome for money with veiled threats of publishing a memoir. He finally produced a slim volume in the 1930s that did nothing more than present Stanley as a wonderful employer and himself as a model servant ever ready to serve his master. Wellcome stopped receiving begging letters when Hoffmann died in a hostel for London's destitutes in 1936.

The most disturbing letter came from Lewis Noe, who informed Dolly that he possessed numerous correspondences and photographs from Stanley, which he might be prepared to surrender for $100. There was no suggestion of blackmail, but Dolly thought it best to obtain the material, particularly as Noe's letter alluded to experiences 'good and bad' with Stanley on the ill-fated visit to Turkey with Harlow Cook in 1866. A member of Wellcome's New York staff was sent to visit Noe and paid the asking price for the material.

Dolly could now get on with the job of finishing the story of her husband's life. Using material Stanley had completed plus a thousand other fragments, she produced a credible but flawed book called *The Autobiography of Henry Morton Stanley, Edited by his Wife, Dorothy Stanley*. The early part was a frank admission – with embellishments – by Stanley of the true circumstances of his birth in Wales and life at the workhouse. Dorothy took over where Stanley had stopped, carefully avoiding any mention of Lewis Noe, Kalulu, Katie Gough-Roberts, Alice Pike, her husband's first disastrous American lecture tour, disputes with the establishment over his discovery of Livingstone and methods used during his journey down the Congo and rescue of Emin Pasha. It was published by Sampson Low, Marston & Company in 1909 and in a letter to Dr Scott Keltie at the Royal Geographical Society, Dorothy predicted: 'This book is going to live forever.' The volume was politely received, but many had difficulty remembering exactly who Henry Morton Stanley was and what he had achieved. By this time, Dolly had remarried Dr Henry Curtis, a Harley Street practitioner and Fellow of the Royal College of Surgeons and sixteen years her junior, who had been introduced to her by Wellcome. It was a marriage of convenience. Dolly wanted a father for Denzil and a companion for herself. They enjoyed each other's company, but Dolly made it clear she had no intention of giving up her title of Lady Stanley or homes in London and Furze Hill.

Despite her second marriage, a small handwritten label penned in 1919 shows how much Dolly pined for Stanley fifteen years after his death. The label was attached to a Turkish-made cushion, which Stanley had used for a pillow on African expeditions. On it, Dolly wrote: 'This old cushion was valued by Stanley. He twice carried it across Africa, always using it as his pillow. He had an affection for this old cushion. Dorothy Stanley, his wife – who hopes soon to rejoin him – April 1919.'

Dolly was buried next to her Bula Matari in Pirbright churchyard when she died in October 1926. Dolly's mother, Gertie Tennant, had died aged ninety-nine in 1918. Richmond Terrace passed to Dolly, who in turn left the property to her second husband. Ownership of Furze Hill was passed to Denzil Stanley.

Denzil grew into a fine young man, educated at Harrow before becoming a Sandhurst-trained officer-cadet, rising to the rank of captain. He served with the Guards in India and later retired from the army to manage the Furze Hill estate, where he died in 1959, aged sixty-four. His wife, Helen, and their own son, Richard Stanley who died in 1986, are buried in the same plot at Pirbright under the great granite headstone.

Emin Pasha recovered from his fall at Bagamoyo and threw in his lot with the German government who asked him to mount an expedition to equatorial Africa to secure territories along the southern shores of Lake Victoria to Lake Albert. Soon after the expedition started in 1890, an Anglo-German agreement was signed excluding Lake Albert from German influence. After difficulties with German authorities in Tanganyika, Emin – now almost blind – crossed into the Congo Free State in May 1891. On his journey to the western African coast, near Stanley Falls, and suffering hunger and illness, he was captured by Arab slave raiders. His throat was cut open, his head removed and sent to a slave chief. His body was never found. His daughter, Farida, who had remained at Bagamoyo, was sent to Germany where she was brought up as a well-born German girl.

Three of the four volunteers returning to England with Stanley following the Emin Pasha Relief Expedition, died before their commander. Lieutenant Stairs returned to the Congo Free State, where he died in 1892. Captain Robert Nelson joined the staff of Mackinnon's British Imperial East Africa Company and died in what is today Kenya the same year. Dr Thomas Parke, the devoted physician who had taken care of Stanley's health in Africa and London died in Argyllshire in 1893 and was buried with full military honours in his home town of Drumsna, Ireland. William Bonny, the former army sergeant and Zulu war veteran, died alone in a Fulham workhouse in 1899, his health ruined by drink and poverty. He was buried in London's 'fashionable' Brompton Cemetery – in a pauper's grave. Arthur Mounteney Jephson, the only volunteer to outlive his former commander, longed to return to Africa, but poor health put paid to his attempts. He became a Queen's Messenger in 1895 and a King's Messenger in 1901. He died in 1908.

James Gordon Bennett, proprietor of the *New York Herald* who had instructed Stanley to 'Find Livingstone!' was ostracised by smart New York society after he had sunk one too many drinks and used the fireplace of his fiancée's parents' smart Westchester County home as a urinal. It is said that women fainted and heroic men rushed Bennett from the house – and polite society – by the elbows. He moved to France, from where he continued to rule his newspaper empire with an iron fist via overseas cable. He established a Paris edition of the newspaper, which still exists today as the *New York Herald Tribune* and steered both papers through the difficult years of the First World War. He died in 1918 after milking tens of millions of dollars from the earnings of his newspapers to buy racing yachts, racehorses, mansions, and to have a darn good time. The *New York Herald* name finally disappeared in 1924 when the paper was taken over by new proprietors.

Alice Pike, Stanley's young American fiancée who married another man while he was travelling down the Congo, became a Washington socialite and artist. Her marriage to Albert Barney ended in divorce after she had produced two daughters. In later years she reflected that she should have waited for her 'Morton' to have returned from Africa and set about writing the story of her association with Stanley in the form of a trashy novel which she entitled 'Stanley's Lady Alice by "One Who Knew"'. It was never published and this author located a copy in the Smithsonian Institution's Washington archives. Alice died with Stanley's photograph next to her bedside in 1931, leaving her large home and fortune to the National Museum for American Art.

Dr John Kirk, who had increasingly annoyed Stanley and went to some lengths to discredit his achievements, was knighted in 1881 after spending twenty years as British Consul in Zanzibar. He retired from public office in 1887 to live in Scotland where the National Library recently acquired a large collection of over three hundred photographs and papers belonging to Kirk, with help from a £55,000 Heritage Lottery Fund grant.

Mirambo, the notorious 'Ruga-Ruga' warlord and Stanley's blood brother, ruled a powerful kingdom and was one of the few able to take strategic control of Tippu-Tib's slave trade routes. In 1880, members of an expedition sponsored by King Leopold were killed by one of his chiefs, putting a price on his head. After Mirambo's death in 1884, his kingdom disintegrated. Today he is revered in Central Africa, where streets and public buildings are named in his memory.

The notorious slaver, Tippu-Tib was never paid a penny for his 'work' as the Congo Free State's Governor at Stanley Falls, where he had failed on almost every count to keep Arab traders under control. Arabs resented his alliance with Europeans and in April 1890 he left Stanley Falls and returned to Zanzibar with a large caravan carrying tons of ivory and lived in style in a large house. He died in 1905.

Stanley's home town of Denbigh went into a frenzy of mourning after his death. The Bishop of St Asaph's told his congregation: 'The man, who, above all others, turned the eyes of Europe on Africa, was our own countryman, born at Denbigh and educated under the shadow of this cathedral . . . such a man, the greatest of Welshmen, will always stand out as great among the greatest English men of action.' There was a suggestion in the *Denbigh Free Press* that the town might consider turning itself into a place of pilgrimage to Stanley's birthplace in the same way as Stratford-upon-Avon had done in memory of William Shakespeare. The paper pointed out that although the house where Stanley was born had been demolished, other places connected with his boyhood existed, including Denbigh Castle, the Cross Foxes pub where his mother had been landlady, and St Asaph's workhouse. It called for statues to be built in his memory and for a public subscription to be raised to fund the project, to be managed in the same way as a similar one devoted to African explorers in London's Kensington Gardens, promoted by former Royal Geographical Society president Francis Galton. Nothing became of either statue project, although the building that was once St Asaph's Poor Law Union Workhouse is today the H.M. Stanley Hospital.

Nearly a hundred years after his death, Denbighshire Council attempted to raise £100,000 to buy some of the 1,000 objects, furniture, gifts from kings and emperors, African weapons, rifles, pistols, knives, lantern slides, maps, books and photographs once owned by Stanley and stored in the huge dark attic at Furze Hill and its many other rooms. The majority of the relics were unearthed by specialists from London auctioneers Christie's, who spent months examining the contents of boxes and cupboards, before members of Stanley's surviving family sold the estate which had been owned by the explorer's descendants for over a century. The council approached the National Lottery for a grant to enable the purchase of as many artefacts as possible and house them in part of their local museum to be devoted to Stanley's private life and public explorations.

The auction took place in London on 24 September 2002, where Tom Lamb of Christie's London Book Department remarked: 'there has never before been such a large number of objects, books and artefacts relating to one explorer offered at auction'. Mr Lamb predicted that much of the collection would end up in institutions in America, Stanley's erstwhile adopted homeland.

On the day of the auction, bidding was intense. The top-selling lot was the water-stained map carried by Stanley when he returned to Africa to complete Livingstone's exploration work in 1874–8, complete with his pencil additions filling in the uncharted Congo as he descended the great river. It sold for a staggering £77,675 ($120,396) – more than twice the estimated price – and was purchased by a private buyer in the United States.

Travelling equipment used on Stanley's 1871 search for Livingstone fetched strong prices including the Winchester rifle he was holding when he reached out and shook the doctor's hand for the first time at Ujiji. It raised £19,120 ($29,636) and was bought by a private British buyer. Livingstone's sextant, presented to Stanley by Agnes Livingstone, was bought by another private British buyer for £17,925 ($27,784). The entire collection raised £891,709, and Tom Lamb said the sales 'reflected the rarity of the items offered and the extraordinary fascination that Stanley's name generates throughout the world'.

Denbighshire Council's attempt to buy items connected with Stanley's Welsh childhood was a success. Representatives purchased a handwritten testimony Stanley had produced in memory of his grandfather, Moses Parry, plus a plaster cast of his hand, some photographs and wedding presents given to Dolly and Stanley by Welsh people. They are now housed in the Denbigh Library, Museum and Art Gallery. As Tom Lamb had predicted, the majority of items at auction are now in private ownership.

Denbigh's undertaking to honour its most famous son with a collection of his artefacts for their museum was a modest attempt to celebrate a man who had little to thank Wales and the Welsh for in his lifetime. After all, Henry Morton Stanley was American born and bred . . . was he not?

ACKNOWLEDGEMENTS

Many people and organisations provided valuable information for this book. I am grateful to them all for their assistance, enthusiasm and efficiency; in particular I should like to thank Dafydd Hayes of the Clwyd Family History Society for information about Stanley's early life in Wales; Flintshire Records Office, Hawarden, keepers of records for St Asaph's Poor Law Union Workhouse; www.familysearch.org for information on Henry Hope Stanley's parents; C.B. Pritchett Jr for information on the Camp Douglas civil war prison camp, near Chicago; the US National Park Service for material on the attack on Fort Fisher in January 1865; Jason D. Stratman of the Missouri Historical Society, St Louis, for material on Stanley's time as a reporter on the American frontier for the *Missouri Democrat*; staff at the *Southwest Review*, Southern Methodist University, Dallas, Texas, for data on Stanley's life in New Orleans and Cypress Bend; William Cox at the Smithsonian Institution Archives, Washington DC, for information on Alice Pike Barney (Record Unit 7473); Clare Roberts at Christie's (London) for background material on the auction of Stanley's artefacts in September 2002 and Emma Strouts of Christie's Images for finding several photographs used in this book; R.O. Tough of Tough's Boatyard, Teddington and Hon. Sec. of the British Motor Yacht Club for information on boatbuilder James Messenger and construction of the *Lady Alice*; Peter Speller, Liz Brown at the National Monuments Records Office, London, for historical material about 2 Richmond Terrace, Whitehall; Jane Crompton and Rick Mitcham at the National Archives, Kew, for steering me in the direction of Dr John Kirk's correspondence and reports from Zanzibar to the Foreign Office in London (Ref: FO 841373); Gary Symes for drawing the map; my editors at Sutton Publishing, Christopher Feeney and Clare Jackson; Sarah Strong of the Royal Geographical Society, London, for access to their collection of documents, images and artefacts on Stanley; Zoë Stansell of the manuscripts department at the British Library which houses Stanley's journals on microfilm plus other documents relating to his life and work; Surrey History Centre, Woking, for archive material on Stanley's estate at Furze Hill, Pirbright and funeral; the British Library's Newspaper Library in London where I spent many happy hours reading Stanley's historical dispatches to the *New York Herald*, *Daily Telegraph* and other publications reporting and commenting on his actions. My sincere thanks to each and every one.

BIBLIOGRAPHY

Books by Henry Morton Stanley (all published in the UK by Sampson Low, Marston & Company and in the United States by either Charles Scribner's Sons or Harper & Brothers)

How I Found Livingstone in Central Africa, 1872
My Kalulu, Prince, King and Slave, 1873
Coomassie and Magdala – the Story of Two British Campaigns in Africa, 1874
Through the Dark Continent, 2 vols, 1878
The Congo and the Founding of its Free State, 1885
In Darkest Africa, 2 vols, 1890
My Dark Companions and their Strange Stories (also known as *Tales from Africa*), 1893
My Early Travels and Adventures in America and Asia, 2 vols, 1895
The Autobiography of H.M. Stanley, Edited by his Wife Dorothy Stanley, 1909

Books about Stanley's Life, Times and Adventures

Barttelot, W.G. (ed.), *The Life of Edmund Musgrave Barttelot*, London, Richard Bentley, 1890

Bennett, N.R. (ed.), *Stanley's Dispatches to the New York Herald (1871–77)*, Boston University Press, 1970

Bierman, John, *Dark Safari*, London, Hodder & Stoughton, 1990

Blaickie, William Garden, *The Life of David Livingstone*, London, John Murray, 1880

Jameson, James S., *The Story of the Rear Column of the Emin Pasha Relief Expedition*, ed. Mrs James S. Jameson, London, Pater, 1890

Jeal, Tim, *Livingstone*, London, William Heinemann, 1973

Jephson, A.J. Mounteney, *Emin Pasha and the Rebellion at the Equator*, London, Sampson Low, Marston, 1890

Livingstone, David, *Narrative of an Expedition to the Zambezi and its Tributaries (1858–1864)*, London, John Murray, 1865

——, *The Last Journals of David Livingstone in Central Africa*, ed. Horace Waller, 2 vols, London, John Murray, 1874

Manning, Olivia, *The Remarkable Expedition – the Story of Stanley's Rescue of Emin Pasha from Equatorial Africa*, London, William Heinemann, 1947

Maurice, Albert, *H.M. Stanley: Unpublished Letters*, London and Edinburgh, W. & R. Chambers, 1955

Parke, Thomas Heazle, *My Personal Experiences in Equatorial Africa as Medical Officer of the Emin Pasha Relief Expedition*, London, Sampson Low, Marston, 1891

Stanley, Richard and Neame, Alan, *The Exploration Diaries of H.M. Stanley*, London, William Kimber, 1961

Ward, Herbert, *With Stanley's Rear Column*, London, Chapman & Hall, 1890

——, *My Life with Stanley's Rear Guard*, London, Chatto & Windus, 1891

Other Works

[Alice Pike Barney], 'Stanley's Lady Alice by "One Who Knew"', unpublished MS, Smithsonian Institution archives, Washington DC (Record Unit 7473), n.d.

Christie's, *The Africa Sale, Including the Henry Morton Stanley Collection, September 24, 2002*, catalogue, London, Christie's, 2002

Owen, Bob, 'Stanley's Father, I Presume?', *Hel Achau (Journal of the Clwyd Family History Society)*, Llansannan, Clwyd, Spring 1985

Perham, Margaret and Simmons, Jack, *African Discovery*, London, Penguin, 1942

Shuey, Mary Willis, 'Stanley in New Orleans', *Southwest Review*, Southern Methodist University, 25 (4), Dallas, Texas, July 1940

——, 'Young Stanley: Arkansas Episode', *Southwest Review*, Southern Methodist University, 27 (2), Dallas, Texas, winter, 1942

Turner, Helen, *Henry Wellcome, The Man, His Collection and His Legacy*, London, the Wellcome Trust and William Heinemann, 1980

Wheeler, Douglas L., 'Henry M. Stanley's Letters to the *Missouri Democrat*', *Bulletin of the Missouri Historical Society*, St Louis, Missouri, April 1961

Wynne-Woodhouse, Bill, 'Elizabeth Parry of Denbigh, an Extraordinary Woman and H.M. Stanley, Her Son, an Extraordinary Man', *Hel Achau (Journal of the Clwyd Family History Society)*, Llansannan, Clwyd, Spring 1985

Letters of Queen Victoria (1886–1901), London, John Murray, 1930

David Livingstone and the Victorian Encounter with Africa, London, National Portrait Gallery, 1996

Other newspaper and magazine sources are identified in the main body of the text.

INDEX